D0406015

GUARDIANS
OF
THE GULF

A History of America's
Expanding Role in the Persian Gulf,
1833–1992

———•———

Michael A. Palmer

THE FREE PRESS
A Division of Macmillan, Inc.
New York

Maxwell Macmillan Canada
Toronto

Maxwell Macmillan International
New York   Oxford   Singapore   Sydney

Copyright © 1992 by Michael A. Palmer

All rights reserved. No part of this book may be reproduced or transmitted in any form or by any means, electronic or mechanical, including photocopying, recording, or by any information storage and retrieval system, without permission in writing from the Publisher.

The Free Press
A Division of Macmillan, Inc.
866 Third Avenue, New York, N.Y. 10022

Maxwell Macmillan Canada, Inc.
1200 Eglinton Avenue East
Suite 200
Don Mills, Ontario M3C 3N1

Macmillan, Inc. is part of the Maxwell Communication Group of Companies.

Printed in the United States of America

printing number
1 2 3 4 5 6 7 8 9 10

Library of Congress Cataloging-in-Publication Data

Palmer, Michael A.
  Guardians of the gulf : a history of America's expanding role in the
Persian Gulf. 1833–1992 / Michael A. Palmer.
      p.   cm.
  Includes bibliographical references and index.
  ISBN 0-02-923843-9
    1. Persian Gulf Region—Foreign relations—United States.
  2. United States—Foreign relations—Persian Gulf Region.
  I. Title.
  DS326.P36   1992
  327.73053—dc20   92-10789
                                                                CIP

To Ryan and Lisa

CONTENTS

TO THE VALLEY OF THE EUPHRATES

—•—

On February 25, 1991, as the day gave way to evening, forward elements of the U.S. Army's 24th Mechanized Infantry Division exploded into the valley of the Euphrates River, cutting Iraq's Highway 8 south of An Nasiriya. After securing a major ordnance storage complex and the military airfields at Tallil and Jalibah, the lead brigades of the division struck east toward Basra in a drive that trapped the remnants of Saddam Hussein's once-mighty army in a desolate corner of southeastern Iraq and northern Kuwait.

The speed and scope of the Allied victory in the Gulf War brought a seven-month-long crisis to an end on a note of triumph and political consensus in the United States. But between Saddam's August 2, 1990 invasion of Kuwait and the final ground operations of late February 1991, many had wondered why the United States was deploying military forces in such massive strength so far from home. Politicians, the media's talking heads, and millions of Americans in their homes and workplaces, debated involvement in the gulf. Whether or not they supported the policies of President George Bush, Americans wanted to know why the United States was risking a potentially bloody war with Iraq.

Bush administration pronouncements that offered myriad reasons for the stand in the gulf represented neither duplicity nor confusion. No single American "interest," not even concern about petroleum supplies, determined U.S. policy during the Kuwait crisis of 1990–91. The United States confronted Saddam to deter further aggression, foster a new world order, support the United Nations, safeguard

vii

American interests, insure the flow of Persian Gulf oil, save American jobs, and as a response to Iraqi human rights abuses in Kuwait.

But how had the United States amassed such broad interests in the region? And when had Americans become the protectors of the Persian Gulf?

Most Americans view their country's interest in the gulf as a relatively recent phenomenon, one rooted in the Reagan defense buildup of the 1980s or the cold war confrontation between the Soviet Union and the United States. But the origins of American involvement go much deeper. Over the course of two centuries, commercial and strategic interests and religious and political expectations merged to impart a distinctive shape to American policy. Pragmatism, self-interest, and naiveté characterized the American approach to the gulf.

Throughout the nineteenth century Americans cursed British domination of the gulf and sought to displace them commercially, while undermining them politically. But by the twentieth century, as American traders and businessmen deepened their stake in the region, they became increasingly sympathetic to the role played by Britain in the gulf. Americans also discovered, as had the British centuries earlier, that as commercial interests expanded, strategic responsibilities became difficult to avoid.

Steadily deepening interests combined with diminishing resistance to involvement in the affairs of a volatile region. Slowly during the nineteenth and early twentieth centuries, more quickly in the decades following the Second World War, and with astounding celerity after the late 1970s, the United States accepted ever greater responsibility for the security of the Persian Gulf. At each step along the way, decisions regarding deeper American involvement were made deliberately and reluctantly by administrations that considered themselves faced with Hobson's choices. Year after year, decade after decade, American responsibilities increased until, finally, the United States had replaced Great Britain, not just commercially, but also politically and militarily. The United States had become the guardian of the Persian Gulf. Operation Desert Shield/Desert Storm was the logical, though by no means inevitable, consequence of two centuries of American Persian Gulf policy.

CHAPTER ONE

AN OPEN FIELD FOR AMERICAN CAPITAL AND INDUSTRY

—•—

1833–1939

The origins of American involvement and interest in the gulf are to be found in the early history of the United States. Over two hundred years ago, commercial necessity, revolutionary political passions, and missionary zeal carried representatives of "God's American Israel" to the four corners of the globe.[1] Commercial interests (greed, if one prefers) combined with a drive toward political and spiritual prose-lytizing to shape American foreign policy. The United States sought not an economic or political imperium, at least not beyond the confines of the North American continent, but open, reciprocated access to markets unencumbered by diplomatic and military responsibilities, as well as an opportunity to preach the American message—both civil and religious—to those peoples of the world who still had the mis-fortune to labor under the political and economic domination of Eu-ropean powers.

Commercial and political policies were (and remain) inextricably linked in the American mind. Commercial expansion was a necessity as an emerging American nation confronted old, established imperial systems. The Treaty of Paris of 1783 secured the political, but not the economic independence of the United States. Americans, no longer part of the British mercantilist system, now had to make their own way in a harsh world, seeking opportunities in those corners of the globe not entirely controlled by the established European powers. Americans believed that the Old World's imperial systems had to be

1

undermined if the United States was to survive and prosper. That goal could be accomplished by Yankee merchants and missionaries revolutionizing the world with the message of American economic and political freedom. Timothy Dwight, president of Yale College, asked, "Could stupid heathens, or hardened Jews, sit silent and unmoved, under such mighty interpositions as these, by which Providence hath distinguished this land?"[2]

American policy was thus simultaneously pragmatic and naive. Americans correctly understood that to survive they had to break open the European powers' imperial systems. But American expectations that their commercial activity could crack European-dominated regional power structures without the entire edifice collapsing on their heads, or without the United States having to accept any diplomatic or military responsibilities, were ingenuous. So, too, was the belief that the peoples of the world would be so astounded by American political and economic achievements that they would rise up against European domination and cast aside culture and religion in a headlong effort to emulate the example of the United States.

Such interests and ideals motivated the Americans who first entered the waters of the Indian Ocean in the years after the Revolution. For most Yankee merchants, that ocean was just an obstacle to be crossed on the way to the Orient, but a few saw opportunities, albeit limited, for trade.[3] By the end of the eighteenth century American merchants, sealers, and whalers were active in the Indian Ocean basin, though few chose to pursue commercial opportunities in the Persian Gulf itself.[4]

This trade was substantial enough that during the undeclared "Quasi-War" with France (1798–1801) the United States dispatched a pair of frigates to protect American commerce east of the Cape of Good Hope.[5] A winter gale dismasted one of the men-of-war, but in 1800 Captain Edward Preble's frigate *Essex* became the first U.S. Navy warship to enter the Indian Ocean. In his journal Preble noted the evidence of the growing American presence in the region. While sailing past the nominally French islands of St. Paul and Amsterdam, he saw the American flag flying from the huts of Yankee sealers.[6]

In the first quarter of the nineteenth century, American trade in the Indian Ocean continued to expand, prompting the United States government to consider the establishment of a formal commercial relationship with the sultan of Muscat.

The sultanate harked back to an era when the Arabs had dominated the trade of the Indian Ocean, a period that had lasted until the arrival

2

of the Portuguese in the late fifteenth and early sixteenth centuries. The Portuguese, in fact, had ruled Muscat from 1507 until its capture by the Omanis in the mid-seventeenth century.[7]

The British, who helped drive the Portuguese from the Indian Ocean and were somewhat less imperious in their policy, allowed the coastal Arabs to resume their traditional commercial activity. Muscat, which had not been a port of note before the Portuguese conquest, became a major Indian Ocean trading center and the sultan's power expanded to such an extent that he controlled much of what had comprised the Portuguese empire in the Persian Gulf, the Arabian Peninsula, and the eastern coast of Africa.

While the gulf Arabs no doubt resented the European presence, for the most part they never suffered direct colonial rule comparable to that experienced by their fellow Arabs elsewhere in the Middle East and in North Africa (a fact that helps explain the modern gulf Arabs' greater willingness to cooperate with the West). Thus the Arabs the Americans contacted along the southern and gulf coasts of the Arabian Peninsula were not subject peoples living under the heel of European colonialism, but commercially oriented societies comprised of ruling families closely aligned with local merchant communities who governed successfully and profitably and were eager to expand their trade.[8]

While the Arabs had centuries of experience dealing with Europeans, the Americans who first reached the Indian Ocean, after tiring voyages that lasted several months, found themselves in a strange, climatically inhospitable region.[9] Alfred T. Mahan, who visited Muscat in 1867 as a young naval officer, noted that conditions confirmed "the association of the name Arabia with scorching and desert."[10]

While many people in the United States considered those of the Islamic world heathen barbarians living in darkness, the Americans who rounded the Cape of Good Hope found the Arabs to be shrewd businessmen whose societies were generally well ordered and civil. In the nineteenth century American naval officers considered "Mohammedan" ports unusually safe, if somewhat boring, venues for sailors. Mahan noted that when a party of men from his ship went ashore he "had the unprecedented experience that they all came back on time and sober."[11]

Muscat was situated on a mere cove, but was nonetheless a fine harbor with a natural breakwater. From a distance, one could make out the high cliffs and forts that encircled and protected the town, although Muscat itself, Mahan wrote, "was hardly to be descried, the gray color of the stone used in construction blending with the background of the mountains, from which it had probably been quarried." Only when one neared the town did it appear "imposing . . . there being several minarets, and some massive buildings, among which the ruins of a Portuguese cathedral bear the mute testimony to a transitory era in the long history of the East."[12]

In 1833 U.S. special agent Captain Edmund Roberts, a Salem, Massachusetts, merchant who represented the commercial community interested in the eastern trade, arrived in Muscat, accompanied by a small naval show of force—Master Commandant David Geisinger's two-ship squadron, the sloop-of-war *Peacock* and the schooner *Boxer*. Americans had found ready markets for their cotton textiles, furniture, and the occasional cargo of rum in Muscat and Zanzibar, major Indian Ocean entrepôts controlled by the sultan. For their return voyages, Americans could purchase valuable cargoes of ivory, dates, and pearls from Africa and Arabia, as well as spices and other goods from the Far East. But the American market could absorb limited quantities of ivory, dates, and pearls, and many of the products transhipped from the Far East could be had more cheaply at their source. Indeed, until the development of the oil industry in the Persian Gulf in the twentieth century, the Arab states had little of value to sell. Roberts thus found the sultan eager to trade and the two men signed a treaty of amity and commerce on September 21, 1833, establishing the United States' first tie to a Persian Gulf state and a diplomatic relationship still extant between the United States and Oman.[13]

The negotiations between Roberts and the sultan took place beneath the shadow of Great Britain's eastern empire. Muscat was the strongest indigenous maritime power in the region, but both Roberts and the sultan understood that the latter's far-flung commercial empire—which extended from the east African coast into the gulf—survived only because of British forebearance.[14]

In fact, the newcomer Americans, had they not been so quick to dismiss British colonial experiences, might have learned a lesson or two from the history of Great Britain's involvement in the region. British merchants had reached the Indian Ocean and the Persian Gulf in the 1500s, seeking not the imperium of the Portuguese who had preceded them, but, much like the Americans two centuries later, commercial opportunity in the east.[15] But the British had inexorably been drawn into the region's affairs. In 1622 they joined the Persians in the successful assault on Hormuz island that broke the Portuguese grip in the gulf.[16] France's short-lived occupation of Egypt in 1798, seen in London as a threat to India, led Great Britain to establish formal diplomatic and military ties with strategically placed Muscat.[17] Gradually, but steadily, the British found themselves ever more deeply involved in the affairs of the region, a trend that would continue throughout the nineteenth century.

Not surprisingly, given their position in the region, the British were fully aware of the American overture to Muscat. When British representatives questioned the sultan about the arrangements, he offered to tear up the treaty. But since the accord was purely a commercial arrangement and the Americans had displayed no interest in involving themselves in the sultan's affairs, the treaty survived. American trade continued to expand and in short order the United States had achieved a virtual monopoly of trade with Zanzibar. The American presence was so extensive that when in 1841 a British consul arrived in Zanzibar, he found the sultan's palace decorated with prints of the U.S. Navy's victories over the men-of-war of Britain's Royal Navy in the War of 1812.[18]

Americans thus continued to expand their commercial opportunities in the Indian Ocean, in part, at least, at the expense of the British, while at the same time benefiting from the order Britain brought to an unstable region. Throughout the nineteenth century, Americans watched passively as the British struggled to prevent the entire region from descending into chaos. Trading patterns underwent dramatic change as European steamers and commercial companies gradually displaced Arab dhows and traders. Britain's well-intentioned and successful campaign to end the slave trade also disrupted established commercial patterns and threatened the old order of the region. Dynastic instability led to internal strife, economic decline, disorder, and frequently the establishment of a British protectorate. The ebb and flow of Wahabism—fundamentalist Sunni Islam later championed by the Saudis—threatened the maritime Arab chieftains around the periphery of the Arabian Peninsula and intensified the piracy that generally troubled the gulf's waters. Nineteenth-century expeditions to suppress gulf piracy, and diplomatic and military support to the imperiled states, led Britain into ever deeper involvement in the affairs of the gulf.

British imperial success in the Indian Ocean and the gulf allowed Americans to further expand their commercial operations in the region. By the mid-1850s, American trade in the gulf itself had become substantial enough that the United States sought a commercial treaty with the Persian empire. The Americans, who already had reached a similar accord with neighboring Turkey in 1830, were anxious to gain a consulate at Bushire in the upper gulf.[19]

The negotiations between representatives of the United States and the Persian monarchy were far more difficult, and the issues involved far more complex, than had been the case in Muscat in 1833. In Istanbul in October 1851, Persian and American negotiators signed a commercial treaty. The U.S. Senate ratified the agreement but in Teheran "the influence of England at the Persian Court" allowed the accord to die a slow death.[20]

The treaty fell victim to the "Great Game" then already underway in the Near East and Central Asia between Britain and Czarist Russia. As the British had been steadily expanding their position in the gulf, around the periphery of the Arabian peninsula, and in India, the Russians had been pushing south from the steppe. Throughout the seventeenth and eighteenth centuries, Russian southern expansion came primarily at the expense of the Ottoman Turks and the khanates of Central Asia. But in 1722–23, during the reign of Peter the Great, the Russians first waged war against the Persians, gaining, temporarily, a foothold on the Caspian Sea. Between 1804 and 1813, the Persians fought their northern neighbor again, this time for control of Georgia. Once more, the Russians triumphed. The Treaty of Turkmanchai, which ended a third Russo-Persian struggle—1826 to 1828—secured the Russian position in the Caucasus.[21]

The Russian threat from the north drove the Persians temporarily, and begrudgingly, into the arms of the British. In the early 1850s, Shah Nasir ud-Din, and especially his chief adviser Mirza Taki Khan, were unwilling to do anything that might put at risk future British support against a Russian attack from the north. The British, anxious to preserve and expand their position in strategically located Persia, viewed American commercial penetration of the country as a potential threat.

But in the mid-1850s, relations between Persia and Britain soured because of the latter's domination of the region's trading routes and disputes over the border between Persia and Afghanistan. Moreover, the outbreak of war in 1854, and the concentration of both Russian and British military forces in the Crimea, gave the Persians much greater freedom of maneuver.

In the fall of 1854, at the instigation of the Czar of Russia, the Persians reopened negotiations with the United States. The shah was now eager not only to establish a commercial relationship with the Americans, but also "to buy or have constructed in the United States several vessels of war and to procure the services of American officers and seamen to navigate them."[22]

As the negotiations began, once again in Istanbul, the American representative, Carroll Spence, soon realized that the shah hoped to draw the United States not only into commercial, but also political and military relationships. The first draft treaty advanced by the Persians included articles that called for the United States to protect Persian merchant vessels and "ports and isles" in the gulf from attack.[23] In a subsequent draft, the shah's representatives requested American assistance for Persian attacks against Muscat and Bahrain and included an article that would permit the shah to reflag his ships with the Stars and Stripes (as would the Kuwaitis in the late 1980s to protect their ships, ironically, from Iranian attacks). Another article called for the United States "to protect the Persian seas from the bad conduct and evil designs of the enemies of Persia."[24]

The proposed articles were clearly aimed at Great Britain, for no other power threatened the shah's ports and shipping, and Britain alone was the protector of Bahrain and Muscat. The shah was undoubtedly already planning the war that he would begin in 1856 with an attack against Herat in Afghanistan. The British would reply as he feared, striking back in the gulf, cuting off trade, and seizing Kharg Island, Bushire, and other Persian ports.

The Americans were fortunate that they possessed neither the military capability nor the desire to play the role in the gulf proposed by the Persians. The British, who were aware of the shah's desire to strike while Britain was occupied elsewhere, recognized that the draft treaty, a copy of which they secured despite the secrecy of the negotiations, would have led to another Anglo-American war.[25]

It is unclear whether or not Spence fully recognized the scope of the Persian game, but he was wise enough to know the limitations of American policy and informed his Persian counterpart that the suggested articles would be totally unacceptable to the president and the Senate. The Persian proposals would inevitably entangle the United States in the shah's affairs. Moreover, the United States could not join an attack against Muscat, a friendly country which was all but an ally of Britain. The Persians agreed to drop the Muscat articles, but their next proposal still included provisions for the reflagging of merchant ships and empowered the shah to call for the services of an American naval squadron to reassert his control in the gulf, specifically over Bahrain.[26]

7

Again, Spence rejected the offending articles. In an effort to convince the Persians that a purely commercial treaty was in their interest, he stressed the economic strength of the United States, "a power of equal commercial resources as Great Britain," and pointed out that "the merchants of the United States are particularly fitted to destroy the monopoly of the English trade in Persia."[27]

The Persians, apparently disappointed by their inability to draw the Americans into the affairs of the gulf, withdrew from the negotiations. But Spence patiently waited for them to reopen the discussions, believing that they would return if he held firm. The shah, he noted, had "a desire to introduce into [his] territories a counterbalancing influence to that of England, which had of late become rather too powerful."[28]

When the Persians did, in fact, resume the negotiations, Spence once again stressed the benefits that would accrue to Persia from a relationship with a country "destined one day to control the commerce of the world."[29] This time the shah's negotiator agreed to accept a purely commercial treaty, which was signed on December 13, 1856. Spence, for his part, agreed to pass on to the secretary of state a verbal request from the Persians that the United States send a minister to Teheran and a ship of war to the gulf as soon as possible.

The Senate ratified the treaty on March 12 of the following year. Ratifications were exchanged in June and the treaty went into effect on August 18, 1857. At the request of the State Department, in 1858 the U.S. Navy sent a ship to the region, but inexplicably, to Muscat, the capital of the shah's nemesis the sultan, and not into the gulf.[30] Another twenty years would pass before an American man-of-war passed through the Strait of Hormuz, and a quarter-century before an American minister reached Teheran.

Nevertheless, the United States had at last become a party, if only in a commercial sense, to the intrigue of the gulf. The treaty negotiations demonstrated that even in the mid-1850s Britain, Russia, and Persia viewed the United States as a potentially powerful force in the affairs of the gulf. It is evident from Spence's letters and instructions that the Americans expected ultimately to displace the British in the region commercially, although the United States was loathe to take on the political and military responsibilities borne by Great Britain. Of course, the Americans were naive in their belief that commercial opportunities and diplomatic and military burdens could somehow be kept distinct. As long as Great Britain remained the dominant economic power in the region, the United States could freely reject proposals for reflagging, arms sales, advisers, and the stationing of a U.S. Navy squadron in the gulf. But as the American economic stake in the gulf grew, so, too, would the pressures to take on added responsibilities for the security and stability of the region.

But such considerations lay in the future. In the interim, as Yankee merchants sailed into the Persian Gulf via the Indian Ocean they joined a small group of American missionaries who had worked their way into northern Persia via Ottoman Turkish Armenia and Russian Georgia. In December 1830, an expedition led by two Presbyterian missionaries—Harrison Gray Otis Dwight and Eli Smith—reached Persian Azerbaijan. By the end of the decade, an American missionary presence had been firmly established in Urumiah in northern Persia and by the 1870s had spread to Tabriz, Teheran, and Hamadan. The Presbyterians provided spiritual, educational, and physical ministrations to Nestorian, Chaldean, and Armenian Christians, and a few, very few, Muslims.[31]

For the next half-century, these Protestant missionaries represented the principal American presence in Persia, since trade between the United States and the gulf remained limited. The missionaries were the first Americans to face the reality of the Middle East, for they quickly discovered that the local "heathens" were not overly impressed with American commercial, political, and religious ideas. As Britain's Lord Curzon, in his 1892 review of the "Persian Question," noted: "It is against the impregnable rock-wall of Islam, as a system embracing every sphere and duty, and act of life, that the waves of missionary effort beat and buffet in vain."[32]

While American ideals were not in great demand in the gulf, American goods most certainly were. By the late 1870s the United States was beginning to take fuller advantage of commercial opportunities in the region. In 1879, Commodore Robert Wilson Shufeldt, in the man-of-war *Ticonderoga*, visited Muscat en route to Asia and his successful mission to open Korea to American commerce.[33]

Shufeldt discovered that much had changed since the Roberts mission of 1833. Muscat's power had waned.[34] But American commercial interests remained strong, constituting two-third's of the sultan's trade.[35] Shufeldt learned that elsewhere in the gulf, opportunities flourished, despite the American government's reticence to support commercial activity diplomatically or militarily.

In December 1879, the *Ticonderoga* passed through the Strait of Hormuz and became the first American man-of-war to enter the gulf. Shufeldt visited Bushire and Basra, steaming seventy miles up the

Shatt-al-Arab.[36] "There is no place in the world," he wrote of the gulf, "where the physical manifestation of power is so necessary for the diffusion of the knowledge of the moral power of a civilized Nation as among the semi-barbarous and barbarous peoples that dwell upon these shores."[37] He also discovered that the British were understandably less than enthusiastic about the growth of American commerce in the region.[38] Great Britain, Shufeldt recognized, viewed the Persian Gulf as an "English Lake."

But the evident manifestations of British power failed to impress the American commodore. Shufeldt considered Britain's imperium a facade. Arabs, Turks, and Persians were eager to see another power replace Britain in the gulf. Ultimately, a challenge in European waters, Shufeldt hypothesized, would weaken, perhaps fatally, the British empire in the east. The commodore believed that the United States could dominate the gulf if it wished, provided Americans challenged the British commercially and diplomatically and refused to "continue to play the role long ago assigned to us in China—of No. 2 Englishmen."[39]

Shufeldt also was the first American to look beyond mere commercial interests to broader strategic or geopolitical concerns in the Persian Gulf. He recognized that Persia was one of the principal focal points of the Anglo-Russian imperial struggle in the east—"the Great Game."[40]

The old struggle between Britain and Russia grew more intense when, during the reign of Czar Alexander II, the Russians completed the pacification of the Islamic tribes in the Caucasus and undertook the conquest of khanates of Kokund, Bokhara, and Khiva. By 1881, Czarist Russia fronted Persia's entire northern border.[41]

Faced with this new Russian threat from the north, and the old British threat from the south, the Persian leadership searched the horizon for a protector—a diplomatic counterweight. As they had during the treaty negotiations of the 1850s, the Persians offered Americans expanded economic prospects in return for diplomatic support. In June 1883, after years of suggestions from Persian representatives in Europe, an American minister at last arrived in Teheran to establish a formal diplomatic relationship.[42]

The Persians were more than eager to foster American economic activity and involvement. The shah told the U.S. minister in Teheran, E. Spencer Pratt, "the field is opened to American capital and industry, which have but to come and reap its fruits." The shah looked to American know-how to help develop Persia's natural resources and

10

to expand commercial activity.[43] The shah viewed the United States, a country distant from Persia, and a nation with no evident territorial ambitions, as a third force, far less dangerous to Persian interests than Great Britain or Russia.

But if Americans found themselves offered the riches of Persia, they also confronted a seriously unstable situation. American diplomats spent a great deal of their time looking after the physical security of their countrymen, principally missionaries. During the 1880s and 1890s sectarian strife was rife, especially in the northwest around Tabriz, where Kurds routinely murdered Persian Christians and occasionally threatened or actually killed Americans.

In early 1892 Americans in Teheran witnessed at first-hand the power of the Persian mullahs, nearly a century before the rise of Ayatollah Khomeini! The previous year the shah had awarded a British consortium a monopoly for the import and export of tobacco, a substance widely used in Persia. The shah's decision prompted a popular reaction, led by the mullahs who reasoned that foreign control made the tobacco "unclean" and unfit for use by the Islamic faithful. A popular boycott spread across the country. Faced with such strong opposition, the shah ended the monopoly on imports, hoping to diffuse the situation, and ordered one of Teheran's leading mullahs to smoke in the main mosque in a symbolic effort to demonstrate to the people that they should end their "strike." When the mullah refused, the shah ordered him into exile.

The mullah's preparations to leave Teheran provoked a popular reaction that brought the people into the streets. An angry mob marched on the palace, intent on killing the shah. The mullahs told the people that the monarchy was selling the country piece by piece to the Europeans. Soldiers manning the palace gate joined the crowd. Only the intervention of a regiment of troops personally led by the shah's son saved the monarchy. Shots rang out killing two mullahs, green-turbaned descendants of the Prophet.

The people milled about, threatening to march to the foreign compounds and massacre the Europeans. Fortunately, before Teheran erupted into complete turmoil, the shah agreed to negotiate with the mullahs, avoiding catastrophe. Britain's tobacco monopoly was over.

The report of the incident sent to Washington by the American minister in Teheran, Truxtun Beale, could easily have been written nearly a century later, when in 1978 and 1979 the mullahs once again challenged a shah. Beale wrote:

11

This affair has brought forth a power in this country that the oldest Orientalist and even the Persians themselves did not dream of, to wit, the extent of the power of the mollahs. A mollah is simply a priest and not a member of any organization like the Church of England, or one of our own churches, but by common consent a body of them came together, carried on negotiations with the Shah, made demands and concessions, and concluded an understanding with him.

A means was suddenly found for the expression of popular discontent and for the redress of popular grievances.

In a despotism more like that of Cyrus and Xerxes than that of any government existing elsewhere to-day, a parliament seems to have risen from the ground.[44]

The situation remained unstable in Persia for the next two decades. In 1896, the shah was assassinated. The following year his successor banned the importation of foreign books, fearing the spread of Western ideas.

Nevertheless, the Persian monarchy eventually recovered its balance and once again turned to the United States for financial assistance and expertise. In 1910, the Persians suggested the appointment of an "impartial" American to control Persian finances. The following year, W. Morgan Shuster arrived in Teheran and became Treasurer General of Persia. Under Russian pressure he was quickly forced out.[45] But the Persians continued to look to Americans for assistance, assistance of even greater importance since it was becoming apparent that Persia possessed a great natural resource—petroleum—that would earn the state income, but that would also make Persia a more attractive target for British and Russian imperialists.

By the turn of the century, many Americans were aware of the "great game" being played by Britain and Russia in Eurasia. An American naval officer, Alfred Thayer Mahan, noted the importance of the Persian Gulf, especially the significance of Turkey and Iran as bulwarks against Russian expansion to the south.[46] In fact, it was Mahan, who viewed the region as a strategic locale sandwiched between Europe and the Orient, who coined the term "Middle East."[47] But for all of his foresight, Mahan missed one fundamental development then underway in the world—the gradual shift from coal to oil by industry and navies. The master of sea power and strategy overlooked a factor that would markedly alter strategic geography.

Indeed, the industrial revolution transformed the face of the world. By the turn of the century machine power had replaced that supplied by animals or nature. Coal had long since replaced wood, and was being displaced by petroleum, yet another fossil fuel. Neither Mahan nor anyone living in 1900 would have envisioned that industrialization in Europe, North America, and the Far East, and the growing demand for oil to fuel that industrialization, would in a half-century make the Persian Gulf critically important to the world.[48]

After 1900, the strategic significance of the Persian Gulf increased steadily, even at a time when the Middle East's oil production was limited and the region's known reserves were marginal. The reason was simple. Of the world's industrial and military powers, only the United States and Czarist Russia were major producers and exporters of oil.[49] The other powers—Germany, Japan, France, and Great Britain—relied on foreign, usually American imports, and eagerly searched abroad for new sources of oil.

In May 1901 an Englishman, William Knox D'Arcy, gained an oil concession from the shah that covered the whole of Persia, except the five northern provinces. The first major strike at Masjid-i-Sulaiman seven years later heralded the beginning of the oil age in the Persian Gulf. In April 1909 the newly established Anglo-Persian Oil Company (APOC) began work on a pipeline to transfer the oil from the fields to the gulf for shipment. In 1913 the APOC refinery at Abadan began production.[50]

By the eve of the First World War, access to petroleum had also become an element of sea power. Great Britain, the world's preeminent naval power, needed a secure supply of oil for the mighty Royal Navy. Admiral Sir John Fisher was the Royal Navy's main proponent of oil as the replacement fuel for coal in warships. As early as 1886, Fisher's advocacy of petroleum had earned him the sobriquet "Oil Maniac."[51] Fisher recognized that oil-fueled ships were cleaner, faster, had superior endurance, and were more easily refueled and maintained.[52] Accordingly, in 1914 the British government became the controlling partner in the management of APOC.

Great Britain's need to secure access to the petroleum of the Middle East extended beyond Persia. In 1912, the British began to develop the oil resources of the Ottoman Empire in concert with German and Dutch companies, principally in the area that in the 1920s would be-

13

come Iraq. In the gulf, under British pressure, the sheiks and emirs of Kuwait, Bahrain, Qatar, Oman, and the Trucial Coast—city states that adhered to an 1853 maritime truce enforced by Britain—agreed not to grant oil concessions to non-British companies.[53]

While the major threats to Britain's strategic position in the region came from the Germans and Russians, American interests, as they had throughout the nineteenth century, continued to pose a challenge. American oil men targeted the Ottoman Empire, long the focus of United States–based commercial and missionary activity. Several American consortiums gained rights to explore for oil in the Ottoman Empire. Retired Rear Admiral Colby Chester put together an American syndicate that negotiated railroad, mining, and oil concessions (1909–10) with Constantinople.[54] Standard Oil Company of New York (SO-CONY) obtained licenses for oil exploration in northern Anatolia and Palestine. Unfortunately for the Americans, before drilling could begin, the First World War spread to the Near East.[55]

The 1914–18 war demonstrated the increasing importance of oil to the industrial world and intensified interest in the potential of the Persian Gulf. By 1918 partially motorized armies and air forces had joined navies in their reliance on petroleum. Britain's Lord Curzon remarked shortly after the end of the Great War that the Allies had "floated to victory on a sea of oil."[56] Over 90 percent of that oil had come from the United States.[57]

The Allied victory left Great Britain supreme in the Persian Gulf. Alliance with Germany and Austria-Hungary led the Ottoman Empire to defeat and dissolution. The British drove the Turks from Palestine, Mesopotamia, the Red Sea, and the Persian Gulf coasts of the Arabian Peninsula. The Mesopotamian campaign, despite early setbacks, covered British positions in the gulf and APOC interests in southwestern Iran, where oil production and refinery capacity increased 400 percent during the war. By 1918 the German threat epitomized by the planned Berlin to Baghdad railway had disappeared. In the early 1920s, the Russian menace ebbed amidst revolution and civil war.[58] Palestine, Iraq, and Kuwait came under Great Britain's control. No foreign power other than France, entrenched in Lebanon and Syria, could threaten Britain's seemingly supreme position in the Middle East.[59]

There remained only the internal threat. A newfound sense of Arab nationalism had developed during the war and had played a large part in helping the British drive the Turks from the region. To secure this assistance, Britain and France had made innumerable promises to recognize Arab national rights. But at the end of the war the Allied powers refused to yield their gains. The Arabs turned to the United States and its president, Woodrow Wilson, for help. But Americans were reluctant to get involved in the affairs of the Middle East. The British, aware that the politically divided Arabs lacked a Western protector, ignored the nascent nationalist movement's hopes and desires, though not without cost.[60]

The British moved quickly to make the most of their victory. Britain adopted a national oil policy to secure control of a vital strategic resource—petroleum.[61] APOC expanded its Persian concession.[62] In newly independent Iraq, the British considered their former concession with the Ottoman Empire still valid and pressed further development. Anglo-French cooperation in the Middle East, conspicuous in the 1915 Sykes-Picot agreement to divide the Ottoman Empire, became obvious at the April 1920 San Remo Conference. French companies gained a 25 percent share in the Turkish Petroleum Company (TPC), soon to become the Iraqi Petroleum Company (IPC), in return for an agreement to permit the construction of a pipeline from the northern Iraqi fields across French-controlled Syria to the Mediterranean.[63]

Finding themselves barred from Iraq and Arabia, Americans looked to Persia where the situation appeared somewhat more promising. During the course of the war, Britain, Turkey, and Russia had violated Persian neutrality. When civil war erupted in Russia, Britain had staged its intervention in the Caucasus from Persian territory in near-complete disregard of the host nation's wishes. As the Bolsheviks began to consolidate their power throughout Russia and to reassert themselves in the south, the British withdrew and the Persians were left to face their traditional northern nemesis now operating under the Bolshevik guise. In February 1921, with Red Army troops occupying the northern province of Gilan, the Persians concluded a treaty with the Soviet Union that gave the latter the right to intervene if a "third party" moved forces into Persia.[64]

As they had so many times before, the Persians turned to the United States—a "disinterested" party—for help. As the situation in the Caucasus deteriorated, Persian leaders offered an oil concession in the north of their country, the region threatened by the Soviets and being evacuated by the British, to American petroleum interests. When British control of the area had seemed secure, APOC officials had blocked American efforts to develop the petroleum resources of the northern provinces. But now, with Great Britain's military forces withdrawing from the Caucasus, APOC relented.[65] An American oil concession in the north would act as a deterrent to any Soviet advance into Persia. Unfortunately, when an American company finally gained the concession, the Russians refused to allow transport of the oil through the Caucasus to Black Sea ports, making the deal worthless.

Thus in the Middle East, the results of the Great War seemed to have reduced, rather than enhanced American commercial opportunities.[66] Representatives of American oil companies returned to Palestine and Mesopotamia to find themselves excluded from commercial activity. And to the annoyance of American oil men, the State Department appeared to provide little assistance and not much more in the way of sympathy. The government–petroleum industry cooperation that had worked so well in the United States during the war ended abruptly with peace.[67]

Despite the fact that Americans in 1919 were gripped by a panic about the state of their oil reserves (only ten years remaining according to official government estimates), the administrations of Woodrow Wilson and Warren G. Harding did not develop any national petroleum policy. To the chagrin of American oil men, U.S. diplomats at the Versailles peace conference preferred to wait until the fate of the Ottoman Empire was decided before they pressed for concessions from the victorious allies. Subsequent American diplomatic efforts on behalf of the oil industry were limited to outraged protestations of British behavior, declarations of the Open Door Policy of equality of commercial opportunity for all nations, and a refusal to recognize the legitimacy of an Iraqi Petroleum Company concession based on arrangements that predated the establishment of Iraq.[68]

The diplomatic failure to insure the participation of the American petroleum industry in the development of the Middle East is understandable, for the Wilson and Harding administrations did not have a strong hand to play in that region. The United States had been an "associated," not a fully Allied power during the Great War and had never declared war against the Ottomans. The British, who had borne most of the cost of defeating the Turks, rightly saw no reason to allow Americans to share the spoils of victory. Nor did the United States ratify the League of Nations Treaty under which the mandates of the Middle East were administered. Moreover, any State Department effort to gain a concession for an individual American oil company would be seen by the other companies, correctly, as favoritism.

Despite its reluctance to play a major role in world affairs, the United States was an international power, and American oil companies remained the largest and most powerful in the world. Middle Eastern

16

doors did eventually open for Americans during the 1920s. In 1923, A. C. Millspaugh, a former State Department official, became the shah's financial adviser. Gradually, both Great Britain and the United States adopted more conciliatory positions regarding access to Middle Eastern oil.[69] Faced with a resurgent nationalist Turkey that seemed intent on recovering the oil-rich Mosul district, Great Britain sought American involvement in the development of the petroleum industry in Iraq, to which the district ultimately was given.[70] More importantly, British oil companies lacked the capital to develop the vast area staked out for them by their government.

Following the settlement of the boundary between Turkey and Iraq, new agreements between the IPC and the Iraqi government, and major oil strikes in 1923 and 1927, several American oil companies signed the infamous Red Line agreement on July 31, 1928.[71] The accord established a cartel operating within the area bound by a red map line drawn around the former Asiatic territories of the Ottoman Empire, an area that included much of the Arabian Peninsula. For the United States, the agreement marked the end of its diplomatic fight against recognition of the IPC as the legitimate successor of the TPC, a decision that would leave in force the pre-World War I agreements that had excluded American oilmen.

While the inclusion of some American oil companies marked an improvement in the commercial opportunities open to U.S. companies, the establishment of a cartel was a major setback for the Open Door policy in the Middle East. Nevertheless, American oil companies, principally through their own efforts, had established themselves in the Persian Gulf and, not for the last time, challenged Britain's preeminence.

Americans sought and obtained concessions in Kuwait, Bahrain, and the Arabian Peninsula. Despite the fact that British companies, most notably the Eastern and General Syndicate represented by Major Frank Holmes, held the concessions to explore for petroleum throughout the region, efforts to find British companies willing and able to purchase these rights often failed. Capital-rich American firms were soon on the scene with ready cash.

Bahrain had been a British protectorate since 1880. Following the identification of oil seepages in 1910, the British had obtained an agreement that gave Britain a veto on future oil development. When Holmes, whose December 1925 agreement expired after four years, was unable to interest any British developers, he sold his rights in Bahrain to Eastern Gulf Oil, a subsidiary of American Gulf Oil.

17

Gulf, a partner in the IPC, was bound by the restrictions of the Red Line Agreement, which covered the Bahrain archipelago. The British-dominated IPC refused to undertake the development of oil on Bahrain or to allow Gulf to exercise the option. So Gulf sold the rights to Standard Oil of California (SOCAL) for $50,000.

SOCAL, an American company, fell afoul of the Nationality clause of the Anglo-Bahraini agreement of 1914, but circumvented the restriction by establishing the Bahrain Petroleum Company (BAPCO) as a wholly owned Canadian subsidiary. Drilling began in 1932 and the company exported the first barrel of Bahraini crude three years later. Ultimately, SOCAL sold half its shares to the Texas Oil Company and formed CALTEX, chartered in the Bahamas, as a company to market BAPCO product internationally.[72] Thus, by the early 1930s, the development of the oil industry in Bahrain, which had become a strategic base for British military forces in the Persian Gulf, was firmly in the hands of the United States.[73]

Kuwait, strategically placed at the head of the gulf, and purposefully excluded from the Red Line agreement, also became the focus of American interest. Gulf Oil bought Major Holmes's concession and the British scrambled to insure that APOC became a partner to Gulf in the formation of the Kuwaiti Oil Company (KOC).[74]

The most significant American penetration into the region came in the formerly British-dominated and politically divided Arabian Peninsula. Abdul Aziz, later known as Ibn Saud, the sultan of Najd, ruled the central and eastern peninsula, and Sherif Hussein of Mecca the western Hejaz. To prosecute the war against Turkey between 1914 and 1918, Britain had allied with Hussein and insured internal peace in the peninsula with a £5,000 monthly subsidy to Ibn Saud and a December 1915 treaty that established a protectorate over his domains. Ibn Saud agreed not to attack Hussein nor to grant mineral or trade concessions without British approval.[75]

After the war, British concern about rising Arab nationalism and discontent with Hussein's leadership led to the end of the subsidies to, and the effective unleashing of, Abdul Aziz. In January 1926 the king's Bedouin tribesmen conquered the Hejaz. The 1927 Treaty of Jidda ended the British protectorate and removed the economic restraints of the 1915 agreement.[76]

Ibn Saud, who needed cash to consolidate his hold over the tribes of his newly established Saudi Arabian state, looked eagerly for the loans and the royalties that came with oil development. In 1923 Major Holmes negotiated an oil concession with Ibn Saud for al-Hasa, in the

18

northeastern part of the peninsula along the Persian Gulf, but failed to interest any British company in undertaking the development. The prospects of finding oil in Saudi Arabia appeared bleak until the 1932 Bahrain strike in a formation that geologists believed extended into the adjoining al-Hasa region of the peninsula. Since al-Hasa lay within the Red Line, Gulf Oil could not seek to develop the region, but SOCAL, already operating in Bahrain, moved in, outbid the IPC, and won a major sixty-year concession for the newly formed California-Arabian Standard Oil Company (CASOC).[77]

By the late 1930s, the pace of development of the petroleum industry in the Middle East was accelerating. Oil production in the Persian Gulf region increased 900 percent between 1920 and 1939. Iraq, Bahrain, and Saudi Arabia joined Iran as major producers. Whereas less than 5 percent of non–United States produced oil had come from the gulf in 1920, by 1939 the figure had grown to 14 percent.[78]

Increasingly, American corporations fueled the region's development. Britain may have held a monopoly on military and political power in the gulf, but American financial capital challenged the British economically during the 1920s and 1930s. British-dominated Iran remained the source of about two-thirds of Persian Gulf oil, but American participation in the IPC and control of the oil concessions in Bahrain and Saudi Arabia demonstrated a growing American role in the region.

Thus, on the eve of the Second World War, the United States, while certainly not a military force in the Persian Gulf, was nevertheless an economic power of the first rank. Kurds, Arabs, and Persians all held a favorable view of the as yet untainted United States. To offset the power of Britain and Russia, the Persians, the most politically developed of the peoples of the region, continued their nearly century-old policy of offering commercial concessions to Americans in an effort to draw the United States into Persian affairs. And control of the petroleum concession for Bahrain, the strategic center of the British position in the gulf, by American oil companies clearly demonstrated the extent of U.S. economic penetration of an ostensibly British-dominated region.

Policymakers in Washington had thus far rejected any diplomatic or military involvement in the gulf. But the increasingly rapid expansion of American economic interests, already evident during the interwar years, could not forever be secured with a hands-off policy toward the region.

19

CHAPTER TWO

THE WORLD OIL CENTER OF GRAVITY

---•---

1939–1946

Before the Second World War, U.S. interests in the Persian Gulf were economic. The rapidly expanding presence of American oil companies in the region represented purely commercial concerns, because the United States remained the world's largest oil producer and exporter. The petroleum American-owned companies pumped from the gulf flowed not back to the United States, but to overseas markets.

While more Americans, like Shufeldt and Mahan before them, recognized the strategic importance of the Persian Gulf, and appreciated the stability British political and military dominance brought to the region, few in the United States expressed any desire to see their country either replace or support Great Britain. Americans still believed that they could undermine Britain's economic position without having to accept any political or military responsibilities.

The course of the Second World War in the Middle East led the United States, albeit reluctantly, to play a larger role in the affairs of the Persian Gulf. The global conflict both highlighted the growing importance of petroleum and exposed the weaknesses of Britain's strategic position in the Persian Gulf.

During the First World War British and Imperial forces had sufficed to defend the Middle East, but between 1939 and 1945 a variety of threats compelled Britain to rely on Soviet and American forces to redress the regional imbalance of power. Early in the war, pro-Axis sentiment in Iran and Iraq threatened the security of Britain's major sources of oil. British and Indian Army forces crushed the short-lived Iraqi coup of May 1941 at the expense of the prosecution of the campaign in Libya against the Germans and Italians.[1] Then in June, Axis forces invaded the Soviet Union. Overland communications through strategically placed Iran assumed great importance and the presence of German advisers in Teheran led to a crisis in the late summer. When Reza Shah Pahlavi refused to expel the Germans, British forces invaded Iran from the south, while Soviet troops struck from the north. The Allies forced Reza Shah to abdicate in favor of his son, Muhammad Reza Shah Pahlavi. The new shah signed the Anglo-Soviet-Persian Treaty of January 1942, which legitimized the joint occupation but guaranteed the territorial integrity and political independence of Iran.

External threats also imperiled Britain's position in the Middle East. Between June 1940 and December 1942, the British faced dangers from the north, where the Germans nearly broke through Soviet positions in the Caucasus; the west, where German-Italian forces in Libya menaced Egypt; the south, where Italian-controlled Ethiopia and Somalia fronted the Gulf of Aden and the Red Sea; and the east, where Japan's army invaded India and the Imperial Japanese Navy sortied into the Indian Ocean.[2]

By early 1943, the British had secured their position in the Middle East but, unlike their experience in the First World War, not without major assistance from their allies. Russian troops were entrenched in northern Iran. American sea, ground, and air forces had engaged the Axis in North Africa and had arrived in the Persian Gulf to secure the overland lend-lease route to the Soviet Union.

These early Axis threats against the Middle East also impeded the development of the petroleum industry in the Persian Gulf, despite the importance of oil to the prosecution of the war, and further weakened Britain's position in the region. Fears that the oil fields might be overrun by Axis forces, the absence of British capital, political instability, and the interruption of overland and sea communications slowed, and in some cases reversed, development trends. In Iraq, annual oil production fell from 32,643,000 barrels in 1938 to 12,650,000 in 1941, before rising to 32,112,000 barrels by 1945.[3] Iranian oil production declined from 213,737 barrels per day in 1938 to 138,704 in 1941, before rising to 280,000 in 1944.[4] The Trucial states, Qatar, Oman, and Kuwait, all latecomers to oil development and reliant on British capital, also suffered.[5] British-dominated companies capped wells and postponed development. Only late in the war did Kuwait, where the consortium included capital-rich American concerns, resume production.[6] Decreased production and reduced royalties exacerbated tensions between the gulf states and the British, especially in Iraq and

Iran. Only in late 1942 and early 1943, with the Allies cut off from oil supplies in the southwestern Pacific, the Middle East secure, the Mediterranean reopened to sea communications, and the Western Allies' economies and military forces expanding, did demand for Persian Gulf oil force production increases.

Bahrain and Saudi Arabia, where the controlling interests were American, fared noticeably better. In Bahrain, with well-developed facilities and an in-place refinery, production declined, but not as markedly as it did elsewhere.[7] Activity in Saudi Arabia continued to increase into 1940, when annual production reached 5,075,000 barrels, up from 580,000 barrels in 1938. Production then fell to 4,310,000 in 1941, but rose to 21,311,000 by 1945![8] An IPC official at the time noted that the marked decline in oil production in British dominated areas "gave throughout the Middle East an impression . . . that the tempo of American development far exceeded the British."[9]

If the Second World War weakened Great Britain's position in the Persian Gulf, it heightened American strategic concern for the security of the region. American wartime strategy could succeed only if the Soviet Union kept fighting. The route through the gulf and Iran was vital for the shipment of Lend-Lease aid to Stalin's Russia. Toward the end of the war, gulf oil became a strategic commodity, fueling Allied planes, tanks, ships, and trucks deployed overseas. As a result, by the end of the war the United States had dramatically increased its economic stake in the region and, for the first time, deployed military forces to the gulf.

American oil policy also changed markedly during the war. In the 1930s, as part of the "New Deal" programs to lift the country out of the depths of the Great Depression, President Franklin D. Roosevelt had initiated a new era of government-business cooperation, aimed primarily at controlling prices through production restraint.[10] The war caused the administration to switch gears and seek expanded domestic production. As a result, between December 1941 and August 1945, the United States was able to supply 80 percent of the oil that fueled the Allied war effort. Petroleum products constituted more than half the total tonnage of war material shipped from the United States.[11] Harold Ickes's Petroleum Administration for War (PAW), a further development of earlier bureaucratic regulatory agencies created by Roosevelt during the 1930s, made the government the arbiter of the oil industry.

In an effort to insure a sufficient supply of oil for the Allied war effort, the United States sought to exploit not only domestic, but also foreign sources of petroleum.[12] American policymakers hoped both to increase production and refinery capacity during wartime, and to insure American participation in postwar overseas oil development. Ickes believed that these goals could best be achieved if the United States government became an actual partner in the oil industry, much as the British government was a stockholder in APOC.[13] Had Ickes's policies been pursued, the United States would have become Britain's partner, committed diplomatically and militarily to securing the nation's stake in the oil industry in the gulf.

In the Persian Gulf, Ickes achieved his first goal. PAW assigned the gulf both production and refining increases under its 1941 Foreign Production Program. Military concerns about the security of the region, voiced early in the war, retarded the execution of plans to expand local refining. Nevertheless, Persian Gulf refinery capacity increased by 89 percent between 1938 and 1944. Moreover, by the end of the war specialized refined products, such as high octane aviation gas, Navy Diesel, and Navy Specialized Fuel Oil were produced in the Persian Gulf at Abadan, Bahrain, and Ras Tanura.[14] The expansion was so significant, in fact, that the Middle East assumed a special prominence in American eyes. A February 1944 PAW technical report labeled the Persian Gulf "the center of gravity" for future oil development.[15]

While the effort to increase overseas production was markedly successful, Ickes was unable either to formalize a government-industry alliance, or to secure an Anglo-American petroleum agreement to govern postwar development in the Middle East. American businessmen were anxious to see the U.S. government play a larger role promoting the interests of American oil companies in the Persian Gulf. But Ickes's plans for joint government-industry participation raised concerns about government regulation, intervention, and control, and in August 1944 American oil industry representatives rejected the initial petroleum accord worked out by British and American negotiators. While industry representatives accepted a revised September 24, 1945, agreement, peace ended the sense of wartime urgency and the treaty lay before Congress unratified.[16] American oil companies remained independent, and no formal agreement existed to insure the United States government's participation in the development of Persian Gulf oil.

Nevertheless, the growth of American diplomatic, economic, and military involvement in the Middle East during the war insured that American oil companies would play a leading role in the Persian Gulf.

The Lend-Lease programs extended to Britain, the Soviet Union, and ultimately to Iran and Saudi Arabia, brought the American military into the region to train local forces. Throughout the Persian Gulf, the United States constructed pipelines, built and improved airfields, roads, railroads, port and storage facilities, and improved communications. The war strengthened the newly established American positions in Bahrain and Saudi Arabia, and provided the United States ingress to Iran, Britain's major oil supplier. Only the Roosevelt administration's restrictions against negotiating new oil concessions, wisely meant to prevent distrust among the Allies, prevented American oil companies from reaping a windfall of new commercial opportunities in the gulf.

The situation in Iran best exemplified the new political reality in the region. The Anglo-Soviet invasion and occupation and the forced abdication of the shah left many Iranians understandably concerned about their nation's future. The arrival of an Anglo-American team in Teheran in 1941 to plan improvements to the Iranian State Railway, encouraged many Iranians to look to the United States as a source of support, much as the hard-pressed Persian monarchy had since the 1850s.[17] The Iranians once again proposed an American oil concession in the north, but the United States, reluctant to take any action that might upset the British or Soviets, chose to delay negotiations until after the war.[18]

Nevertheless, the United States did take several steps during the war to support Iran. Although the Tripartite agreement of January 1942 prevented Iran from entering the conflict on the side of the Allies, the United States declared Iran eligible for Lend-Lease. In late 1942 and early 1943 the United States established American military advisory missions in Iran to build up the nation's gendarmerie and army to insure internal security.[19] Such support was indispensable if the young shah was to reassert governmental authority when, and if, the Soviets and the British withdrew. In addition to this advisory presence, by 1945 the American Persian Gulf Service Command, responsible for improving communications in the region and moving Lend-Lease material to the Soviets, Iranians, and Saudis, grew to a force of 30,000 men, most of whom were in Iran.[20] At the time of the Teheran Conference of late 1943, the United States upgraded its diplomatic mission in Teheran from a legation to an embassy. And at the conference itself, at Iranian prompting, the United States drafted and backed the "Declaration of the Three Powers Regarding Iran." The document, signed on December 1, 1943, by Churchill, Stalin, and Roosevelt, regularized

24

the presence of American forces in Iran, noted the special hardships and indignities imposed by foreign occupation, and guaranteed Iranian postwar territorial integrity and independence.[21] As payment for tolerating the Anglo-Soviet occupation and an extensive American presence, Iran received a promise of support from the United States.

Across the Persian Gulf in the Arabian Peninsula, Ibn Saud, much like the young shah, increasingly looked to the United States for assistance. The war reduced Saudi oil revenues and depressed the usually lucrative pilgrimage traffic to Mecca. Ibn Saud's financial problems were evident to British and American observers who were also concerned about the possible pro-German sympathies of the monarch.[22]

Early in the war, Ibn Saud viewed Britain as the more important power in the region and considered the United States a nation with but a passing interest in the affairs of the gulf.[23] Thus Britain initially bore the financial costs of supporting Ibn Saud's rule when CASOC proved unable, and the United States government proved unwilling, to supply the advances and loans demanded by the king. The British quickly increased aid to Ibn Saud after the Iraqi revolt of the spring of 1941. President Roosevelt, despite the position of the American oil companies in Saudi Arabia, still considered the peninsula a British sphere of interest.[24]

While American oil men were concerned by the increasing British wartime presence and clout in Riyadh, their main worry remained the potential internal collapse of the Saudi monarchy.[25] Not until early 1943, with British economic power waning, and British skepticism about Ibn Saud's ability to govern growing, did American aid reach significant levels.

As Americans became increasingly aware of Great Britain's incapacity, the strategic significance of the Middle East, and the importance of access to the oil in the Persian Gulf during the war, and perhaps after as well, they began to reassess longstanding United States policies toward the region. During the final years of the Second World War the Roosevelt and Truman administrations demonstrated much greater interest in the gulf, an interest based on a newly developed national petroleum policy for the postwar world formulated by the State Department in late 1943 and early 1944. That policy called for the "conservation of Western Hemisphere petroleum reserves" through the "curtailment, in so far as practicable, of the flow of petroleum and its products from Western Hemisphere sources to Eastern Hemisphere markets" concurrent with the "substantial and orderly expansion of production in Eastern Hemisphere sources of supply, principally in the Middle East." The report also called for full American participation in this development, both to insure its success, and to "create a potential outside source of supply for the United States in the event that the recent unfavorable curve of domestic discoveries should not take a turn for the better."[26]

The American decision to take the leading role in the postwar development of the petroleum industry of the Middle East was based on a sober, but realistic assessment of British capabilities—diplomatic, economic, and political. Since the end of the First World War, Great Britain had demonstrated that it lacked the capital to develop the region, certainly to the extent that the United States now considered necessary. Nor had the British taken "adequate steps to look after the welfare of the masses" in an area where national and anticolonial sentiment was on the rise. American policymakers were concerned about instability in the region, instability that might threaten the continued expansion of the oil industry or tempt the Soviets into a potentially destabilizing and dangerous involvement or intervention.[27] Roosevelt and Truman administration officials believed, in keeping with their liberal democratic principles and the political traditions that had motivated American missionaries and many merchants in the Middle East since the late eighteenth century, that the best guarantor of stability in the gulf would be rapid and comprehensive economic development. This would lead to a higher standard of living for the people "and to consequent increased purchasing power and greater political and economic stability."[28]

The growing awareness of Great Britain's imperial decline posed problems for United States policy. Britain's weakened position in the Persian Gulf and throughout the Middle East presented Americans with unparalleled economic and diplomatic opportunities, but also threatened to lead the United States into deeper political and military involvement in an unstable region. From his post in Cairo, Lincoln MacVeagh, American ambassador to the Greek government in exile, wrote in October 1944:

I doubt if in any other part of the world it can appear so clearly as here,—along its principal artery [the Suez Canal],—that, militarily speaking, the British Empire is anachronistic, perfect for the eighteenth century, impossible for the twentieth. Every day brings its evidence of weakness and dispersion, of consequent opportunism, and dependence on America's nucleated strength. No one, I feel,

26

can keep his eyes and ears open here and fail to believe that the future maintenance of the Empire depends on how far England consents to frame her foreign policy in agreement with Washington, and how far in our turn we realize where the Empire, so important to our own security, is most immediately menaced.[29]

Nevertheless, American policymakers had no desire to commit United States military assets to the support of the British Empire or the defense of the Middle East. During the Second World War, American planners envisioned a world in which U.S. military power would be exercised in the Western Hemisphere and the Western Pacific. The Mediterranean and the Middle East would remain areas of British responsibility. In December 1943, then Secretary of the Navy Frank Knox spoke of a postwar "working agreement between the British and the American navies which assigns to the British fleets control of the Eastern Atlantic, the Mediterranean and the Indian Ocean. The U.S. Navy guards the Western Atlantic and the entire Pacific. . . . There is the backbone of the postwar naval police force, already organized and functioning."[30] As a result, while Americans were aware that great-power troubles were brewing, and knew that the British wanted, and expected, American postwar assistance, the U.S. military planned and began to execute a complete withdrawal from European waters.[31]

New directions in American policy toward the gulf states became evident in the relationship between the United States and Saudi Arabia, where as late as 1943 Americans had resisted playing a larger political role. By the following year, the Americans were actively engaged in a struggle with the British for the favor of King Ibn Saud. The Americans, who approached the Saudis regarding rights to construct an air base at Dhahran along the Persian Gulf coast, attempted to capitalize on their leading role in the development of the oil industry in Arabia. The British, who were also seeking rights to a base, worked to make the most of their long-established political position in the Arabian Peninsula. But the United States gained the upper hand. The extension of Lend-Lease to the Saudis in 1944 and increased CASOC oil production and royalties abated the immediate threat of the collapse of the monarchy and raised American stock in the Saudi capital.[32]

During the final year of the war, the United States labored diligently to insure American commercial and political influence in postwar Saudi Arabia. Preparing to return from the Yalta Conference in February 1945, President Roosevelt invited King Saud to a meeting on an American cruiser in the Great Bitter Lake of the Suez Canal.[33] The U.S.

27

Navy destroyer *Murphy* transported Ibn Saud and his retinue from Jidda to the face-to-face meeting with Roosevelt on the cruiser *Quincy*. The Americans outfitted the *Murphy* with a tent that covered the forward part of the ship. Live sheep—fresh meat on the hoof—were penned aft.[34] While the topic of discussion was ostensibly Palestine, not the future of Saudi oil, the meeting confirmed the growing importance of Saudi Arabia to the United States and demonstrated to Ibn Saud that the Americans were determined to play a postwar political role in the region.[35] Roosevelt also favorably impressed Ibn Saud, who also met with Winston Churchill on his return from Yalta. The Saudi king later compared the American president's extremely diplomatic approach with the "deviously" evasive British prime minister's use of the "big stick"—namely commercial and military threats.[36]

Unfortunately, Roosevelt's untimely death in April 1945 and the end of the war in Europe in 1945 threatened to undercut the Saudi-American relationship. The debate over whether or not the United States would remain diplomatically engaged in the postwar affairs of the gulf focused on the question of the continued construction of the air base at Dhahran.

Possession of an air base at Dhahran was no longer a military necessity. The base had originally been intended to provide a link between Cairo and Karachi for the "redeployment of U.S. forces to the Far East and to increase the efficiency of present and contemplated military air transport operations through the Middle East."[37] Nevertheless, after the end of the European war, proponents of the base argued that construction should continue.

> The oil resources of Saudi Arabia, among the greatest in the world, must remain under American control for the dual purpose of supplementing and replacing our dwindling resources, and of preventing this power potential from falling into unfriendly hands. . . . The U.S. should have preferred nation status in Saudi Arabia in the event that the construction of military and naval bases in the Persian Gulf area becomes necessary.[38]

Even the impending end of the Pacific war failed to shake the resolve of those advocating the construction of the air base.[39] The State-War-Navy Coordinating Committee's (SWNCC) Near and Middle East Subcommittee concluded:

Thus the world oil center of gravity is shifting to the Middle East where American enterprise has been entrusted with the exploitation of one of the greatest oil fields. It is in our national interest to see that this vital resource remains in American hands, where it is most likely to be developed on a scale which will cause a considerable lessening of the drain upon the Western Hemisphere reserves. . . . evaluation of the airfield project cannot be based wholly on questions of utility as an airfield. There are ramifications in the realm of U.S.–Saudi relations that make this issue complex.[40]

The argument for the completion of the base was political, not military. Acting Secretary of State Joseph C. Grew had counseled President Harry S. Truman in June:

If, after having conducted successful negotiations with King Ibn Saud to obtain permission to construct the field, this Government would be compelled to inform him that it had decided not to build it, King Ibn Saud would be likely to gain the impression that our policies with regard to Saudi Arabia are of a wavering character. This would contribute to his existing uncertainty as to the extent to which he may rely upon the United States.[41]

So advised, on September 28, 1945, Truman approved the completion of the air base at Dhahran.[42] The basic insecurity of a Saudi monarchy fiscally unstable and militarily weak, and the growing American awareness of the significance of the Arabian peninsula's oil led to the construction of the airfield that would play a key role in Operation Desert Shield/Storm forty-five years later. Truman's decision symbolized the fusion of American diplomatic and economic interests in the Persian Gulf and demonstrated American intent to retain what was expected to be a limited, residual postwar military presence in the region.

The full import of the U.S. decision to play a larger political role in the Persian Gulf was, unfortunately, not readily apparent to most Americans, Britons, Arabs, Iranians, or, more importantly, the leadership of the Soviet Union. At the end of the war, Joseph Stalin chose to test the resolve of his former allies in a fashion that insured that the postwar world would be characterized not by global harmony, but by chronic confrontation between the Soviets and the West—the Cold War. Whatever his motivations, Stalin clearly sought no conflict and proceeded cautiously, especially in Europe and Asia where American military forces remained, backed up by the U.S. nuclear arsenal. But the Americans had withdrawn almost completely from the Persian Gulf and when Stalin looked south, he saw only Great Britain standing in his path.

Soviet military moves in northern Iran marked the culmination of an extended campaign of intimidation that had begun in the summer of 1945. At the Potsdam Conference, the Soviets had resisted American and British efforts to force a withdrawal of Russian troops from Iran before the deadline—six months after the end of the war—agreed to in Article Five of the Anglo-Soviet-Iranian Treaty of January 1942. When the Japanese surrendered on September 2, 1945, the deadline became automatic—the Soviets had to withdraw by March 2, 1946.[43]

Concerns over Soviet intentions in Iran were heightened when not long after the Potsdam meeting, Soviet-sponsored separatists in Azerbaijan and Kurdistan, under the political mantel of the Democratic Party of Azerbaijan, began seizing control. When the Iranian government sent troops north to reassert central authority, Soviet forces blocked the way and "threatened to fire if [the] stop order [was] not obeyed."[44]

American diplomats in Teheran and Washington understood that governmental authority in Iran was tenuous. Many political elements in Iran were less than enthusiastic about the increasing authority of the monarchy that had begun under Reza Shah and would continue under his son.[45] There were legitimate nationalist sentiments, especially among the non-Iranian Turkic, Armenian, and Kurdish peoples of the northern and western provinces. The Russians themselves had several legitimate grievances with the Iranians.[46] But it was clear that the Soviets had both exacerbated and manipulated these tensions to create a puppet regime in the area under their control. From Moscow, George Kennan warned that "nationality" tactics had been used before "in Bessarabia, Ruthenia and Eastern Poland and [were] currently evident with respect to Sinkiang and Turkish Armenia."[47]

As the crisis came to a head in March 1946, Moscow simultaneously pressured Iran's neighbor Turkey.[48] Soviet ground and air forces concentrated in Bulgaria and began to prepare for offensive operations. The movement of Russian troops through northern Iran toward eastern Anatolia appeared to be part of a concerted effort to attack, or at the minimum unnerve, the Soviet Union's two southern neighbors.[49] As Truman later wrote: "Iran would be required to negotiate with Russia while a gun was at her head."[50]

30

Soviet threats against Turkey and Iran prompted American poli-cymakers to reassess their assumptions about Allied postwar coop-eration, but failed to bring about any immediate shifts in policy.[51] Despite concern among the State Department's Middle East experts, Secretary of State James F. Byrnes decided not to press the Soviets regarding their behavior in the Near East at an Allied foreign ministers conference held in Moscow in December 1945.[52] Nor was the American military eager to adopt a tougher line in the Near East. A Joint Intel-ligence Committee report of January 31, 1946 virtually wrote off Soviet-occupied northern Iran.

> Current Soviet moves with respect to Iran and Turkey appear to
> include the establishment of governments "friendly" to the U.S.S.R.,
> and to bring these areas within the limits of the Soviet security zone.
> The recent *fait accompli* in Iranian Azerbaijan has virtually achieved
> Soviet aims in northern Iran.[53]

Three weeks later, the Joint Chiefs of Staff approved a memorandum that recommended that the United States stick to its plans and avoid military commitments in the Near East, despite obvious Soviet pres-sures on Great Britain's position in the region.[54]

The absence of American strategic concern over Soviet actions in the Near East may, in fact, have helped to precipitate the crisis in Iran. Stalin, well served by an effective intelligence apparatus in the West, may have been aware of the American Joint Chiefs of Staff's assess-ments. He certainly had little reason to suspect that the United States, demobilizing rapidly and withdrawing its forces from Europe, would stand fast in Iran.

But in early March, the policy of American restraint ended abruptly when Stalin overstepped himself in northern Iran. On March 4, 1946, American Vice-Consul Robert Rossow, Jr., observed Soviet mecha-nized troops moving into Tabriz in the northern Iranian province of Azerbaijan. The Russian forces passing through Tabriz were headed south, "Tehranward," and not north towards the Soviet border. De-spite the March 2 deadline for the withdrawal of Soviet troops from Iran, Stalin had decided to reinforce his army in northern Iran.[55] Ros-sow later wrote: "One may fairly say that the Cold War began on March 4, 1946."[56]

So, too, did American concerns for the security of the Middle East. Over the course of the next few days, Soviet-American relations de-teriorated rapidly and an atmosphere of crisis and near war hysteria

31

swept through the United States. On March 5 in Fulton, Missouri, Winston S. Churchill delivered his famous "Iron Curtain" speech. Churchill spoke of the "shadow" that had fallen "upon the scenes so lately lighted by the Allied victory."[57] Iran, the former British prime minister noted, was "both profoundly alarmed and disturbed" by Soviet "claims" and "pressure."[58] From Washington that very evening, Secretary of State Byrnes sent a telegram to Moscow for the American Chargé George F. Kennan to deliver to Soviet Foreign Minister Vyacheslav Molotov, asking the Soviets to clarify their intentions with regard to Iran.[59] On March 6 the State Department announced that the battleship *Missouri* would carry the remains of the late Turkish ambassador Mehmet Münir Ertegün to Istanbul. Although state had rejected the navy's proposal to send Vice Admiral Marc A. Mitscher's Eighth Fleet, including an aircraft carrier, to the Mediterranean, the dispatch of *Missouri* was still a significant demonstration of American interest in the region.[60]

Throughout March 7, the State Department's Office of Near Eastern and African Affairs (NEA) monitored the deteriorating situation in Iran. Director Loy Henderson ordered his special assistant, Edwin M. Wright, to prepare a large map of Azerbaijan on which to plot Soviet moves. Wright showed the map, covered with arrows indicating the depth of the Russian penetrations, to Secretary Byrnes at six that evening. Byrnes remarked: "Now we'll give it to them with both barrels." The following morning, the now updated map was used to brief other State Department officials. Undersecretary of State Dean Acheson, alarmed by the Soviets' failure to respond to Byrnes's telegram and by continued reports from Rossow in Tabriz of Russian moves towards Teheran, eastern Turkey, and Kurdistan, decided that the United States had best make certain that the Soviet Union understood that Washington was aware of what was going on in Iran.[61]

Unfortunately, many prominent American historians have confused the record of the events that took place in Iran in late 1945 and early 1946 which precipitated the first crisis of the cold war. Many label Rossow's accounts exaggerated or simply ignore the evidence of Soviet activity in Iran. In his account of the crisis, Melvyn P. Leffler, for example, fails to mention that the Soviets not only refused to evacuate Iran, but also sent additional troops into the country.[62] Walter LaFeber, in his widely used text on American diplomacy, writes: "Russian tanks rumbled towards the Iranian border in early March."[63] In fact, the Russian tanks rumbled over the border and to within a score of miles from the Iranian capital. Joyce and Gabriel Kolko write of "rumors of

32

a massive Soviet troop build-up."[64] John Lewis Gaddis notes that *New York Times* reporter James Reston indicated in a March 20, 1946, column that the reports were exaggerated.[65] Robert L. Meeser follows a similar line, writing: "It seems in retrospect that, though there was some truth to the reports of a Soviet buildup within its zone, the contemporary diplomatic and press reports of a massive Soviet offensive beyond the zone into the rest of Iran were in part deliberate Iranian fabrications and partly the work of self-proving prophets in the State Department bureaucracy."[66] Meeser's source for his account is Stephen L. McFarland, who writes:

> The government of Iran continued the pressure on Washington by passing reports of large Soviet troop movements all over northern Iran. The American consul at Tabriz, capital of Azerbaijan, reported similar movements, although some of his reports were based on sightings passed to him by Iranian sources. The New York *Times*'s reporter in Iran wrote that he saw no sign of Soviet troops concentrations or movements at Qazvin, based on a reconnaissance flight over Azerbaijan, but he found fourteen tanks and other vehicles at Karaj. . . . The Soviet advances certainly occurred, but the reports of them probably were exaggerated.[67]

But Karaj is only twenty miles from Teheran, and while some of Rossow's reports of an increased Soviet presence were supplied by Iranians, most were the result of his own observations, as a reading of his dispatches makes clear. Gene Currivan, the *Times* reporter who took to the air in search of the Soviets, did write that no concentrations were spotted, but he also noted: "Aerial observation is ineffectual because the Russians invariably move at night."[68] Moreover, after initial skepticism caused by a lack of similar reports from its diplomats in Iran, the British embassy in Teheran asserted that Rossow's reports were not exaggerated.[69] United States Army Captain Alexis M. Gagarine, the assistant military attaché in Iran, traveled by road from Teheran to Tabriz and reported "having seen personally Soviet column of 25 tanks moving direction of Teheran. Says Soviet garrison Qazvin increased and Soviet infantry unit in Zenjan. Observed armed Red troops in same trucks with armed Azerbaijan 'Democrats.' "[70] Archie Roosevelt, an American intelligence officer who arrived in Iran at the height of the crisis, also saw Russian soldiers and equipment on the roads between Teheran and Tabriz.[71]

A more interesting question is why the Soviets allowed American

33

diplomatic and military personnel to gather firsthand intelligence of Russian movements. Rossow expected the Soviets to cut communications from Tabriz to prevent him from reporting about their actions, but they never did. Far from trying to conceal their movements, whatever public pronouncements they might make, or whatever American historians might subsequently write, the Soviets clearly wanted American, British, and Iranian officials to observe Soviet troops and equipment moving into Iran. Intimidation could only succeed if a visible, or at least a perceived, threat was apparent.

And it was this threat to which the United States responded. At Acheson's direction, Alger Hiss "scribbled" a draft statement for Byrnes's signature that would convey American concerns to Moscow but leave the Kremlin "a graceful way out" of what was becoming a major crisis. That afternoon the department forwarded a second telegram for Kennan to deliver to the Peoples' Commissar for Foreign Affairs.[72]

The Govt of the US has the honor to inform the Govt of the Soviet Union that it is receiving reports to the effect that there are considerable movements of Soviet combat forces and materials of war from the direction of the Soviet frontier towards Tabriz and outward from Tabriz in the direction of Tehran, Mahabad and various points in Northwestern Iran.

The Govt of the US desires to learn whether the Soviet Govt, instead of withdrawing Soviet troops from Iran as urged in the Embassy's note of Mar 6, is bringing additional forces into Iran. In case Soviet forces in Iran are being increased, this Govt would welcome information at once regarding the purposes therefor.[73]

In Moscow, Kennan cautioned that no attack was imminent. Stalin had not prepared the Russian people for any such undertaking. Kennan reported that the Soviet moves were part of a coordinated plan meant to succeed "by sheer force of intimidation." He believed that the Soviets would remain "just this side of the line" to avoid "a complete diplomatic break with [the] British," whom apparently the American chargé and the Soviets saw as the major bulwark against Russian expansion toward the Mediterranean and the Persian Gulf. Acknowledging that such a war of nerves was fraught with danger, Kennan reminded Byrnes that the Kremlin did not "blunder casually into situations, implications of which it has not thought through."[74]

In his famous "Long Telegram" of February 22, Kennan had advised what course the United States should follow:

> Soviet power, unlike that of Hitlerite Germany, is neither schematic nor adventuristic. It does not work by fixed plans. It does not take unnecessary risks. [It is] impervious to logic of reason, and it is highly sensitive to logic of force. For this reason it can easily withdraw—and usually does—when strong resistance is encountered at any point. Thus, if the adversary has sufficient force and makes clear his readiness to use it, he rarely has to do so. If situations are properly handled there need be no prestige-engaging showdowns.[75]

As Kennan had predicted, on March 24 Stalin, faced by a resolute response from the Iranians, Americans, and the British, ordered Soviet forces to withdraw from Iran.[76] By the end of May, Russian troops had recrossed the border and the Azerbaijani regime was left on its own.

Nevertheless, the crisis continued as the Iranian government tentatively attempted to reestablish its control over the northern provinces. No one could be sure how Stalin would respond as the Tabriz regime gradually, ingloriously, and ultimately bloodily collapsed at the approach of the Iranian army. And despite the apparent diplomatic victory in Iran, an Office of Naval Intelligence report of September 1946 pessimistically concluded:

> Russian political exploitation of Iranian Azerbaijan, widespread clandestine penetration of rest of Iran, equivocal attitude of Premier Ghvam, wholly amorphous politico-economic situation, degeneracy all aspects of Iranian national life suggest inevitability of eventual Russian suzerainty whole country.[77]

The Iranian crisis of 1946 had a significant impact on both United States–Soviet relations and American policy in the Near East. After March 1946, Truman adopted a more confrontational approach towards the Soviets and the Cold War became an unfortunate reality that the world would live with for the next forty-five years. Truman decided the time had come to stop playing "compromise." But he had not based his decision on any assessment of the strategic importance of the Persian Gulf or its oil; a frustated president had simply grown "tired of babying the Soviets."[78] Truman's new hard line approach was applicable not just to the Middle East, but to other points of contention in Europe and Asia as well.[79]

Nevertheless, the crisis did cause Americans to rethink their policy. Stalin's moves in Iran and along the Turkish border demonstrated that the strategic importance of the Near East to the United States had not, as wartime planners had assumed, ended with the conclusion of the war against the Axis. In Iran in March 1946 Americans found themselves teamed with the British playing the "Great Game," contesting the movement of Russian forces toward the south.

The United States' postwar recognition of the strategic significance of the Near East did not translate into an immediate revolution in American policy in the Gulf. While Iran had been the focus of the March 1946 crisis, American diplomats and strategists were far more concerned about Turkey. By the end of the year, the United States had reversed its military withdrawal from European waters and had become an eastern Mediterranean naval power, establishing what would become the Sixth Fleet. The Turks became the chief recipients in the Near East of American military aid. But no comparable naval buildup occurred in the Indian Ocean or the Persian Gulf and Iran received far less military and economic assistance than its western neighbor.

The Turkish focus of American policymakers became evident early during the March 1946 confrontation with the Soviets. On the sixth, in the midst of the Iranian crisis, Secretary of State Byrnes asked the Joint Chiefs of Staff for "an appraisal from the military point of view" of Soviet demands on Turkey, "bearing in mind the possible effect on the security interests of the United States of any undue threat to the security interests of the British Commonwealth of Nations in that area."[80] The JCS reply concluded that the Soviets sought to dominate the Middle East and the Mediterranean as a means to defend their own southern resource regions, to secure control of additional areas, and to undermine the prestige of Britain and the United States in "the Moslem world." Turkish concession to Soviet control of Kars and Ardahand in eastern Anatolia would weaken Turkey and provide a springboard for further moves into that country, Iraq, or toward the Persian Gulf. Regarding the Turkish straits, the JCS noted: "A demand for additional bases in or near the Dardanelles cannot be based on a purely defensive attitude since the Soviets now possess and undoubtedly will retain the military capability of closing the Straits at will." Britain's fate in the Middle East particularly troubled the Joint Chiefs. "The defeat or disintegration of the British Empire would eliminate from Eurasia the last bulwark of resistance between the United States and Soviet expansion." Soviet success against Turkey would also un-

36

dermine the effectiveness of United Nations Organization. The Joint Chiefs recommended that the United States not acquiesce in meeting any of the Soviet demands.[81]

Unfortunately, the military prospects for the United States in the event of a war with the Soviet Union were dismal. A March 13 estimate of the "Availability of Land, Sea and Air Forces in the Event of Emergency" pessimistically concluded that even if the Truman administration halted demobilization on April 1 and canceled or postponed Operation Crossroads, the atomic test scheduled for the Pacific that required commitment of Navy and Air Force assets, little could be done to defend the Middle East.[82] An April 1946 outline of the course an "unlikely" Soviet-American war might take was particularly bleak. The JCS concluded that the Soviet Union had "the capability of overrunning Iran, Iraq and possibly the Suez Canal area, European Turkey, and making major inroads into Asiatic Turkey."[83] Not surprisingly, the Chiefs were concerned about the inadequacy of the American military should the on-going Near Eastern crisis lead to war.[84]

Not until September did the State Department ask the JCS for an analysis of American "strategic interests in Iran" comparable to the one requested by Byrnes on Turkey the previous March.[85] The initial report, prepared by the Joint Strategic Survey Committee (JSSC), focused on petroleum. In the event of a Soviet-American conflict, the JSSC estimated that the United States could wage war for two years without Middle Eastern oil, but thereafter, shortages would handicap operations. "If, during a major war, the United States and her allies are deprived of the oil resources of the Iran–Near and Middle East area it is highly improbable that other sources can supply the United States military and economic requirements together with those of her possible allies." The Soviets, too, the JSSC concluded, needed Middle Eastern oil. "In a major war the USSR would at present require oil from the Iran–Near and Middle East area to meet her military and economic requirements." A sound American strategy would seek "*a.* To deny the oil resources of the Iran–Near and Middle East area to the USSR as long as possible, and *b.* Ultimately to regain the use of these resources for herself and her allies." The JSSC recommended that the Joint Chiefs forward to SWNCC an enclosed memorandum stating that Iran was considered "of vital strategic interest to the United States" and that the United States provide the Iranians with "non-aggression" military assistance and advice as a "token" measure of goodwill and support.[86]

At Fleet Admiral William O. Leahy's direction, the Joint Chiefs

37

toned down the draft memorandum. The JSC's October 11 response to SWNCC termed Iran "an area of major strategic interest," a defensive "cushion" that offered opportunities to delay any Soviet drive toward the Persian Gulf and provided "one of the few favorable areas for counteroffensive action." The JCS stressed the need to support Iran if the United States was to maintain its reputation in the Middle East and throughout the world. To secure Iranian central authority and to prevent Soviet moves into the area, defensive military equipment could be provided to the Iranians. Nevertheless, the October 11 memorandum was restrained in its call for assistance and ended with the reminder that "the military implications in the existing international situation concerning Iran are closely related to the military implications of the current Turkish situation, on which the Joint Chiefs of Staff furnished their views to the Secretaries of War and the Navy on 24 [sic] August 1946."[87]

In mid-October, the State Department issued revised policy positions on Iran and Turkey.[88] As the crisis in Iran dragged on, and Britain appeared to weaken in its support of Iranian territorial integrity, the Near Eastern and African Affairs Office completed a memorandum on the "Implementation of United States Policy Toward Iran."[89] The State Department's policy paralleled, but went somewhat farther than the JCS's recommendations with regard to the provision of defensive military equipment to the Iranians. Three days later, a draft memorandum on Turkey was ready.[90] Like the Iran statement, it was "partially based upon the JCS memorandum." Recognizing that the Soviets' "unrelenting war of nerves" forced Turkey to keep large military forces in the field and posed "a dangerous drain on the nation's economic strength," NEA proposed diplomatic, moral, economic, and military support for the Turks. Nevertheless, the memorandum suggested that military support for Turkey should come from the British, "because the world in general has become accustomed to the fact that Turkey receives arms from Britain." If Britain proved unable to supply such assistance, NEA suggested that American military aid be channeled through the British.

In Iran and Turkey, as elsewhere in the region, the United States was gradually supplanting Great Britain as the preeminent external power in the diplomatic arena. The Iranian policy elite continued, as it had for nearly a century, to view the United States as central to any effort to maintain the integrity of Iran. Through their "century-old strategy of *movazaneh* (equilibrium)," writes Stephen L. McFarland, the Iranians "endeavored to attract the United States to act as a buffer and counter-balance the Anglo-Soviet threat."[91]

In the spring of 1946, the United States demonstrated its willingness to play the role of "buffer" in Iran. Americans agreed to provide substantial political and economic support to Great Britain, Turkey, Iran, Saudi Arabia, and other states in the Near East. The United States took the diplomatic lead and faced down the Soviets at the United Nations and in Iran and Turkey. The promises made by President Roosevelt to the Iranians at the Teheran Conference in 1943 had been kept, although the Americans found themselves far more deeply involved in the affairs of the gulf than they had expected.

But despite its increasing economic stake in the region and newly discovered diplomatic leadership in the affairs of the Persian Gulf, the United States, its armed forces already stretched thin by commitments in Europe and Asia, steadfastly refused to contribute to the defense of the Middle East. Americans continued to look to the British to shoulder near total military responsibility for the region's defense.

CHAPTER THREE

MIDDLE EAST OIL AND THE DESTINY OF EUROPE

———•———

1947–1950

For American policymakers, the Second World War and the Iran crisis of early 1946 made manifest the strategic importance of the Middle East. Despite the expectations of wartime planners, the gulf remained the pivotal position that Mahan had described a half-century before—a region where the British had blocked Russian expansion to the south throughout the nineteenth century.

Initially, such basic strategic considerations overshadowed American concerns about the petroleum of the Persian Gulf. Policymakers in Washington were cognizant of the growing importance of the oil of the Middle East, but petroleum was just one, and by no means the most significant, factor in the regional strategic equation.[1]

Americans were beginning, gradually and reluctantly, to assume responsibility from the British for the security of the Middle East. Great Britain's strategic interests in the region, and clashes with the Russians, predated the development of the oil industry in the Persian Gulf. For Great Britain, and for the United States, the Middle East was a strategic midway point between east and west. Great Britain's imperial lifelines—most notably the Suez Canal in Egypt—ran through the region. The canal was (and remains) a vitally important international waterway. And in both British and American contingency plans developed in 1946 and 1947 for a Third World War, air bases in Egypt were assigned critical roles in a strategic air campaign against the Soviet Union.

The petroleum resources of the Middle East are so much a part of

40

modern life that it is hard for Americans in the 1990s to consider the strategic importance of the Persian Gulf in terms other than oil. Nevertheless, a focus on oil interests alone is insufficient to explain the directions taken by American policy in the years immediately following the Second World War.[2] NEA's memorandum of October 1946 on United States policy toward Iran, for example, never once mentioned oil.[3] Of the three northern tier states—Greece, Turkey, and Iran—only the last-named actually possessed petroleum, but nevertheless received the least American diplomatic, economic, and military support between 1946 and 1953. Soviet behavior in Iran in early 1946, not concern about the oil of the Persian Gulf, prompted President Truman to take a forceful line against Stalin in the Near East. And, despite the supposed criticality of oil, American strategists continually resisted efforts to make a major military commitment to the defense of the Persian Gulf, which remained a theater of tertiary importance after Europe and Asia.[4]

The Near East became a battleground in the Cold War initially and principally to contain the Soviets. The United States and its allies had to block Communist expansion by appropriate means, be they diplomatic, political, economic, or military. When the expansion came in the Middle East, the United States responded promptly.

Nevertheless, in the late 1940s, the petroleum riches of the Persian Gulf became an increasingly important consideration in the strategic calculations of the United States. The trends in the global oil situation foreseen in the State Department's spring 1944 foreign oil policy statement altered the focus of American diplomacy in the Persian Gulf. The United States saw its share of world oil production fall from 70 to 51 percent, while that of the Persian Gulf states rose from 7 to 16 percent.[5] An Office of Naval Intelligence assessment of 1949 concluded that "the center of world oil-producing activity is slowly but steadily shifting from the Western Hemisphere to the Middle East."[6] The United States, long the world's premier oil exporter, proved unable to maintain its position in the postwar world, a development that occurred far more rapidly than American policymakers had expected. In 1946, American petroleum exports totalled 119,687,000 barrels, more than twice the 51,610,000 barrels imported, but by 1950 imports were almost twice as high as exports.[7]

Concern about dwindling American oil reserves did not become acute until 1947 and 1948.[8] The problem was not the availability of domestic supplies, but the inability of the United States to resume its pre-1939 role as the major oil exporter to the world. At a May 2, 1947, lunch, Secrtary of the Navy James Forrestal and Senator Owen Brewster discussed these concerns.

I [Forrestal] said that Middle East oil was going to be necessary for this country not merely in wartime but in peacetime, because if we are going to make the contribution that it seems we have to make to the rest of the world in manufactured goods, we shall probably need very greatly increased supplies of fuel.

Brewster said that . . . Europe in the next ten years may shift from coal to an oil economy and therefore whoever sits on the valve of Middle East oil may control the destiny of Europe. He expressed considerable misgivings about the capacity of American forces to keep Russia out of Arabia if they decided to move there.[9]

Forrestal had long been concerned about the security of Persian Gulf oil.[10] He was one of many American policymakers who believed that it was in the long-term interest of the United States to draw upon extensive Middle Eastern reserves to the greatest extent possible in an effort to conserve American petroleum reserves for the future. Soviet moves in Iran, as well as Forrestal's belief that American support for Zionism would threaten the American position in the Arab world, only increased his apprehension.

During the Iran crisis, the Navy's Political-Military Policy Division began a study of the world oil situation and in October presented Forrestal with a report. During the Second World War, Persian Gulf oil had been critically important and had "supplied the British 8th, 9th, 10th, and 14th Armies, the Mediterranean and Indian fleets, as well as India, Africa and the Middle East, and the U.S. Persian Gulf command, the 9th U.S. Air Force, the Eastern Bomber Command, the China-India-Burma A.T.C., the Flying Tigers, the 20th Air Force and the African Middle Eastern Service Command." Although the report dismissed many of the fears of an impending domestic oil shortage, it stressed the long-term need for secure reserves, and the growing importance of Middle Eastern supplies. The report reiterated previous recommendations that the United States draw on Middle East oil to preserve American reserves.[11]

But in late 1947, as the United States continued to export oil, domestic shortages developed. On January 17, 1948, President Truman announced stringent government-wide standards meant to conserve fuel in the midst of an energy-short winter. Federal office buildings and residential quarters were not to be heated above 68°F during working hours, nor above 60°F at other times. Installation of new equipment that consumed petroleum products was barred without the approval of the Bureau of Mines. Government buildings were to be insulated to preserve energy; lighting and other uses of electricity were to be reduced. Government vehicles were not to be driven above forty miles per hour, except in emergencies. No vehicles were to use premium grade fuel unless required by design.[12]

Truman acted in response to a growing national perception that the United States was in the midst of an energy crisis. Four days before, Secretary of the Interior Julius Krug had warned that the nation faced a critical petroleum situation in twenty-four of the forty-eight states, especially in the Northeast. Rationing was a possibility. American oil reserves would be exhausted within ten years. Krug recommended government support for programs to extract oil from shale and to find alternate supplies of energy. At a January 16 cabinet meeting, Krug had indicated that postwar American domestic demand for oil was 50 percent higher than the prewar level. While the United States was importing 450,000 barrels of oil a day to meet the demand, exports, mostly to Europe, had already risen to almost 100 percent over the prewar levels and about 450,000 barrels a day were being exported.

Forrestal, now secretary of defense, focused on the strategic implications of the domestic oil crunch. He noted "that the Marshall Plan for Europe could not succeed without access to the Middle East oil, that we could not fight a war without access to it and that even in peacetime our economy would be unable to maintain its present tempo without it."[13] On January 19 he warned Congress that the oil shortage threatened American national security. The United States would find itself short 2,000,000 barrels of oil a day if a Third World War broke out. Forrestal also publicly voiced his concerns about the administration's decision to support the partition of Palestine, which, in his view, threatened not only American supplies, especially those upon which the U.S. military was increasingly relying, but also the oil that would have to fuel the planned European Recovery Program (ERP)—the Marshall Plan. Forrestal hoped that increased American production, especially from newly discovered fields in Alaska, would help ease the situation, but he expected that the United States would itself have to rely increasingly on Persian Gulf suppliers. He suggested that it would be a "good approach" for President Truman to establish a special commission to draw up a national energy program.[14]

The oil scare of 1948 was less a harbinger of a dramatic oil shortage than a result of a short-term imbalance between production and demand. The booming postwar United States economy had recovered and had begun to expand faster than the world's oil companies had increased their output and adjusted from wartime to peacetime production and distribution realities.

The Truman administration's effort to maintain oil exports at increasingly high levels had exacerbated the situation. Despite the growing petroleum shortfall in the United States throughout 1947 and into 1948, the administration continued to permit the export of oil, even to the Soviet Union. Not until February 1948, after initial Truman administration opposition, did the Commerce Department respond to congressional calls for a halt to petroleum exports. The situation had become critical, so critical that the navy was forced to turn over 1,000,000 barrels of oil for domestic use.[15]

The oil shortage increased the American military's interest in the Middle East. In the fall, Secretary of Defense Forrestal told Congress that further development of Saudi oilfields, and the construction of a pipeline from those fields to the eastern Mediterranean, was "essential."

> I took the position that because of the rapid depletion of American oil reserves and an equally rapidly rising curve of consumption we would have to develop resources outside the country. The greatest field of untapped oil in the world is in the Middle East. . . . We should not be shipping a barrel of oil out of the United States to Europe. From 1939 to 1946 world oil reserves . . . went up about 60 per cent while American discoveries added only about 6 per cent to ours.[16]

But by early 1949, the oil shortage had evaporated. In January, Truman ended Federal conservation measures. Even Forrestal began to sound less pessimistic, noting "that we could, by the application of strict rationing in the United States, fight a war for a considerable period of time without access to the Middle East."[17] Some Congressmen began to ask whether there had ever really been a shortage and blamed the oil companies for the previous year's problems. In June, Texas state regulators restricted production, fearing a glut.

Nevertheless, the oil fright of 1948 forged the connection between American energy needs, national security, and the Middle East.[18] By 1948 the oil of the Persian Gulf had become a strategic, not just a commercial commodity for the United States. The reconstruction of war-torn Western Europe, the fundamental imperative of the containment of Soviet expansionism, depended upon the continued and expanded flow of oil from the Persian Gulf. An Office of Naval Intelligence confidential report concluded:

> Considering the paucity of oil-bearing regions and the insufficient rate of production from the United States and South American fields, and in view of the United States commitments under the European Recovery Plan, it is essential that Middle East production, conditions permitting, increase its output in order to prevent serious depletion of United States strategic reserves.[19]

As policymakers in Washington debated American Middle East policy, the U.S. Navy, its "black oil" stocks diverted to civilian use, sought out new sources of supply. The pressing need for fuel for the fleet, not long-term strategic interests, first brought the ships of the U.S. Navy to the Persian Gulf in the postwar era. Domestic shortages, lower prices, and geographic propinquity to naval operating areas increasingly led the navy to look to the gulf for fuel produced in the refineries built or expanded by the British and the Americans during the Second World War. In mid-1947 the U.S. Navy began to purchase large quantities of fuel overseas from the refineries constructed to supply military quality naval fuel during the Second World War. The navy contracting with CALTEX in the Persian Gulf to purchase just short of 100,000,000 barrels of refined product over five years, at rates lower than those available domestically.[20]

By the end of the 1940s, while the United States imported insignificant amounts of Persian Gulf oil, the American military had become heavily dependent on Middle Eastern supplies. From 1946 to 1950, between 30 and 42 percent of the petroleum products moved by the U.S. Navy came from the Persian Gulf.[21] American men-of-war in the Mediterranean and the Western Pacific relied heavily on Persian Gulf fuels. Moreover, the majority of some critically important products came from the gulf.[22] During the Korean War, the American war effort was fuelled extensively from Persian Gulf refineries.[23]

Each month, the navy transported between 1.5 and 5 million barrels of product from the Persian Gulf to the Mediterranean or the Pacific in its own oilers and in chartered tankers. The movement of as many as two dozen ships through the Persian Gulf necessitated the establishment of facilities to monitor and control such a large-scale logistical effort.[24] The possibility that the United States might have to defend the region in wartime also led the navy to conduct extensive surveys of what was for it a new area of operations.

Admiral Richard L. Conolly, Northeastern Atlantic and Mediterranean commander in chief based in London, controlled all American naval forces in European and Indian Ocean waters, including those of the Persian Gulf.[25] Conolly believed that it was imperative that the U.S. Navy assure the nations of the Old World that the United States would not revert to its "policy of isolationism, as we had after World War I, but would continue to maintain a potent interest, an interest that we would back up with force, if necessary—by the show of force, the presence of force—in that area, and thereby hearten them in their opposition to the spread of Communism."[26]

Establishing Task Force 126 on January 20, 1948, Conolly formalized and improved the navy's command structure in the Persian Gulf. The task force consisted solely of tankers in the gulf to take on oil and was commanded by the Senior Officer Present Afloat (SOPA). Conolly reported that "the formation of this new command reflected the navy's increasing interest in this area as evidenced by additional oilers operating from the Bahrein–Ras Tanura area and the scheduled visits of one or more carrier task forces later in the year."[27]

Throughout 1948 and 1949, Conolly continued to reorganize the command. On June 26, 1949, he turned over operational command of American naval forces in the gulf to the commander of the renamed Persian Gulf Forces.[28] On August 16, 1949, the command was renamed yet again—Middle East Force.[29]

Conolly struggled to place the small command on as firm a basis as possible. In both London and Washington there was a growing sense that the U.S. Navy's role in the Persian Gulf area should be "an operation similar to that now enjoyed in the Mediterranean."[30] At a conference held in Washington in June 1948, Conolly recommended the appointment of a flag officer and the stationing of a permanent command vessel in the Gulf/Indian Ocean area.[31]

But neither the Truman administration nor the Joint Chiefs of Staff were prepared in the late 1940s to commit the United States to the defense of the Persian Gulf. The deployment of the navy's Middle East Force (MEF) symbolized the United States' increased interest in the region, but was not meant to herald the arrival of a force comparable to the Sixth Fleet deployed in the Mediterranean. Despite the modest growth of the Middle East Force in size and significance, and the deployment of a flag ship to the gulf, three years passed before a rear admiral assumed command. The U.S. Navy captains in command remained grossly outranked by the vice admirals who commanded British forces in the region. Nevertheless, under Conolly's guidance, MEF was established on a firm basis and the United States has since maintained a permanent naval presence in the Persian Gulf.

United States Navy ships operating in the Indian Ocean basin immediately confronted the logistical realities inherent in operations in an area with few good ports, fewer airfields, and almost halfway around the world from the United States. Central to the control and smooth functioning of the American effort in the Persian Gulf/Indian Ocean area was the extension of naval support and logistics facilities to the region. In the summer of 1947, the navy established a plan for its oilers "to facilitate communications between ships and INSMAT [Inspector of Naval Material] Bahrein and to expedite loading these oilers."[32] By mid-1948, the navy had established stations at Asmara, Ethiopia, and Dhahran, Saudi Arabia, and had leased facilities for fuel storage at Massawa, Ethiopia; Aden; and Trincomalee, Ceylon.[33] These first steps to improve communications and logistics facilities initiated a forty-five-year effort to expand the American support infrastructure in the region.

Recognition that the U.S. Navy would continue to operate for the foreseeable future in the Persian Gulf, as well as the realization that the region could become an area of operations in the event of a Soviet-American confrontation, led the Office of the Chief of Naval Operations (OPNAV) in October 1947 to plan a Persian Gulf cruise for August 1948. The navy wanted to test its equipment and personnel under the extreme conditions of the gulf, to conduct visits to suitable ports, and to gather amphibious data and other intelligence.[34] The initial plan called for a force of ten ships, including an aircraft carrier, to conduct hydrographic, photographic, and other reconnaissance of the area stretching from the Suez Canal to the Persian Gulf.[35]

Although commitments elsewhere forced the navy to alter its plans for 1948, a carrier task force and other naval units did visit the Persian Gulf during the year. The resultant extensive reconnaissance and scientific surveys indicated that environmental conditions in the gulf posed significant, though not insurmountable, problems. Because of the "unbearable heat," work was best performed early in the day and only essential watches were stood in the afternoon. One captain wrote that the heat was so intense that he did not believe that his crew "could think straight."[36] Another reported:

47

It was found that all berthing and messing spaces for the crew were untenable with temperatures up to 115°F and high humidity. The officers and crew slept topside on cots or on the deck. Sick Bay was moved topside. The crew was fed on the fantail with mess gear set up, and chow lines passing through the galley. Officers and CPOs ate in their messes, but meals were short and the Wardroom and CPO messes were deserted except for fifteen minutes at meal hours. The uniform aboard, except when rendering honors, was shorts and undershirts. . . . The shower water was too hot to use except for short periods. The alterations submitted to BuShips were based on those incorporated in HMS Wild Goose and HMS Wren, of the British Persian Gulf Squadron. These ships were fairly comfortable.[37]

Ashore, conditions were somewhat better. The navy operated from Bahrain, the major British base in the Persian Gulf. American sailors played softball with oil company personnel and had access to the British recreation facilities for both officers and men at Jufair, outside Manama. The Royal Navy even shared its beer, despite short supplies, but U.S. Navy commanders reported that American sailors were less than enthusiastic about the "poor quality" of the two bottles of "Scotch beer" allowed each man and recommended that "Navy tankers destined for the Persian Gulf load a supply of American beer for use by recreation parties."[38] Another source of complaint and a cause for poor morale was irregular mail service.

Americans found the Arabs of the Gulf hospitable and impressed by displays of U.S. Navy might. When the carrier Valley Forge visited Ras Tanura in the spring of 1948, bad weather unfortunately forced the cancellation of most of the planned flight operations, including the standard flyover by the carrier's aircraft—in a formation that spelled S-A-U-D. Nevertheless, the tour of the Valley Forge, a limited air demonstration, and a showing of the film "Fighting Lady" greatly impressed Crown Prince Saud of Saudi Arabia and his retinue.[39]

The visit of the seaplane tender Rendova to Bahrain was similarly well received. About twenty members of the Bahraini royal family came aboard the Rendova for a demonstration that included several catapult launchings and a navy film about carrier operations. But a more prosaic piece of technology most interested the Bahrainis: "Drinking ice water from numerous ship's water coolers seemed to be the prize indulgence on the parts of the royal retinue, young and old." The congenial mode continued ashore when the sheik threw a massive dinner for the Americans that was marked by inordinate amounts of food (including Sunkist oranges) served in splendid Arab fashion.

By April 21, 1951, when Rear Admiral Harry D. Felt relieved Captain Ernest M. Eller as commander, the Middle East Force had become a symbol of U.S. military and diplomatic interest in the region. A flag-ship, a pair of destroyers, command aircraft based at Bahrain or Dhah-ran, tankers, and occasionally additional combat, support, and survey vessels cruised the strategic shipping lanes of the gulf and the Indian Ocean, "supplied much needed intelligence, maintained liaison with all allied military and diplomatic forces present, conducted both in-formal and official calls on civilian and military dignitaries in all coun-tries and pursued an active type people-to-people program."[40]

The U.S. Navy's Middle East Force was not, nor was it meant to be, as capable a deterrent as the Sixth Fleet in the Mediterranean. In a Third World War scenario, MEF was capable of doing little more than evacuating American civilians.

Nevertheless, the small U.S. Navy force based at Bahrain repre-sented a permanent military presence in the Persian Gulf. Every year, MEF men-of-war monitored the movement of more and more tankers from the gulf. Many of these tankers carried refined product to Europe or Asia for the American military, which by 1950 drew as much as half of its fuel from the gulf. Other tankers carried crude to the United States, which each year began to import more and more oil from the gulf. But most of the tankers were bound for Europe where Persian Gulf oil fueled a dramatic economic recovery.

The Cold War and the economic needs of the United States and the West had brought the U.S. Navy into the Persian Gulf. How long that presence would continue, and how the American military role in the region would change over time could not be foreseen. But early in 1951, Captain Ernest M. Eller, commander of the Middle East Force, wrote Chief of Naval Operations Admiral Forrest P. Sherman: "Great nations are stirring and great events are shaping up in this part of the world. I hope the United States will comprehend them and will be equal to the opportunity."[41]

By 1950, the formative period of the American relationship with the gulf had come to an end. The basic outlines of the policy that would lead the United States into ever deeper involvement in the Persian Gulf had been established. United States policy called for the rapid expansion of oil production in the gulf. In the short term, that oil would fuel economic recovery in Western Europe and thereby contain the political threat posed by Soviet-sponsored communism. In the mid- and long-term, Persian Gulf oil would provide the United States with an alternative source of supply, one that would allow Americans to husband their own domestic petroleum reserves for the future. In the oil-producing states, economic prosperity would be accompanied by political development along traditional liberal democratic lines. For example, during Anglo-American talks held in London in September 1950, diplomats spoke of the need to encourage the development of "progressive" governments in the Near East.[42] As a result, the gulf would become more stable and pro-Western. While Great Britain was expected to provide for the military defense of the region, backed by the ever-expanding American nuclear capability, the United States would take the political and economic lead in the affairs of the gulf.

The most noteworthy aspect of American Persian Gulf policy as formulated in the 1940s is that the United States had a coherent policy at all. Over the ensuing decades many Americans expressed doubts about whether or not their government knew what it was doing in the Middle East. In fact, the United States pursued its goals fairly faithfully. American policymakers *planned* to increase the world's dependence on Middle Eastern oil and *expected* to have to shoulder political and economic responsibility for the security of the gulf. The United States *chose* to become the political guardian of the oil supplies that would flow, for the most part, not to the United States, but to Europe. And the concept of "energy independence," an attractive political catchword in the United States since the 1973 Arab oil embargo, was exactly what policymakers in the 1940s *sought* to avoid. To them, energy independence meant the rapid exhaustion of American oil reserves. Their long-term vision of energy security called for *increased* reliance, or if one prefers "dependence," on Persian Gulf oil.

In retrospect, American Persian Gulf policy, as developed in the 1940s, was remarkably successful. The United States achieved its most important goals: the economies of Western Europe recovered from the ravages of the Second World War, fueled by the oil from the Gulf; Soviet communism was contained; and Americans increased their reliance on Middle Eastern oil.

Unfortunately, this policy did not, nor could it have anticipated all future developments. Great Britain ultimately proved unable and unwilling to sustain its military commitment to the defense of a region increasingly dominated by the United States. Oil revenues and economic development brought not stability, but rapid modernization and instability to the region. The United States found itself increasingly reliant on petroleum from, and was forced to bear an ever-larger military burden in, a region of endemic volatility. In that sense, as early as 1950 the United States had embarked on the road to Desert Storm, and had an appointment to keep on the Euphrates.

CHAPTER FOUR

THE CHIMERA OF REGIONAL DEFENSE

———•———

1950–1967

For the United States, by mid-1950 the security of the Middle East had become a conundrum. The defense of the region was an important, if not yet vital, component of a comprehensive system of Western security. American policymakers recognized the geostrategic significance of the Middle East and the geoeconomic importance of the oil of the Persian Gulf. They accepted the fact that the United States had to take the diplomatic lead in the Middle East to protect Western interests. But Americans still looked to Great Britain to actually defend the region, since the Truman administration continued to reduce the size of a military establishment already more than fully committed to the defense of Europe and Asia. Even the effectiveness of the U.S. nuclear deterrent had diminished. The Soviet Union's explosion of an atomic weapon in 1949 brought the short-lived American atomic monopoly to an end and reduced the likelihood that Truman would risk a nuclear exchange to halt a Russian attack confined to the Middle East. Then in June 1950, the outbreak of war in Korea intensified concerns in Washington, London, Ankara, and Teheran about the possibility of a Soviet drive south into Turkey or Iran, but at the same time the extensive commitment of United States forces to the defense of the Korean peninsula all but ruled out American military support for the British.

As the reality of the Soviet threat to Western interests in the Middle East became manifest in the late 1940s and early 1950s, the British, upon whom primary responsibility for the defense of the region rested, sought help in the form of a multinational defense arrangement. An effective regional security structure, what in 1952 would become known as the Middle East Defense Organization (MEDO), would legitimize and formalize the continued stationing of British forces in the Middle East, especially in Egypt; provide a weakened Great Britain with a set of allies, albeit of uncertain quality; and establish a regional command structure into which, the British hoped, American forces would be introduced should the Soviet Union undertake an offensive south from the Caucasus.

The British effort to organize a Middle Eastern command met with little success. The Middle East was not Western Europe. Only in Turkey and Iran, states that physically bordered the Soviet Union, were there any real concerns about the threat emanating from Moscow. Whereas most of the original NATO countries had only a few years before worked together as allies during the war with Germany, many of the Middle East states had until recently been subjected to British colonial rule. To a country such as Egypt, Britain appeared a more likely menace than the Soviet Union and any scheme that called for the stationing of European forces in the Middle East held little appeal. As Egyptian President Gamal Abdel Nasser explained to Secretary of State John Foster Dulles in 1952: "How can I go to my people and tell them I am disregarding a killer with a pistol sixty miles from me at the Suez Canal to worry about someone who is holding a knife 5,000 miles away?"[1] To the extent that the Arab states in the region wished to band together, they hoped to establish a Pan-Arab framework, not a security relationship dominated by Great Britain.

The United States, which during the war had worked to distance itself from its Allies' legacy of imperial rule in the Middle East, initially was less than enthusiastic about British efforts to institute a regional defense structure. As the war ended, American policymakers on the whole were somewhat slower than their British counterparts at discerning the Soviet threat in the Middle East. Americans were more concerned about ending British and French colonial rule. Moreover, the United States, which was unwilling to join a European defense structure until late 1949, was even less eager to risk involvement in the volatile Middle East.

In the immediate aftermath of the Second World War, Americans, much like the Arabs, were more concerned about the realities of Arab nationalism than any potential Soviet threat to the Middle East. The pressures of war had accelerated and strengthened the forces of nationalism and anticolonialism already at work in the Islamic world. The states of the Middle East had struggled to assert themselves nationally, and often collectively as Arabs, to protect their Islamic culture, and to survive in what was demonstrably a dangerous and rapidly changing environment.

The United States entered the post–World War II era without any "imperialist" baggage in the Middle East. Unlike the British, French, and Russians, Americans had no history of territorial aggrandizement in the region. The anticolonial tenor of American wartime policy had appealed to the Arabs. The United States had supported Arab governments in Beirut and Damascus during the Levant crisis of 1945 when the French attempted to reimpose colonial control in Lebanon and Syria.[2] As a result, much like the Iranians and the Turks who benefitted from similar American support in 1946, the Arabs initially viewed the United States as a counterweight to those powers intent on asserting or reasserting colonial influence and control.

Nevertheless, as the United States played an ever larger role in the region, attempts to achieve American policy aims were bound to lead to occasional conflicts with Arab governments. In the Middle East, the United States could not forever escape the opprobrium that came with its new-found international leadership.[3]

The most pressing problem facing the United States in the Middle East was what Dean Acheson termed "The Puzzle of Palestine."[4] The debate over Palestine was highly charged. In the Middle East Jews imbued with Zionist aspirations and post-Holocaust determination sought a secure homeland. There they confronted both Great Britain, which still administered Palestine, and Arab nationalists who violently opposed such settlement. In the United States the politics of the debate frequently overwhelmed the more pragmatic concerns of American foreign policy.

The extent to which domestic political concerns shaped American policy toward Palestine has been and will continue to be debated. President Truman's motivations may well have "represented a deep conviction," as believed by Acheson, or "the disastrous and regrettable fact that the foreign policy of this country was determined by the contributions a particular bloc of special interests might make to party funds," as Secretary Forrestal presumed.[5] What is certain is that American political leaders controlled the debate and overruled the politico-military bureaucracy. Dean Acheson later wrote, "It was clear that the President himself was directing policy on Palestine."[6]

The military had expressed misgivings about the possible impact of the Palestine question on American policy in the Middle East in early 1946.[7] The Joint Chiefs of Staff were concerned that a pro-Zionist policy might inevitably force an already overstretched military establishment to commit forces into Palestine, would drive the Arabs into the Soviet camp, complicate American Near Eastern policy, threaten the West's strategic position in the region, and, most importantly, provoke the Arabs to deny the United States access to Middle Eastern oil.[8]

This last point was critical. American policymakers recognized the connection between Palestine and the Persian Gulf. An Arab-Jewish crisis in the Levant had the potential to undermine the West's position in the Gulf. As the crisis deepened, so, too, did the apprehensions of the JCS. An October 1947 paper concluded:

> The Joint Chiefs of Staff are of the opinion that implementation of a decision to partition Palestine, if the decision were supported by the United States, would prejudice United States strategic interests in the Near and Middle East and that United States influence in the area would be curtailed to that which could be maintained by force. Further, there is grave danger that such a decision would result in such serious disturbances throughout the Near and Middle East area as to dwarf any local Palestine disturbances resulting from the decision. As a consequence the USSR might replace the United States and Great Britain in influence and power throughout the area.[9]

As they considered the problems of evacuating Americans from the region, the Chiefs reiterated a June 1946 recommendation that the United States not take any decision that would lead to the commitment of American forces into Palestine or would "orient the peoples of the Middle East away from the United States, since the United States has a vital security interest in the Near and Middle East."

American military leaders grew even more alarmed when the diplomatic debate at the United Nations appeared likely to lead to a proposed United States–Soviet Union trusteeship and occupation of Palestine. To the prospect of American military intervention in a region torn by violence and terrorism, was added the possibility of Soviet diplomatic involvement in the Middle East.[10] In early February 1948, Chief of Naval Operations Admiral Louis E. Denfeld argued that such an outcome would lead to all kinds of problems and the continued "deterioration" of the American position in the Arab world.[11] Nevertheless, the JCS dutifully prepared contingency plans that projected extensive force requirements for Palestine (100,000 troops) as well as a plan to secure control of Jerusalem.[12]

The surprising, if not shocking, victory of the newly established

Israeli Defense Forces over the Arabs in the 1948 war dramatically altered the character of United States Middle East policy. The American military establishment performed a rather dramatic about-face. The JCS, which no longer had to concern itself with the possible dispatch of American forces to Palestine, stopped producing papers that argued against American support for a Jewish state and began studying "U.S. Strategic Interest in Israel."

> Existing Joint Chiefs of Staff policy on this subject appears now to have been overtaken by events. The power balance in the Near and Middle East has been radically altered. At the time the state of Israel was forming, numerous indications pointed to its extremely short life in the face of Arab League opposition. However, Israel has now been recognized by the United States and the United Kingdom, is likely soon to become a member of the United Nations, and has demonstrated by force of arms its right to be considered the military power next after Turkey in the Near and Middle East.[13]

Early 1949 American military assessments were as overoptimistic as previous appraisals had been alarmist. JCS reports began to extol the advantages of a strategically located base in Palestine. A May 1949 report concluded that U.S. policy ought to endeavor to assure Israel's Western orientation, seek to reconcile the differences between Israel and its Arab neighbors, and work to include Israel in any regional defense pact.[14]

In September and October 1949, the National Security Council formalized more sober and realistic assessments that established the basic outlines of American Middle Eastern policy for the next four decades. NSC 47/2 concluded that the "Eastern Mediterranean and the Near East" were critically important to American security. The United States had to engage in "impartial" but "constructive leadership" to promote pro-Western ties, to prevent Soviet penetration of the region, and to insure that disputes internal to the region did not prevent Middle Eastern states from acting "in concert to oppose Soviet aggression." Regarding the Palestine problem, the NSC argued that Israel and its Arab neighbors had to reach an accord on their own and that the Arabs were unlikely to welcome Israel into any Middle Eastern defense structure.[15]

Far from being eager to build up the Israeli military machine, the NSC sought to closely control the flow of arms to the Near East, and especially to the Israelis and their Arab neighbors. NSC 65/3 of May

19, 1950 ("United States Policy Towards Arms Shipments to the Near East") quickly gained British and French support and on May 25, Washington, London, and Paris released the text of the Tripartite Declaration regarding arms transfers.[16] The thrust of the declaration was simple.

> This policy provides for the export of arms to the Near East on a restricted basis for the purposes of internal security, self defense and defense of the area as a whole. Shipments of light material should continue as an indication of our interest in the area.[17]

American fears about the impact on Western interests of the establishment of a Jewish state in Palestine and the possibility of a regional arms race were justified. The Arabs, stung by their defeat at the hands of the Israelis, vented much of their anger and frustration at the West, especially the United States. Nevertheless, American policymakers, despite the worst fears of many in the politico-military bureaucracy in the 1940s, managed (and continue to manage) to juggle the interests of "the competing nationalisms" in the Middle East with fair success. The realities of American political, economic, and military might insured that the United States remained a recognized and respected, if not loved, power throughout the Middle East. Nevertheless, those same realities were themselves menacing. The United States, as a world power and as a purveyor of materialist mass culture, threatened traditionalist, rapidly modernizing Islamic states. And American support for Israel placed the United States in direct conflict with the dreams of Arab nationalists.

As a result, these dual realities gave, and continue to give, the postwar Arab-American relationship a schizophrenic character. Parallel interests combined with underlying tensions generally have led the Arab states to welcome a very circumscribed American presence in the region. In times of crises, a threatened state might well set aside its pan-Arab concerns and allow, or even request, an expanded American presence. But should the crisis in question involve Israel, the Arab reaction could very easily take an opposite course and seek the expulsion of an American military, diplomatic, and even commercial presence.

Thus between 1946 and 1950, the legacy of British colonialism, the Arab-Israeli problem, and the political chaos evident in the Arab world, convinced American policymakers not to support British efforts to establish a Middle Eastern command.[18] As late as the March 1950 Cairo

57

conference, American representatives argued that "it would be impractical and undesirable for the United States to encourage any Near Eastern regional defense pact."[19]

But by late 1950, with the situation in the Middle East becoming increasingly unstable, American thinking about Great Britain's proposed Middle East Command (MEC) began to change. With its membership in NATO, the United States had broken with its historic tradition of avoiding peacetime "entangling" alliances. The war that had begun in Korea in June 1950, and the subsequent Chinese communist intervention, had raised the specter of a possible Soviet attack against the Middle East. The worst of the crisis over Palestine appeared to have passed. George C. McGhee, assistant secretary of state for Near Eastern, South Asian, and African Affairs, and a leading proponent of MEC/MEDO, noted that "the UK, which has the primary responsibility for the defense of the area, lacks both manpower and resources successfully to defend the area and has no plans for defense of Saudi Arabian oil fields and the Dhahran Air Base." McGhee proposed:

> To establish (for political as well as military reasons) a combined US-UK command structure in the Middle East which would stimulate basic cooperation among the states of the area not now possible through indigenous organizations or groupings such as the Arab League. This structure would not alter the fact that the UK and Commonwealth have primary responsibility for the defense of the area.[20]

In the summer of 1951, the American military, although still unwilling to commit forces to the region, fell into step with the State Department and supported the establishment of MEC.[21] American and British political and military representatives quickly worked out satisfactory preliminary agreements on the nature of a regional command structure, to be headed by Great Britain.

American policymakers unfortunately failed to completely grasp the dichotomy of their new policy. The effort to erect a Western-oriented security structure led by Britain—the bête noire of Arab, Iranian, and Israeli nationalists—exacerbated tensions, heightened anti-Western sentiment, and, far from strengthening the British position in the Middle East, accelerated Great Britain's decline.

Britain, which as the power "responsible" for the Middle East took the diplomatic initiative within the region, found few Middle Eastern countries eager to align themselves with the West. The Turks were an exception, and as the only Near Eastern power with a sizable, effective military, were indispensable to any effective regional defense organization. Unfortunately, they were reluctant to join a Middle Eastern security framework until they had been accepted within the European defense community—NATO.[22] In Iran, because of disputes over oil, and in Egypt, because of disagreement over the status of the Suez Canal, the British faced strong nationalist challenges. Rising Arab and Iranian nationalism, the still-fresh legacy of colonial rule, and the somewhat antagonist attitude of British diplomats, handicapped efforts to reach settlements with Teheran and Cairo.

For Great Britain, Egypt was the strategic key to the Middle East, a historic bastion of imperial strength, and in the postwar world a military complex that could serve as a base for a buildup of United Kingdom, Commonwealth, and American forces and for a strategic bombing campaign against the Soviet Union. But British-Egyptian negotiations, far from leading to an agreement over the Suez Canal and basing rights, a necessary precursor to any regional alliance, led instead to disorder and outright military action in early 1952. The outbreak of violence not only dashed hopes for an accord, but actually sparked nationalist emotions that brought down the heretofore relatively pro-Western Egyptian government and ultimately led to the July 1952 overthrow of King Farouk by army officers, among them Gamal Abdel Nasser.[23] Subsequent efforts to interest the new Egyptian government in MEDO were destined to fail.

In Teheran the British and Americans also faced challenges, for the Arabs held no monopoly on nationalist and anti-colonial sentiment. Iranian nationalism manifested itself in a variety of forms, at times conducive and at times harmful to Western interests in the Persian Gulf.

The March 1946 Iranian crisis led the United States to support Iran aginst Russia, its traditional imperialist foe to the north. The imbroglio forced the United States to reassess its interests and commitments in the Mediterranean and the Middle East and led to a shift in American policy toward the region. In the Persian Gulf, the United States gave its wholehearted diplomatic support to the principle of Iranian territorial integrity. Iran became the recipient of increased, though still meager, economic and military assistance.

Five years later, another Iranian crisis led the United States to again reassess its Middle Eastern policies. On March 8, 1951, the Special Oil

Commission of the Iranian Majlis (parliament) submitted a resolution proposing the nationalization of the oil industry—principally the wholly British-owned Anglo-Iranian Oil Company (AIOC). On the fifteenth, the Majlis voted unanimously to approve the commission's recommendation. The Iranian Senate followed suit five days later.

Nationalization of the AIOC sparked a two-and-one-half-year crisis that ultimately led the United States to depart markedly from the policies initially pursued by the Truman administration toward Iran. In the summer of 1953, President Dwight D. Eisenhower ordered direct American intervention in Iranian internal affairs and decided to support the shah in his efforts to build a modern state internally stable and capable of deterring a Soviet overland drive toward the Persian Gulf. These U.S. actions in Iran in the early 1950s helped to shape the nature of the challenges faced by Americans in the Persian Gulf and throughout the Middle East in the late 1970s, 1980s, and 1990s.

Several factors led to the nationalization crisis of 1951–53 in Iran. Throughout what would come to be called the Third World, the growth of nationalist and anticolonialist movements sparked the reassessment of existing economic arrangements. Most Iranians viewed the long-standing agreements with the AIOC as symbols of British imperial political and economic domination. During the early stages of the negotiations that began in 1948, the British were understandably unwilling to weaken their control of such strategically important concessions, but after the December 1950 American oil rights settlement with the Saudis, in which ARAMCO agreed to a 50/50 split of net operating revenue (retroactive to January 1, 1950), there should have been little hope that the proud Iranians would agree to anything less. Continued AIOC recalcitrance fed Iranian intransigence and generated popular support for nationalization.[24]

The United States did not "in general" favor nationalization, although it recognized the right of sovereign states to nationalize provided "just compensation" was made. "However, this policy [was] not publicized abroad as it might encourage fon [foreign] states to nationalize." Moreover, with regard to Iran, the State Department did not oppose AIOC nationalization because to do so would "jeopardize politically US and West in Iran and might result in loss of Iran to Sovs."[25]

American concern over the situation was genuine, for Iran was no longer considered strategically expendable. "Strictly from the United States military point of view," a 1951 JCS memorandum noted: "Iran's orientation toward the United States in peacetime and the maintenance of the British position in the Middle East now transcend in importance the desirability of supporting British oil interests in Iran. The Joint Chiefs of Staff would be forced immediately to reexamine their global strategy in the event that the USSR breached the Truman Doctrine in regard to Iran by measures short of war."[26]

While Iran had not been named in President Truman's 1947 policy statement (prompting Iranians to characterize the American effort as an attempt to build a dam across two-thirds of a river), American policymakers *did* consider the Truman Doctrine applicable to Iran.[27] American diplomats assured the Iranians that their country was considered as strategically important to the United States as Greece and Turkey. John D. Jernegan, acting chief of the Division of Greek, Turkish, and Iranian Affairs, wrote George Allen, the ambassador in Iran, on December 9, 1947:

> I think we can say that we in NEA, at least, regard Iran as completely on par with Greece and Turkey so far as its importance to the United States is concerned. This attitude is, I believe, shared by the Service Departments, and is concurred in by our own high command in the Department. I do not know what the Army and Navy think about the relative strategic importance of the Persian Gulf and the Turkish Straits, but my own inclination would be to agree that the oil fields are at least as important as the Straits. The big question is: what can we do about it, and what are the best methods to employ in trying to protect Iran? . . . I am far from convinced that Iran's safety can best be promoted by arraying her unequivocally and irrevocably in the Western camp in opposition to the Soviet Union. If I could think of a way to give real assistance to Iran without automatically forcing her into open opposition to the USSR, I would start pushing it immediately.[28]

In a July 1947 telegram, Secretary of State George C. Marshall had offered a simple explanation for what the Iranians saw as a lack of even-handedness in American Near Eastern policy. The extensive American aid extended to Greece and Turkey had been meant to replace that previously supplied by Britain and to maintain the "status quo," whereas an extensive military and economic aid package for Iran, which faced no similar immediate threat, could "worsen present Iranian-Soviet relations [and] might bring about the very situation which we seek to avoid and would not be in interest of Iran, US, or world security generally."[29]

61

Despite Iranian fears, the United States did consider Iran's security a vital issue. A mid-March 1951 draft report prepared by the National Security Council (NSC) reiterated points made in earlier assessments—Iran was a "key strategic position" and a screen for Middle Eastern oil producing areas. "Iranian oil resources are of great importance to the economies of the United Kingdom and Western European countries," the report argued, and the "loss of these resources would affect adversely those economies in peacetime." Moreover, if Iran "fell," neighboring countries, with the exception of Turkey, would probably also succumb to Soviet pressure. The draft concluded: "For these reasons, the United States should continue its basic policy to take all feasible steps to assure that Iran does not fall victim to communist control," to strengthen the Iranian government, and, in the event of communist internal subversion, consider options such as "correlated political action by the United States and United Kingdom."[30]

Significantly, the final version of the report, approved by President Truman, equated the Iranian government with the person of the shah. NSC 107/2 of June 1951 appraised the "Shah as the only present source of continuity of leadership . . . ," and spoke of the need to "strengthen the leadership of the Shah and through him the central government."[31]

Despite the language of NSC 107/2, not all American policymakers considered the shah a strong leader, or the prospects for a stable Iran good. Few Americans considered Iran a national and governmental entity comparable to Turkey or Greece.[32] Iran could at best be viewed as a country in transition from absolute monarchy to a constitutional form of government. In the interim, unfortunately, it possessed neither the attractions of a democracy nor those redeeming attributes of stability and strength often associated with a despotically ruled state. The Iranian Majlis was seen as the bastion of the landowning class, not the voice of the people; and the military as corrupt and incompetent, incapable of providing either effective internal security or even slowing a Soviet attack. In January 1951 Admiral Robert B. Carney, commander, Northeast Atlantic and Mediterranean, offered a dismal "appraisal of Persian capabilities." Carney wrote:

The key to Persian intentions and capabilities is to be found in the character of the Persians; there is nothing in the analysis of Persian character which gives rise to any reason for placing dependence of Persian intentions nor confidence in Persian ability to resist major Russian armed aggression.[33]

62

Loy Henderson, the American ambassador in Teheran during the critical period of 1953, considered the shah "indecisive and weak, though well intentioned," a man who held "no confidence in his own influence."[34] The shah of the 1950s was not the Shah of Shahs familiar to Americans in the 1960s and 1970s.

Not all the reports coming from Iran and the Persian Gulf were negative. Captain Ernest Eller, Middle East Force commander in 1950, provided a rather optimistic picture of the situation in Iran and advised the navy's senior leadership to reject the views of those who warned that the Iranians were useless and incapable of improvement. Eller recommended that the United States provide Iran with aid and loans on the same scale as Turkey.[35]

Eller's recommendations paralleled those of the shah, who blamed the unstable internal political situation in Iran partly on the lack of American aid.[36] The shah believed that only the provision of an aid package similar to that provided Greece and Turkey would give Iran "something dependable to rely on."[37]

American support for Greece and Turkey would extend even to armed hostilities if either of those countries were the victims of open Soviet aggression. [The Iranians] are not certain with regard to Iran and feel that their greatest danger lies in this uncertainty. If the Soviet Govt knew definitely that an attack on Iran would mean armed hostilities with the United States, they feel that the Soviet Union would not attack. They are afraid, however, that if any doubt on the subject is allowed to continue in the Kremlin, Iran may become the victim of aggression.[38]

The shah and many Iranians also felt that American military assistance ought to be provided free, rather than as part of a loan package, and on a much more extensive scale than the United States considered necessary.[39] The shah and pro-Western Iranians saw the extension of the Truman Doctrine, the Economic Cooperation Administration, and extensive economic and military aid packages to Greece and Turkey, but not to Iran, as an expression of an unwillingness on the part of the United States to commit itself to Iran's defense.

The American military was, in fact, reluctant to obligate itself to the defense of Iran, or to any other Middle Eastern country. As they had between 1946 and 1949, JCS studies conducted in the early 1950s routinely outlined the strategic importance of the Near East, but habitually rejected calls for any formal American commitment to the region's defense. A Joint Strategic Survey Committee report of October 1950 concluded that

> the loss of Europe would represent a most serious blow to the Western Powers. The loss of the Middle East in the early stages of a global war would not in itself be fatal, although the recapture of the Middle East would be essential for victory. The strategic defense contemplated for the Far and Middle East indicates that those areas are, for planning purposes, now considered to be in a lower category than Western Europe.[40]

The Persian Gulf was geographically remote. Estimates of the resources necessary to conduct an effective defense far exceeded the capability of the American military, which was already fully committed elsewhere in Europe and the Pacific, including, until mid-1953, the stalemated war in the Korean Peninsula. The JCS supported the much talked about establishment of a multinational Middle East Defense Organization, but refused to commit American forces to it and recommended that the obligation for the defense of the Middle East "should be accepted by the British as a British responsibility, and that they should develop, organize, and as necessary provide forces for an effective defense thereof."[41]

But as the Iranian internal situation deteriorated rapidly in 1952, the National Security Council adopted a more forceful policy. NSC 136/1 of November 20, 1952, concluded:

> Present trends in Iran are unfavorable to the maintenance of control by a non-communist regime for an extended period of time. In wresting the political initiative from the Shah, the landlords, and other traditional holders of power, the National Front politicians now in power have at least temporarily eliminated every alternative to their own rule except the Communist Tudeh Party. However, the ability of the National Front to maintain control of the situation indefinitely is uncertain. The political upheaval which brought the nationalists to power has heightened popular desire for promised economic and social betterment and has increased social unrest. At the same time, nationalist failure to restore the oil industry to operation has led to near-exhaustion of the government's financial reserves and to deficit financing to meet current expenses, and is likely to produce a progressive deterioration of the economy at large.
>
> It is now estimated that communist forces will probably not gain

control of the Iranian Government during 1953. Nevertheless, the Iranian situation contains very great elements of instability. . . . It is clear that the United Kingdom no longer possesses the capability unilaterally to assure stability in the area. If present trends continue unchecked, Iran could be effectively lost to the free world in advance of an actual communist takeover of the Iranian Government. Failure to arrest present trends in Iran involves a serious risk to the national security of the United States.[42]

To "check" these "trends" in Iran, the NSC proposed that the United States continue and expand ongoing economic and military assistance, prepare to offer technical help to the Iranians when they chose to resume oil production, to assist them in marketing their oil, plan to include Iran in any regional defense pact, and in

the event of either an attempted or an actual communist seizure of power in one or more of the provinces of Iran or in Tehran, the United States should support a non-communist Iranian Government, including participation in the military support of such a government if necessary and useful. Preparations for such an eventuality should include:
a. Plans for specific military, economic, diplomatic, and psychological measures which could be taken to support a non-communist Iranian Government or to prevent all or part of Iran or adjacent areas from falling under communist domination.

The NSC decision placed the American military in a difficult position. During the fall of 1952, as the debate over NSC 136 continued, the Joint Chiefs demonstrated increased concern over the situation in Iran, but stressed the difficulties inherent in military action in the region and the low priority accorded the Middle East in American war plans. The latter was an important consideration since the Chiefs were concerned that any overt American move into Iran could provoke Soviet intervention under the terms of their 1921 treaty with Iran.[43]

Ultimately, the JCS supported an NSC draft that envisioned possible American military intervention if, as the result of external invasion or internal subversion, Iran went communist.[44] In the interim, the JCS called for the services and the Strategic Air Command and the staff of CINCNELM to draw up plans for air demonstrations, the movement of air force units to southern Turkey, and of ground forces to Basra, Iraq, stressing that no decision had yet been made to deploy forces.[45]

While the American military debated the possibilities of intervention, the Truman administration began a final diplomatic effort to resolve the crisis. Paul H. Nitze, then director of the State Department's Policy Planning Staff, wrote:

> As a result, by the end of 1952, it appeared that a solution was at last in sight. Early in January 1953, [Iranian prime minister Mohammed] Mossadegh gave his final approval and we thought everything was settled. A few days later, however, Mossadegh changed his mind, probably in the mistaken belief that he could cut a better deal with the incoming Eisenhower administration.[46]

The negotiations appeared to be nearing a settlement in January 1953, but Mossadegh, when presented with a formal draft agreement, continually altered and reinterpreted his demands.[47] In early February, the frustrated British recommended breaking off talks and leaving the next move to Mossadegh.[48] The new American secretary of state, John Foster Dulles, also grew pessimistic about the chances of an ultimate solution.[49]

The Iranian Prime Minister himself suddenly changed course, set the negotiations aside, and began a vociferous campaign against the shah, the royal family, and the institution of the monarchy.[50] In late February, American diplomats in Teheran reported that the shah was about to abdicate. Only appeals by the British, Americans, members of the Iranian general staff, Mossadegh's enemies in the Majlis, and, most importantly, popular demonstrations in support of the monarchy (the fervor of which surprised both Iranian and American observers) convinced the shah to remain in Teheran.[51]

Mossadegh's decision to embark on an anti-shah campaign came at a critical moment as American policymakers wrestled with the few remaining policy options. If Mossadegh believed that Iran could get a better deal from the Eisenhower administration, and that increased pressure on the shah would move the Americans to push the British to make further concessions, he was mistaken.[52] Attacks on the monarchy and threats to sell oil to the Communist bloc instead convinced the Eisenhower administration that Mossadegh's leadership posed dangers to the United States and the West. After all, Mossadegh himself had taunted Ambassador Henderson that "Iran would prefer to go Communist rather than cause any trouble between the United States and the United Kingdom."[53]

Washington policymakers saw Mossadegh's late February failure to force the shah's abdication as a sign of the prime minister's weakening power. Americans were surprised to find Iranians taking to the streets in strength in support of the Shah.[54] A March 1 CIA report concluded: "The institution of the Crown may have more popular backing than was expected," presenting the monarch with an opportunity to act, although "his past record does not suggest that he will act."[55]

At a March 4, 1953, NSC meeting, John Foster Dulles concluded that the shah had, in fact, missed his chance and that the monarchy would continue to be a target for attack. Dulles also expressed concern about Mossadegh's future. His political strength was obviously waning. Soviet broadcasts into Iran had become disturbingly anti-shah *and* anti-Mossadegh. According to the minutes of the meeting:

> The probable consequences of the events of the last few days, concluded Mr. Dulles, would be a dictatorship in Iran under Mossadegh. As long as the latter lives there was but little danger, but if he were to be assassinated or otherwise to disappear from power, a political vacuum would occur in Iran and the communists might easily take over.

When Treasury Secretary George M. Humphrey asked Dulles if he had concluded "that we are going to lose that country," the secretary of state "replied in the affirmative." President Eisenhower interjected that a military option, the movement of American troops into Iran, would likely provoke Soviet intervention under the terms of the 1921 treaty.[56] With the situation in Iran clearly deteriorating, what options remained?

The possibility of taking "political action" in Iran had been raised within the Truman administration as early as March 1951. NSC 107 had listed as an option "correlated political action by the United States and United Kingdom."[57] C. M. "Monty" Woodhouse, a British intelligence officer, discussed the coup with CIA and State Department representatives in Washington in October and November 1952, at the time that the NSC was developing NSC 136, the not yet fully declassified document that superseded NSC 107/2.[58] The CIA responded favorably to Woodhouse's proposal; the State Department coolly. But at a subsequent meeting in December, also held in Washington, Truman administration representatives nevertheless refused to rule out a coup, although they intended to wait to see how Mossadegh responded to the proposal for a settlement painstakingly worked out by the negotiators.[59] Mossadegh's rejection of the American plan and his mounting attacks against the monarchy, thus came at a critical moment—as the Eisenhower administration in the late winter and early spring of 1953 weighed its options in Iran.[60]

Throughout the spring and summer of 1953, Mossadegh's popularity declined as the failure of his policies became increasingly evident. The prime minister's mismanagement had led Iran to economic and political ruin. In a March 1953 assessment, Ambassador Henderson wrote:

> His career [Mossadegh's] has been based on negative activities and slogans. As Prime Minister he has not been able accomplish anything of constructive character. When frustrated he searches for some new opponent to blame and destroy. He has thrown out British; emasculated Majlis; eliminated Senate; forced all well-known politicians out of public life; deposed all prominent civilian and military officials; sent various members Royal Family into exile, etc. Now he places blame his failures on court and takes measures against Shah. He may later blame rump Majlis and take steps get rid of it. [Mossadegh dissolved the Majlis on August 15, 1953.] If coop [coup] of kind desired not forthcoming he may give Americans same treatment as that given British.[61]

In early March, the possibilities of a coup were being weighed in Washington, London, and Teheran. On March 6, Ambassador Henderson wrote from Iran: "Difficult for us believe Shah really would have courage or resolution to take part in movement to effect either by force or peacefully downfall Mossadeq government. He would undoubtedly be frightened at thought of military coup being attempted in his name and if given the opportunity would probably try discourage it."[62] Nevertheless, planning and preparation for a coup continued. Barring some change in the situation in Iran, the United States and Britain were committed to political action.[63]

Perhaps the most dramatic moment came in May when Mossadegh personally appealed Iran's case to President Eisenhower. Far from eliciting increased American aid or breaking the stalemate in the oil negotiations, the Iranian prime minister's letter drew only a rebuff, increased Iran's diplomatic isolation, and served to "belie carefully nursed 'myth' US supporting Mossadeq."[64] The United States, long Iran's ally, had taken the side of Great Britain.

Eisenhower's reasoning was simple. In the summer of 1953, he feared an Iranian internal collapse. To Churchill, Ike confided that he considered Iran an "area of potential disaster for the Western world."[65] The administration viewed Mossadegh not as a communist, nor even a communist sympathizer, but as an incompetent leader and administrator whose policies had so undermined Iranian stability that ultimately the only remaining organized force in the country would be the Tudeh party. Of course, the United States, far from attempting to support Mossadegh, was actively pursuing a policy meant to destabilize his government.[66] But Mossadegh himself foolishly played up the communist threat, warning Henderson that the United States had best realize that "drastic measures must be adopted if Iran not fall Commie hands."[67]

Several factors had, indeed, led the Eisenhower administration to adopt "drastic measures" and a policy toward Iran that the Truman administration had avoided, though never rejected. Eisenhower and his senior advisors brought a more militant view of the Cold War to American policy. The impending end of the Korean War, Stalin's death, and the Soviet Union's apparent lessened interest in pursuing southward expansion, all afforded the United States a freer hand in the region.[68] And the need for tough policy choices regarding Iran had also become more pressing. As the new administration took office, the internal Iranian situation deteriorated rapidly as Mossadegh adopted dictatorial measures, began to cozy up to the Soviets, and either rejected or felt politically unable to accept the diplomatic proposal worked out by the Truman administration. In the spring and summer of 1953, the time seemed ripe for an effort to "save" Iran.

Nevertheless, although the decision to act in Iran was taken by Eisenhower, the critical policy premises on which he acted had been shaped by the Truman administration. In the spring of 1951 the NSC had identified the shah as the focus for American support and the hope for a stable Iran. NSC 107/2 and 136/1 ruled out the "loss" of Iran and mandated military or political operations if diplomatic efforts failed. By the spring of 1953, all such efforts had failed and the situation in Iran continued to deteriorate.

In its execution of Truman administration policy in Iran, Eisenhower had few options. A diplomatic solution appeared impossible since Mossadegh was either unwilling or unable to reach any agreement the Americans or British considered reasonable. Because of the existence of the 1921 Soviet-Iranian treaty, American military intervention posed the risk of world war. Continued inaction, the administration feared, as had Truman's, would allow conditions to deteriorate to the point that the government in Teheran lost control, either as the result of a domestic coup or through the breakdown of central authority. Centrifugal forces would lead to the breakup of Iran and possibly civil war. Both the United States and the Soviet Union would receive calls for assistance. The United States would then be forced to sit back and watch the Soviet Union move into Iran, or to intervene itself and risk a third world war.[69] To the administration, a coup appeared to be the least risky course to pursue.[70]

Another factor central to the Eisenhower administration's decision to conduct political action in Iran was the conviction that Mossadegh was losing support and, had the shah been more forceful, might well have been removed from power in the late winter. The planners of the Anglo-American coup assumed, correctly, that the shah still had a fair amount of support in Iran, but that he would refuse to act without the United States holding his hand.[71] As Kermit Roosevelt later wrote: "If our analysis had been wrong, we'd have fallen flat on our, er, faces."[72]

Operation Ajax—the codename for the coup—owed its success in no small measure to the extent of the shah's residual popularity and Mossadegh's relative unpopularity.[73] On the evening of August 15, the initial stage of the planned coup miscarried when Mossadegh loyalists arrested the commander of the Imperial Guard after he had delivered the shah's decree (firman) removing the prime minister from power.[74] The shah had, in the meantime, fled the country "as planned," going to Iraq, and subsequently Rome, a location somewhat further from Teheran than originally envisioned. The situation in the Iranian capital looked rather bleak. On the seventeenth, Mossadegh's supporters, including a bogus Tudeh mob reportedly in the pay of the Central Intelligence Agency, took to the streets in displays of anti-monarchical fervor.[75] But Mossadegh hesitated, fearing overreliance on his most fervent supporters—Tudeh. The pro-shah forces used the time to reorganize. They published copies of the Royal firman removing Mossadegh from power and naming General Zahedi as prime minister. On the morning of the nineteenth, pro-shah demonstrators took to the streets and routed both the Mossadegh and Tudeh mobs.[76] Woodhouse wrote: "In fact, probably for the first time, the Communists' technique of spontaneous demonstration was successfully turned against them."[77] A British postcoup assessment concluded:

> It is widely believed that the success of the coup was due to the fact that it was well planned, that it was kept secret, and that plenty of money was made available to carry it out. . . .

The general feeling in Tehran among influential people was one of jubilation that the U.S.A. should have come to the country's rescue when Dr. Musaddiq was about to deliver it to the Tudeh Party. There was general agreement that, were it not for America's assistance and guidance, its financial contribution, and its encouragement to the Shah to withstand further humiliation, the plan for the overthrowing of Musaddiq's government could not have succeeded. Unfortunately it appeared that these influential persons regarded American support as something obligatory and continuous, which would enable them always to shelter behind it and continue, as in the past, without paying any real attention to the basic needs of the country.[78]

The Iran coup was a watershed event in Iranian-American affairs. American involvement caused deep resentment on the part of those who opposed the shah in 1953 and would come to oppose him over the following decades.[79]

Nevertheless, as Iran expert James Bill writes:

the American intervention of 1951–1953 did not determine the revolutionary events of 1978–79. Although the American image was tarnished severely by its actions against Musaddiq, the United States had numerous opportunities to rethink and revise its policy towards the shah's Iran in the quarter-century before the revolution.[80]

Homa Katouzian, author of a recent biography of Mossadegh, writes that "Iran's later troubles were largely due to dictatorship (later, arbitrary rule), corruption and feeble political leadership rather than sinister interferences in its domestic affairs by foreign powers."[81] Indeed, the shah had twenty-five years and ample opportunities to prove himself a capable ruler.

But the most important aspect of Operation Ajax was that it signaled the adoption by the United States of a new policy toward Iran and the Persian Gulf, one that involved not only "political action" to rescue the shah, but also a decision to provide greater political, economic, and military support. Secretary of State John Foster Dulles wrote:

We believe that if the present opportunity is seized we can capitalize on the existing favorable situation in Iran and make a significant advance toward bringing Iran into closer cooperation with its neighbors in a free world and changing it from a liability to a positive asset in the Middle Eastern area.[82]

The decision to use political action in Iran also saved the American military from having to confront the difficulties of operations in the Persian Gulf region. United States military forces, most noticeably the U.S. Navy's MEF in the gulf, played no role in the coup.[83] The United States did not even reinforce MEF in the months before Ajax. The CINCNELM staff's involvement consisted of preparing contingency plans should the coup fail and should intervention become necessary, to support the shah or because of a Soviet move into Iran.

Nevertheless, as the events of mid-August unfolded in Teheran, the Eisenhower administration pushed the military to consider greater involvement in the region. On August 19, as the second stage of the coup began, the NSC directed the chairman of the JCS to consider possible military responses, beyond those outlined in JCS 1714/50, to support the shah in the event of the failure of the coup or a counter-coup. Since the final months of the Truman administration, the NSC, unlike the JCS, had been prepared to risk Soviet intervention in Iran. And now, with the Korean War ended, and with new leadership on the JCS, the military was more willing to consider such contingencies.[84]

By end of the year, the JCS had developed a plan for a multiservice operation that, over the course of several months, would draw on forces deployed all over the world to build up substantial American military strength in the Persian Gulf.[85] Fortunately, the coup's success made intervention unnecessary.

The Eisenhower administration, as it demonstrated in Iran, brought a more forceful brand of American diplomacy to the Middle East as well as a somewhat different conception of Britain's proposed Middle East Defense Organization. Secretary of State John Foster Dulles acknowledged that many "of the Arab League countries are so engrossed with their quarrels with Israel or with Great Britain or France that they pay little heed to the menace of Soviet communism." But Dulles, who had just returned from a tour of the region, reported that he had found "more concern where the Soviet Union is near. In general, the northern tier of nations shows awareness of the danger."[86] American policy henceforth focused on these states—Turkey, Iran, Iraq, and Pakistan—in an effort to foster the development of an indigenous Middle Eastern security arrangement.[87]

Initially, Eisenhower administration policies in the Middle East were less expressions of a major shift in direction, than indications of the more dynamic leadership of the United States in the region and within the context of the Anglo-American relationship.[88] Long before 1953, the United States had focused on an "outer ring" for Middle East defense—for example, Turkey and Iran in 1946—but had deferred to Britain because Americans were unwilling to supply the forces necessary to defend such a line.[89] But the British fixation on Egypt, what the Americans considered an "inner ring" concept, had become a dead issue by 1953. A fiercely nationalist Arab government in Cairo refused to become a party to any agreement that by definition served Western interests, and, moreover, involved non-Arab states such as Britain, the United States, Iran, and Turkey. In Egypt, and in Iran as well, British policies had done little but fan the flames of nationalist fires.[90] Thus by late 1953, the Eisenhower administration had little choice but to play a more forceful role in the Middle East.[91] With the shah seemingly secure on his throne, and with the American military freed from the albatross of the war in Korea, the United States pursued an "outer ring" concept for the defense of the Middle East.[92]

The more aggressive U.S. Middle Eastern policy quickly bore fruit. On February 24, 1954, Turkey and Iraq signed a bilateral security agreement—the Baghdad Pact. Great Britain joined the pact in April 1954, Pakistan in September 1955, and Iran in October 1955. The United States, which sat on various alliance committees, never signed the accord but played a crucial role, providing necessary military assistance.

Historically, the Baghdad Pact has been considered a cheap imitation of NATO, the political and military strength of which the Middle Eastern alliance never attained. The Baghdad Pact remained a loose alignment of states, many of which were internally unstable, that viewed the alliance primarily as a means to acquire the Western armaments deemed necessary to insure internal security and to enhance their own positions within the Middle East. In the view of some critics of American policy, in exchange for a marginally improved capability to defend the region, the United States intensified internal Middle Eastern discord, increased domestic political pressure against the governments of the signatory states from nationalist and anti-Western groups, and facilitated and accelerated Soviet penetration of the Middle East. For example, the July 1958 nationalist coup in Iraq—the only Arab member state—took the Baghdad out of the Pact, and opened the door of the heart of the Middle East to the Soviets.

But the United States considered the possibility of a direct Soviet invasion remote, never expected the Baghdad Pact to substantially improve regional defense, and most certainly did not expect the pact to become a Middle Eastern version of NATO. A National Security Council statement of policy concluded:

> In the Near East the current danger to the security of the free world arises not so much from the threat of direct Soviet military attack as from a continuation of the present unfavorable trends. Unless those trends are reversed, the Near East may well be lost to the West within the next few years.[93]

American policymakers hoped to reverse these trends by strengthening the morale of Middle Eastern states and by reinforcing whatever pro-Western sentiments existed. An April 1952 State-Defense Working Group paper noted:

> The United States supports the establishment of a Middle East Command Organization in the belief that such an organization may make an early contribution to the political stabilization of the vitally important Middle East area, and in the long run increase the capacity of the area to resist Soviet aggression.[94]

Paul Nitze admitted quite frankly that MEDO would be "in its initial phases merely a paper organization."[95] A June 22, 1954, National Intelligence Estimate noted: "The immediate effects of a loose regional defense grouping based on the Turk-Pakistani agreement and backed by US military aid programs would be primarily political and psychological rather than military."[96] The shah of Iran once remarked: "CENTO has never been really serious, you know."[97]

Perhaps the most credible impact of the Baghdad Pact was the indirect link, through the participation of Turkey, of NATO to the defense of the Middle East.[98] In fact, American diplomats in Western Europe made a conscious effort to play down such a connection.[99] But for Soviet planners, the fact that a Middle Eastern war might lead to hostilities with three NATO members—Britain, the United States, and Turkey—certainly complicated planning.

Because American policy sought primarily political, not military, benefits from MEDO, and because the United States had despaired of enticing Arab states into a pro-Western defensive alignment, the Baghdad Pact survived the Iraq coup of 1958. Renamed the Central Treaty Organization (CENTO) on March 5, 1959, the pact—now comprising the Islamic, but non-Arab states of Turkey, Iran, and Pakistan—survived for another twenty years thanks to British membership and American political, economic, and military assistance.

Although American military expectations for CENTO were low, the alliance, such as it was, remained a framework within which the United States worked to improve the defensive capabilities of the northern tier states. Coordinated aid programs, much like those accorded to Greece and Turkey under the Truman Doctrine, sought to strengthen the internal, regional, and external security of Turkey, Iran, and Pakistan.

The Baghdad Pact–CENTO was no substitute for active American political and military involvement in the defense of the Middle East. While the pact did marginally improve the prospects for regional defense, the alliance did, as critics charged, exacerbate tensions within the region. Egyptian President Nasser, for example, viewed the pact as the first step in a Western scheme to isolate his country and denounced the agreement, in the words of George V. Allen, assistant secretary of state for Near Eastern, South Asian, and African Affairs, as "a new form of imperialism . . . designed to imprison all of the Arab people."[100]

Nasser's attacks on the Baghdad Pact reached a crescendo in 1956 as the crisis over the Suez Canal came to a head. The pan-Arab Nasser, desperate for economic and military assistance denied by the West, turned to the Communist bloc for support and became increasingly anti-Western in his rhetoric. On July 26, 1956, he announced the nationalization of the Universal Company of the Suez Maritime Canal, "an edifice of humiliation."[101] Negotiations to resolve the dispute made little headway.[102]

The Israelis broke the subsequent diplomatic deadlock on October 29 when they attacked the Egyptians in the Sinai and drove westward toward the canal. The British and French, who themselves had been planning and preparing to intervene since August and who had agreed beforehand to cooperate with the Israelis, promptly issued a ceasefire ultimatum that called for both Israeli and Egyptian withdrawal and temporary Anglo-French occupation of Port Said, Ismailia, and Suez. On October 30, following the expected and desired Egyptian rejection of the ultimatum, France and Great Britain began operations against Egypt, bombing military installations and seizing about 40 percent of the canal zone area.

American policymakers, who had been closely monitoring the situation, responded quickly to the Anglo-French aggression. In August, the Joint Chiefs had argued that the United States ought to support Great Britain and France politically and logistically if they attacked Egypt.[103] Admiral Arthur W. Radford, chairman of the Joint Chiefs of Staff, had suggested that such a course would prevent the spread of war, an eventuality that he feared might lead to conflagration in the Persian Gulf, a region critical to the support of United States operations in the Far East.[104] But both President Eisenhower and Secretary of State Dulles, while they expressed an understanding of the dilemma in which British and French leaders found themselves, demonstrated no inclination to take sides against Egypt in a showdown. While Eisenhower and Dulles were anxious to lessen Nasser's influence in the Arab world, they believed that the dispute over the Suez Canal was not the issue on which to confront the Egyptian president.[105] The administration took its even-handedness seriously, so much so that in June it had initiated Operation Whiplash, the prepositioning of ships in the eastern Mediterranean loaded with arms that could be delivered to the victim of aggression, be it Israel or a neighboring Arab state.[106] Not surprisingly, when hostilities began the United States, working through the United Nations, forced a cease-fire and complete withdrawal from Egyptian territory.

The Eisenhower administration's decision not to support the Anglo-French-Israeli invasion was the coup de grace for an operation that even at the time was considered a debacle. As retired Air Chief Marshal Sir David Lee wrote in his history of the Royal Air Force in the Mediterranean in the postwar period: "It is impossible to look back upon the Anglo-French intervention in Egypt without coming to the conclusion that it was a fiasco."[107] Nasser survived, the canal, far from being secured, remained closed for months after the war, and in Egyptian hands. British prestige plummeted throughout the Middle East. In his diary, David Ben-Gurion, the Israeli prime minister, wrote: "60,000 British and 30,000 French troops participated in the Anglo-French campaign, as well as 1,200 jet planes and two-thirds of the active British navy. If they had only appointed a commander of ours over this force—Nasser would have been destroyed in two days."[108] Even Secretary Dulles, recovering from cancer surgery at Walter Reed Hospital, remarked to Eisenhower that

> the British having gone in should not have stopped until they had toppled Nasser. As it was they now had the worst of both possible

worlds. They had received all the onus of making the move and at the same time had not accomplished their major purpose.[109]

The Anglo-French-Israeli attack, as American policymakers had expected and feared, provoked violent reactions throughout the Arab world. Because the United States supported United Nations calls for cease-fire and withdrawal, and refused to support "the use of force as a wise and proper instrument for the settlement of international disputes" it avoided, for the most part, Arab wrath.[110]

Nevertheless, the reaction against Britain in the Middle East demonstrated the depth of Arab emotions, Arab willingness to use oil as a weapon against the West, and the possible repercussions events that took place elsewhere in the Middle East could have in the gulf. The Saudis mobilized their armed forces, began training volunteers, broke off diplomatic relations with Britain and France, banned the refueling of their ships in Saudi ports, and embargoed oil shipments to both countries. Rioting and demonstrations broke out in Kuwait and Bahrain, both still British protectorates. For nine days Bahrainis rioted in Manama and Muharraq, attacking British nationals, as well as a few unfortunate Americans, and destroying property. A work stoppage by BAPCO workers quickly became a general strike. As the situation deteriorated, Britain airlifted troops into Bahrain.[111] In Kuwait, while the demonstrations were somewhat less violent, the repercussions of the Suez affair were longer lasting. Arabs sabotaged British-owned and -controlled oil fields and facilities and subjected British firms to a boycott that lasted for two months.[112]

The Suez affair led to deeper crises in the Middle East. The failure of the Anglo-French assault increased the legitimacy and strength of Nasserite, anti-Western forces and led to the formation on February 21, 1958, of the United Arab Republic (UAR) of Egypt and Syria, headed by Nasser. Those Arab states that continued to resist Nasser's brand of Pan-Arabism—most notably Iraq, Saudi Arabia, Jordan, and Lebanon—quickly found themselves threatened by internal and external forces.

The situation was most critical in Iraq which suffered major economic losses as a result of the Suez crisis.[113] Syria had shut down the oil pipelines that crossed its territory from Iraq to the Mediterranean and the West. With the Suez Canal closed as well, Iraqi oil revenues fell and King Feisal of Iraq, a pro-Western leader, found himself isolated and weakened. Feisal's efforts to develop a counteralignment of

Arab nations met limited success in the form of the short-lived Iraqi-Jordanian Arab Federation of February 14, 1958.[114]

The Suez affair had made apparent the American strategic dilemma in the Middle East. Support for Britain inflamed anti-Western emotions; support for nationalist movements undermined the position of Britain, the power responsible for the defense of the region. The obvious alternative was for the United States itself to play a larger role in the Middle East, not just politically, but also militarily. Accordingly, after the Suez crisis, Eisenhower, sensing the deteriorating situation in the region, found himself faced with potential situations where American political or military intervention appeared to be the best means to secure Western interests. The United States began yet another policy reevaluation that led to the initial development of military forces capable of large-scale operations in the Middle East.

The first sign of this new direction in American policy, as ultimately adopted on March 5, 1957, in a joint resolution of the House and Senate, was the Eisenhower Doctrine, which provided for increased economic and military assistance.

> Furthermore, the United States regards as vital to the national interests and world peace the preservation of the independence and integrity of the nations of the Middle East. To this end, if the President determines the necessity thereof, the United States is prepared to use armed forces to assist any such nation or group of such nations requesting assistance against armed aggression from any country controlled by international communism: Provided that such employment shall be consonant with the treaty obligations of the United States and with the Constitution of the United States.[115]

The United States also began to reevaluate its military plans for the region. Joint Middle East Defense Plan 1-57 of May 1957 sought to meet a possible Soviet move into the region without expanding the existing U.S. force structure. An American "strategic defense" of the Middle East would shield "the NATO right flank, airbase sites, the Turkish Straits, the Eastern Mediterranean, the Cairo-Suez-Aden area, and the Persian Gulf and contiguous oil-bearing area." Depending on the course of events elsewhere, significant ground, air, and naval forces would move to the Gulf–Indian Ocean area where they would be directed by a Commander-in-Chief Middle East (CINCME) to be designated by the Joint Chiefs.[116]

During the Suez crisis, the JCS had drawn up contingency plans to rush ground forces from Germany to the Persian Gulf in the event of escalation.[117] Following the crisis, the army began to develop a reserve force in the United States capable of deployment overseas and in 1958 established the U.S. Strategic Army Corps (STRAC), a corps headquarters for the control of assets, among them the 82nd Airborne Division, not already committed under existing plans to a specific theater in wartime.

These preparations had not fully matured when, in the spring and summer of 1958, the United States observed with growing concern UAR aid to rebels in Iraq, Lebanon, and Jordan. The situation appeared most threatening in Lebanon, where a virtual civil war erupted in May and the American military busily prepared contingency plans for possible intervention.

But the expected Middle Eastern crisis originated in Baghdad, not Beirut. On July 14, Iraqi Army officers engineered a successful coup d'état. Pro-western King Feisal and the senior political leadership of the linchpin of the Middle East's regional defense organization—the Baghdad Pact—were brutally slaughtered.

The coup surprised the Eisenhower administration and many of Iraq's neighbors. The Saudis, Iranians, and Turks favored intervention to topple the new regime. But the United States ultimately ruled out such actions as reports from Iraq indicated that little or no royalist resistance had materialized, and that the populace, displaying antiroyalist, anti-Western, and pro-Arabist sentiments, had embraced the revolution. The Iraqis also wisely kept the oil flowing to the West and did not immediately nationalize foreign companies. Moreover, the United States had little interest in risking a wider war—within the Middle East with the UAR, or globally with the Soviet Union.[118]

Nevertheless, the Eisenhower administration considered a forceful display of American resolve necessary to forestall further moves against other pro-Western regimes. When only hours after the Iraqi coup President Camille Chamoun of Lebanon requested American, French, and British military support, President Eisenhower decided to send troops into Lebanon. At 1:30 P.M. Beirut time on July 15, a battalion landing team of U.S. Marines hit the beach south of the Lebanese capital. On the sixteenth, King Hussein of Jordan requested the assistance of Great Britain and the following morning British paratroopers began landing at Amman as American carrier aircraft from the Sixth Fleet flew demonstration missions over Jordan's West Bank.[119] Anglo-American military forces remained in Lebanon and Jordan into late October 1958.

Despite the focus on Lebanon and the eastern Mediterranean, the crisis of the summer of 1958 was regional in scope and global in character. The United States placed its military forces throughout the Atlantic, Pacific, and European commands at higher states of readiness and alert. On the afternoon of July 14, the Chief of Naval Operations, Admiral Arleigh Burke, directed that a Middle East Force destroyer remain near Dhahran, Saudi Arabia. On the fifteenth, the MEF flagship *Greenwich Bay* moved into the northern Persian Gulf nearer Kuwait. On the seventeenth, CMEF, with CNO approval, ordered the destroyer *Holder*, in the Strait of Tiran at the mouth of the Gulf of Aqaba between Egypt and Saudi Arabia, to operate so that it would be visible from the shore, a move that would hopefully help to stabilize the situation. That same day, Admiral Burke directed the commander of the Pacific Fleet to load and steam a Marine battalion from Okinawa to the Persian Gulf. On July 21, the British strengthened their garrison on Bahrain, which was also the major base for the U.S. Navy's Middle East Force, with 1,000 additional troops.[120]

The wisdom of intervening in the Lebanese civil war escaped many Americans at the time and Eisenhower's decision to send in the marines has since been the subject of historical debate. There was a comic-opera quality to the affair, with armed marines scrambling up a beach crowded with sunbathers, hounded by ice cream and soft-drink vendors. Without a doubt, the administration oversold the nature and the extent of the communist menace throughout the Middle East. And the ultimate settlement in Lebanon between the various factions owed as much to their own cool-headedness and to effective American diplomacy as it did to the display of U.S. military muscle.

Nevertheless, an assessment of American Middle Eastern policy in the summer of 1958 must acknowledge that the Eisenhower administration based its decisions not only on a determination to restore orderly government to Lebanon, but also, and most importantly, on the assumption that the failure of the United States to respond to Chamoun's call for help would have disastrous consequences for American relationships with those countries still friendly to the United States. King Hussein of Jordan waited until American troops were ashore in Lebanon before he requested help from Great Britain to secure his throne. Nor was the United States more hawkish than its most important regional allies. The Turks, Iranians, and Saudis all supported American moves, and also favored intervention in Iraq.

However one chooses to assess the admittedly debatable results of the Lebanon operation, the lessons that can be drawn from the crisis are, nonetheless, much more obvious. First, the July 14, 1958, coup, despite a plethora of reports about internal problems in Iraq, surprised and shocked the American military, diplomatic, and intelligence communities. A country which had been the centerpiece of Anglo-American hopes for regional defense suddenly became anti-Western in outlook and policy, leading a president to use force to protect American interests and to demonstrate resolve. Twenty-one years later, the fall of the shah of Iran, then the linchpin of CENTO, the successor of the Baghdad Pact, would similarly catch the United States by surprise and ultimately lead to the commitment of American military forces into the midst of an intraregional dispute. Second, the use of marines in Lebanon marked a departure from past American policy, which, until July 14, 1958, had resisted the commitment of military force in the Middle East. Moreover, the Lebanon landing, the establishment of STRAC, and the effort by the Joint Chiefs of Staff planners to develop a contingency plan for the defense of the Middle East illustrates the Eisenhower administration's drift toward a more formal American military role in the Middle East. During the Lebanon crisis the United States, not Great Britain, took the lead both politically *and* militarily. Third, the Lebanon experience highlighted the effectiveness of naval assets in the Middle East, not only as a crisis management tool, but also as a force well tailored to meet contingencies in the region. During the operation, the absence of modern landing facilities handicapped efforts both to move land-based combat aircraft and to airlift troops into the region, and placed a premium on carrier aircraft and ship-based marines.

For the United States, the Middle East remained relatively quiescent for nearly a decade after 1958. Neither the Eisenhower nor Kennedy administrations faced crises that tempted them to use American military forces in the region, although both enhanced the United States' conventional military capabilities.

Nevertheless, regional instability, anti-Westernism, anti-Americanism, Nasserism, and expanding Communist influence continued to threaten U.S. interests. Nasserite supporters persisted in their attempts to undermine the Saudi monarchy. Egyptian forces intervened in the civil war in North Yemen in the early 1960s. The United States countered with increased military assistance to Saudi Arabia, including Operation Hard Surface, which brought American fighters to Dhahran, and the comprehensive expansion of Saudi military facilities and armed forces that began in 1965.[121] Through such efforts the United

States, and Great Britain, maintained positions in the Middle East that had appeared to be on the verge of collapse in the mid-1950s.

But in 1967 the state of crisis gave way to civil unrest and conflict. In April and May, MEF ships were sent to Yemen to help evacuate American civilians. Simultaneously, tensions between Israel and the UAR intensified. On May 16, Nasser called for a partial withdrawal of United Nations peacekeeping forces from the Sinai Peninsula. United Nations Secretary General U Thant rejected the idea of a partial pullout but then surprisingly acceded to Nasser's subsequent demand for a complete withdrawal. On May 22, Nasser announced the closing of the Tiran Strait to Israeli shipping, a move Israel had heretofore considered a casus belli.

Unfortunately, by 1967 the United States was politically, militarily, and emotionally trapped in the quagmire of Indochina. The Johnson administration had consigned the American military's improved conventional capabilities to the war in Vietnam. Because it was so committed, politically and militarily, in Southeast Asia, the Johnson administration failed to respond promptly and unambiguously to the increasingly deteriorating situation in the Middle East. Not until the crisis was virtually out of control did Johnson begin to seek a multilateral approach to avoid another Arab-Israeli confrontation.

Because of earlier tensions in the Yemens, the U.S. on-scene assets—those of the U.S. Navy's Middle East Force—were, however, concentrated near the Red Sea and were well positioned to respond to the new Arab-Israeli crisis. On June 4, the American destroyer *Dyess* raced to reinforce the small command and passed through the Suez Canal "just in time," jeered by anti-American crowds during its passage.[122] But a weak American naval presence was no deterrent to war. That very day Israel decided to strike and on June 5 simultaneously attacked Egypt and Syria.[123]

The lightning Israeli victory, since known as the Six Day War, was a complete debacle for the frontline Arab states. Israeli forces overran the Gaza Strip, the Sinai, the West Bank (following Jordanian intervention), the Golan Heights, and decimated Arab air and ground forces. Despite the fact that the Israelis had chosen to preempt, the United States did not call for an immediate withdrawal as it had in 1956, but instead sought a negotiated settlement—land for peace. The United States became the major player in the diplomatic struggle to end the Arab-Israeli conflict.

Unlike the situation during the crisis of 1956, the United States also found itself drawn dangerously toward the vortex of the new Middle

Eastern war. The Hot Line, connecting Washington and Moscow, came alive for the first time since its installation after the Cuban Missile crisis of October 1962. MEF forces were among those that went on alert on June 5, 1967. In the eastern Mediterranean Israeli planes attacked the U.S. Navy's intelligence ship *Liberty*. Fabricated tales of American aircraft supporting the Israelis sparked anti-American demonstrations throughout the region.

Particularly violent demonstrations occurred in Bahrain and Dhahran, outbursts of emotion that threatened American lives, property, and perhaps even the United States' postwar position in the gulf. Arab leaders responded differently to these outbursts of anti-Americanism from locale to locale. To American eyes, the ruler of Bahrain "demonstrated genuine leadership" during the crisis, allowing carefully controlled demonstrations for several days. The sheik also took action to undercut the enthusiasm of the crowds by offering free transportation to the battle zone for those who were determined to fight. Few, apparently, accepted the offer. The Saudis proved unable or unwilling to counter demonstrations and at Dhahran "uncontrolled mob violence" resulted in several hundred thousand dollars worth of damage to U.S. property and forced the evacuation of many dependents.[124]

Despite these anti-American outbursts, the impact of the crushing Israeli victory dampened the enthusiasm of Arab nationalists and led to a relatively rapid resumption of routine in the Middle East. On June 12 MEF returned to its regular operating status. By the end of the summer the situation in the Indian Ocean basin had slowly returned to near normal.

Nevertheless, the immediate aftermath of the 1967 war demonstrated that anti-Western and anti-American sentiments, the latter exacerbated by United States support of Israel, were growing stronger in the Arab world.[125] Americans had tasted Arab wrath, popular and economic, as had the British after the Suez crisis of 1956. Soon after the war began, the Arabs embargoed oil sales to the United States. But the embargo proved ineffective. The United States still imported little petroleum from the Persian Gulf. A jump in prices tempted several major oil producers, among them Libya, Iran, and Venezuela, to plan to increase production to reap the windfall. And, because of preexisting low prices, the embargoing countries had limited cash reserves. A fortnight after the embargo had begun, the Saudis were broke. The Arabs quickly realized that the boycott hurt them more than the United States.

But they also learned several lessons that would allow them to use

83

their oil weapon successfully six years later. In 1973 the Arabs would have the political unity and the cash reserves to stay the course.

Despite the apparent rapid return to business as usual, the United States faced difficult times ahead. American policy, still burdened by the Vietnam war, struggled to head off another Arab-Israeli conflict and to limit Soviet diplomatic, economic, and military penetration into the Middle East. By the early 1970s, one-third of the countries of the Indian Ocean basin suffered from internal or external crises that manifested themselves in anti-American policies.

Nevertheless, the United States had weathered the storm of the 1967 war, and the turbulent post-Suez decade, fairly well. Nasser's defeat led to an abrupt end to most internal machinations against the Saudi regime and the withdrawal of Egyptian support from the rebels in North Yemen. The core American relationships with Turkey, Iran, Saudi Arabia, and Israel remained intact, and the military strength and internal stability of all four states had significantly improved. Unfortunately, American policy in the Middle East was headed for a fall of monumental proportions.

CHAPTER FIVE

A TALE OF TWO DOCTRINES

———•———

The Nixon and Carter Doctrines, 1968–1980

To most Americans, the foreign policy of the administration of President Lyndon B. Johnson is synonymous with the American defeat in Southeast Asia. The Vietnam War weakened the U.S. economy, divided the American people, almost destroyed the postwar foreign policy consensus in the country, and cost the lives of 50,000 Americans and untold numbers of Vietnamese.

Unfortunately, Johnson administration policies also prepared the stage for a decade of crises in the Middle East. Few Americans at the time (or since) recognized that among the myriad costs of U.S. involvement in the Vietnam War was a shift away from more active efforts to assure the security and stability of the Middle East. Had the United States been more actively engaged in the affairs of the region, there might not have been a 1967 war.

Johnson's fixation on Indochina led him to reverse the trend of the late 1950s and early 1960s toward deeper American political *and* military involvement in the Middle East. Eisenhower had considered the security of the Persian Gulf a far more vital concern than the containment of the spread of communism in Southeast Asia. Ike had intervened militarily in the Middle East but had rejected a similar course in Indochina. Johnson reversed Eisenhower's policies, intervened in the ongoing conflict in Southeast Asia, and, in an effort to win the war, redirected American political, economic, and military capital away from the Middle East.

Initially, Israel's crushing military victory over the Arab front-line states in the Six Day War masked many of the dangers Americans faced in the Middle East. The Arabs' defeat had a short-term dampening effect on anti-Western agitation. The rapid return to normalcy allowed the Johnson administration to continue to focus its foreign policy on Indochina, while fighting a rear-guard diplomatic action in the Middle East.

But not long after the immediate crisis of the 1967 war passed, dramatic events shook the Middle East and forced the Johnson administration to reassess its policy toward the region. Three factors forced this reappraisal: the British pullout from east of Suez announced in January 1968 and completed in 1971; the appearance of the Soviet Navy in the Indian Ocean in March 1968; and the physical and psychological consequences of the Vietnam War for the U.S. government and the American people. Once again, American policymakers wrestled with the more than two-decade-old question—who should be responsible for the defense of the Middle East? Once again, Americans answered "not us." But if not Americans, who?

Great Britain's determination to relinquish its already diminished position east of Suez marked the end of a "Long Retreat"—the withdrawal from imperial positions that began almost immediately after the Second World War.[1] Whatever the cause, the British pullout unraveled existing concepts for the defense of the Middle East. Britain, backed by the American atomic deterrent, had been the principle Western power responsible for the security of the region and her military strength was still the major source of stability within the volatile Persian Gulf.[2] Great Britain had intervened in newly independent Kuwait in July 1961 when Iraq threatened invasion (not for the last time), and British troops and aircraft were engaged in the suppression of radical forces in Aden and the Yemens.[3] The unwelcome prospect of Britain's sudden retreat from the region led several of the smaller Persian Gulf states to offer to finance a continued British military presence, but to no avail.[4]

To further complicate matters for the United States, the British announcement was almost immediately followed by the appearance of the Soviet Navy in the Indian Ocean. The arrival of Russian warships was a clear indication of Moscow's expanding influence in a region rife with nationalist and anti-Western sentiments.[5] By the end of the year, Soviet men-of-war had spent more time in the Indian Ocean than had those of the U.S. Navy.[6]

As the Western position in the gulf deteriorated, President Johnson's focus remained fixed on events in Indochina, especially after the start of the Communists' Tet offensive on January 31, 1968. Two months later, Johnson announced that he would not seek reelection.

86

What little attention the lame-duck administration gave to the Middle East focused on the Arab-Israeli dispute, not the question of who would replace Britain in the Persian Gulf.

When Richard M. Nixon became president in January 1969, he inherited not only the Indochina War from his predecessor, but also a not so slowly disintegrating Western security position in the Middle East. In charting the policy course for his administration, Nixon understood that the American people, deeply divided by the Vietnam war, were no longer willing to "bear any burden." The domestic political consensus necessary to support a larger American role in the Middle East, that is, to return to the Eisenhower administration's policies, no longer existed. Speaking to reporters on July 25, 1969, during a stopover on Guam, the president remarked that in the future Asian nations would have to accept greater responsibility for their own defense.[7] Nixon soon expanded on his concept in what became known as the Nixon Doctrine. In his State of the Union Address of January 22, 1970, he stated:

> Neither the defense nor the development of other nations can be exclusively or primarily an American undertaking.
>
> The nations of each part of the world should assume the primary responsibility for their own well-being; and they themselves should determine the terms of that well-being.
>
> We shall be faithful to our treaty commitments, but we shall reduce our involvement and our presence in other nations' affairs.[8]

The Nixon Doctrine had a profound impact on American policy in the Middle East, and its consequences are still being felt in the 1990s. In its search for a regional power willing and able to insure stability in the Persian Gulf the United States turned to Iran. The Iranians, not the Americans, would replace the British in the region. Henry Kissinger, then Nixon's National Security Adviser, wrote:

> It was imperative for our interests and those of the Western world that the regional balance of power be maintained so that moderate forces would not be engulfed nor Europe's and Japan's (and as it later turned out, our) economic lifeline fall into hostile hands. We could either provide the balancing force ourselves or enable a regional power to do so. There was no possibility of assigning any American military forces to the Indian Ocean in the midst of the Vietnam war and its attendant trauma. Congress would have tol-

erated no such commitment; the public would not have supported it. Fortunately, Iran was willing to play this role. The vacuum left by British withdrawal, now menaced by Soviet intrusion and radical momentum, would be filled by a local power friendly to us.[9]

American policymakers understood that reliance on Iran, an Islamic but non-Arab state frequently at odds with its neighbors, would be viewed as a threat by most of the gulf Arabs. To provide some balance within the region, and to assure the pro-Western Arab states of the gulf that they would not be abandoned to an Iranian hegemony, the United States identified Saudi Arabia as a second, on paper at least, coequal regional power in a policy that became known as the Twin Pillars.[10] But the Saudis, with a population of less than five million, could hardly be anything but a junior partner in the evolving security structure in the region.

The shah was more than willing to play his new role as protector of the gulf. From an Iranian perspective, Nixon's doctrine represented nothing more than U.S. acceptance of an existing regional reality. Following Great Britain's announced withdrawal from east of Suez, the shah immediately declared Iran the new power in the region. Through quick diplomatic moves he meant to insure that Iran, and not the United States, would replace Great Britain in the Gulf.[11]

To salve Arab sensibilities, late in 1968, before Nixon's inauguration, the shah began a diplomatic offensive that settled several, though by no means all, outstanding issues with the Saudis. During a November visit to Riyadh, the shah and King Faisal issued a joint communique that spoke of Arab-Iranian friendship and cooperation in the gulf.[12] In late December 1967, a joint Iranian-Turkish-Pakistani communique "affirmed that the responsibility for the preservation of peace and stability in the Persian Gulf rested only with the littoral states."[13]

Thus the Nixon Doctrine, as implemented in the Persian Gulf, was actually little more than an Iranian policy eagerly embraced by an administration caught in the morass of the Vietnam War. The gulf policy of Nixon and Kissinger reversed a quarter-century-old approach to Middle Eastern security that had rejected as destabilizing and counterproductive a massive military buildup of any state within the region, with the exception of NATO-ally Turkey. The United States had been rejecting the shah's schemes to build up the Iranian military since 1946. CENTO had been primarily a political, not a military pact.

The new directions in American Persian Gulf diplomacy invited criticism. Senator Edward Kennedy argued that the policy encouraged an arms race in the gulf and increased the risk of internal instability.[14] Other observers expressed strong concern about the internal situation in Iran.[15] And not all such doubts came from Nixon administration critics. During Anglo-American talks held in Washington in October 1974, a British official and Middle Eastern expert warned his American counterparts that they had "better watch out," because "the Shah may have overreached himself."[16]

The buildup of Iran was also likely to exacerbate problems with the Gulf Arabs, despite the shah's best efforts. Iraq, already being armed by the Soviet Union, felt threatened as its non-Arab neighbor, three times as populous, built up its armed forces. Soviet arms shipments to Iraq increased. On April 9, 1972, Iraq and the Soviet Union signed a friendship treaty aimed, in part at least, to offset Iran's arms buildup.[17]

Statistics for arms expenditures and imports between 1969, when the Nixon administration took office, and 1978, the last complete year of the shah's rule, support the view that the buildup of the Iranian military did prompt a regional arms race. Iranian defense expenditures increased 580 percent; those of the Iraqis 260 percent.

The Nixon administration's decision to make Iran a regional power also complicated efforts to establish a smoothly working relationship between Iran and oil-rich, pro-Western Saudi Arabia. The Saudis viewed both Iraq and Iran as potential threats and the developing arms race between the two boded ill for the Saudis. A 1973 Department

Iranian and Iraqi Arms Expenditures and Imports, 1969–78
($ millions)

Year	Total Defense Expenditures		Arms Imports	
	Iran	Iraq	Iran	Iraq
1969	1,828	826	220	70
1970	2,045	822	160	50
1971	2,505	857	320	40
1972	3,093	977	525	140
1973	3,729	1,304	525	625
1974	6,303	1,686	1,000	625
1975	8,646	1,738	1,200	675
1976	9,521	1,837	2,100	1,000
1977	8,747	2,007	2,400	1,500
1978	10,598	2,136	2,100	1,500

Source: Anthony Cordesman, *The Gulf and the Search for Strategic Stability*, p. 160.

of State report on Iranian-Saudi relations, entitled "The Odd Couple," noted that the two countries' concerns about Arab radicalism and the increasing Soviet presence in the Middle East had not been translated into effective cooperation.[18] Traditional problems, such as religious discord between the predominantly Shia Iranians and the Sunni Saudis, territorial disputes over several small islands in the gulf, and differences in scale and internal development divided the United States' "Twin Pillars."

> The Iranians, who tend to look down on the Arabs anyway, consider the Saudi regime's approach to its problems simplistic and ultra-conservative. The Saudis have their own doubts about the stability of the Iranian regime, which they consider dangerously dependent on the survival of the Shah.[19]

Another State Department report concluded: "The upshot of all these cross-currents is that the logic of Iranian-Saudi cooperation is being undercut by psychological, nationalistic, and prestige factors, which are likely to persist for a long time."[20]

Saudi and British concerns about the stability of the shah's regime and about his reliability as an ally were shared by many in the United States. A Defense Intelligence Assessment noted that since the shah was dependent on Americans for military and economic support, he had little choice, for the short term at least, but to accept "that aspect of the Nixon Doctrine dealing with the responsibility for regional powers to provide the primary protection for their own areas as tacit agreement by the United States to help provide Iran the wherewithal to do so."[21]

But the shah made no secret of his policy objectives. His military buildup was meant to forestall an American effort to replace the British in the gulf. In fact, the shah opposed the basing of the U.S. Navy's Middle East Force, which had operated from Bahrain since the late 1940s, in the gulf. At a January 29, 1972, press conference, when asked about the American presence in Bahrain, the shah responded: "Well, you know what we declared long ago that we should not like to see a foreign power in the Persian Gulf. Whether that power be Britain, the United States, the Soviet Union or China our policy has not changed."[22]

Nor were the shah's pretensions limited to the gulf. In 1974, following Indian Prime Minister Indira Gandhi's call for a "zone of peace" in the Indian Ocean, the shah announced his own similar plan for the region.[23] In October 1974, a British foreign ministry official warned the United States that "in the long run the Shah may be more audacious than shrewd and may not even be an ally." He was a man, the British official concluded, who suffered from "delusions of grandeur." A DIA estimate raised the possibility that the shah "might himself embark on adventures" after he completed his military buildup in 1980.[24] A State Department assessment noted the shah's leading role in hiking up oil prices in 1973 and 1974, to the detriment of the West, noting "heretofore his ambitions, though grandiose, have been limited to his own region, but he now seems to envision a global reallocation of capital resources and industry."[25] According to 1975 press reports, a CIA psychological profile of the shah termed him "a dangerous megalomaniac, who is likely to pursue his own aims in disregard of U.S. interests."[26] Senator Kennedy, who visited Iran in 1975, later wrote: "As I was told during my visit to Iran in May, leaders of that country now see it as part of both the Gulf and West Asia, with wider interests and ambitions, extending even to the Indian Ocean."[27] The U.S. Navy shared these concerns. When in 1974 the shah expressed an interest in purchasing three of the U.S. Navy's Sturgeon-class nuclear-powered attack submarines, the navy successfully opposed the sale.[28] But the shah was able to buy the navy's top-of-the-line fighter, the F-14 Tomcat, along with the long-range Phoenix air-to-air missiles.

While the scale of the Iranian military buildup in the mid-1970s was impressive, it was by no means evident that Iran, a Third World nation, could effectively absorb the vast amount of war material flowing into the country. The shah believed so and planned to make Iran not only a Middle Eastern, but also a Southwest Asian power. The Imperial Iranian Navy would become the dominant naval force in both the Persian Gulf and the Indian Ocean. But a Department of Defense assessment termed the Iranian endeavor "superficial," an effort "outside and far in advance of the Iranian industrial base." The report concluded: "By 1978, Iran's military machine may actually turn out to be a 'parade ground army,'—physically impressive but incapable of prolonged military action."[29]

An interesting contrast can be made of the nature of the respective buildups in Iran and Saudi Arabia. As Anthony Cordesman has pointed out, Saudi levels of defense expenditures equaled those of the Iranians. But the shah spent his money on tanks, planes, and ships—hardware that would increase the firepower of the Imperial Iranian armed forces. The Saudis, with a population only one-tenth that of Iran, almost obsessively, but understandably, concerned about internal stability, spent their money on major infrastructure improvements, training, modernization, and only carefully measured expansion. The air defense of Saudi Arabia became the top priority of the buildup. The effort to improve the Saudi air force and air defense system—the Peace Hawk program—met with great success and continued into the 1980s. Saudi military expansion reflected the wisdom and long-term thinking of a monarchy that survived the turbulent decades of the 1960s, 1970s, and 1980s. Conversely, the Iranian arms buildup had all the appearances of a crash program not all that well thought through.[30]

Despite significant enhancements to Saudi security, overall, Nixon administration policy in the gulf proved to be short-sighted and calamitous. Admittedly, the Vietnam War imposed such political and military restraints on the Nixon administration that it had little choice but to make virtue of necessity—to adopt as its own, policies that originated in Teheran. In the Persian Gulf, Nixon and Kissinger faced a Hobson's choice. But if the adoption of the administration's policy was understandable, and perhaps unavoidable, that did not make it wise. Nor was it necessarily executed as well as it might have been.

There was an enthusiasm for the shah, one shared by other American presidents including Jimmy Carter, that was undeserved. The shah of the 1940s and early 1950s—indecisive, prone to flight in a crisis, less than politically astute, unable or unwilling to organize a coup, despite obvious domestic support, to secure his own throne—had been forgotten. In his place Americans of the 1970s found the shah as statesman, adviser of presidents, and to some the ruthless despot of the Peacock throne. Unfortunately, when the crisis of the 1970s began, the shah reacted as he had in the early 1950s—indecisively. But this time no American-organized coup would save him or his regime.

The decision to build up Iran militarily was also a marked departure from past American policy, such as the May 1950 Tripartite Declaration, and had disastrous consequences for the United States. The State and Defense Departments could no longer veto arms transfers to Iran on the grounds that a given request from the shah, if fulfilled, represented an unnecessary increase in capability or was beyond the capacity of the Iranian military to employ effectively. Thanks to Nixon and Kissinger, what the shah wanted, he now got. Yet, even had the shah completed his military buildup, the Defenses Department estimated that his military would still have lacked the strength to do much more than slow a determined Soviet drive through Iran. As the Iraqis have recently learned in Kuwait, Third World countries, however well armed, are no match for First World powers.

While the Iranian buildup was not, nor could it be, substantial enough to block a Russian drive to the south, the shah's expanding military was more than sufficient to balance the only major regional threat—that posed by Iraq. Clearly, if an Iranian military torn by revolution was able to hold the Iraqis in 1980, the shah's military machine, had the monarchy survived, would certainly have possessed the capability to march to Baghdad. Such a regional imbalance created instability, not stability. And that instability made a Persian Gulf arms race, primarily an Iraqi arms buildup, inevitable. In that sense, Operation Desert Storm was, to a significant extent, an American effort to destroy an Iraqi military arsenal that the United States' own policies had helped create in the 1970s. The application of the Nixon Doctrine in the Persian Gulf bore no better results than did the doctrine's original offspring—Vietnamization—in Indochina.

While Nixon and Kissinger shared the shah's desire to avoid having American military power replace that of Great Britain in the gulf, the administration, despite the war in Vietnam, had no intention of reducing the already limited American presence in the region. Between 1969 and 1977 the U.S. role actually expanded. The Nixon administration's predilection to avoid the use or commitment of ground forces, and the lack of support facilities in the Indian Ocean basin, shaped that expansion and led to an increased reliance on naval forces.[31]

Following Great Britain's announced withdrawal from east of Suez, American policymakers had to decide whether or not the U.S. Navy's Middle East Force would remain in the Persian Gulf, and if so, where it should, or could, be based. The Johnson administration initiated, but did not complete, an interagency review of the question. The change in administrations did little to accelerate the process. Nor did complicating factors in both domestic and international politics. A continued U.S. presence in the gulf might well imply, given the British withdrawal, an increased leadership role, an unattractive proposition to many Americans for whom foreign commitments had become anathema. The shah's forceful policy further complicated the matter. The Iranians came to Washington with their long-standing claims that soon-to-be-independent Bahrain was part of Iran, while in the American capital there was a clear understanding that "no assertion of influence in the area by the Americans or others was desired or acceptable" by the shah.[32] Thus the increasing reliance on Iran as America's regional policeman appeared to rule out a continued U.S. presence in the Persian Gulf, certainly one based at Bahrain.

But the U.S. Navy had no wish to withdraw Middle East Force from the gulf, or from its base at Bahrain. In fact, the navy hoped to expand its capabilities in the Indian Ocean. Officially, the navy refrained from formal negotiations with the British or the Bahrainis, although Middle East Force officers in Bahrain began "informal discussions with the British." "However," the Chief of Naval Operations stressed, "you are still cautioned to avoid any action or commitment that could lead the British to believe that we intend to pick up their commitments in the area."[33] By early 1969, the navy had gained the support of the Joint Chiefs of Staff to keep Middle East Force at Bahrain.[34]

Nevertheless, the Nixon administration, its attention focused on Indochina, only slowly came to grips with the issue. On June 5, 1970, the National Security Council recommended that Middle East Force remain "at about its present strength [four ships], homeported in Bahrain."[35] Final presidential approval came only in December 1970, two years after the British announcement of their proposed withdrawal from the gulf.[36]

On Christmas Eve 1970, the Middle East Force commander finally received permission to discuss officially with Royal Navy personnel, the British Political Resident, and with the Bahrainis themselves, a continued American presence in Bahrain. A plan earlier prepared by the Middle East Force staff called for the United States to take over 10 acres—about 10 percent of the existing British base at Jufair—including a receiving antenna, priority use of Berth No. 1 on the Mina Sulman jetty, a small waterfront facility for work and recreation boats, landing rights for aircraft with suitable hanger and office space at the Muharraq airfield, and a radio transmitter building with a transmitting antenna.[37] The staff had also developed plans for various withdrawal contingencies should the negotiations with the Bahrainis fail. By the time that the Americans learned (August 19, 1971) that the British expected to complete their withdrawal by December 1971, the negotiations were well underway. On December 23, 1971, a week after Bahrain became independent and assumed full control over both its administration and international affairs, it signed a lease basing agreement with the United States. Both countries reserved the right to end the agreement one year after serving an official notice of intent.

The agreement met with opposition in the United States and the Arab world. On June 29, 1972, the United States Senate approved the arrangement, but only after a tough and spirited debate during which the senators received guarantees from the administration that the lease implied no political or military commitment to the security of Bahrain.[38] Throughout the Middle East, Arab nationalists viewed the Bahraini's basing arrangement with the United States as a new form of Western colonialism. But the Bahrainis, concerned about Iranian designs on the archipelago, not only stuck by their deal, but also hinted "that there would be no objection to an increase in the US presence provided it could be done quietly, at a politically realistic time and in such a way not to force the Government of Bahrain to make a choice between the US and the Arab world."[39]

The U.S. Navy faced a much more difficult and drawn out domestic political struggle over the development of the American base at Diego Garcia. The navy's interest in an Indian Ocean complex began in the late 1950s during the Eisenhower administration, when long-range planning conducted under the direction of Chief of Naval Operations Admiral Arleigh Burke identified the small atoll as a possible base. In 1959 the navy secretly suggested that the British break off Diego Garcia from the Seychelles and establish the island as a separate political entity.[40] The Indian Ocean base concept resurfaced during the early 1960s, with strong support from Paul Nitze, then assistant secretary of defense for international security affairs. As the navy had years before proposed, the British in November 1965 split off the Chagos Islands, including the Diego Garcia atoll, from the Seychelles and organized the British Indian Ocean Territory (BIOT). On December 30, 1966, the United States and the United Kingdom signed an executive agreement authorizing the U.S. military to construct a communications facility on Diego Garcia. Under Nitze, first as secretary of the navy (1967) and then as assistant secretary of defense (1968), the pace of development quickened. In June 1968, Congress approved funding for a modest base. Thereafter, base development continued, slowed by the need for constant political debate concerning the nature of the American role in the Persian Gulf, but hastened by the expanding Soviet presence in the region.

The development of a base on Diego Garcia was, and remains, central to a continued United States role in the Indian Ocean. Given the historic international and domestic difficulties inherent in an American effort to establish a base in one of the littoral states, the development of the virtually unpopulated atoll was a politically acceptable and attractive alternative. While Diego Garcia is a long way from everywhere (or, as some have said, a long way from nowhere), it is centrally placed to support operations throughout the Indian Ocean

95

basin and has proved its worth during several regional crises, the American involvement in the latter stages of the Iran-Iraq tanker war of 1987–88, and Operation Desert Shield/Storm. The base will likely play an expanded role in the future, especially when the United States loses its base rights in the Philippines.

Despite the construction of basing facilities at Diego Garcia, the U.S. position in the Indian Ocean basin remained weak in the early and mid-1970s. The Soviets had arrived and the British, on whom the Americans had depended for over thirty years, were packing for home.[41] One U.S. Navy assessment admitted that the British withdrawal

> resulted in the loss of a huge reservoir of historical knowledge, political expertise and analytic ability on events in the Persian Gulf and Arabian Peninsula that previously had been available to COM-IDEASTFOR. Additionally, the withdrawal of Royal Navy ships and the Royal Air Force removed the only available assets for maritime reconnaissance in the Persian Gulf and Gulf of Oman. Prior to withdrawal, U.K. sources and analysts had contributed about 80% of the political intelligence on the Persian Gulf area available to COM-IDEASTFOR.[42]

The collection of military intelligence on Soviet activity in the region posed problems for the United States. The intelligence tasks confronting the four ships of the Middle East Force were intimidating. For example, in late 1971 MEF assets monitored the Soviet anchorages off Socotra, Cape Guardaufi, Coetivy Island in the Seychelles, and Speakers Bank in the Chagos, and a Soviet Indian Ocean squadron (SOV-INDRON) that included two cruisers, two destroyers, an LST, a minesweeper, seven submarines, nine support vessels, an intelligence collector, and four space and research ships.[43]

The British withdrawal prompted the Americans and the French, who operated from Djibouti and Réunion, to cooperate more closely. By 1972, the French and Americans were informally exchanging information. On February 15, 1973, the two countries reached a formal agreement and established improved communications and a direct link between CMEF and the French Indian Ocean Commander (ALIN-DIEN) at Réunion.[44]

Franco-American cooperation enabled the U.S. Navy's Middle East Force's to maintain an efficient intelligence collection effort during the critical years of the mid-1970s. The October 1973 war, during which the two superpowers placed some of their respective forces on alert, stretched American capabilities to the limit. So, too, did the Soviet Union's April 1975 global naval exercise OKEAN during which twenty-three warships of various types operated in the Indian Ocean. About the same time Soviet long-range aircraft, flying from Indian Ocean bases, began performing reconnaissance duties of their own. Soviet activity symbolized a growing presence and increased capability in a volatile region, critically important to the United States and the West.[45]

Middle Eastern volatility became evident on October 6, 1973. The fourth Arab-Israeli conflict—the Yom Kippur War—began when Syria and Egypt attacked Israeli positions in the Golan and the Sinai. Once again, events took the United States by surprise and Americans found themselves engulfed by both regional and global crises.

Initially, Washington expected a quick Israeli victory and adopted a low profile hoping to avoid Arab wrath and to maintain a position as a postwar "honest broker." But on October 9, reports from the Golan and Sinai fronts indicated that the Israelis were in trouble. Rumors abounded that they were readying their not-so-secret atomic arsenal. The United States responded with a sizable resupply effort that, in combination with the fighting power of the Israeli Defense Force, allowed Israel to regain the initiative. The Soviet Union reacted by beginning its own aerial resupply effort to Syria and placed several airborne divisions on alert. The Arabs, led by Saudi Arabia, responded with an effective embargo against oil sales and shipments to the United States.

The active diplomatic efforts of American Secretary of State Henry Kissinger led to an October 22 U.N. resolution calling for an in-place cease-fire that was ostensibly accepted by all parties that same day. But continued Israeli efforts to destroy the Egyptian Third Corps, isolated in the Sinai, threatened the agreement. By the 24th, the administration was concerned enough about Soviet military moves that President Nixon, early on October 25, placed American military forces on a higher state of alert. Fortunately, the situation deteriorated no further, the cease-fire held, and difficult negotiating led to disengagement on all fronts.

The October War forced the United States to confront a new reality in the Middle East. Following the successful resolution of the 1970 Jordanian crisis, the United States had increased military and economic aid to Israel. Nixon and Kissinger believed that a secure Jewish state, freed from the specter of Arab attack, would become a force of stability

97

in the region. The administration would then be free to focus on what Nixon and Kissinger considered the truly important foreign policy problems of the day—the ongoing struggle in Indochina, the Soviet-American detente, and the American relationship with Communist China.[46] But reliance on Israeli military superiority had secured neither peace nor stability. The improved fighting capability of Egyptian and Syrian forces did much to obliterate the memory of the Arabs' 1967 defeat and rekindled their pride and nationalism. The Arabs also demonstrated the will to use their oil as an effective political weapon and inflicted a shock on dependent Western economies by an embargo that continued into the spring of 1974. Soviet influence in the region, which had been expanding since the mid-1950s, not only challenged American interests, but also threatened to turn regional crisis into superpower confrontation, despite détente.

The 1973 war, and its aftermath, also imperiled the operations of the only U.S. military assets actually deployed in the region—the U.S. Navy's Middle East Force.[47] The fallout from the war further restricted already limited American access to Persian Gulf and Indian Ocean ports, in the midst of a crisis during which the United States needed to increase its naval presence in the region. On October 20, the Bahrainis announced the termination of their lease agreement with the United States.

The political debate over a continued American naval presence in the gulf began once again. The navy studied the possibility of basing the Middle East Force at Diego Garcia or at an Iranian port inside, or perhaps outside, the gulf. But in Bahrain, MEF personnel sensed that they might not be going anywhere, noting the "absence of any immediate pressure" from the Bahrainis to pull out.[48] The Middle East Force commander, Rear Admiral Robert Hanks, advised Washington that the Bahraini decision appeared to be reversible.[49]

In fact, the Bahrainis did quietly drop their demand for immediate withdrawal. The Americans may well have been the allies of the hated Israelis, but the shah was just across the narrow Persian Gulf. In July 1975 the United States agreed to amend certain provisions of the 1971 agreement, and on August 12, 1975, the Bahrainis extended the provisional agreement to June 30, 1977.[50] Continued negotiations resulted in a further exchange of notes (June 28, 1977) in which both parties agreed to abide by the amended terms of the 1971 agreement. According to the 1977 accord, the United States no longer retained the right to base the Middle East Force in Bahrain, although American civilian and military personnel could be assigned to an administrative support unit in Manama, Bahrain, to back up American ships in the gulf.[51] Officially, U.S. Navy warships were no longer homeported in Bahrain and most of the staff were considered to be on temporary duty. Eighteen years after being told to leave, U.S. Navy ships continue to operate from Bahrain.

While the navy did retain access to base facilities in Bahrain, by mid-1974 twenty-eight ports in eleven countries were closed to American warships. Only Manama (Bahrain), Port Louis (Mauritius), Karachi (Pakistan), Colombo (Sri Lanka), and the "dependable" Iranian ports of Bandar Abbas and Bandar Shahpur continued to supply U.S. Navy ships.[52]

The absence of port facilities handicapped American naval operations in the Indian Ocean basin, but the Arab oil embargo threatened to disrupt the operations of the U.S. Navy in the Indian Ocean, the Mediterranean, and the Western Pacific.[53] The navy found itself relying on Iranian sources of supply. The shah personally directed the Iranian National Oil Company to divert fuel to the Iranian Imperial Navy, which, in turn, transferred the fuel to the U.S. Navy. The shah's assistance allowed the American navy to continue to operate in the Indian Ocean, a development that many viewed at the time, and continue to view, as a vindication of the Nixon administration's decision to rely on the shah.[54]

The Arab reaction to the October 1973 war—the Bahraini decision to evict the Middle East Force and the efforts of other littoral states to close their ports to American ships—further strengthened and accelerated American efforts to develop a secure basing infrastructure to support an American presence, however limited, in the Indian Ocean basin. Moreover, as the impact of the embargo and the higher OPEC-driven prices on Western and Third World economies became apparent, the United States reassessed its strategy for the unstable region.[55] American policymakers sought some chimerical formula that would allow a solution of the Arab-Israeli dispute, permit the United States to strengthen its ties with "moderate" Arab countries, secure the flow of oil to the West and Japan, and limit Soviet power and influence in the region.

One of many options American leaders considered was a new correlation between military strength and diplomacy. In late 1974 and early 1975, the Western press and many senior American officials speculated openly about a possible United States military operation—an "oil grab" scenario—to secure critical oil producing areas in the event of an embargo. In a January 1975 *Business Week* interview, Secretary of State Kissinger commented on such a possibility.

A very dangerous course. We should have learned from Vietnam that it is easier to get into a war than to get out of it. I am not saying that there's no circumstance where we would not use force. But it is one thing to use it in the cause of a dispute over price, it's another where there's some actual strangulation of the industrial world.[56]

Despite official denials, American planners were conducting preliminary studies on a variety of options to an Arab cutoff of oil to the United States, Western Europe, and Japan. Navy planners estimated the probable impact of an increased naval presence in the Indian Ocean, of a blockade of Arab ports, of the diversion or sinking of tankers headed to non-embargoed countries, of air strikes against non-oil related facilities, and of a direct amphibious assault. Unfortunately, none of the proposals appeared practical or effective. Then Chief of Naval Operations, Admiral James L. Holloway, III, wrote on the cover letter of one such study: "It becomes evident that there is little we can effectively accomplish in M.E."[57]

Nevertheless, despite the practical difficulties of projecting American military power into the Middle East, a new factor had been added to the strategic equation, one that could not be ignored by the Arabs, and one that would soon become a central element in American strategic thinking. Since the end of the Second World War, the United States had routinely weighed and rejected the idea of committing American military forces to the defense of the Middle East. The Eisenhower administration had demonstrated a willingness to intervene in the region militarily, and it is possible that had it not been for the Vietnam war the military developments initiated in the late 1950s could have led to an ultimate American commitment to defend the region. But now, in the mid-1970s, the United States once again began to contemplate the use of military force, not to shield the region from the Soviet Union, but to insure the flow of oil to the West.

Concerns about the stability of the Middle East, the growing reliance of the West on Persian Gulf oil, the British pullout from east of Suez, and the Soviet Navy's entry into the Indian Ocean contributed not only to a growing American recognition of the importance of the gulf, but also to the continued emphasis on strengthening the American position in the region. The Nixon and Ford administrations, encumbered as they were physically and psychologically by the war in Vietnam, sought marginal improvements in infrastructure and, given the turmoil in the region, ordered occasional carrier forays into the Indian Ocean. American naval forces in the Persian Gulf proper were not reinforced.

It fell to the administration of President Jimmy Carter to confront in a realistic fashion the dynamics of the United States strategic dilemma in the Middle East. Carter was the first elected president since Truman to take office without having to face an Indochina crisis. The former Georgia governor came to Washington determined to focus less on the global Communist peril and more on the regional problems facing the United States. While Carter was premature in his dismissal of Americans' "inordinate" fear of the Soviets, his concern about the deteriorating American position in the Middle East was fully justified.

The Carter administration moved quickly to strengthen the American position in the region. In mid-1977, Presidential Review Memorandum 10 identified "the Persian Gulf as a vulnerable and vital region, to which greater military concern ought to be given."[58] Presidential Directive 18, signed by Carter on August 24, 1977, called for the establishment of what would become the Rapid Deployment Force—a " 'deployment force of light divisions with strategic mobility' for global contingencies, particularly in the Persian Gulf region and Korea."[59] In a December 1977 address, Secretary of Defense Harold Brown stressed the importance of naval and tactical air forces and improved strategic mobility, assets that would give the United States the capability "to respond effectively and simultaneously to a relatively minor as well as a major military contingency."[60] These Carter administration policies led directly to the establishment of the Rapid Deployment Force.

The concept of a rapidly deployable force had deep roots in American military thinking. The army had established the Strategic Army Corps (STRAC) in 1958. STRAC's assigned units—the XVIII Airborne Corps headquarters and the 82nd Airborne Division—would ultimately provide the core for the RDF and U.S. Central Command and were deployed to Saudi Arabia during Operation Desert Shield/Storm. Under Admiral Burke, the navy in the late 1950s had also begun thinking about expanding its presence in the Indian Ocean at Diego Garcia. Similarly, the Joint Chiefs of Staff began to search for a command structure to oversee operations that fell outside the bounds of the existing geographically focused, multiservice, unified commands—the European Command (EUCOM) and the Pacific Command (PACOM). CINCNELM, temporarily designated Commander in Chief

Specified Command, Middle East (CINCSPECOMME), had controlled Operation Bluebat, the 1958 intervention in Lebanon. In the July 1960 Congo crisis, the possibility of American intervention once again led the services to argue over who should plan for such a contingency.[61]

The following year, the Kennedy administration arrived in Washington with myriad new defense-related concepts, among them flexible response. To direct possible contingency operations in areas such as the Middle East, the administration on January 1, 1962, directed the Joint Chiefs to establish Strike Command (STRIKCOM), headquartered at MacDill Air Force Base in Tampa, Florida, under which the Middle East Force subsequently operated during times of crisis. Special operations capabilities also improved and the expansion of strategic air and sealift assets began.

Unfortunately, American involvement in Vietnam retarded many of these developments.[62] In December 1971, when the Nixon administration directed the Joint Chiefs to disestablish STRIKCOM (which sounded too aggressive and interventionist to American ears), the responsibilities of the newly established Readiness Command did not include the Middle East. Responsibility for planning for contingency operations reverted to SACEUR and his naval component commander, Commander-in-Chief, U.S. Naval Forces Europe (CINCUSNAVEUR). The debate over the command structure only ended, at least temporarily, in 1983 with the establishment of Central Command at MacDill AFB.

In demanding yet another strategic review, and quite obviously directing the Joint Chiefs of Staff to conclude that the United States ought to accept, at long last, responsibility for the defense of the region, the Carter administration was resuming policy directions sidetracked in the 1960s and early 1970s. In response to PD-18, the Joint Chiefs of Staff oversaw a methodical—that is, slow—review of American strategy for the Middle East. On September 7, 1978, the JCS approved the "Review of US Strategy Related to the Middle East and the Persian Gulf" and that same day forwarded it to Secretary of Defense Brown.

This document highlighted three major American interests in the region.

1. To assure continuous access to petroleum resources.
2. To prevent an inimical power or combination of powers from establishing hegemony.

3. To assure the survival of Israel as an independent state in a stable relationship with contiguous Arab states.

The Joint Chiefs recommended expanding basing facilities at Diego Garcia, in Oman, Saudi Arabia, and Djibouti and projected naval force augmentation to include increases in carrier battle group (CVBG) deployment from one-to-three months to three-to-four months of the year. At times when CVBGs were absent, the Joint Chiefs recommended that an amphibious assault ship (LHA or LPH) with AV-8A Harriers and an embarked Marine Air-Ground Task Force (MAGTF) patrol the Indian Ocean.

> These forces will be capable of supporting US and allied interests in contingency situations by conducting a variety of tasks (not necessarily simultaneously) at several levels of intensity. These tasks would include: a range of conventional air operations; amphibious operations; SLOC protection; naval gunfire support; protection and evacuation of US and designated third-country nationals from crisis/conflict areas; surveillance of Soviet and other maritime operations; operations and exercises with allied forces; and port visits.[63]

Given the strain on American resources, especially the naval assets of the Seventh and Sixth Fleets, and because the security of the area was vital not only to the United States, but also to its allies, the report recommended that the British, Dutch, Germans, and Australians be encouraged to increase their naval deployments to the Indian Ocean. The French, the report noted, already had deployed a sizable force to the region. The "Review of US Strategy Related to the Middle East and the Persian Gulf" also suggested the possibility of establishing a numbered fleet in the Indian Ocean—a Fifth Fleet. But the services, even the U.S. Navy, remained unenthusiastic about the plan. For the sea service, the Indian Ocean was "a bitch," a theater that offered a harsh climate, and few ports for sailors and marines to enjoy shore leave.

The JCS review was soon overtaken by events—the Iranian revolution and the collapse of the existing American security structure in the gulf. For Americans, 1979 was a year of crisis. In January the shah abdicated. The centrist government that replaced the monarchy quickly demonstrated its ineffectiveness and the radical mullahs increasingly dominated Iranian politics. In November, the Iranians seized the American

103

embassy in Teheran and the interminable hostage crisis began. Then in December, the Soviet Union began moving troops into Kabul, Afghanistan. Some interpreted Moscow's move as Brezhnev Doctrine aid to a threatened Socialist state. Others saw the invasion as the first step in a Communist masterplan to drive toward the warm waters of the Indian Ocean and to secure the oil of the Persian Gulf. Whatever the cause of the decision taken by the Soviet leadership, apparently in a drunken Kremlin stupor,[64] for the first time since the end of the Second World War the Soviet Union had used force beyond its own borders or those of the Eastern European countries "liberated" by the Red Army in 1945.

For the United States, the fall of the shah in early 1979 was a disaster for American policy in the Middle East. Not surprisingly, following the shah's fall there was no shortage of "I told you so" analysis. In a history of Iranian-American relations, Professor James Bill, who had long held a pessimistic view of the shah's prospects for survival, quoted from a paper he delivered to the State Department in early 1978 in which he painted a rather "grim," but realistic assessment of the state of affairs in Teheran.[65]

In his memoirs, Henry Kissinger attempted to refute the ex post facto attacks on Nixon administration policy. Kissinger stressed the continuity of U.S. policy toward Iran and noted the shah's oft-demonstrated cooperation with and friendship for the United States, most notably his sale of oil to Americans during the 1973–74 Arab embargo.[66] Kissinger rejected the idea that extensive American arms sales imposed a guns or butter dilemma for Iran, writing: "nor can it be said that the shah's arms purchases diverted resources from economic development, the conventional criticism of arms sales to developing countries. The shah did both."[67] The shah fell, in Kissinger's view, not because his reforms were proceeding too slowly, but because they were moving too fast. The shah was a victim of a modernization crisis.

But the shah's American-supported modernization drive—the rapid military buildup, and just as rapid attempt to drag Iran into the twentieth century—exacerbated internal tensions and hastened or perhaps even precipitated his downfall. In an article written shortly before the revolution, Theodore H. Moran noted that "in the first years of euphoria following the fourfold oil price increase in 1973–74, Iranian planners felt that they had the financial resources needed for all aspects of development. This proved not to be the case."[68] Controlled food prices, meant to keep urban supplies cheap, were not matched by controls in the countryside and led to a drop in agricultural production and a multibillion dollar food import bill. The shah's defense expenditures totalled about a third of his budget and despite the country's oil wealth, the Iranian government actually ran a deficit in 1976.[69] Incredibly, by 1977 Teheran, the capital of oil-rich Iran, was enduring six-hour-long blackouts because of lack of fuel and inadequate generating capacity.

Moreover, the shah's evident willingness to support American policy heightened internal xenophobic pressures, as did the ever-expanding American presence in Iran. The Ayatollah Ruhollah Khomeini first gained national notoriety as a vociferous critic of the shah's acceptance of a 1964 Status of Forces Agreement that gave American military personnel in Iran virtual extraterritoriality. Khomeini denounced an agreement that "reduced the Iranian people to a level lower than that of an American dog," and was shortly thereafter exiled.[70] While the Nixon Doctrine called for a reduced American involvement and presence in the gulf, the extensive assistance needed to oversee military and economic aid programs necessitated just the opposite. A mid-1970s Department of Defense estimate projected that about 150,000 Americans would be in the Middle East by 1980.[71] When President Carter visited Iran in December 1977, there were already 30,000 Americans in the country, as many as there had been during the height of the American presence during the Second World War.[72]

During the mid-1970s, the modernization process in Iran reached a crisis stage. Inflation, rapid internal development, and the expansion of the Iranian military beyond realistic security needs (and beyond what it could usefully absorb) exacerbated the crisis. As the modernization process accelerated and internal pressures mounted, the shah himself was increasingly preoccupied with supervising the military buildup and directing Iranian foreign policy.[73]

The shah was not an American puppet and he bore the ultimate responsibility for his own fate.[74] If the Iranian government was unresponsive to the needs of its people, that government had been fashioned by the shah, configured to insure his own security by preventing the development of any rival center of political power. If the Iranian military was unwilling or incapable of rescuing or replacing their monarch, it was because the shah had insured that the military was divided and led by men unlikely to seize power themselves in a military coup. The system placed all authority in the hands of a man who in 1978–79 was dying of cancer and under chemotherapy.[75] Ultimately, the shah, as he had many times before, fled the country in the midst of crisis. James Bill writes: "[The Shah] in the end understood better than disgruntled Western critics and his own hard-line military generals that such a national uprising could not be put down by force indefinitely."[76] Even Kissinger later admitted:

Wise is the ruler who understands that economic development, far from strengthening his position, carries with it the imperative of building new political institutions to accommodate the growing complexity of his society. It cannot be said that either the Shah or his friends possessed this wisdom; but, it must be remarked, neither did his enemies.[77]

After the fall of the shah, the Carter administration moved quickly to strengthen the U.S. position in the region. In January and March 1979, unarmed U.S. Air Force F-15s and Airborne Warning and Control System (AWACS) aircraft deployed in a Carter-style show of force in Saudi Arabia.[78] A carrier battle group built around the *Midway* steamed into the Indian Ocean from the western Pacific. Following the seizure of the hostages in November in Teheran, the *Kitty Hawk* CVBG left Subic Bay in the Philippines for the Arabian Sea.[79]

Coming on the heels of the revolution in Iran, the Soviet invasion of Afghanistan provoked a sharp response from the West. The Carter administration embargoed grain shipments to the Soviet Union and withdrew the U.S. team from the forthcoming Moscow Olympics. Carter decided that forceful action was necessary to deter further Soviet moves to the south. In his January 23, 1980, State of the Union address, the president annunciated what became known as the Carter Doctrine.

Let our position be absolutely clear: An attempt by any outside force to gain control of the Persian Gulf region will be regarded as an assault on the vital interests of the United States of America, and such an assault will be repelled by any means necessary, including military force.[80]

To put teeth in the new policy, the administration continued to deploy military force to the region. U.S. Air Force AWACS deployed to Egypt and B-52 bombers from Guam overflew the Arabian Sea in a demonstration of American air power. But the U.S. Navy bore most of the burden. By mid-January, when Carter delivered his address, the navy had twenty-five ships, including three aircraft carriers, in the Indian Ocean, a force more powerful than that deployed by the Reagan administration during the 1987–88 tanker war with Iran.[81]

In a March 6, 1980, address, Secretary of Defense Harold Brown outlined the military aspects implicit in the Carter Doctrine. Brown listed American interests in the region: "to insure access to adequate oil supplies; to resist Soviet expansion; to promote stability in the region; and to advance the Middle East peace process, while insuring—and, indeed, in order to help insure—the continued security of the State of Israel." Regarding oil, the secretary of defense emphasized the importance of conservation as an element of national security, but he also stressed

that no conceivable combination of measures—conservation, stockpiling, or alternative energy sources—can totally eliminate the near term security problem that is created by threats to the Gulf and its oil. The hard fact is that there is nothing the United States—or our industrial world partners or the less developed countries—can do in the coming decade, or probably even the next, that would save us from severe damage if the bulk of the oil supply from the Persian Gulf were cut off for a sustained period.

Increases in U.S. Navy Strength in the Indian Ocean, 1976–88

	Surface Ship Days	Carrier Ship Days	% of Deployed Carriers	Average Yearly Carrier Strength
1976	1279	19	3	0.1
1977	1439	100	7	0.3
1978	1207	35	3	0.1
1979	2612	153	9	0.4
1980	6993	836	51	2.3
1981	5651	646	39	1.7
1982	5361	443	27	1.2
1983	4704	406	24	1.0
1984	5335	410	28	1.1
1985	5136	475	36	1.3
1986	3580	185	13	0.5
1987	6760	412	30	1.1
1988	7991	412	30	1.1

Source: Adam Siegel, Karen Domabyl, and Barbara Lindberg, *Deployment of U.S. Navy Aircraft Carriers and Other Surface Ships, 1976–1988*, pp. 13, 15, 21, 26–27.

Accordingly, the United States, Brown announced, was developing rapid deployment forces and increasing its capability to project military power into the region.[82]

Unfortunately for the United States, and for the Carter administration, 1980 proved to be as difficult a year as 1979. The April attempt to rescue the hostages ended in disaster at Desert One, a rendezvous site on the Iranian plateau. The hostage rescue fiasco further weakened the administration's credibility and appeared to illustrate American military incapacity in the region.

The history of the hostage rescue attempt is replete with examples of American ineptitude, lack of determination, and insufficient intelligence. Within a week of the November 4, 1979, seizure of the American embassy in Teheran by Iranian "students," the United States military was at work developing a variety of plans for the use of force either to free the hostages or to retaliate should the Iranians begin to execute or otherwise harm the captives. The planning effort demonstrated the physical and political limitations facing the United States in the region. Other than Oman, none of the gulf states were willing to allow American aircraft to operate from their territory to support any effort against Iran. And the difficulties in moving substantial forces to the region were daunting. Nevertheless, by early 1980, three U.S. Navy carrier task forces and a small Marine Corps amphibious-capable contingent were in the Indian Ocean, strengthening the Middle East Force.

The Carter administration rejected several less risky, more militarily feasible retaliatory strike options, such as a plan to seize Kharg Island, an important oil terminal in the northern Persian Gulf. Instead, on April 11, 1980, Carter issued an execute order for a hostage rescue option which heretofore had borne the cover name RICE BOWL.

On April 24, the operation, codenamed EAGLE CLAW began.[83] Unfortunately, the on-scene commander aborted the mission when three of the eight U.S. Navy RH-53 helicopters developed mechanical problems.[84] The failed rescue mission seemed at the time to underscore the helplessness of the United States in the Gulf.

As the hostage crisis continued, the already hard-pressed Carter administration faced yet another major challenge. In September, deteriorating relations between Iran and Iraq led to open warfare. Most Western analysts, and no doubt the Iraqis themselves, expected a quick Iraqi victory, a World War II-type blitzkrieg, and early initial Iraqi successes seemed to support that view.[85] But the advance slowed after the first few weeks and the war continued for eight years.

The Iran-Iraq war presented the United States with a new dilemma. The Carter Doctrine had addressed the issue of external, "outside," that is Soviet, threats to the gulf. But what about an "inside" job? In his March 1979 speech, Secretary of Defense Brown, echoing the conclusions of the JCS's "Review of US Strategy Related to the Middle East and the Persian Gulf," had termed "access to adequate oil supplies" the primary American objective in the region. Would the United States respond with military force if the threat to the West's oil supplies came from a Middle Eastern state?

As the Carter administration's policy evolved, the answer proved to be affirmative. The president reacted promptly to the Iran-Iraq conflict, continuing the military buildup that had begun in early 1979. Two more American men-of-war entered the Persian Gulf bringing Middle East Force to a strength of seven ships.[86] U.S. Air Force AWACS and tankers returned to Saudi Arabia. A pair of carrier battle groups remained in or near the North Arabian Sea, bringing the U.S. Navy's strength in the region to over thirty ships. Carter also discovered that strong American leadership attracted support. In a pattern that would be followed throughout the decade, and during the 1990-1991 Gulf War as well, Western European nations sent their men-of-war to the gulf to support the United States. By October about sixty American, French, British, and Australian warships were in the Indian Ocean or the gulf, keeping a close eye on the belligerents as well as nearly thirty Soviet warships in the region.[87]

This Western show of force was meant to impress not just the Soviets, but the gulf states, too. Speaking to reporters at the White House on September 24, Carter noted that the loss of both Iranian and Iraqi oil would not have a major impact on the world's supply. But he emphasized:

Of course, a total suspension of oil exports from the other nations who ship throughout the Persian Gulf region would create a serious threat to the world's oil supply and consequently a threat to the economic health of all nations. Therefore, it's important that I add my own strong support and that of my Nation to the declaration which the nine European Community nations made yesterday. Freedom of navigation in the Persian Gulf is of primary importance to the whole international community. It is imperative that there be no infringement of that freedom of passage of ships to and from the Persian Gulf region.[88]

Three weeks later, Secretary of State Edmund Muskie reiterated the president's position: "We have pledged to do what is necessary to protect free shipping in the Strait of Hormuz from any interference."[89]

By late 1980, the Carter administration had brought about a radical transformation of American policy in the Persian Gulf. Carter and his National Security Adviser, Zbigniew Brzezinski, examined the conundrum of Middle East defense and concluded that, with the British gone and the shah overthrown, the United States could no longer avoid primary responsibility for the defense of the Middle East. The only other option was to withdraw, a policy that was politically, economically, and militarily unthinkable.

Carter's clarity of thought on this subject was not solely the result of narrowed options. From the start his administration focused on regional problems, such as those of the Middle East, problems that had too long been ignored. That focus bore fruit in the form of the Camp David accord that brought peace to Egypt and Israel and secured the Middle East's most populous Arab nation as an American ally. While Carter achieved no comparable success in the gulf, his failure had more to do with the sins of his predecessors than the shortcomings of his policies.

By 1980 the United States had embarked on a new course in the Middle East, one that reversed not only the Nixon Doctrine, but also conceptions that had long ruled out direct American military commitment in the Middle East. The Carter Doctrine, Secretary of State Muskie's "pledge" to keep open the Strait of Hormuz, and the development of the Rapid Deployment Force broadened American policy responsibilities and options. The United States had not only committed itself to military action against any Soviet move into the region, but had also raised the possibility that it would react with force to a threat of Middle Eastern origin to the West's oil supply.

Such considerations were not voiced as loudly or as clearly in Washington as was concern over the Soviet threat. While the development of the capability to project American power into the Middle East to stop a Russian attack could expect to receive the support of the moderate Arab states, the development of the capability to move United States military force into the region for use against the oil-producing states themselves was hardly conducive to American efforts to build a foundation for an increased role and presence in the region. As former Secretary of Defense Harold Brown noted in a study written shortly after he left office: "the differing but related attitudes of the

Persian Gulf states toward being defended from Soviet forces and being intimidated by Western forces make an explicitly declared policy on defense against local threats unwise."[90]

The period from 1968 to 1980 was, indeed, a tale of two doctrines. Many of the problems the United States faced (and will face in the Persian Gulf during the 1990s) were the legacy of the Nixon Doctrine, while the means with which the United States successfully confronted these problems were largely the legacy of the Carter Doctrine.

CHAPTER SIX

NOT WHILE THIS
PRESIDENT SERVES

—•—

The Reagan Administration and the Gulf,
1981–1987

W hile the Carter administration had brought about a dramatic redirection in United States Persian Gulf policy and had set in motion
the political and military developments necessary to support that policy, the continuing crisis atmosphere in the gulf all but insured the
president's electoral defeat in 1980. Higher Persian Gulf oil prices
helped lock the economy in what seemed a permanent recession.
Shocks to the American psyche, such as the shah's fall, the hostage
crisis, and the Soviet invasion of Afghanistan, fed the "malaise" that
even Carter admitted gripped the American people. Suddenly, and
unexpectedly, the security of the Persian Gulf, a region already commercially, strategically, and geoeconomically vital to the United States,
had become politically crucial to the domestic electoral survival of
American presidents.

That lesson was not lost on Carter's successor, Ronald Reagan.
Reagan brought a renewed sense of optimism to the American presidency in January 1981. He promised to end the American people's
"malaise," get the economy moving, rebuild the military, give new
direction to American global policy, and reverse what many had perceived to be a period of decline for the United States.[1] He also arrived
in Washington in January 1991 determined not to allow events in the
gulf to undermine his administration the way they had Carter's.

Historians and political analysts will long debate the extent to which
Reagan gave new direction to the nation, or simply reflected and
capitalized on an existing American mood. But with regard to United

112

States policy in the Persian Gulf–Indian Ocean region, Reagan inherited clearly defined and annunciated diplomatic and military policies from the previous administration, namely the Carter Doctrine and the Rapid Deployment Force.

The Reagan administration built on, and ultimately executed these inherited policies. The continued development of the Rapid Deployment Force led in 1983 to the establishment of a new unified command—United States Central Command. And in 1987, President Ronald Reagan chose to act on Secretary of State Muskie's 1980 pledge to do what was necessary to keep tanker traffic safe from "interference" in the Persian Gulf.

At first, Reagan administration spokespersons generally attempted to dissociate themselves from anything that bore the "Carter" label.[2] Only gradually did the new administration embrace some of its predecessor's policies. In a January 28, 1981, appearance before the Senate Armed Services Committee, Secretary of Defense Caspar Weinberger called for a navy "capable of maintaining a three-ocean commitment," implying a continued buildup of naval forces in the Indian Ocean.[3] The administration's first defense guidance projection stressed the need "to assure the continued flow of oil" from the Persian Gulf and to "make a heavier investment in the near term in upgrading our capabilities to project forces to, and operate them in, this region."[4] In an interview with *Time* magazine, Secretary of State Alexander Haig, questioned about the Carter Doctrine, responded:

Western industrialized societies are largely dependent on the oil resources of the Middle East region and a threat to access of that oil would constitute a grave threat to the vital national interest. That must be dealt with; and that does not exclude the use of force.[5]

During an appearance before the Senate Armed Services Committee on March 9, Deputy Secretary of Defense Frank Carlucci spoke of American concerns for the security of the gulf region and outlined several responses, including an increased American naval presence in the Indian Ocean of one or two carrier battlegroups and an afloat Marine Air Ground Task Force (MAGTF), continued development of the Rapid Deployment Joint Task Force (RDJTF), diplomatic efforts to increase access to local ports and airbases, expansion of facilities at Diego Garcia, and the prepositioning of equipment and supplies.[6]

The new administration's reluctance to forthrightly embrace existing policies was both philosophical and political. Having assailed the

113

Carter presidency during the campaign, Reagan well understood that his inheritance came with a fair amount of political baggage.[7]

From the start, both the Carter Doctrine and the Rapid Deployment Force had come under bipartisan attack. Senator Edward Kennedy, long an opponent of the American role in the region, had questioned the wisdom of the Carter commitment to the defense of the gulf. Others had expressed doubts about the substance of the policy. Some had called Carter's doctrine a bluff. Analysts charged that the Rapid Deployment Force concept was so dependent on nonexistent airlift and sealift capabilities that the RDF was neither rapid, deployable, nor a force.

The most substantive criticisms were those that focused on the logistical problems an American effort to project military force into the region would face. Logistical shortcomings led military analyst Jeffrey Record to argue that the RDF was "a standing invitation to military disaster" because "the Rapid Deployment Force currently envisaged by the Department of Defense is a fatally flawed instrument for effective U.S. military intervention in the Persian Gulf."[8]

Joshua Epstein, in a balanced and cogent examination of the Rapid Deployment Force concept, attacked what he viewed as the underlying precepts of the Carter strategy—that the RDF was a tripwire backed by the threat of American horizontal or vertical escalation.[9] Successful deterrence, Epstein argued, had to be based on a conventional capability to check a Soviet move into Iran. And Epstein, unlike most other critics of the RDF concept, demonstrated that because the Soviets also faced enormous logistic difficulties in the Middle East, the United States could, in fact, develop a small, deployable force capable of effective action in the Persian Gulf arena.[10]

Many of the criticisms of the Carter Doctrine and the Rapid Deployment Force were merited. The military force necessary to support stated policies did not exist in the early 1980s. There were conceptual problems with the idea of nuclear deterrence, or even conventional deterrence. Would Americans really risk war with the Soviet Union, be it nuclear or conventional, to save revolutionary Iran? And the logistical realities inherent in operations halfway around the world were exacting.

Nevertheless, in a democracy, as Brzezinski noted in the memoir of his service as Carter's National Security Adviser, pronouncements such as the Carter Doctrine had to be issued in advance of the development of capabilities. Only through such means could an administration garner sufficient public and political support for the long-term programs ultimately needed to implement the policy. The American military had been no better prepared to defend Greece and Turkey when Truman announced his doctrine in 1947, or to defend Western Europe when the NATO treaty was signed in 1949.

And the idea behind the Rapid Deployment Force was not some half-brained, hastily concocted public relations effort of the Carter administration. The RDF concept evolved from a lengthy process of strategic thinking about the Middle East, and about the nature of the American military, that had deep roots in the United States. Secretary of Defense Brown remarked in early 1980: "The United States has been in the rapid deployment and power projection business for a long time. If you doubt that, ask the Marines who 5 years ago celebrated their 200th anniversary."[11]

The Carter Doctrine and the RDF were evolving concepts. In 1980, Secretary of Defense Brown, while he acknowledged the weakness of available forces, specifically rejected the notion that the RDF was meant to be no more than a "trip wire." The administration's planned improvement of conventional airlift and sealift capabilities was meant to develop the Rapid Deployment Force, over time, into a true conventional deterrent.[12]

Nor was the American military blind to the logistical problems connected with the projection of power into the Indian Ocean. A 1979 JCS strategic mobility study on the Persian Gulf concluded that even "the most productive alternatives" currently available for the support of forces deployed to the Persian Gulf were "inadequate."[13] The Carter administration, the Congress, the Department of Defense, and the services worked diligently to upgrade the assets necessary to deploy and support a sizeable force in the Persian Gulf.

Nor was the military satisfied with the command structure for the Middle East. When Jeffrey Record suggested in 1981 that the United States should establish a unified command for the Persian Gulf region, the Department of Defense was already considering just such a proposal.[14] A Navy memorandum of 1981 acknowledged that the "present command arrangements for the RDJTF are cumbersome." Planning was divorced from peacetime control and responsibilities. Among the myriad options under consideration was the creation of a unified command.[15] Indeed, the eventual establishment of the United States Central Command on January 1, 1983, was, to quote Lieutenant General Robert C. Kingston, its first commander, "the product of an evolutionary process which sought the best methods for integrating our nation's military and security interests with those of nations of the region and our allies."[16]

From his MacDill AFB headquarters in Tampa, Kingston oversaw the formative period of the new unified command, the first established in twenty-one years.[17] CENTCOM's marching orders were consistent with the policy objectives that had been annunciated in the JCS Middle East review of 1978–79: to assure Western access to oil, preserve regional stability, deter Soviet aggression, and halt and reverse the spread of Soviet influence. Identified threats included local instability, intraregional conflicts, and outright Soviet aggression. To secure these objectives, Kingston controlled, on paper, substantial, multiservice forces, although in the event of a wider war with the Soviet Union, not all would be available for deployment in Southwest Asia. CENTCOM also managed and coordinated the security assistance programs in the nineteen countries located within the command's area of responsibility (AOR).

While the establishment of CENTCOM marked a step forward in the development of a coherent defense policy for the Middle East, the existence of the new command just as certainly did not immediately resolve those problems that had hampered American efforts to project military power into the region since 1979. In a January 1984 lecture delivered to the Royal United Service Institute in Great Britain, Kingston noted:

Notional Central Command Forces

Army	Air Force
1 Corps Headquarters	7 Tactical Fighter Wings
1 Airborne Div	2 Strategic Bomber Wings
1 Airmobile Air Assault Div	
1 Mechanized Infantry Div	**Marine Corps**
1 Infantry Div	1 Marine Amphibious Brigade
1 Mechanized Brig	
1 Cavalry Brig (Air Combat)	**Special Operations Forces**
	1 Special Forces Group
Navy	1 Ranger Regiment
	1 Special Operations Aviation Bn
3 Carrier Battle Groups	1 Navy Special Warfare Task Group
1 Surface Action	1 Air Force Special Ops Base
5 Maritime Patrol Squadrons	

It would be less than prudent to advise you that in my Command, now one year old, that all the problems confronting us have been solved. Consider for a moment, by comparison with the European and Pacific Commands, some of the challenges facing the US Central Command. There are sizeable US forces in place in the European and Pacific theaters. The Central Command area has almost none. There are in-place Command and Control Communications systems in both the European and Pacific theaters. In the Central Command area there is none. There is an extensive logistic infra-structure in place in Europe and the Pacific. But in the Central Command area there is none. There are extensive host support agreements between the United States and the nations of Europe and the Pacific. In the Central Command area we have none. And we have long-term alliance with Western Europe and many nations of the Pacific. We have none with nations in the Central Command area. In short, if we had to send a combat force in the Central Command area we would start from almost zero in terms of combat power and support structure in the region.[18]

Nevertheless, the Central Command demonstrated the U.S. commitment to provide not only diplomatic, but also military leadership and a military presence in the Middle East. Other nations—both regional and extraregional—with economic or security interests in the area were invited to cooperate. But reliance on Britain, CENTO, and the Twin Pillars had finally given way to the realization that the United States had to do the job itself.

As the Reagan administration refined its politico-military policy toward the Middle East, the situation in the region steadily deteriorated. In Egypt, Muslim fanatics assassinated President Anwar Sadat on October 6, 1981. In the Levant, the Lebanese civil war dragged on and in June 1982, Israel invaded southern Lebanon. In August, the United States sent 800 Marines into Beirut as part of a multinational peace-keeping force. The following April, terrorists struck at the U.S. embassy in Beirut, killing sixteen Americans. In October, a terrorist drove an explosives-laden truck into the barracks at Beirut International Airport killing 241 Marines, more Americans than were killed in action in Desert Storm! President Reagan promised not to be "intimidated by terrorists." But a disastrous naval air strike in December cost the United States two aircraft, downed by the Syrians. One American aviator was killed and a second captured but released. By March 1984, the Marines had been withdrawn. The civil war in Lebanon continued. In the Mediterranean, United States naval forces clashed repeatedly with forces of Muammar al-Qadhafi's Libya. On April 14, 1986, during Operation El Dorado Canyon, U.S. Navy and U.S. Air Force planes struck targets in Tripoli and Benghazi in retaliation for a terrorist bombing of a West German disco frequented by Americans. To the east, the Soviets persisted in their unsuccessful efforts to subdue Afghanistan. The stalemated conflict threatened to spill over into neighboring Pakistan, which served as the base for Western aid to the Afghan resistance fighters. And in the Persian Gulf, the Iran-Iraq war continued without cease.[19]

As the stalemate persisted in the gulf, the Reagan administration's concern deepened. In September 1981, Iranian aircraft bombed a Kuwaiti oil facility, highlighting the possibility of escalation and the air defense problem confronting the gulf states.[20] The Iranian attack was timely, because the administration faced tough Congressional opposition to the completion of the AWACS sale to Saudi Arabia, a program initiated by President Carter.

Among the arguments employed by the opponents of the sale was the possibility that the Saudi Arabian monarchy might go the way of Iran's Pahlavi dynasty. The Reagan administration, wishing to send a clear signal of American concern over the course of events in the gulf, used the AWACS debate as an opportunity to assure Congress and other interested parties in the gulf that there would be no repetition of the Teheran revolution in Riyadh. At a press conference, President Reagan remarked: "there is no way . . . that we could stand by and see [Saudi Arabia] taken over by anyone that would shut off the oil."[21] Subsequent press conferences and interviews with administration officials made evident the Reagan administration's commitment to the security of Saudi Arabia, a pledge that went beyond the bounds of, and ultimately became known as the Reagan corollary to, the Carter Doctrine.[22]

Tough talk was not about to end the war in the gulf. Testifying before Congress in September 1983, Deputy Assistant Secretary of State for Near Eastern and South Asian Affairs Robert H. Pelletreau remarked:

> The longer this war of attrition lasts, the greater the risks will be that either Iran or Iraq will risk some desperate military escalation in the Gulf that would widen the war. We would regard as especially

118

serious any threat by either party to interfere with free navigation or act in any way that would restrict oil exports from the Gulf.

I wish to emphasize, as we have made clear to both Iran and Iraq, that the unrestricted flow of oil from the Gulf is vital to the entire international community. Our commitment to freedom of commerce and navigation in the international waters of the Gulf is firm. Even if Iran and Iraq cannot come to grips with the basic issues that divide them and to make peace, we expect them to respect this principle.[23]

In 1984, as American policymakers feared, the war escalated. In an attempt to break the stalemate, the Iraqis began using chemical weapons, launched air and missile strikes against Iranian cities (the war of the cities), and stepped up attacks against ships bound to or steaming from Iranian ports (the tanker war).[24] The Iranians responded as best they could. Their aircraft raided Baghdad and other Iraqi cities. And while the tanker war initially was a one-sided affair, Teheran eventually retaliated by striking at the shipping of the gulf Arab states, which were providing financial support for Saddam Hussein's war effort.[25]

The United States responded promptly to the spillover of the war to the gulf and supported a June 1, 1984, United Nations Security Council Resolution (552) condemning Iranian attacks on ships bound to neutral Kuwaiti and Saudi ports.[26] That same month, Richard W. Murphy, the assistant secretary of state for Near Eastern and South Asian affairs, warned Congress that the widening war threatened Western oil supplies and the security of America's "moderate Arab friends."[27] The United States would seek a negotiated settlement through the United Nations, strengthen the defenses of the gulf states, and weigh the option of the use of military force. In a July statement, Murphy made clear that while the United States did not seek to become involved in hostilities, it was not prepared to see the gulf's oil traffic threatened.[28] And when it became obvious late in the year that the Iraqis had given up any hope of achieving victory and were eager to find a diplomatic solution to the conflict, the United States "tilted" toward Baghdad, resuming diplomatic relations with Iraq. The United States announced publicly that in its view the war continued primarily "at insistence of Iran."[29]

Unfortunately, 1985 witnessed little movement toward peace, although the tempo of the tanker war slowed. While the Iraqis continued their assault against Iranian oil facilities, the number of ships bound to or steaming from Iran attacked by Iraqi aircraft fell from fifty-three

119

to thirty-three. The Iranians showed similar restraint (eighteen to fourteen), although they warned that renewed Iraqi attacks would lead to retaliatory strikes against tanker traffic headed to the ports of the Arab nations of the gulf.[30]

The administration expressed continued concern. In a June 11, 1985, interview, President Reagan remarked that the United States had "a vital interest in maintaining freedom of navigation in the gulf and stability in the region generally."[31] On October 1 in New York City Secretary of State George Shultz commented on the effectiveness of the Iraqi attacks and the Iranian policy of stopping and searching ships in the gulf: "The United States stands by its commitment to the right of international access to the gulf and free transit passage of neutral shipping through the Straits of Hormuz. We take seriously any infringement on these rights and are ready to work with the G[ulf] C[ooperation] C[ouncil] in areas such as joint contingency planning."[32]

For the United States, 1986 proved to be a critical year in the Gulf War. In a February–March offensive, Iranian troops overran the Fao Peninsula and Iran appeared to be on the threshold of victory. The Arabs were weakening: Iraq militarily, the gulf states economically. As a result of the oil glut of the early and mid-1980s, the oil revenues of Saudi Arabia, Kuwait, and United Arab Emirates fell from $186 billion in 1982 to $57.6 billion in 1985 and were headed lower.[33] The loss of income combined with the cost of subsidizing the Iraqi effort and the impact of the war on commercial activity in the gulf, sent economic and political shock waves through the region that increased the risks of internal problems and tensions.

With the Iranians now possessing the whip hand and threatening to march on Baghdad, the Iraqis stepped up their attacks on tankers carrying Iranian oil. The Iranians, apparently sensing the shift in the war's momentum, responded, as they had warned they would, in kind.[34]

For Iran, the asymmetry of the tanker war posed special problems. Because of the closing of the Shatt-al-Arab, the Iraqis had no access to, and had virtually no naval forces in, the Persian Gulf. Nevertheless, Iraqi aircraft could strike at vessels bound to or from Iranian ports within a declared war zone in proximity to the Iranian coast. The Iraqis could justify these actions as attacks against belligerent ships or vessels headed to a belligerent port. By comparison, Iran was geographically far better situated to conduct the tanker war, fronting as it did the entire Persian Gulf and the Gulf of Oman approaches to the Strait of Hormuz. The Iranian Navy, while it had not recovered from the turmoil of revolution, remained the most powerful in the gulf. Unfortunately for Teheran, despite its inherent advantages at sea, there were no Iraqi ships, nor vessels bound to or from Iraqi ports, at large in the gulf. Iraq exported its oil via pipelines that ran through Turkey,[35] or via transshipment through Kuwait and Saudi Arabia.[36] Imports, including war material, arrived in neutral ships and were unloaded at neutral ports in Kuwait and Saudi Arabia. To strike at the economic underpinnings of the Iraqi war effort, the Iranians had several options, all of which involved considerable risk: to attack the pipelines in Turkey; to attack neutral, including Western and especially Soviet, ships carrying war material to Kuwaiti ports; or to strike indirectly at Iraq by attacking tankers carrying oil from the gulf states that were supporting Saddam Hussein.

The Iranians chose this third option as the least dangerous and late in 1986 began to attack Kuwaiti and Kuwaiti-bound ships in the gulf. While only three Kuwaiti ships were hit during 1986, ten tankers headed to or from Kuwaiti ports were attacked, and the number rose precipitously to forty in 1987.[37]

The Reagan administration was aware of, and was alarmed by, the renewed escalation in the tanker war. In February, Secretary of State Shultz spoke of the need to help the gulf states defend themselves, and the importance of improved bilateral relations, noting the U.S. access agreement with Oman, "a vital element of our Central Command strategy."[38]

Unfortunately, 1986 was a year of political division and debate over Middle Eastern policy, not consensus and decision. Congress, principally because of concerns related to Israeli security, complicated the administration's efforts to strengthen the Arab states' military forces. After bitter and acrimonious political debate in 1981, the Reagan administration successfully concluded the Saudi AWACS deal and delivered the aircraft in 1984. But the subsequent sale of air-defense weaponry foundered, as did various planned transfers to other states, most notably Kuwait.[39]

But the Reagan administration had only itself to blame when in early November 1986 reports of arms transfers to Iran became public. The subsequent debate and investigations—Irangate or Iran-Contra—diverted attention from the worsening problem in the Persian Gulf and undermined the administration's policy concerning the war.

Whatever one's view of the legal niceties of the Iran-Contra dealings, within the context of American policy in the Persian Gulf, the "strategic opening" toward Iran was inconsistent with the existing

U.S. policy of embargoing arms shipments to Iran, and, to quote former Secretary of Defense Weinberger, was "one of the more absurd proposals" undertaken during the Reagan administration.[40] At a critical moment in the Iraq-Iran war, when the United States, fearing an Iranian victory, was publicly "tilting" toward Iraq and privately assuring the Gulf Arabs that if they supported American policy they would not be left hanging, the National Security Council was secretly shipping arms and providing intelligence to the Iranians.[41] How seriously were the Iranians to take the Reagan administration's public warnings against stepping up the tanker war when planeloads of antitank and antiaircraft missiles were arriving into Teheran, even as late as October 1986, after the Iranians had begun their attacks on Kuwaiti ships? And what were the Gulf Arabs to think of American declarations of support?

Not surprisingly, the Reagan administration entered the new year struggling to focus the debate on the deteriorating situation in the gulf. On January 27, 1987, Secretary Shultz told Congress that the Persian Gulf was "critical to the economic health of the West" and that Iran had been so warned.[42] In February, President Reagan spoke of the American commitment to the "free flow of oil through the Strait of Hormuz."[43] But behind the scenes, the administration debated its response to a Kuwaiti request for more than another restatement of American policy.

In late 1986, the frequency of attacks on Kuwaiti-bound ships, evidence of Iranian attempts to foment trouble among Kuwait's Shia minority, the presence of Iranian troops in the Fao Peninsula, and intelligence about Iranian planning for a possible invasion, alarmed not only the Kuwaitis, but also the United States. "By September of 1986," Caspar Weinberger noted, "it had become increasingly clear to U.S. Defense Intelligence officials that Iran had singled out Kuwait as the focal point of the pressure it elected to use against the Gulf Arab states."[44] On December 10, 1986, the Kuwaitis asked the U.S. Coast Guard to provide information regarding registration requirements for merchant vessels. Since the beginning of the Gulf War, the United States had been escorting American flagged ships in the gulf, and the Kuwaitis obviously viewed reflagging as a means to protect their most valued tankers.

The Kuwaiti request sparked a series of high-level meetings in Washington as the Reagan administration faced a rapidly deteriorating situation in the gulf. The administration was aware that the Kuwaitis had also approached the Soviets about reflagging tankers.[45] In February, satellite imagery and overflights showed that the Iranians were installing Chinese-built Silkworm antiship missiles opposite the Strait of Hormuz. Given the situation, Secretary of Defense Weinberger and National Security Adviser Frank Carlucci recommended reflagging the Kuwaiti ships. Secretary of State George Shultz disagreed.[46] After considerable debate, during the first week of March President Reagan decided to protect eleven reflagged Kuwaiti tankers. Weinberger, the "advocate" of the decision, recalled:

> I recognized that the option of American reflagging would be more politically difficult to fulfill, but the basic effect was the same. . . . [A]nd it seemed immaterial to me whether the Kuwaiti ships were reflagged or not. To my mind the main thing was for us to protect the right of innocent, nonbelligerent and extremely important commerce to move freely in international open waters—and, by our offering protection, to avoid conceding the mission to the Soviets.[47]

After providing classified briefings to key congressional members and staff, on April 21, 1987, Assistant Secretary of State Murphy announced that the United States was "consulting" with Kuwait about the registration of certain Kuwaiti ships under the American flag.[48]

The Iraqi attack on the frigate *Stark* on May 17, 1987, demonstrated to the administration, the Congress, and the American people the dangers inherent in an increased United States role in the Persian Gulf. Two French-made Exocet missiles, errantly fired by an Iraqi Mirage F-1, nearly sank the *Stark* and left thirty-seven Americans dead. Thus, as the administration worked to implement the reflagging decision, it faced a political debate over not only the concept of an expanded American role, but also the wisdom of a continued American presence in the war-torn Persian Gulf.

Despite the *Stark* debate, the United States had little choice but to follow through on its March 7 offer to Kuwait to reflag the tankers and the official pronouncement came on May 19. The United States viewed Kuwait as "the weakest link on the Arab side of the Gulf." Assistant Secretary of State Murphy announced:

> Consistent with longstanding U.S. commitment to the flow of oil through the gulf and the importance we attach to the freedom of navigation in international waters, as well as our determination to assist our friends in the Gulf, the President decided that the United States would help in the protection of Kuwaiti tankers.[49]

Moreover, Murphy emphasized that the administration had no intention of allowing the Soviet Union to increase its role in the region, a development that American policy had long sought to preclude. The prospect of the Soviets safeguarding the West's oil was not an attractive alternative.

The continued flow of Middle Eastern oil remained the focus of the administration's policy. Murphy pointed out that in 1986 the gulf had supplied Western Europe with 46 percent of its oil; Japan 60 percent, and the United States itself 15 percent.[50] In a May 19 White House statement, President Reagan reiterated the same points and recalled the gas lines, rationing, and economic dislocations of the 1970s "that shook our economy to its foundations."

> But this will not happen again, not while this President serves. I'm determined that our national economy will never again be held captive, that we will not return to the days of gas lines, shortages, economic dislocation, and international humiliation. Mark this point well: The use of the sea lanes of the Persian Gulf will not be dictated by the Iranians. These lanes will not be allowed to come under the control of the Soviet Union. The Persian Gulf will remain open to navigation by the nations of the world.[51]

The American decision to escort the Kuwaiti ships, later termed by Secretary of Defense Caspar Weinberger as *"very real military action"* taken to meet a *"very real military threat,"* was part of a "two track" policy.[52] The second track was diplomatic. On June 30, 1987, the United States called on the United Nations to take immediate action to pressure the combatants to agree to a cease-fire.[53] On July 20, the U.N. Security Council adopted Resolution 598 demanding that "Iran and Iraq observe an immediate cease-fire, discontinue all military actions on land, at sea and in the air, and withdraw all forces to the internationally recognized boundaries without delay."[54]

As part of its military and diplomatic efforts, the United States sought the support of friends and allies. Many of the Arab states of the gulf responded cooperatively, if cautiously, keeping a low profile, for obvious political reasons, but providing crucial assistance. At the June European economic summit, the United States received firm, public support from its European allies and ultimately, French, British, Italian, Belgian, and Dutch naval forces would play significant roles in the effort to keep the sea lanes open and the oil tankers moving through the gulf.[55]

124

Nevertheless, in deciding to reflag and escort the tankers, the United States risked further escalation and heightened tension, not only with Iran, but also with the Soviet Union. The Soviets, who had built up their own force in the region to a dozen ships, responded harshly, attacking the American presence in the gulf as "sinister," "impermissible from the standpoint of contemporary humanitarian international law," and "fraught with far-reaching negative consequences."[56] The somewhat restrained rhetoric from Iran indicated that there was little desire in Teheran to provoke the United States, although Ali Akbar Hashemi Rafsanjani, then speaker of Iran's parliament, threatened: "If even one single drop of blood is shed by the United States in the Persian Gulf, there will be rivers of blood throughout the world."[57]

Those in the United States who opposed the Reagan administration's policy were deeply concerned about the possible ramifications of the reflagging decision. Senator Edward Kennedy remarked during a hearing: "I do not think that the American people are prepared to see an administration with an itchy trigger finger loose in the Persian Gulf."[58] A staff report prepared for the Senate Foreign Relations Committee concluded:

> The United States seriously risks being drawn into the war in the Persian Gulf. Although the stated purpose of the huge American fleet in the region is narrowly defined—to escort U.S.-flagged vessels through the Gulf—this mission, given the circumstances, is dangerously nebulous.
>
> The U.S. is perceived by Iranians and Arabs alike as having sided with Iraq, and the expanded U.S. naval presence is likely to invite more Iranian attacks of increasing severity. Moreover, the greater the Iraqi assault on Iranian shipping, the greater the likelihood of Iranian retaliation against U.S. forces. Thus, American naval forces in the Gulf are now, in effect, hostage to Iraqi war policy.[59]

The report's authors also noted that the world oil glut and the increasing percentage of the region's petroleum output that went to the Mediterranean by pipeline made the tanker escort mission superfluous; that despite the administration's oft-stated policy of reducing Soviet involvement in the region, by siding with Iraq, the United States increased the chances that the Iranians would be driven into a closer relationship with the Soviets; that the gulf states needed to upgrade their air defenses; that the reflagging decision had been hastily reached; and that the navy was "ill prepared" to execute its new role in the Persian Gulf. The report concluded by recommending a diplomatic offensive focused on the United Nations.

Nor was the administration of one mind with regard to the decision. Caspar Weinberger, who considered the Kuwaiti request "an opportunity," noted that Secretary of State Shultz "did not share my enthusiasm for this mission."[60] And new Secretary of the Navy James Webb voiced concerns about the open-ended, Vietnam-like nature of the commitment.[61]

Such fears were well founded, as was much of the critical analysis of the Foreign Relations Committee's staff report. The administration's hope that a strong American response would deter further Iranian escalation was just that—a hope. The tanker war had ebbed and flowed according to decisions taken in Baghdad, not Teheran. And the world's dependence on oil supplies shipped through the gulf was declining.

Nevertheless, even a minor shortfall in oil supplies could have a dramatic impact. In 1973 and 1974, during the Arab oil embargo, disruptions of world petroleum supplies totaling no more than 5 percent had led to severe adverse economic consequences.[62] The possibility of the Soviet Union drawing closer to Iran, at a time when Soviet freighters regularly delivered war material to Kuwaiti ports for shipment to Iraq, was unlikely. The reflagging decision, made over a period of six months, could hardly be termed impetuous. If the gulf states felt vulnerable in the area of air defense, Congress had increased that sense of vulnerability by routinely killing administration-sponsored arms sales to Arab states. The United States had not "generally ignored" a diplomatic approach, but rather continued to push the United Nations to take a firmer stand. And if, as the report posited, the major threat to American interests in the region was an Iranian victory on land, why chide the Reagan administration for taking action that made such a victory less likely?

The administration recognized the risks it was running in the gulf. The Chairman of the Joint Chiefs of Staff, Admiral William Crowe, assured Congress that the United States armed forces could "carry out" the mission, although he admitted that there were "no absolute guarantees that such an operation will be casualty-free" or that Iran would not "escalate the sea war, which will present us with further difficult choices."[63] The administration readily admitted that it could not "predict with absolute certainty" how the Iranians would respond.[64] Secretary of Defense Weinberger noted:

126

There is no risk-free way to safeguard our longstanding vital interests in the Persian Gulf, which today is an increasingly volatile region. We can only do our best to minimize and manage the risks, chart a steady course aimed at our strategic goal of ending the war, and reassure our friends—and our adversaries—of our resolve as we move ahead.[65]

Whether the gulf Arabs piped or shipped their oil to the West, developments in the region, exacerbated by the Irangate fiasco, had led to calls for a firm American commitment to the gulf. Weinberger, admitting the difficulties the administration faced, nevertheless remained "convinced that the risks of alternative courses of action or inaction are even greater."[66]

CHAPTER SEVEN

THE TANKER WAR

1987–1988

While President Reagan was prepared to risk escalation with Iran, he did not seek it. The administration believed that it had little choice, given the extent of the Western interests at stake and existing American commitments to the security of the region, but to play the role of protector or guardian of the gulf Arabs. The administration was also fully cognizant of the popular forces at work in the Middle East, especially fundamentalism epitomized by Khomeini's rise to political power in Iran. The ideological expectations that Yankee missionaries and merchants had first carried to the Middle East in the late eighteenth and early nineteenth centuries, and the liberal democratic assumptions of Roosevelt and Truman administration policymakers that oil revenues would lead to the development of "progressive" societies in the gulf, appeared incredibly naive against the backdrop of the course of events in the Middle East in the late 1970s and early 1980s. This, probably healthy, recognition of the limits of American power narrowed Reagan administration goals and insured that the concept of military operations in the gulf minimized the risk of a larger war that could entail political problems the solution of which would transcend American willingness, understanding, and capabilities.

Attacks on Ships in the Persian Gulf by Month, 1987

	Jan	Feb	Mar	Apr	May	Jun	Jul	Aug	Sep	Oct	Nov	Dec	Tot
Iran	6	3	4	4	10	5	4	5	16	7	10	17	91
Iraq	6	8	5	7	5	2	3	4	12	13	8	15	88

Source: Ronald O'Rourke, "The Tanker War," U.S. Naval Institute *Proceedings* 114 (May 1988), p. 32.

Initially, the Reagan administration's hope that tough talk and a small show of force would deter further Iranian escalation appeared well founded. Secretary of Defense Caspar Weinberger and Chairman of the Joint Chiefs of Staff Admiral William Crowe, appearing before a congressional committee, noted the drop-off in both Iranian and Iraqi attacks against shipping following the *Stark* incident.[1] Public statements emanating from Teheran seemed indicative of a cautious response to the American actions. Michael H. Armacost, undersecretary of state for political affairs, told the Senate Armed Services Committee:

Iran has not attacked any U.S. naval vessel. It has consistently avoided carrying out attacks on commercial ships when U.S. naval vessels have been in the vicinity. In its recent actions, it has displayed no interest in provoking incidents at sea with the United States. Of course, it would be foolhardy for them to attack an American flag vessel. Those ships would have American masters—that is, the reflagged vessels. They will carry no contraband. They pose no danger to Iran. They will be defended if attacked.[2]

Should deterrence fail, the American military, both in Washington and the gulf, viewed the Strait of Hormuz as the most likely focus of an Iranian attack. Accordingly, U.S. Navy forces in the theater concentrated their efforts on the narrow passage where ships would steam within range of Chinese-manufactured Silkworm antiship missiles. The Strait of Hormuz also seemed to be the most logical place for an Iranian mine campaign.[3]

Not that the Joint Chiefs of Staff and the U.S. Navy considered the Iranian threat serious. During Congressional hearings then-Senator Dan Quayle asked about the menace posed by mines. "Do we have any minesweepers that are going to go up in there?" Quayle asked? "No, we do not," Undersecretary Armacost admitted. Armacost downplayed the danger of Iranian attack.

I can tell you what the Chairman of the Joint Chiefs [Crowe] told me in answer to that question. He said, it was very small, because we do not feel that they are there yet. If they are there, then obviously we would have to reconsider how we were going to go about transiting the Gulf.[4]

Armacost also stated that the Silkworm, a Chinese version of the old Soviet Styx missile, posed few problems for the U.S. Navy. "We can defeat, and have defeated, the Styx missile with the weapons systems that are on board," the undersecretary assured Quayle, although "the protection of a protected [convoyed] ship is somewhat more difficult."[5]

American disregard for the possibility of Iranian military action and the U.S. focus on the Strait of Hormuz is understandable. The U.S. Navy traditionally concentrated its attention on maritime choke points and the Strait of Hormuz was an obvious point of transit for all ships entering or leaving the Persian Gulf. But the strait, while narrow, was also deep and swept by strong currents that made effective mining difficult.[6] Nor were the Iranian Silkworm sites near the strait operational, while those located further north, near Kuwait, were.

Unfortunately for the United States, the political geography of the war made the entire Persian Gulf a narrow strait. Iran had declared a wartime exclusion zone, within which all non-Iranian ships were subject to attack, extending south and west into the gulf from the Iranian coast and Iran's many island possessions. Since the bottom of the Persian Gulf is not concave, but deepens toward the Iranian coast, deep-draft vessels such as the large reflagged Kuwaiti tankers were effectively confined to a relatively narrow corridor of deep water in the central gulf that hugged the boundary of the exclusion zone. There were numerous locations where the Iranians could seed minefields through which the American-flagged tankers and escorts were likely to pass.

The potential Iranian threat of mine warfare in the gulf should have been apparent to American military leaders. In 1973, following a CENTO exercise, U.S. Army General George J. Eade, deputy commander in chief of U.S. Forces Europe and the senior American observer at MIDLINK 73, informed the chairman of the Joint Chiefs of Staff, Admiral Thomas H. Moorer, that the Iranian exercise commander had "expressed some concern to me privately about the vulnerability of the Persian Gulf to Guerilla mine warfare. He remarked that this tactic 'could play havoc with merchant ships and flow of oil' "[7] The shah's naval officers had obviously given much thought to the possibilities of mine warfare in the gulf and their mining plans probably remained in the files of the various Iranian naval commands.

In the summer of 1984, the Iranians also had monitored the Western response to the mining of Red Sea shipping routes.[8] Between July and September 1984, nineteen ships struck mines in the Red Sea. Islamic Jihad, a pro-Iranian fundamentalist Shiite faction in Lebanon, claimed responsibility, although the terrorist group clearly lacked the resources to mine such an extensive area. Western analysts were unsure whether

Iran or Libya had sown the mines, until the British retrieved a Soviet-made mine of recent manufacture and the examination of Suez Canal shipping records provided strong, though circumstantial, evidence of Libyan responsibility.

The confused Iranian response to the incident revealed division among Iran's leaders. Teheran first praised, but then condemned the mining. Then the Iranians declared that the United States had laid the mines in an effort to tarnish the reputation of the Islamic Republic.

Indeed, the lessons that Teheran could have drawn from the incident were contradictory. Although the impact of the mine effort had been more psychological than real, since no ships were actually sunk, the threat posed by the mines sharply reduced shipping in the Red Sea and the Suez Canal, striking an economic blow against Egypt. And despite fairly obvious Libyan complicity, the United States and its allies had taken no retaliatory action.

But the West had responded promptly to the threat to international shipping. The United States, Great Britain, France, Italy, and the Netherlands, cooperated closely with Egypt and Saudi Arabia in what proved to be a painstaking but very successful effort to clear the mines. And the incident hardened the Reagan administration's stance towards Libya, leading ultimately to the April 1986 air strikes.

Perhaps as they had in 1984, Iranian leaders in the summer of 1987 reviewed the pros and cons of a mine campaign in international waters. Initially, Teheran appeared cautious; then in late July, more daring and confrontational. On the twenty-fourth, the reflagged tanker *Bridgeton*, the first Kuwaiti ship the U.S. Navy escorted through the Persian Gulf, struck an Iranian mine during the transit. On July 31, Shia pilgrims making the traditional Haj pilgrimage to Mecca in Saudi Arabia rioted. In the melee that erupted between edgy Saudi security forces and a massive crowd driven by Iranian provocateurs, hundreds were killed. Iranian official statements issued before and after the Mecca riots indicated that Teheran remained a threat to the gulf Arabs.[9] Then in August, Iranian television broadcast the "Martyrdom Maneuvers," a fairly extensive, dramatically staged (and well scored) extravaganza depicting mock attacks by Iranian patrol boats and commandos obviously directed at the United States. In Teheran, according to Robin Wright, a sign that adorned the Revolutionary Guards' headquarters read: "The Persian Gulf will be the graveyard of the United States."[10]

Since the United States had failed to deter Iran's escalation of the war in the gulf (although the Iranians had avoided direct attacks on

131

American ships), the Reagan administration decided to accelerate the military buildup in the region. "We had to put some capability there that we had hoped to avoid," Chairman Crowe admitted.[11] Minesweeping helicopters and ships rushed to the gulf and Middle East Force, which began 1987 at a strength of six ships, grew to thirteen by year's end. The warships of the battlegroup in the Gulf of Oman brought American strength to between twenty-five and thirty vessels, a level at which it would remain until late 1988. Other forces operating in and over the gulf included nearly a dozen-and-a-half Navy patrol boats, several P-3 Orion patrol aircraft, two mobile sea bases—barges outfitted as forward bases from which SEALs, patrol boats, and helicopters conducted surveillance operations—in the northern Persian Gulf, about eight Marine Corps helicopters with a 400-man Marine Air Ground Task Force, several U.S. Army MH-6 "SEABAT" and "AHIPS" helicopters operating from naval platforms, and U.S. Air Force ELF One AWACS and aerial tankers flying from Saudi Arabia.[12] To control this expanding force, on August 21, 1987, the Department of Defense established a new command—Joint Task Force Middle East (JTFME). Rear Admiral Dennis Brooks, flying his flag with the carrier battlegroup in the Gulf of Oman, became JTFME's first commander. Brooks answered to Marine Corps General George Crist, Commander in Chief, U.S. Central Command (USCINCCENT), in Tampa, Florida.

The Reagan administration also worked to gain substantial international support for the newly acquired American role in the Persian Gulf. Virtually all of the Arab gulf states granted the United States temporary support or access of some kind. Former Secretary Weinberger noted:

> Kuwait was the primary source of contract fuel for all of our naval aircraft and ships in the region during the actual escort operations. The government of Kuwait also partially absorbed the cost of fuel for our ships and aircraft involved in escorting the American-flagged Kuwaiti oil tankers.[13]

By the end of 1987 over half the "Allied" ships operating in the region were European. Western naval forces in or en route to the gulf included the United Kingdom's ten-ship Armilla Patrol, two Dutch, two Belgian, seven Italian, and thirteen French (including a carrier) ships.[14] With the Americans concentrating more and more naval forces in the gulf and Indian Ocean, the West Germans sent three warships to the

Mediterranean. The Japanese agreed to fund the installation of improved navigation equipment in the gulf essential to accurate bottom surveys and minehunting. A February 1988 Center for Naval Analyses (CNA) symposium on the Gulf War concluded that the ability to mobilize such international support would compel the Iranians to recognize their isolation and could become a critical factor in forcing them to end the war.[15]

As American military strength in the region increased in early 1988, the United States adopted a less passive concept of operations in the Persian Gulf. To deter further mining and to demonstrate to the international community that despite denials Iran was responsible for the threat to shipping in the gulf, the United States planned an operation to catch the Iranians in the act of laying mines. Using a variety of intelligence assets, American forces in the gulf were able to identify, monitor, and ambush an Iranian minelayer. On the night of September 21, U.S. Army helicopters flying from the U.S. Navy frigate *Jarrett* caught the small Iranian amphibious ship *Iran Ajr* laying mines in the shipping channel and attacked the vessel with rockets. U.S. Navy SEALs then boarded the *Iran Ajr* and her cargo of mines were photographed and made public.[16]

Following the *Iran Ajr* incident, the United States kept up the pressure on Iran. On October 8, Navy-based Army helicopters surprised four Iranian speedboats operating fifteen miles southwest of Farsi Island.[17] After the Iranians opened fire, the Army copters attacked, sinking one speedboat and damaging and capturing two others.

The Iranians struck back on October 15 and 16, firing Silkworm antiship missiles from launching sites in the Fao Peninsula against tankers at Kuwait's Mina al-Ahmadi terminal. One of the missiles struck the reflagged KOTC tanker *Sea Isle City*. Admiral Crowe proposed a retaliatory attack on an Iranian ship, but the Reagan administration rejected the plan and directed U.S. Navy forces in the gulf to attack and destroy two Iranian oil platforms used as military outposts.[18]

As the pace of operations accelerated, and the size of the American multiservice force grew, the United States improved its somewhat cumbersome command structure in the region. Since September 1987, the overall command of American forces in the North Arabian Sea and the Persian Gulf had been vested in Rear Admiral Brooks, who rode with the battlegroup, while a second Rear Admiral, Harold Bernsen, commanded the Middle East Force within the Persian Gulf. In February, Rear Admiral Anthony A. Less became commander of the

JTFME as well as MEF commander and shifted his flag to the *Coronado* in the gulf.[19] Less recalled:

> In order to streamline location, command and control functions, it was decided to consolidate the two geographically separated staffs and install a single commander who would be responsible for the region. . . . My job was to plan, coordinate and direct joint and combined operations in the Arabian Gulf, the Gulf of Oman, and the Northern Arabian Sea. This included protecting U.S. flagged ships, and others as directed, providing a military presence in the region and coordinating operations and training with allied and friendly forces. We were tasked to operate a regional joint force.[20]

Rear Admiral Less directed what by early 1988 were established operational procedures developed to counter myriad threats that included aerial, missile, small boat, naval, and mine attacks.

The principal danger in the air came from the Iraqis. The accidental attack on the frigate *Stark* exemplified the nature of the threat to American forces in the gulf. The continued significance of the problem was driven home on February 12 when an Iraqi aircraft mistakenly attacked, fortunately without success, the destroyer *Chandler*.[21] Throughout the Gulf War, the United States worked with the Iraqis to improve "deconfliction" procedures meant to make such attacks unlikely, although the threat was never totally eliminated. Nevertheless, while Iraqi fighter-bombers posed a genuine and dangerous threat to American ships and seamen, because such attacks were accidental in nature, rather than planned, they did not represent an operational challenge to the successful execution of the U.S. Navy's mission in the Persian Gulf.

The Iranians posed the greatest threat to American operations in the gulf. Weapons in Iran's military arsenal included aircraft, Silkworm missiles, Boghammers and other small fast attack boats manned by the Pasdaran (Revolutionary Guards), and the remnants of the shah's Imperial Iranian Navy. The Iranians' few attempts to use aircraft against American forces failed completely. Nor were the Iranians able to execute any successful small boat or naval attacks against navy ships. After the American rataliatory strike of October 19, 1987, against the Rashadat oil platform, following the Silkworm attack on the *Sea Isle City*, the Iranians chose not to employ antiship missiles against American or American-escorted ships. Only in the area of mine warfare did the Iranians' achieve even marginal successes.

134

For many critics and analysts, the mine problem became, and has remained, central to any discussion of the American naval campaign in the Persian Gulf. Analysts have portrayed the U.S. Navy as a service unprepared to deal with a "primitive threat" from "World War I–design" weapons.[22] The United States was, in fact, caught woefully unprepared in the gulf by the Iranian mining campaign. Naval mine countermeasure (MCM) forces were not on hand to meet the threat when escorting began in July 1987. In fact, until late in the year, the United States relied less on the deterrent effect of its still expanding forces within the gulf, than it did the hope that the Iranians would avoid potential confrontation with Americans. It is not inconceivable that in 1987 the U.S. Navy would have had difficulty protecting escorted tankers from Silkworm attacks in the Strait of Hormuz had the Iranians been prepared and chosen to employ the antiship missiles. The true significance and most troubling aspect of the mining of the *Bridgeton* was not the U.S. Navy's apparent inability to counter the mine threat, but the quite obvious American failure to deter Iran from attacking at all.[23]

While the Iranian mine campaign in the gulf did surprise the United States, mine warfare was not a risk-free option for Iran. Iranians talked of the "hand of God," and many Reagan administration critics viewed Teheran's mining effort as "an effective way to confront the U.S. Navy and other navies at low risk of immediate discovery and retaliation."[24] But there was never any actual doubt about who was laying mines in the gulf. Nor did the Iranians have any guarantee that their mines would only damage or destroy reflagged Kuwaiti or American vessels. Blowing up British or Soviet ships would hardly have advanced Iran's war aims. And Iran's mine warfare campaign ultimately proved to be a dismal failure. The Iranians were quickly caught in the act when U.S. Army helicopters observed the *Iran Ajr* laying mines in the gulf in September 1987. The retaliatory operation that followed the April 1988 mining of the frigate *Samuel B. Roberts* costs Iran half of its operational navy.

Iranian mining of shipping routes also prompted the dispatch of an international armada to the gulf. In 1987 and 1988 several NATO navies deployed MCM vessels, and accompanying warships. There the European MCM vessels cooperated with American minesweepers in clearing the shipping lanes. The European MCM ships were newer and more capable than the 1950s–vintage U.S. Navy minesweepers operating in the gulf and its approaches. But American technological capability was up-to-date, if not state of the art. The MCM job in the gulf involved not minesweeping in the traditional sense, but mine-hunting—using remote-controlled devices to locate, identify, and record the location of bottom debris and mines. The latter would then be destroyed by Explosive Ordnance Disposal (EOD) divers.

Moreover, the U.S. Navy's concept of operations for the Persian Gulf and the Gulf of Oman recognized that the counter to the Iranian mine campaign was not simply technical MCM. Minehunting was, and is, a slow, dangerous, costly process. MCM is a capability that a navy wishes not to have to use, because the last place one wants to deal with a mine is in the water. Thus, to say that the U.S. Navy ignored the mine threat is incorrect, since American operations in the gulf were designed to preclude mining as well as other "guerrilla" methods of naval warfare.

The navy's philosophy of operations involved deterrence, intelligence, surveillance, presence, retaliation, and, last, MCM. The United States hoped to deter attacks by establishing a military presence in the gulf and through a not so veiled threat of retribution. If deterrence failed, intelligence and reconnaissance would hopefully reveal Iranian preparations for an attack, as they had in the case of the *Iran Ajr*. To counter such Iranian efforts throughout the gulf, Joint Task Force Middle East established a presence from Kuwait to the Gulf of Oman that included aerial reconnaissance from E-3A Sentry AWACS flying from Saudi Arabia, E-2C Hawkeyes flying from the carrier battle group in the Arabian Sea, and P-3C Orion patrol aircraft. JTFME divided the gulf itself into several sectors, each of which was usually patrolled by a destroyer or frigate. In the northern Persian Gulf, two mobile sea bases, accompanied by minesweepers and a frigate, operated as floating islands from which MK-III patrol boats and helicopters conducted mine-hunting and surveillance activities. Cruisers in the gulf coordinated the antiair warfare effort to provide safety from air attack—Iraqi or Iranian. Additional frigates performed the actual escort of the reflagged tankers (and occasional tagalongs) during the 127 Earnest Will missions that ran between the Gulf of Oman and Kuwait between July 1987 and December 1988.[25]

The most significant aspect of the U.S. Navy's operations during 1987 and 1988 was its ability to establish a presence throughout the gulf, not the actual conduct of individual Earnest Will missions. By the end of 1987, every tanker that transited the gulf passed through areas patroled and secured by American naval forces and thereby benefitted from the protection of the U.S. Navy. The passage along shipping routes that were neither mined nor subject to harassment or attack by Iranian small boats or men-of-war was the principal fruit of the navy's work in the gulf. By early 1988, the navy focused less on the physical escort mission itself, which had become more symbolic than real, than on the safety of the corridor through which the tankers steamed. The shift from multiship escorts during the early Earnest Wills to single frigate escorts later in the war marked this transition in the American naval effort.

Such extensive operations in the Persian Gulf placed an enormous strain on the U.S. Navy. While the number of ships deployed—thirty-plus—was not that large, the distance from the United States at which the ships had to operate was a critical factor. The navy placed high value on its Operational and Personnel Tempo (OPTEMPO and PERS-TEMPO) objectives, goals designed to keep reenlistment rates high by preventing the service's volunteers from being kept too long at sea. For the navy, operating within peacetime restrictions required the commitment of about seven ships for every one deployed in or near the gulf. Thus the maintenance of a single carrier in the North Arabian Sea effectively tied down six or seven of the U.S. Navy's fifteen carriers. The four cruisers in the region represented an effective commitment of about twenty-eight of the thirty-six ships of that type in the navy. A half-dozen guided-missile frigates on station accounted for forty-two of the navy's fifty-six of that type. Operating in a inhospitable region, with no good ports for leave, with long cruises to reach the area, without any well-developed forward bases proved to be a tremendous administrative, logistical, and human burden.

Not surprisingly, there were many in the U.S. Navy who were concerned about just how long the effort would have to be maintained. The successful, but reactive, nature of the operations in the gulf offered no avenue to force an end to the war. In early 1988 some navy leaders began to ponder: "How do we get out?" The answer was as frank as it was pessimistic. United Nations efforts were critical to the peace process, but unlikely to produce a quick resolution of the conflict. A navy study concluded that the "outcome/resolution of Iran-Iraq war is the key. . . . The sheer scale of the land war makes it apparent that the Persian Gulf war is, ultimately, a *sideshow* to the war that counts for the two protagonists."[26]

What troubled many in the navy, the administration, and the Congress in early 1988 was that, unfortunately, the end of the Iran-Iraq war seemed to be nowhere in sight. The tempo of the tanker war slowed after December 1987, although Iranian attacks rose from seven in February 1988 to thirteen in March. The Iraqis, following their accidental attack on the *Chandler* in February, suspended, temporarily, their shipping strikes. While the Iranian effort slowed as well, Iraq continued, as it had late in 1987, to be responsible for most of the antishipping attacks in the gulf.

But despite American concerns about the prospects of a prolonged struggle in the gulf, the war was actually approaching a climax. On February 27, the "war of the cities" resumed, reaching a new level of destruction. On February 29, seventeen Iraqi Scud-B surface-to-surface missiles hit Teheran. By April 20, when the barrage ended, over 140 SSMs had hit the Iranian capital.[27] In March, the Iraqis began using deadly chemical weapons—mustard gas and nerve agents—along the front in Kurdistan. On April 18, the Iraqis retook the Fao Peninsula, again using gas. That same day in the gulf, the U.S. Navy fought its largest surface action since the Second World War.

The American action came in retaliation for the near-sinking of the frigate *Samuel B. Roberts*, which hit a mine in the gulf on April 14 fifty-five miles northeast of Qatar.[28] The mine blew a 30 by 23 foot hole in the ship's port side below the engine room, snapped the keel, and nearly broke the frigate in two. Fires and extensive flooding threatened the *Samuel B. Roberts* but effective damage-control efforts by the ship's officers and men saved the vessel. No Americans died, although the explosion injured ten sailors.

The near-loss of the *Samuel B. Roberts* demonstrated that Iran had resumed its attacks against international shipping and was perhaps purposefully targeting U.S. Navy men-of-war. A few days later, American and Allied MCM units discovered additional mines, all of Iranian manufacture, in areas of the central Persian Gulf frequented by U.S. Navy vessels and transited by tankers.

In response to the mining of the *Samuel B. Roberts*, the Reagan administration directed General Crist to plan and execute a retaliatory strike. On the flagship *Coronado*, moored along Mina Sulman pier in

Attacks on Ships in the Persian Gulf by Month, 1988

	Jan	Feb	Mar	Apr	May	Jun	Jul-Aug	Tot
Iran	7	7	13	7	5	3	10	52
Iraq	8	5	6	0	7	1	11	38

Bahrain, the staff of Rear Admiral Less's Joint Task Force Middle East quickly developed several offensive options which they sent back up the chain of command through Tampa to Washington.

The options presented covered a broad range of possible retaliatory scenarios. One option, understandably attractive to the personnel of the Joint Task Force who braved the dangerous waters of the gulf, was to strike directly at those Iranian assets capable of laying the mines, the depots where mines were stored, and other facilities, the destruction of which would make further mining more difficult. But such an option entailed direct attacks against Iranian territory, a step the Reagan administration considered too escalatory.

The retaliatory option chosen involved actions solely against Iranian forces at sea in the gulf. Joint Task Force Middle East ships and aircraft would "take out" a pair of gas/oil separation platforms (GOSPs) and target a single Iranian warship to compensate for the damage inflicted on the *Samuel B. Roberts*. If no man-of-war could be located and attacked, a third GOSP would be struck. Despite the Reagan administration's rhetoric about never fighting another conflict the way the United States had fought in Indochina, the planned "proportional response" against the Iranians was, in fact, a Vietnam-like controlled, marginally escalatory use of military force. Unwilling to risk a wider war with Iran, the administration avoided to the greatest extent possible, actions that could lead to further escalation.

The CENTCOM and Joint Task Force Middle East staffs picked their targets carefully. The Sassan and Sirri GOSPs in the central and southern Persian Gulf were, like the Rashadat oil platform destroyed in response to the Iranian Silkworm attack on the *Sea Isle City* in October 1987, manned by Iranian forces and used to coordinate attacks on shipping. Both GOSPs were armed with ZSU-23mm automatic guns, and their garrisons with rocket-propelled grenades and small arms. Sirri was also an active platform still producing about 180,000 barrels of oil per day. In selecting a naval target, attention focused on one of Iran's four British-built 1,350-ton Vosper Mark 5-class frigates—the *Sabalan*. The frigate had gained quite a reputation in the gulf during 1987 and 1988. Under the command of "Captain Nasty," the *Sabalan* established as its trademark concentrated fire on the crew quarters of the tankers and other merchant vessels it attacked.

Less's staff completed final planning on the *Coronado* on the night of the sixteenth and the early morning hours of the seventeenth of April as American ships from the Middle East Force and the battle-group in the North Arabian Sea rushed into position. To provide air support and cover for the operation, the *Enterprise* steamed to within 120 nautical miles of the Strait of Hormuz. To execute the plan, code-named Praying Mantis, Joint Task Force Middle East formed three Surface Action Groups (SAGs):

SAG Bravo—to neutralize or destroy the Sassan GOSP and, if no Iranian surface ships offered themselves as targets, the Rahkish GOSP;

SAG Charlie—to neutralize or destroy the Sirri GOSP;

SAG Delta—to sink the frigate *Sabalan*, or any other warship that might attempt to sortie from Bandar Abbas.

The attacks on the GOSPs were to be preceded by a warning that would give the Iranians five minutes to evacuate the platforms. After any resistance had been silenced by naval gunfire, Marines would seize the Sassan GOSP, and U.S. Navy SEALs the Sirri GOSP, both of which would then be destroyed. These operations would be covered by four F-14A Tomcats, a pair of A-6E Intruders, and two EA-6B Prowlers flying Surface Combat Air Patrol (SUCAP) from the carrier *Enterprise* on station in the North Arabian Sea. The carrier also prepared a war-at-sea strike group that would be kept on alert status, ready to take off in fifteen minutes or less, throughout the operation. United States Air Force KC-10 tankers flying from Saudi Arabia would be airborne to provide air refueling capabilities for the navy planes. Air Force AWACS would also cooperate with the *Enterprise*'s carrier-based E-2C Hawkeyes to provide a continuous radar picture of the gulf and Iranian air space.

Order of Battle: April 18, 1988

SAG Bravo	SAG Charlie	SAG Delta
Merrill	*Wainwright*	*Jack Williams*
Lynde McCormick	*Bagley*	*O'Brien*
Trenton	*Simpson*	*Joseph Strauss*

The operation began about 7:55 A.M. local time on April 18, 1988, when SAG-Bravo warned, in Farsi and English, the occupants of the Sassan GOSP to evacuate the platform. Intercepted radio transmissions indicated that the Iranians were panic-stricken, frantically asking their command ashore for direction, and the Americans for more time.

About thirty Iranians quickly disembarked in two tugboats, but about as many remained, manning the platform's weapons, apparently intent on defending their positions. The *Merrill* and *Lynde McCormick* opened fire at 8:04, using well-placed air bursts to silence the Iranian ZSU-23mm multipurpose gun. When an approaching Iranian tugboat radioed for permission to retrieve the other crewmen—"a large crowd of converted martyrs gathered at the northern end" of the GOSP—the Americans held their fire and allowed the evacuation to proceed. When the Iranians had cleared the platform, an assault element of Marine Air-Ground Task Force 2-88, an EOD detachment, and an intelligence gathering team fast-roped from helicopters to Sassan. After securing the platform, the Americans found anti-aircraft guns, rocket-propelled grenades, ammunition and communication gear. The boarding party then departed and, by remote control, destroyed the Sassan GOSP with explosives.

SAG Charlie began its morning operations somewhat behind schedule, delaying until 8:15 to give the Iranians additional time to evacuate the Sirri GOSP. As at Sassan, not all the Iranians chose to leave and several remained behind. SAG Charlie accordingly opened fire in an effort to eliminate the defenders. At one point in the ensuing barrage, American forces momentarily held their fire to allow Iranian forces to pick up personnel who had refused, initially, to abandon the platform. An American helicopter even dropped a raft to six Iranians. In the end, the few defenders who remained on the GOSP were unintentionally incinerated when an inadvertent round struck a compressed gas tank on the platform setting it ablaze and making it impossible, and unnecessary, for the SEAL platoon to board the platform.

With both GOSP platforms destroyed, the three American SAGs continued operations in search of a worthwhile target. SAG Bravo, after checking out an unidentified surface contact that turned out to be a patrol craft from the United Arab Emirates, steamed north to position itself to engage the Rahkish GOSP, since no Iranian surface combatants appeared willing to play their assigned role in the American plan. SAG Bravo encountered a second unidentified contact, initially considered a possible Iranian frigate. But the ship was a Soviet Sovremenny-class destroyer whose captain just wanted to take a picture "for history."

During the morning hours of April 18, while SAGs Bravo and Charlie attacked the GOSPs, SAG Delta cruised into the Strait of Hormuz hoping to encounter the *Sabalan*. But with the American strikes underway, the Iranian frigate chose to remain in Bandar Abbas where it sought safety between a pair of tankers that provided convenient protection against sea- or air-launched Harpoon anti-ship missiles. Strike aircraft from the *Enterprise*'s SUCAP group were unable to get a clear target confirmation on the *Sabalan* and could not engage the frigate without risking an inadvertent hit on the civilian tankers.

But not all the Iranian men-of-war remained in port on the morning of April 18. About 11:00, Iranian speedboats ventured into the southern gulf, attacking oil facilities and commercial vessels. At 11:46, Iranian Boghammer speedboats attacked the American-flagged supply ship *Willie Tide* with rocket-propelled grenades. Not much later, other Iranian speedboats shot up the *Scan Bay*, a Panamanian-flagged ship with fifteen Americans on board near the Mubarak oil field, and the British-flagged tanker *York Marine*. The SAG Delta frigate *Jack Williams* vectored SUCAP A-6E Intruders into attack positions. At the direction of Rear Admiral Less, two A-6Es engaged the Iranians and dropped Rockeye cluster bombs on the lead Boghammer. The surviving speedboats sped off and ran themselves aground on Abu Musa Island.

Further to the west, the Iranian Combattante II fast attack craft *Joshan*, armed with a 76mm gun and an American-made Harpoon antiship missile, closed to within thirteen nautical miles of SAG Charlie. The sortie of the *Joshan* presented the Americans with a dilemma. Under the operational plan approved by the Reagan administration, JTFME was allowed to strike only a single Iranian surface combatant. The 275-ton *Joshan* was not the designated surface target and sinking her might end the day for the U.S. Navy with Captain Nasty's much larger 1,350-ton *Sabalan* still at large. Rear Admiral Less's reluctance to engage the *Joshan* was understandable, but questionable, since the fast attack craft was armed with a functioning Harpoon. The *Joshan* continued to close on SAG Charlie, ignoring four separate warnings to turn away. After several tense minutes, Rear Admiral Less granted SAG Charlie "weapons free" permission to engage. The *Wainwright*'s commanding officer directed his counterpart on the *Joshan*: "Stop your engines and abandon ship; I intend to sink you."

The *Joshan* responded by launching her lone Harpoon at the *Wainwright*. For Rear Admiral Less, the "most tense moment" of his command in the gulf was at hand as the American-made Harpoon missile sped towards the cruiser. Fortunately, the Harpoon passed harmlessly down the starboard side of the *Wainwright*, either as the result of a malfunction, or having been fired at so close a range that the missile's homing mechanism had insufficient time to activate. The *Wainwright*

142

and the *Simpson* responded promptly, firing five SM-1 missiles in sur-face-to-surface mode at the *Joshan*. The *Bagley* followed with a Har-poon. All the SM-1s found their mark, leaving the *Joshan* a burning, sinking hulk over which the *Bagley*'s Harpoon passed.

In the midst of this short but sharp engagement, an Iranian F-4 Phantom II sortied from Bandar Abbas and approached SAG Charlie. As the aircraft maneuvered to attack the *Wainwright*, ignoring repeated warnings, the cruiser launched a pair of SM-2 surface-to-air missiles, damaging the Phantom which limped back to its base.

The sortie by the *Joshan* indicated an Iranian decision to respond to the American strikes in the gulf. By noon, the Americans possessed intelligence that Iranian warships were preparing to come out of Ban-dar Abbas. The *Enterprise* promptly launched elements of her war-at-sea strike group.

While operating with the SAG Delta frigate *Joseph Strauss*, the strike leader observed what he believed to be a Saam-class frigate near Larak Island, proceeding on a southwesterly course at 25 knots. She was, in fact, the *Sahand*, sister ship to the *Sabalan*. At 2:59 P.M. the frigate had steamed out of Bandar Abbas to confront elements of SAG-Delta. Three American aircraft now circled the *Sahand*. The two Intruders were equipped with forward-locking infrared (FLIR) sensors, and the accompanying Tomcat carried an on-board television system. The Americans were convinced that the vessel was, in fact, an Iranian man-of-war, but under the rules of engagement (ROE), needed a visual identification before they could attack. Accordingly, one of the In-truders approached the *Sahand* at low altitude in an effort to "VID" the contact. The Iranians responded with anti-aircraft fire and launched several heat-seeking SAMs. The Intruder released flares to confuse the SAMs and broke hard to avoid fire. The Americans then counterattacked firing two Harpoons, four Skippers, and several laser-guided bombs, while the *Joseph Strauss*, in a coordinated attack, fired another Harpoon. In all, two Harpoons, three Skippers, one Walleye, and several 1,000-pound bombs struck the *Sahand*, leaving the frigate dead in the water with decks ablaze. On the *Joseph Strauss*, crewmen felt the shockwaves as the *Sahand*'s magazines caught fire and ex-ploded. By early evening, the *Sahand* had disappeared beneath the surface of the Persian Gulf.

As SAG Delta and its supporting aircraft destroyed the *Sahand*, the *Sabalan* at last ventured out of Bandar Abbas. The SUCAP Intruders that had earlier attacked the Boghammers near the Mubarak oil field, had just completed refuelling from a U.S. Air Force KC-10 and were directed to an intercept position south of Larak Island. Again, in an effort to get the required visual identification, one of the Intruders flew low over the Iranian frigate, drawing fire and three SAMs, all of which missed. The lead A-6E dropped a 500-pound Mk-82 laser quided bomb. The LGB struck the *Sabalan* amidships and exploded inside the frigate. A second war-at-sea strike group was en route to the stricken frigate when the Secretary of Defense, Frank Carlucci, called off the attack. U.S. forces stood by as Iranian tugs took the *Sabalan*, dead in the water with stern down, in tow to Bandar Abbas.

Operation Praying Mantis was a clear success for the United States. Two GOSPs, a frigate, a fast attack craft, and several Boghammers had been sunk. The *Sabalan* had been badly damaged, possibly beyond repair. American weapons systems, defensive countermeasures, communications, and personnel had all functioned extremely well. The only American casualties were two Marine crewmen lost when their AH-1T *Sea Cobra* helicopter failed to return from a reconnaissance mission on the evening of April 18. The Iranians later claimed that they had downed the helicopter during the fighting in the afternoon. But examination of the recovered wreckage on May 15 showed no evidence of hostile fire.

By late April, most Iranian leaders probably understood that the war had taken a decided, and probably decisive turn. Ashore, the Iraqis had regained the initiative in the ground war and in the air continued to strike Teheran at will. On April 29, Secretary of Defense Carlucci announced the expansion of the rules of engagement governing the operations of American forces in the gulf.[29] Henceforth, U.S. Navy ships would provide "distress assistance" to requesting friendly and neutral nonbelligerent shipping operating outside recognized war exclusion zones. American forces would no longer tolerate hostile attacks on any innocent commercial shipping transiting the international waters of the Persian Gulf. Since most Iraqi strikes took place inside the declared war zone, but most Iranian attacks occurred outside the zone, the implications of the new American policy were not lost on Iran's Supreme Defense Council. In the past, Iranian patrol boats had attacked foreign commercial vessels, even those in the vicinity of U.S. Navy warships, with the foreknowledge that United States protection extended only to American-flagged vessels.

The American hard line in the gulf and, most importantly, the turn of the tide in the ground war against Iraq, ended Iranian hopes of victory in what had been a long, costly conflict. War weariness became increasingly evident to the governing regime. Antiwar demonstrations broke out in Isfahan and Tabriz. While foreign arms and supplies and Arab petrodollars continued to flow into Iraq, Iran found itself virtually quarantined and headed towards bankruptcy. The economy had all but collapsed under the pressures of eight years of war. Unemployment and inflation rates soared.[30] Iran's efforts to strike at Iraq through the gulf Arab states had failed, drawn the Americans into the war, and left Teheran internationally isolated.

As the Iraqis continued their advance in May and June, the Iranians weakened. A letter critical of the war and of Khomeini's leadership, written by former premier Mehdi Bazargan, circulated openly in Teheran.[31] On June 2 Rafsanjani became commander-in-chief of the Iranian armed forces. In a July 2 speech, he spoke of the possibility of a "nonmilitary" end to the war.[32] The Iranians were gradually moving toward acceptance of U.N. Resolution 598. The next day—July 3— the U.S. Navy cruiser *Vincennes* mistakenly shot down an Iranian civilian airliner, killing 290 people.[33]

Several factors, seemingly unrelated, set the stage for the July 3 tragedy. Naval operations in the relatively narrow Persian Gulf were subject to sudden, violent attack, especially from the air, as the *Stark* incident had demonstrated. Long-range airborne early warning was obviously the best method to preclude such a strike. A force of at least six E-3A Sentries with three airborne and orbiting at any one time was necessary to provide the entire theater with AWACS coverage. Unfortunately, the United States had only four AWACS in Saudi Arabia and the U.S. Air Force was less than enthusiastic about deploying two additional Sentries to the gulf. Nor were the Saudis eager to see an increased American presence. That the southernmost AWACS orbit, the one covering the Strait of Hormuz, would have to overfly the territory of the United Arab Emirates was a further complication.

Nevertheless, the United States and Saudi Arabia were able to solve the problem by securing the permission of the U.A.E. to allow Saudi AWACS to fly the southern orbit. Unfortunately, leaks by congressional members who had been briefed about the secret arrangement prompted the Emirates to withdraw overflight permission and left the United States without AWACS coverage over the Strait.[34]

E-2C Hawkeyes flying from the U.S. Navy's carrier battle group on station in the Arabian Sea were also capable of providing airborne early warning over the Strait of Hormuz and did so, for example, during Operation Praying Mantis. But the navy's Hawkeyes were reportedly plagued by stress fractures in their wings and, most importantly, were bound by peacetime flight-hour restrictions that ruled out the possibility of maintaining round-the-clock coverage over the strait comparable to that supplied further north by the U.S. Air Force's Saudi-based AWACS.

A third option available to the United States was to deploy a U.S. Navy Ticonderoga-class Aegis cruiser into the Gulf. Aegis cruisers, with their phased-array radars, were the most capable mobile, surface-based early warning systems in the United States' military arsenal. While the range of the Aegis system's radar was less than that of an AWACS, it was sufficient to the task in the restricted area of operations in the southern Gulf. Moreover, a Ticonderoga-class cruiser had an advantage over the AWACS in that the Aegis system could not only detect and identify, but also shoot down an attacking aircraft or missile. For these reasons, Admiral Crowe, Chairman of the Joint Chiefs of Staff, ordered the deployment of an Aegis cruiser—the *Vincennes*—into the Persian Gulf.

There were some in the U.S. Navy hierarchy in Washington who disagreed with the chairman's decision. While the cruisers were extremely capable, they had not been designed to operate in an enclosed, green water environment where peacetime air and surface traffic continued in the midst of a twilight war. The Ticonderoga-class cruisers were equipped to defend carrier battle groups operating in a blue water, wartime environment, a hundred or more miles from a hostile coast.

Aegis cruisers were also high-tech, high-value targets, far more costly, and far less expendable, than frigates such as the *Stark* and *Samuel B. Roberts*. The U.S. Navy understood that if the *Vincennes* struck a mine or was otherwise damaged or sunk as a result of a low-tech Iranian strike, the service's critics in Congress and the media would use the incident to attack the navy's Aegis programs, which included the completion of the Ticonderoga-class and a new class of Aegis-destroyers—the Arleigh Burke–class.

These concerns for the safety of the ship placed enormous pressures on the captain and the crew of the *Vincennes*, pressures in addition to existing concerns about striking a mine or getting "Starked." Moreover, the crew of the *Vincennes* may have been less than fully prepared for their mission. The official U.S. Navy investigation of the incident pinpointed several critical human errors that led to the inadvertent shoot down. The author, while in the gulf in June and July 1988, heard frequent references to the *Vincennes* as the "Robocruiser," manned by a "trigger happy" crew.[35]

146

Whatever the true state of training and the frame of mind of the crew of the *Vincennes*, intelligence warnings concerning possible Iranian attacks heightened the tense atmosphere in the gulf at the end of June and in the first few days of July.[36] The situation in and around the strait grew more tense. During an Earnest Will tanker escort mission, the author personally witnessed an Iranian frigate operating in the strait, the first time the Islamic Republic's navy had ventured out of port since April 18.

On July 2, a sudden increase in Iranian activity seemed to indicate that the warnings were warranted. Iranian small boats harassed several neutral tankers, two of which requested distress assistance authorized under the newly established rules of engagement. Early on the morning of July 3, Iranian small boats fired at the *Vincennes*'s LAMPS III helicopter as it investigated a report of hostile activity. In response, the American cruiser closed with the small boats and, with the permission or Rear Admiral Less, engaged the Iranians.[37]

In the midst of this action, the *Vincennes*'s radar detected Iran Air flight 655 at 6:47 A.M. local time, as it took off from Bandar Abbas, a combined civilian and military airfield. The cruiser's Aegis computer recorded a Mode III IFF (identification friend or foe) squawk of 6760, which was the assigned code for the Airbus. But the *Vincennes*'s identification supervisor, after checking the commercial flight schedule, concluded that the detected aircraft, which was twenty-seven minutes behind schedule, was not the Airbus. By 6:50 the aircraft had been tagged on the Aegis display screens as an F-14. The fault lay not with the Aegis system, but with the crewmen responsible for monitoring the air situation. Concerned about the possibility of air attack, and locked in an engagement with Iranian small boats, a few critically placed individuals assumed, not without reason, that the approaching aircraft was hostile and part of a coordinated attack. After all, who in their right mind would send a commercial airliner directly over a naval engagement? Thus, despite the fact that the Airbus was well within its assigned commerical air corridor and was, despite reports to the contrary, climbing, not descending as it neared the *Vincennes* which was itself in the middle of the corridor, the crew of the American cruiser judged the Airbus hostile.

Over the next several minutes, the *Vincennes* issued repeated warnings and requests for identification. But the Airbus, for reasons unknown, never replied and continued on course. The *Vincennes* attempted to illuminate the aircraft with the cruiser's fire control radar, a procedure that might have alerted the Airbus's pilot. But a procedural

147

error, that is a crew failure, delayed the effort and Iran Air Flight 655 was not "locked up" until an instant before it was engaged. Between 6:53 and 6:54, two American surface-to-air missiles left their rails on the *Vincennes* and struck the Airbus, destroying it in midair at a range of about fourteen nautical miles.

While the downing of the Airbus was a tremendous tragedy, according to Robin Wright, the incident provided the Iranians with the "pretext" they needed to end the war.[38] On July 18, with Khomeini's acquiescence, Iran announced that it would abide by the United Nations cease-fire resolution, citing the war's "unprecedented dimensions" and the "engulfing" of the lives of "innocent civilians."[39] The Iran-Iraq war, and the U.S. involvement in the tanker war, were over.

From July 1987 to July 1989, the United States used military force, principally assets of the U.S. Navy, to achieve limited objectives within the context of a larger regional struggle—the Iran-Iraq war. The U.S. Navy's operations in the Persian Gulf and North Arabian Sea frustrated the Iranians' attempt to exercise an escalatory option that would have allowed them to undercut the economic support provided to Iraq by the gulf Arabs, much as Iraq struck at Iran's economic strength by attacking its oil industry. Unfortunately for the Iranians, their actions also directly threatened the relatively pro-Western Arab states of the gulf and indirectly the West's economic well-being. The United States, which had replaced Great Britain as the protector of the gulf Arabs, acted accordingly, much as a century before the British had policed the gulf's waters and prevented the larger states of the region from devouring the smaller.

While ultimately successful, the Reagan administration's policies, sensible and consistent with those of the previous administration, nevertheless involved considerable risk. The American commitment was open-ended, in that the United States had no intention and little capability of forcing an end to a conflict—the Iran-Iraq war—that showed no signs of early termination. Nor did the United States' decision to assist Kuwait deter Iran from further escalation.

Nevertheless, the use of military force in the Persian Gulf furthered U.S. national interests. While the Iranians were not initially deterred, they proved incapable of taking effective measures in the presence of American naval forces. Teheran's actions left Iran, not Kuwait or any of the other gulf Arab states, internationally isolated. Mining international waterways, while it embarrassed the United States, and especially the U.S. Navy, achieved virtually nothing in a military sense and was so indiscriminate in nature that the Iranians paid a steep political price—increased international assistance for the U.S. effort.

How events in the gulf would have unfolded had the United States not taken the actions it did must remain a matter of speculation. Former Secretary of Defense Weinberger has stated that the United States possessed sufficient intelligence to raise reasonable concerns about the path unanswered Iranian escalation would have followed. Given the trend of the Iran-Iraq war through 1986, the Reagan administration had no reason to suspect that either side of the stalemated struggle, both of whom had used chemical weapons more extensively than any combatants since 1918, would show much self-restraint.

Most important, the Reagan administration's decision to reflag the Kuwaiti tankers marked a critical turning point in the history of U.S. involvement in the Persian Gulf. De facto intervention in the Iran-Iraq war demonstrated that Americans took seriously their interests—commercial, strategic, and geoeconomic—in the gulf, and as the Carter administration had pledged, would fight to protect them. Reagan demonstrated that the Carter pronouncements and policies that many critics, both foreign and domestic, had dismissed as bluster and rhetoric were, in fact, earnest statements of American intent.

The Reagan decision was yet another step in the development of progressively deepening American interests and involvement in the gulf. Since the Second World War, there had been a clear consensus among American policymakers that the Middle East, and especially the Persian Gulf, was so vital to the West that its defense was a fundamental strategic necessity. Admittedly, for decades Americans had looked to others to defend the region, but now the Reagan administration had decided that the United States had to take the military lead and execute the Carter administration's policies and pledges. Reagan's decision to reflag and protect Kuwaiti tankers indicated that Americans henceforth would be the guardians of the gulf.

Another important facet of the reflagging decision, and one not widely recognized at the time (and certainly not by Saddam Hussein), was the Reagan administration's focus on Kuwait. Administration supporters and critics made much of the American "tilt" towrad Iraq in its struggle with Iran. But the United States had not risked war with Teheran to defend Baghdad when the Iranians appeared to be on the verge of a crushing victory over Saddam Hussein's forces, whereas Reagan was willing to chance a wider conflict to defend the gulf Arabs, most notably Kuwait.

CHAPTER EIGHT

THE ROAD TO DESERT STORM

—•—

August 1988–August 1990

For the United States, the 1987–88 tanker war marked the end of a two-century-old process—the displacement of Great Britain in the gulf. Americans were no longer "No. 2 Englishmen." The United States had accepted not only political, but also military responsibility for the security of the Persian Gulf. Americans were willing and able to defend their interests, not only against possible Soviet encroachments, but also against the machinations of a power internal to the region. The United States, despite the Irangate scandal, was a reliable power that would not desert its Arab allies in times of trouble. The gulf Arabs understood and, once they saw the Reagan administration take the lead, demonstrated their willingness to work closely, if for the most part behind the scenes, with the United States.

Following the resolution of the crisis and the end of the Iran-Iraq war, the situation in the gulf returned to "normal." Although the cease-fire between the former belligerents failed to develop into a formal and final peace settlement, there was little evidence that either state wished to resume hostilities in the near future. While the United States continued to monitor tanker traffic in the gulf, the Defense Department disestablished the Joint Task Force Middle East and the strength of the U.S. Navy's Middle East Force gradually returned to pre-1987 levels—about five ships. A carrier battle group usually steamed on station somewhere in the Indian Ocean.

American involvement in the tanker war had, quite obviously, done little to improve the state of the relations between Teheran and Washington. Official Iran, even after the death of the Ayatollah Khomeini, continued to view the United States as the Great Satan. Iranian-supported terrorist groups in Lebanon still held American and other Western hostages. Nevertheless, Iran displayed little overt, active hostility toward the United States. The priority for the Iranian leadership was the economic and social recovery of the country.

The U.S. relationship with Iraq, the belligerent that had most benefited from American Persian Gulf policy, was on a somewhat better footing than that with Iran, but was marked by acrimonious disagreements and mutual distrust. The United States continued its efforts to improve relations with Baghdad, especially through expanded trade opportunities, but American policymakers remained concerned about the nature of Saddam's regime. Iraqi support for international terrorism, chemical warfare against the Kurds, and human-rights violations strained the Iraqi-American relationship.

So, too, did the maintenance of Saddam's military on a wartime footing. Iraq is a relatively small country of between 17 and 18 million people. Yet Saddam kept one million men under arms, a military machine that was as large as that of sworn enemies Iran and Syria combined. Such a force imposed a serious economic drain on the Iraqi economy and completely eclipsed the military strength of the pro-Western oil-producing gulf states, which together could field only about 165,000 men.[1]

Nevertheless, the relative calm in a region that has rarely, if ever, been quiescent, allowed American policymakers to focus their efforts elsewhere. The dramatic events of 1989 in eastern and central Europe grabbed and held the attention of most Americans, in and out of government. European affairs, the Soviet-American relationship, and the end of the Cold War completely overshadowed events in the Middle East. To the extent that American policy concentrated on that region at all, the focus, as usual, shifted westward. The United States viewed the continuing civil turmoil in Lebanon and the ongoing *Intifada*—the Palestinian revolt against Israeli rule in the West Bank and Gaza—as the principal threats to stability in the Middle East.

But early in 1990, the Persian Gulf once again became the focal point of American Middle Eastern policy. In late February 1990, the Arab Cooperation Council (ACC)—Iraq, Jordan, Yemen, and Egypt—held its first anniversary meeting in Amman, Jordan. On the twenty-fourth on Jordanian television, Saddam delivered a blistering attack against the United States. He discussed the impact of the waning power of the Soviet Union on the Middle East. This unforeseen development had left the United States the dominant force in the region. To offset American power, Saddam called upon his fellow Arabs to display solidarity, to force the United States to withdraw its naval forces from

151

the gulf, to withdraw investments and funds from banks and corporations in the United States, and to reinvest elsewhere, perhaps in the Soviet Union or Eastern Europe.[2]

The tone of Saddam's remarks, and the use of the ACC as a forum to attack the United States, so troubled Egyptian President Hosni Mubarak that he left Amman a day ahead of schedule. For a year Mubarak had resisted efforts by Saddam and King Hussein of Jordan to turn what was supposed to be a purely economic framework for cooperation into a regional military pact. Indeed, fear that the oil producing gulf states might become the target of the ACC had caused consternation in the gulf. After the invasion of Kuwait, Mubarak speculated that the ACC might have been part of a "conspiracy" designed to isolate the oil producing states of the peninsula and perhaps even prepare the ground, by coopting Egypt with promises of massive economic aid, for the invasion of Kuwait.[3]

In the spring, the crisis atmosphere intensified. In March, Iraq hanged an Iranian-born British journalist accused and convicted of espionage.[4] Shortly thereafter, British and American officials confiscated sophisticated electronic devices and large steel tubes destined for Iraq. The seizures appeared to confirm reports that the Iraqis were developing a long-range supergun and an atomic arsenal. In April, Saddam warned the world that he possessed binary chemical weapons and warned the Israelis that if they attacked Iraq, he would burn half of Israel in retaliation. On May 28, at the Arab League summit, Saddam not only blasted Israel, but also his gulf Arab neighbors, whom he accused of waging "economic war" against Iraq.

Saddam's continued bluster gradually attracted the attention of the United States. *U.S. News & World Report* placed Saddam's image on the cover of its June 4, 1990, issue and labeled him "the most dangerous man in the world." The cover story raised concerns about Iraq's growing nuclear and chemical capabilities, as well as the development of delivery systems such as ballistic missiles and the supergun.[5] In a July 27 *Washington Post* opinion piece, commentator Charles Krauthammer compared Saddam Hussein with Adolf Hitler.

In late June, Saddam granted a rare interview to Karen Elliott House of the *Wall Street Journal*. He warned of the growing risk of war in the Middle East. Israel, he believed, was conspiring against Iraq with the support of the United States. Saddam again called for the withdrawal of American naval forces from the gulf. He also told House that the end of the Cold War had raised American hopes of getting their own way in the Middle East, but in a remark that represented a total misreading of the history of superpower involvement in the gulf and a misappreciation of what the end of the Cold War portended for the future, Saddam stated that the easing of tensions between the Russians and the Americans had ended the division of the Arab world into two camps and had heightened Arab solidarity.[6]

As the summer temperature rose in the gulf, so, too, did the diplomatic tension. On July 16, Foreign Minister Tariq Aziz, in a letter to the Arab League, accused the gulf states of conspiring with the United States to hold down oil prices in a scheme to undermine Iraqi economic recovery, and denounced Kuwait for stealing oil from the Rumaila field that straddled the Iraqi-Kuwaiti border, insisted that the thievery cease, and that Kuwait pay $2.4 billion in compensation. Aziz further demanded that the gulf Arabs forgive Iraq's $30 billion debt; called for the establishment of an Arab "Marshall Plan" to reconstruct Iraq; and demanded support in OPEC for an Iraqi plan to push the price of oil up to $25 dollar a barrel. The next day, July 17, Iraqi Independence Day, Saddam Hussein himself attacked Kuwait and the Emirates, accusing them of conspiring with the Americans and the Zionists. He warned: "If words fail to afford us protection, then we will have no choice but to resort to effective action to put things right and ensure the restitution of our rights."[7] In its July 21, 1990, issue, *The Economist* noted: "[Saddam's] speech, and his foreign minister's letter, sound alarmingly like a pretext for invasion."[8]

There can be no doubt that Saddam's actions in the first half of 1990 caught the United States off-guard. The Iraqi "victory" in the war with Iran should have given Saddam a newfound sense of security. Iran, which for decades had overshadowed its smaller Arab neighbor, had posed a grave military threat under the shah, and then a religious challenge under Khomeini. But now Iran was defeated, its army and economy shattered. Syria was forced to keep the bulk of its forces in the west in Lebanon (in part thanks to Saddam's support for anti-Syrian factional elements) and along the border with Israel. Iraq possessed the fourth largest army in the world, the sixth largest air force, and the largest military arsenal in the Middle East, even larger than that of NATO member Turkey. Yet Saddam, despite the fact that the regional balance of power favored Iraq, continued to display intense, irrational insecurity.

The reasons for Saddam's behavior were psychological and economic.[9] Saddam's victory over Iran had been both narrow and costly. Iraqi dead totaled at least 150,000 and perhaps as many as 340,000. The cost of the war may have topped $560 billion.[10] Iraq ended the war about $80 billion in debt, including $50–$60 billion owed to the gulf Arabs. By one estimate, the cost of the war to the belligerents, calculated in lost oil revenues, infrastructure damage, and actual resources expended, totaled more than twice the combined oil revenues that both Iraq and Iran had earned since they began exporting oil![11]

Such a long war had a deadening impact on the Iraqi economy. Gross national product declined in 1988, although it began to recover in 1989. The inflation rate reached 45 percent in 1990. The fruits of Saddam's "triumphs" continued to elude the Iraqi people.

Nevertheless, Iraq was oil-rich, with a productive agricultural sector, and with one of the most educated and skilled populations in the region. Good administration and reduced defense expenditures could have enabled Iraq to recover.

But Saddam's hold on power made the Iraqi state a family-run concern, a trend that did little to increase administrative efficiency. Moreover, Saddam refused to reduce government outlays and directed a continuation of development projects and the qualitative improvement of the armed forces. He discharged about 200,000 reservists who had been called up during the war, but the size of the active army remained at about the level it had reached in the final year of the Iran-Iraq war.

For Saddam, the economic imperatives were clear: unless he slowed the momentum of economic recovery or sizably reduced his armed forces, he had to convince the gulf Arabs to write off the billions owed to them while simultaneously reducing their oil exports and granting Iraq a larger OPEC production quota. Free from debt, with higher oil production at a $25 per barrel price (an increase of over 50 percent) recovery would be possible.

But the gulf Arabs had their own economic needs. Because of artificially high oil prices in the late 1970s and early 1980s, the Arabs lost market shares to Soviet, North Sea, and Alaskan Slope oil. The Arab gulf states responded by pumping oil in excess of their OPEC quotas.[12] In 1990 oil prices fell from about $22 per barrel in January to $16 by June. Each drop of a dollar in price cost the Iraqis $1 billion annually.

More important, in the 1980s another fault line developed in the gulf. To existing divisions between Arabs and Iranians, Sunnis and Shiites, oil producers and non-oil producers, a new chasm appeared. Iraq and Iran had spent their oil revenues and reserves on war. The other gulf states had spent billions on arms, but held vast reserves invested in the West.[13] As a result, while all oil producers, as suppliers of a vital source of energy, were part of the Western economic system, gulf states with massive investments had become an integral part of the Western financial system. In 1989, for example, the Kuwaitis reportedly earned more from their investments than they did from oil production. For the Iraqis and Iranians, decisions on oil prices and production could be based on relatively simple projections of revenues. But for the gulf Arabs, decisions on oil pricing had to account not only for revenues, but also the impact higher prices would have on Western economies. Slowed economic growth in Europe, Japan, and the United States was no longer in the interest of the gulf Arabs. Saddam recognized this development, but his call for a shift in investment from the United States to the Soviet Union made little financial sense and held few attractions for his Arab neighbors.

Artificially jerking up the price of oil also made little sense. The formation of the Arab Cooperation Council in February 1989 had left the gulf Arabs surrounded by more populous, heavily armed, economic basket cases. Why undermine a relationship with the United States, the nation that had just demonstrated that it alone had the power and the will to protect the gulf states from the designs of their more powerful neighbors?

If the political-military situation in the gulf in early 1990 was so precarious, why did American policymakers fail to recognize the danger? Through their actions, or inactions, did American policymakers give a "green light" to Saddam? Were there initiatives that the United States could have taken that might have prevented Iraq's invasion of Kuwait?

American policy during the 1980s toward Iraq and Saddam Hussein was always somewhat ambiguous in character. The United States did "tilt" toward Iraq during the Iran-Iraq war. The reasons were simple. Iran was perceived to be the more serious threat. Iran is, after all, a true nation, with a population far more homogeneous than Iraq's and about three times its size. Iranians can trace their nation's heritage to the Persian empire that once challenged the city-states of ancient Greece for the supremacy of the Balkans. Despite Saddam's efforts to pose as a modern-day Nebuchadnezzar, king of Babylon and conqueror of Jerusalem,[14] Iraq is an artificial concoction pieced together by Great Britain in the 1920s, not a nation with an ancient heritage, but a state ruled by a Sunni Arab minority at odds with about 70 percent of its population.[15] While Iraq won a narrow victory in its long war with Iran, the Iranians had been weakened by the turmoil of revolution. Their military establishment, which had been built up by

155

the shah, had suffered from gross neglect. What would the shah's pre-revolutionary army have been able to do to Iraq had the war begun in 1977 rather than 1980? As it was, on several occasions the Iranians threatened to break the Iraqi lines, march on Baghdad, and drive south along the southern shore of the Persian Gulf. Such concerns had prompted the United States to reestablish relations with Iraq, to provide the Iraqis with intelligence, and to assist Iraq's Arab allies when their tankers were threatened by Iran.

After the war, American policymakers had a much freer hand in shaping their policies towards Iraq, but little changed. There was a consensus—perhaps it could be called a mindset—in both Washington and the gulf that any move to isolate Iraq diplomatically would prove counterproductive. A man the shah had once termed one of Iraq's "crazy, bloodthirsty savages" seemed to have mellowed during the war with Iran.[16] Saddam had been the first to accept American and United Nations calls to end the war diplomatically. And even when he had regained the upper hand militarily in 1988 and might have achieved greater results, he had abided by the United Nations cease-fire.

There was, of course, evidence that Saddam was still the predator. He had used gas against Iraq's Kurds and his regime was guilty of numerous human-rights violations. He had maintained an enormous army and air force and seemed intent on further strengthening his military power in both conventional and unconventional arms.

Ironically, the Bush administration's policies that in retrospect appear to form a pattern of appeasement, were viewed by Saddam as part of an American conspiracy to encircle and destroy Iraq. The United States was, in fact, sending mixed signals to Baghdad. Even a policy of appeasement requires a fair amount of consistency, but such consistency was lacking in Washington. A February 1990 Voice of America radio broadcast into Iraq had reminded Arab listeners that the tide of history was running against dictators, and had already swept aside several, such as the Ceausescus in Rumania, who had ruled without the consent of their people. Several members of the United States Congress called openly for the reduction of American ties to and support of Saddam's government. But other Congressmen, most notably those from agricultural states, went out of their way to strengthen the growing Iraqi-American economic relationship, commiserating with Saddam about the nature of the American media.[17] Reports also reached Baghdad that the American military, in meetings with the gulf Arabs, had begun identifying Iraq as the major threat to the security of the region.

In the spring of 1990 the State Department did begin to reassess U.S. policy toward Iraq. Unfortunately, the attempt was stillborn as the dramatic events in Eastern Europe grabbed and held the attention of America's senior policymakers.[18]

But in late July, the deteriorating situation in the gulf demanded attention. Following Saddam's blistering verbal threats against his Arab neighbors on July 17, 30,000 Iraqi troops moved into positions along the border with Kuwait. Saddam made no effort to hide the concentration from Western and Arab military attaches traveling the highway between Kuwait and Basra.[19]

The very openness of the Iraqi move convinced most obervers that the display of Saddam's military might was meant to intimidate the Kuwaitis and was not the preparation for an invasion. Nevertheless, the United States declared its willingness to defend its interests in the region and demanded clarification of Baghdad's intentions. On July 21, the Emirates proposed joint military maneuvers with their forces and those of the United States. Two days later, Washington directed the U.S. Navy's Middle East Force, now at a strength of six ships, a pair of U.S. Air Force KC-135 tankers, and a C-141 cargo transport to conduct a military exercise, the first between the forces of the UAE and the United States. But the Kuwaitis, afraid that similar action on their part might provoke, rather than deter an Iraqi invasion, sent no requests for support to Washington. Nor did the United States place in motion those forces that might have signaled American concerns to Saddam. The carrier *Independence* steaming in the Indian Ocean, did not move westward toward the Arabian sea. On July 24, State Department spokesperson Margaret Tutwiler confirmed that the United States did not have any defense agreements with Kuwait, although she also stated that there was no room in the new world order for coercive diplomacy.

The United States took the advice of its friends in the region and waited while Arab leaders attempted to work out an Arab settlement. On July 24, President Mubarak visited both Kuwait and Iraq in an effort to mediate. He received, and believed, Saddam's assurances that war was not imminent. The Iraqi president also agreed to send a representative to an Arab summit to be held on August 1 at Jidda, Saudi Arabia.

On the twenty-fifth, Saddam summoned the American ambassador,

April Glaspie, to what became a famous, or infamous, meeting. According to a "transcript" of the meeting subsequently released by the Iraqis, Ambassador Glaspie told Saddam that the United States had "no opinion on the Arab-Arab conflicts, like your border disagreement with Kuwait," seemingly giving the Iraqis a green light to invade.[20] But in March 1991, Glaspie testified before Congress that the so-called transcript had been edited. While she had informed Saddam that the United States did not consider border disputes its business, she had made clear that "it was emphatically our business that they make the settlement in a non-violent way."[21]

What Glaspie did or did not say to Saddam was probably irrelevant since the Iraqi president had probably already made up his mind to invade Kuwait, despite his protestations to the contrary, and he fully expected some kind of an American riposte. In late May 1991, months after the end of the war, Tariq Aziz, who had attended the July 25 meeting, told Turkish president Bulent Ecevit: [Glaspie] didn't give a green light and she didn't mention a red light." According to Aziz, Saddam went into the meeting prepared for an American response.[22]

Saddam appears to have lied his way through the July 25 meeting. Even the doctored Iraqi "transcript" released in the midst of the crisis reveals that Saddam gave Glaspie no reason to expect an attack on Kuwait. During the meeting, Saddam was called away to take a phone call from President Mubarak. The Iraqi president returned to inform the American ambassador that the Kuwaitis had agreed to attend the Jidda meeting. Relieved, Glaspie told Saddam that while she had intended to remain in Baghdad because of the crisis, she would instead travel to Washington to confer with President Bush.

As Saddam and Ambassador Glaspie met in Baghdad, the OPEC summit opened in Geneva. At the July 25–27 meeting, the Kuwaitis agreed to Iraqi demands to raise the target oil price from $18 to $21 per barrel and to reduce production by 25 percent.[23] Saddam's campaign of intimidation appeared to be succeeding.

But while the final arrangements for the emergency Arab mini-summit were finalized, Saddam continued to mass forces along the Kuwaiti border. By the end of the month more than 100,000 troops were in position. On July 29, the Iraqi air defense system went to a wartime footing.

By August 1, the Iraqi deployment had taken on menacing proportions and doubts about Saddam's sincerity were growing. The CIA, which had been reporting since July 25 that Saddam was not bluffing, was now convinced the attack would begin within twenty-four hours.[24] On the thirty-first, American intelligence analysts had deduced from the logistics buildup behind the front that the Iraqis were about to invade Kuwait. According to Lieutenant General Thomas Kelly, Director of the JCS's Joint Staff, the United States issued a THREATCON 1 warning, indicating that military action was imminent.[25] General H. Norman Schwarzkopf, Jr., Commander in Chief, U.S. Central Command, whose headquarters was responsible for the gulf, briefed Secretary of Defense Dick Cheney and the Joint Chiefs in the Pentagon on August 1. According to Schwarzkopf, he believed that the Iraqis were going to invade Kuwait, although he expected that they would only grab the disputed Rumaila area and Bubiyan and Warbah Islands.[26] In fact, no one in a position of responsibility in the United States seems to have considered the possibility that Saddam might attempt to overrun all of Kuwait.

Nor was there a clear consensus that Saddam was going to invade at all. President Mubarak, King Hussein of Jordan, and King Fahd of Saudi Arabia all reportedly assured President Bush that the Iraqis would not attack. When Secretary of State James Baker informed Soviet Foreign Minister Eduard Shevardnadze that an attack appeared imminent, Shevardnadze assured his American counterpart that Saddam would not march.[27] At 3:00 P.M., when Assistant Secretary of State John Kelly summoned the Iraqi ambassador to the United States to the State Department and demanded an explanation, the Iraqi diplomat denied that Saddam's army was poised to invade Kuwait.[28]

In Jidda, the talks between Kuwait's Crown Prince Sheikh Saad al-Sabah and the Vice-Chairman of Iraq's Revolutionary Command Council Izzat Ibrahim, were fruitless and collapsed in less than two hours. The Kuwaitis, who had already yielded on the questions of their OPEC quota and prices at Geneva, refused to forgive Saddam's war loans, to repay Saddam for the oil allegedly stolen from the Rumaila field, or to lease Bubiyan Island to Iraq.

Only senior Iraqi officials know whether the Jidda talks were genuine negotiations or cover for the final preparations for invasion, but the latter appears to be the case. In addition to Foreign Minister Aziz's remarks to the Turkish president, reports published in the fall of 1990 indicate that the Iraqis had been staging military exercises in preparation for the invasion for two years, including a mid-July rehearsal for a heliborne assault on Kuwait City.[29] General Schwarzkopf later commented:

We pretty well have confirmed that [the Iraqis] had been planning the invasion of Kuwait for 2 to 4 years. . . . We know they had run computer simulations and war games for the invasion of Kuwait. A lot of information indicates they had similar plans for Saudi Arabia.[30]

These may have been contingency plans. But there is additional evidence that by mid-July Saddam had decided to execute such an operation—that is to go to war. Kuwaiti army colonel Said Matar, while on duty as a military attaché in Basra, collected intelligence on the Iraqi military. He noted the first signs of military preparations in April 1990, about the time that Saddam began his verbal attacks on Kuwait and the Emirates. Then on July 25, the same day that Glaspie met with Saddam, and the same day the CIA concluded that Saddam was not bluffing, an officer in a Republican Guard division told Mater that Iraq would invade on August 2.[31]

For the United States, the Iraqi invasion of Kuwait was a classic failure of extended deterrence.[32] To be successful, deterrence, whether simple or extended, requires two fundamental elements—the recognition by the country to be deterred that the deterring state possesses both the will and the capability to react militarily.

Saddam based his decision to invade Kuwait on a gross miscalculation of the willingness and the capability of the United States to defend its interests in the Persian Gulf. Saddam's faulty reasoning is evident in the "transcript" of his July 25, 1990, meeting with Ambassador Glaspie.[33] Saddam told Glaspie that the United States was "a society which cannot accept 10,000 dead in one battle." Such compunctions, in Saddam's mind, ruled out large-scale American intervention in the Arabian peninsula, for he reasoned that such a war would be bloody. Nor did Saddam believe that the Americans possessed the military capability to respond effectively. He knew that the United States could wage an aerial campaign against Iraq, but he did not think that the Americans could deploy and sustain large ground forces in the gulf. "You can come to Iraq with aircraft and missiles," he told Glaspie, but said nothing of American ground forces. Saddam's reasoning is obvious. He told Glaspie that had the Iranians beaten the Iraqis during the Iran-Iraq war, Khomeini's forces would have "overrun" the gulf and the United States could not have stopped them with anything other than "nuclear weapons." If, in Saddam Hussein's mind, the Americans could not move sufficient forces to the Arabian peninsula to halt the Iranians, how could the United States possibly

160

move enough strength to the gulf to check the more powerful Iraqi army?

But why had Saddam miscalculated? Glaspie commented during her congressional testimony that Saddam "was stupid." That stupidity may have been based on bad advice from subordinates or Soviet "advisers"; good, but out of date intelligence; and analysis of the voluminous writings of American critics of United States military policy in the Middle East.

While the extent to which the Iraqis and the Soviets cooperated during the war is unclear, Saddam must have asked the Soviets for an appreciation, however general, of American military capabilities. The Soviets probably did not warn Saddam that the United States would move 500,000 troops, a massive air armada, and over 150 warships, including six aircraft carriers, to the Middle East and then launch a devastating offensive that would make the billions of dollars the Iraqis had invested in their Soviet-equipped military appear to be the largest waste of money in history. One Soviet marshal later admitted, the speed and extent of the American-led victory over Iraq surprised the Russians and "modified the ideas that we had regarding the nature of modern military operations."[34]

Saddam may also have been misled by what appeared at the time to be an intelligence coup. On August 28, 1990, authorities in Bonn arrested a West German records clerk for allegedly supplying classified information to the Iraqi government. The clerk had access to top secret United States military documents that had been shared with the West German Ministry of Defense. According to West German intelligence sources, Iraq had learned of "the U.S. analysis of the Gulf situation" before the invasion.[35] But American plans for the defense of the region were being overhauled in 1990. If the plans and appreciations of and for the gulf did find their way from safes in Bonn to Baghdad, those documents most likely were out of date. They probably did not reflect the changes then underway in the planning process, nor the current state of sea and air lift capabilities.

If Saddam's intelligence analysts scoured the West's open-source defense literature for clues about the United States' military capabilities in the gulf, they probably would have advised Saddam not to worry. Many American military analysts had long questioned the logic that lay behind the RDF and its successor CENTCOM, despite improvements of the command's capabilities during the 1980s. For example, in a March 1990 assessment, military analyst Jeffrey Record doubted that "a sympathetic White House could mobilize timely and sufficient domestic political support for intervention" if Iraq threatened Saudi Arabia.[36] Even within the U.S. Army there were doubts that Americans could take on the Iraqis, and win. A study published shortly before the invasion in the summer of 1990 extolled the strengths of the Iraqi Army. The monograph, published by the Army War College, concluded that "to perform competently" in the Middle East, the U.S. Army had to be "reconfigured, retrained and reequipped."[37] Even as late as February 1991, an article in *Military Review*, an official U.S. Army professional journal published by the U.S. Army Command and General Staff College, noted:

> There is a tendency in the West to disregard Iraq's victory over Iran as the mere ascendence of firepower over human-wave assaults. This is hardly the case, as the Iraqi military has shown a high degree of sophistication in its planning and conduct of operations. The Iraqi Army has shown great tactical improvement since 1980. They are much better fighters than most military analysts formerly believed.[38]

Saddam discounted the decade of improvements in sealift and airlift organization, force structure, and planning overseen by Central Command in Tampa. He misread the U.S. willingness to use force to defend its interests, despite the successful operations in Grenada, against Libya, in defense of Kuwait in the Persian Gulf in 1987 and 1988, and in Panama.

Whatever the mix of paranoia, stupidity, bad intelligence, and miscalculation that shaped Saddam's decisions, his mindset left little room for maneuver by American diplomats. Tougher policies would most likely only have convinced Saddam that the United States was, indeed, conspiring against him. Threats against a man who doubted not only American willingness, but also its capability to defend its interests in the region against a well-armed state such as Iraq, would probably have been ignored. While a bold threat of direct military confrontation with the United States over Kuwait might have convinced Saddam not to strike (after all he did not move into Saudi Arabia once Desert Shield began), without a Kuwaiti request for assistance—a tripwire that would have brought American military personnel into the country and into Saddam's path—there was little the Bush administration could have done.

CHAPTER NINE

SHIELD IN THE DESERT

—•—

August 1990–January 1991

In Washington the evening before the Iraqi invasion, American officials waited apprehensively for the expected news from Kuwait. Only two years after the end of the undeclared tanker war between the United States and Iran, Americans were about to face yet another crisis in the Persian Gulf. The United States had no formal commitment to defend Kuwait. President Bush had not yet drawn any line in the sand. But official Washington understood that if, or more likely when, Saddam moved south, the United States would become involved.

The days when crises in the gulf were someone else's business were long past. It had taken almost two centuries, but the United States had made itself supreme in the gulf. Twenty years had passed since the British withdrawal; eleven since the shah's abdication. For a decade Americans had touted their leadership in the region. And now, that leadership was about to be challenged by a madman with the fourth largest army in the world, a fledgling chemical arsenal, and perhaps even a rudimentary nuclear weapon.

If Saddam's army marched, all eyes would be on Washington. The world would look to George Bush to show the way. American interests, not just in Kuwait but throughout the Middle East, would be at risk. The commercial, strategic, and geoeconomic factors that had led Americans so deeply into the affairs of the gulf would be on the line. So, too, would the president's political future. George Bush the politician well remembered how the Carter administration had run aground while navigating the unpredictable and uncharted political waters of the Persian Gulf.

At 2:00 A.M. (local time) on August 2, 1990, over 100,000 Iraqi troops, led by three "elite" Republican Guard divisions, invaded Kuwait. Special forces units, which had practiced mock heliborne assaults in central Iraq in July, seized important buildings, most notably the palace of the emir of Kuwait, Sheik Jaber al-Ahmed al-Sabah. The Kuwaiti army of 20,000 had been ordered to stand down from full alert days before the invasion to avoid provoking Saddam. Within twenty-four hours, organized armed resistance had ended and the entire country was in Iraqi hands.

The assault was not, however, a complete success. The Republican Guard divisions suffered numerous equipment failures, a factor that may have ruled out an immediate strike against Saudi Arabia.[1] The emir, most of the royal family, and elements of the Kuwaiti armed forces escaped to Saudi Arabia.[2] Subsequent reports indicate that a disappointed Saddam may have had some of the officers responsible for these failures executed.

World reaction to the assault on Kuwait was sharp. Within a week the United States, the Soviet Union, the United Nations, the Arab League, the European Economic Community, and Japan condemned the invasion. On August 6, the U.N. Security Council voted 13–0, with Cuba and Yeman abstaining, to impose economic sanctions against Iraq and Iraqi-controlled territory.[3]

The international community's quick, tough response surprised Saddam. To deflect the mounting pressure he announced that Iraq had invaded to assist revolutionaries who were in the process of establishing a "free revolutionary government of Kuwait." Saddam assured everyone that, as long as no threats were made against Iraq, his forces would begin withdrawing on Sunday, August 5, although the al-Sabahs would not be able to return to Kuwait City.[4] But world outrage continued unabated.

Saddam nevertheless refused to back down. Clear international signals were insufficient to convince him of his folly. For while the world appeared ready to isolate or quarantine Iraq, there was as yet little evidence that it was prepared to force him to yield his conquest. And Saddam also knew that the world would pay for its stand. Crude oil prices jumped another $1.57 to $23.11 a barrel, up from about $17.00 in early July before the crisis had begun.

Saddam's refusal to withdraw in response to unparalleled international pressure placed the United States in a difficult position. On Saturday morning, August 4, President Bush met for two-and-a-half hours with his top national security and military advisers at the presidential retreat at Camp David, Maryland.[5] The situation was bleak.

Intelligence analysts warned that the Iraqi force that had crossed the border on August 2 was larger than necessary to invade and occupy Kuwait. Despite the Iraqi announcement of a withdrawal, Saddam's forces were moving further south and massing along the northern Saudi Arabian border; Saddam had also canceled all leaves and mobilized an additional fourteen reserve divisions.[6] United States forces in the region were few and the immediate options limited. In the Indian Ocean the carrier *Independence*, with its battle group and air wing of eighty-plus aircraft, now sped toward the Arabian Sea. The carrier *Dwight D. Eisenhower*, deployed in the Mediterranean, steamed east. The U.S. Navy's Atlantic Fleet prepared to move the carrier *Saratoga*, the battleship *Wisconsin*, and a Marine Expeditionary Brigade from the east coast to the gulf.

Fear for the immediate safety of Saudi Arabia now totally eclipsed the problem of forcing the Iraqis from Kuwait. Intelligence officials based their estimates of Iraqi intentions on what was taking place on the ground in Kuwait and southeastern Iraq. The movements of the Iraqi army looked threatening. They may have been meant to intimidate the Saudis, since Saddam stated categorically that he had no intention of invading Saudi Arabia. But in July the "experts" had predicted that the Iraqis were just trying to scare the Kuwaitis and Saddam had assured everyone that he was not preparing to invade. The Iraqi president's credibility was rather low in the early days of August 1990, and American intelligence experts who had been burned once, concluded that Saddam was most likely about to invade Saudi Arabia. Secretary of Defense Cheney felt comfortable enough with the evidence to assure Congress in December 1990:

> I personally am convinced that if we had not responded as rapidly as we did, he [Saddam] would, indeed, have continued his aggression, and it was only the speed of the U.S. response that gave him pause and gave us the opportunity to deploy the forces that are now in the field.[7]

If Saddam did send his army south, American military options were limited. A naval blockade of Iraq and occupied Kuwait was unlikely to force Saddam to withdraw and would do virtually nothing to impede an Iraqi drive further south. The carriers *Independence* and *Eisenhower* could launch airstrikes against targets in Iraq or against forces advancing into Saudi Arabia. But aircraft flying from carriers in the North Arabian and Red Seas would be operating at extreme range and would be heavily outnumbered by Saddam's 800-plane air force. The best way to deter an Iraqi strike south, stop that attack should it materialize, and build up a force capable of forcing Saddam to withdraw from Kuwait was to move U.S. ground and air units into Saudi Arabia. But even with full Saudi cooperation, General Schwarzkopf warned the president that it would take seventeen weeks to deploy USCENTCOM's forces—about 225,000 personnel—to the gulf, and eight to twelve months to build up a force capable of driving the Iraqis from Kuwait.[8]

Following the Camp David meeting, President Bush telephoned King Fahd for the second time since August 2. Other American officials conferred with Prince Bandar bin Sultan—the Saudi ambassador to the United States and the king's nephew. These consultations led to a decision on August 5 to send a high-level American delegation headed by Secretary of Defense Cheney and General Schwarzkopf to Jidda to meet with King Fahd.

In the interim, the situation along the Saudi border became more threatening and the crisis atmosphere in the gulf continued to build. Three times between August 3 and 6 Iraqi forces crossed into Saudi Arabia, further heightening Saudi fears.[9] The Arab talks scheduled for August 4 in Jidda collapsed.

Focus shifted to the battle over the Turkish and Saudi pipelines that carried 90 percent of Iraq's exported oil. If economic sanctions against Saddam were to be effective, the pipelines had to be shut down. On August 3 the United States had requested that both Turkey and Saudi Arabia stop the flow of oil. Turkey, a populous nation with defensible borders, a large military establishment, and membership in NATO was relatively secure from Saddam's threats. But Saudi Arabia, sparsely populated, with indefensible borders, a small military establishment, and no formal security ties, was not. On August 5, the Iraqis warned the Turks about the possible consequences if they shut down their pipeline.[10] As the pressure against Saudi Arabia increased, a key aspect of Cheney's mission became to convince the Saudis to halt the flow of Iraq oil, in return for American protection.[11]

Concerns about the safety of foreigners in Kuwait also mounted as reports of the roundup of Westerners reached Washington.[12] The new Kuwaiti government did little to assuage Western fears, warning that it would not necessarily "act honorably" toward foreign citizens.[13] Bush, returning to Washington on Sunday, told the press that the

Iraqi invasion "will not stand," and when asked what the United States could do to reverse it, remarked: "Just wait, watch and learn."[14]

In Jidda on Monday, August 6, Cheney and Schwarzkopf met with King Fahd. The American team laid out for the Saudis the United States' military capabilities. Cheney requested that the king stop the flow of Iraqi oil and allow American forces to deploy to Saudi bases. The secretary of defense also assured King Fahd that the American forces would depart "immediately" at the end of the crisis or whenever directed to do so.[15]

Fortunately for the United States, Secretary Cheney's team did not have a hard sell. As early as August 3, the king, deeply concerned about Iraqi intentions, had made up his mind to request the deployment of American forces into his country, although whether or not he had been prepared to accept ground forces before this point is unclear.[16] But in his meeting with the Americans on the sixth, King Fahd recalled his country's long relationship with the United States, citing the meeting between his father—Ibn Saud—and President Roosevelt in 1945. Fahd announced that ground forces, too, could deploy to the peninsula and that he would close down the Iraqi pipeline. He also offered to increase Saudi oil production to offset the loss of Iraqi and Kuwaiti supplies in an effort to keep prices stable.[17]

After the meeting, Cheney called Bush, who gave the secretary of defense the order to begin the movement of American military forces. Cheney then phoned Army General Colin Powell, chairman of the Joint Chiefs of Staff, and issued the necessary instructions. Cheney gave Schwarzkopf his orders directly.[18] Cheney then flew to Egypt where he met with President Mubarak who agreed to allow the movement of U.S. Navy warships, including the nuclear-powered aircraft carrier *Eisenhower*, from the eastern Mediterranean through the Suez Canal to the Red Sea.

The Saudi decision of August 6 was the sine qua non of Operation Desert Shield/Storm. King Fahd's willingness to cooperate with the United States placed enormous economic, political, and military pressure on Saddam. The possiblity of a military confrontation with American forces increased. Saudi adherence to international economic sanctions gave the anti-Iraqi coalition enormous leverage within the Arab world and in the international oil markets.

While a major political stumbling block had been avoided, the United States still faced an enormous challenge. After August 6, any Iraqi move into Saudi Arabia would lead to a direct confrontation with the United States, a consideration that would, hopefully, deter Saddam. But if the Iraqi dictator was not deterred, the Allies faced a difficult situation.

The entire Saudi army—38,000 men—was far smaller than the Iraqi forces already deployed in Kuwait. Saudi military analysts estimated that the Iraqis could overrun the Eastern Province in six to twelve hours, even with American air cover.[19] Secretary Cheney admitted in December 1990: "As of August 2 . . . the only thing between Saddam Hussein and those oil fields [in eastern Saudi Arabia] was a battalion of the Saudi Arabian National Guard. There was no significant military obstacle to his further move south."[20] The Iraqis probably could have reached Riyadh, the Saudi capital, in three to five days.[21]

The arrival of the first American units scheduled to deploy to Saudi Arabia would do little to immediately shift the balance of power on the ground. U.S. Air Force AWACS, tankers, and F-15 Eagle air superiority fighters would reinforce Saudi air defenses and insure Allied control of the air. The advancing Iraqis would thus be denied air support, but still would have little to fear from above. The initial American ground units slated to arrive in the Arabian peninsula were the three brigades of the 82nd Airborne Division from Fort Bragg, North Carolina. But the airborne troopers were light infantry, armed with only a relative handful of lightly armored tanks. If the Iraqis drove south, they would be hard to stop. Chairman Powell knew that an Iraqi offensive during the first thirty days of Desert Shield would place American forces in "a very, very difficult situation."[22]

The 82nd Airborne Division's initial task would be to secure the airbases and ports through which other American units would later arrive. General Powell considered the retention of these sea and air heads his "number one concern."[23] If the Iraqis overran the ports of Jubayl and Ad Damman and the airbase at Dhahran, the United States' buildup would be considerably retarded. The capture of Ras Tanura, the Saudi's major port for oil export, could prove an economic disaster for the coalition.

Whether or not Saddam intended to follow up his seizure of Kuwait by invading Saudi Arabia, once King Fahd allowed American forces into the country and President Bush announced the commencement of Operation Desert Shield, Iraqi forces *should* have driven south. The Iraqis could hardly have fared worse than they did. Even if United States forces successfully defended the stretch of Saudi coast between Jubayl and Dhahran, a bold Iraqi stroke would at the minimum have overrun much of the oil-producing Eastern Province, have forced lightly armored American units to fight Iraqi armored forces on disadvantageous terms, and might have captured Riyadh. Saddam would have gained enormous political, economic, and military leverage that could have been used to arrange a negotiated settlement that would have left him with part of his conquests.

Why Saddam did not invade Saudi Arabia must remain a topic of conjecture until the Iraqis publish accounts of the war, but there are two factors that probably shaped Saddam's thinking. He most likely did not believe that Operation Desert Shield would ultimately lead to the deployment of an overwhelmingly powerful allied military force in and around the Arabian Peninsula, nor that the coalition would engage in offensive operations to force the Iraqis from Kuwait. Saddam simply did not take American intentions and capabilities seriously. Nor was he a bold military leader. In 1980, when Iraqi forces blitzed into Iran, seized most of their initial objectives, and had the Iranians on the run, Saddam halted his offensive and sought to negotiate a settlement to secure his gains. The Iranians rejected the Iraqi peace overtures and the war continued for eight bloody years.

Similarly, Saddam's response to Operation Desert Shield was not to invade Saudi Arabia, but to hunker down and seek a diplomatic end to the crisis. On August 8 he announced the annexation of Iraq's "nineteenth province." By the ninth, American intelligence reports indicated that Iraqi units were pulling back and taking up defensive positions, although they could go over to the offensive in forty-eight hours.[24] On August 10, Saddam called for a holy war—a *jihad*—against the American-led coalition. Saddam warned his fellow Arabs that Islamic holy sites had been "captured by the spears of the Americans and the Zionists." He issued calls to "save Mecca and the tomb of the Prophet from occupation," to "revolt against the emirs who accept to push the Arab women into whoredom," to "burn the land under the feet of the invaders," to "strike at their interests everywhere," and to prevent the passage of their ships through the Suez Canal.[25] Then on the fifteenth, in an attempt to secure his eastern flank, Saddam offered to return to Iran all territory captured during the 1980–88 war, all prisoners of war, and to accept the 1975 Algiers Agreement that had divided the Shatt-al Arab between Iraq and Iran.[26] The Iranians accepted the Iraqi offer. Saddam was free to transfer additional troops to bolster the defense of Kuwait.

Although some analysts saw Saddam's initiative toward Iran as a masterstroke, the move was, in fact, a tremendous blunder. On August 15 Saddam burned his bridges. He returned to Iran what little Iraq had gained at tremendous cost during an eight-year-long war, in exchange for the prospective, but yet to be realized fruits of the invasion of Kuwait. In effect, Saddam had upped the odds, called the United States' bluff, and gone "double or nothing." For after August 15, if Saddam subsequently chose to withdraw from Kuwait, he would have nothing to show for a decade of war, hundreds of thousands of casualties, and hundreds of billions in treasure. After the fifteenth, Saddam's diplomatic freedom of maneuver was nil.

Both the United States and Iraq were now locked in a desperate confrontation, with each attempting to enlist allies and to build up forces in what the American military labeled the Kuwaiti Theater of Operations (KTO)—the area in and around Kuwait at the head of the Persian Gulf.

Despite Saddam's best efforts, calls for a holy war against the West and its Arab allies produced few adherents. Saddam received little but vocal support from Yemen, the PLO, Cuba, and Jordan. Iraqi troops in occupied Kuwait stood alone, except for a handful of Palestinian militia recruited in Kuwait City.

The United States was far more successful at coalition building, not only in the West, but also among the Arabs and throughout the Third World. The United States secured the support of the international community including that of the Soviet Union, without which the U.N. Security Council would have been powerless. The role of the United Nations in the crisis approximated that which the organization's founders had envisioned during the Second World War. Thirty-eight nations joined the coaltion against Iraq and sent troops, aircraft, ships, medical teams, or money to support the effort.

The American-led military buildup proceeded apace. C-Day—Commencement Day for Operation Desert Shield—became August 7. With President Mubarak's permission, the *Eisenhower* battle group steamed through the Suez Canal. American carriers in the Red Sea and the Arabian Sea were positioned to cover the initial air lift into Saudi Arabia.[27] U.S. Air Force F-15C and D Eagle fighters from the First Tactical Fighter Wing's (TFW) 27th and 71st Tactical Fighter Squadrons (TFS) deployed from Langley Air Force Base in Virginia to Dhahran. Within thirty-eight hours of notification to deploy, U.S. Air Force "F-15s were sitting alert, ready to fly defensive patrols along the Iraqi-Saudi border, 7000 miles from their departure bases."[28] The First Division Ready Brigade (DRB) of the 82nd Airborne Division began loading at Pope Air Force Base, which adjoined the U.S. Army's Fort Bragg in Fayetteville, North Carolina. The next day, August 8, the transports carrying the brigade's personnel began arriving at Dhahran.

On the eighth, the ships of Maritime Prepositioning Ship (MPS) Squadrons 2 and 3 sailed from Diego Garcia and Guam, respectively. These ships carried the equipment and thirty-days supplies for the Marine Corps' Seventh Marine Expeditionary Brigade (MEB) from Twentynine Palms, California, and the First MEB from Hawaii. On August 14, the lead elements of the Seventh MEB flew into Jubayl, already secured by a DRB of the 82nd Airborne. The next day, the ships of MPS Squadron 2 reached Jubayl and the brigade's personnel began "marrying up" with their equipment.[29] Until September, the marines constituted the majority of the American ground forces deployed in Saudi Arabia.[30]

The arrival of the Seventh MEB at Jubayl lessened the dangers the United States faced during the initial phase of Desert Shield. The 17,000-man marine brigade was almost as large as a U.S. Army division. The marines, supported by their own air element, were able to establish a blocking position north of Jubayl covering Ras Tanura, Ad Damman, and Dhahran. The marines also had tanks—M-60A1s—that while inferior to the U.S. Army M1 and M1A1 Abrams, were far superior to the 82nd Airborne's M-55 Sheridans and, in the hands of the well trained Marine tankers, proved to be more capable than anything in the Iraqi arsenal.

Given the importance of the arrival of the Marines' Seventh MEB, one might well ask why the ships of MPS Squadron 2 failed to leave Diego Garcia until C-Day +2 (August 8)? Since Saddam did not invade Saudi Arabia, the question remains academic. But had the Iraqis struck, the delay in moving the MPS ships could have been critical. Lieutenant General Joseph P. Hoar, former deputy chief of staff for plans, policies, and operations, Headquarters Marine Corps, and as of August 1991 General Schwarzkopf's successor as CENTCOM commander, argued that the MPS ships should have moved no later than August 2.[31] Certainly, they should have left Diego Garcia before August 8, if not on the second, perhaps on the third, the day after the invasion, or the sixth, the day King Fahd agreed to allow American units into Saudi Arabia. In *The Commanders*, Bob Woodward states that General Powell killed a proposal to move the Marines' MPS ships toward the gulf before 2 August as a signal to Iraq of American determination.[32] Other Pentagon sources have pointed the finger at the White House or attributed the delay to simple bureaucratic inertia.

In addition to the five ships of MPS Squadron 2, the United States also maintained a dozen Afloat Prepositioned Ships (APS) at Diego Garcia loaded with equipment and supplies for U.S. Army, Air Force,

171

and Navy forces that would deploy to the theater in an emergency. Ten of these ships sped toward the gulf and by September had unloaded their cargoes. Two of the first APS ships to arrive at Saudi ports carried ordnance for U.S. Air Force units.[33] Another of the APS ships, the MV Noble Star, reached Saudi Arabia on August 15 and within two weeks its 400 containers had been unloaded and "the sprawling, 28-acre" U.S. Navy Field Hospital 5 was fully functioning.[34]

The U.S. Navy's Military Sealift Command (MSC) deployed eight Fast Sealift Ships (SL-7s) to Savannah, Georgia, to move the U.S. Army's 24th Mechanized Infantry Division to Saudi Arabia. On August 11, the Capella was the first of the SL-7s to begin the 8,700 mile-long journey to Ad Damman. Having averaged 27 knots during the passage, the Capella reached Ad Damman on 27 August with her cargo of M-1 tanks, Bradley fighting vehicles, trucks, and other equipment. Unfortunately, because of an engine failure in one of the SL-7s—the Antares—the deployment of the 24th Division fell twelve days behind schedule and was not completed until September 13.[35]

Military Sealift Command also mobilized ships from the National Defense Reserve Fleet and United States and foreign chartered vessels to move cargo to the gulf. Sealift Phase I, the buildup of the initial CENTCOM forces, involved over 170 ships, 49 of which (28 percent) were foreign flag.[36] During Sealift Phase II, between December 1990 and March 1991, MSC controlled 220 ships in an effort that by March 1991 saw 84 million pounds of cargo arriving at Saudi ports daily.[37]

Despite the fact that the vast bulk—over 90 percent—of the material shipped to the Arabian Peninsula came by sea, strategic airlift received more attention than sealift during Operation Desert Shield. Video of a giant U.S. Air Force C-5A landing at Dhahran is far more exciting than watching a ship pull into Ad Damman. Airlift did play the critical role in August 1990, rushing the first combat ready brigades of the U.S. Army's 82nd Airborne Division to Dhahran and Jubayl. At the peak of the August–September airlift, a transport landed at Dhahran every ten minutes. Throughout Desert Shield/Storm, the majority of American ground forces deployed to the Arabian peninsula arrived by air. Air force transports and chartered civilian aircraft under Military Airlift Command (MAC) control flew 482,000 passengers and 513,000 tons of cargo into the theater.[38]

But sealift remained the critical element in the overall success of Operation Desert Shield/Storm. Air force transports, even the giant C-5A, could not fly in the equipment for the U.S. Army's heavy divisions. Nor was it cost effective once the initial crisis had passed, to fly in supplies that could otherwise be sent by sea. The 82nd Airborne Division, for example, relied on the Marine Corps during the first few weeks of Desert Shield until the airborne troopers' supplies, coming by sea, caught up with them.[39] Over 3,000 C-141 flights would have been needed to fly the cargo carried by the first three MPS ships to reach Jubayl.[40] The marines, whose equipment came by sea, were the first heavy units to reach Saudi Arabia. By December 1990, when Sealift Phase I concluded, MSC controlled ships had moved 3.5 million tons of fuel and 1.1 million tons of cargo to the gulf. A navy study later noted:

> Sealift moved 2.4 million tons of cargo during the first six months of DESERT SHIELD. By comparison, that is more than four times the cargo carried across the English Channel to Normandy during the D-Day invasion and more than 6.5 times that of the peak force build-up during the Vietnam War during a similar period. On January 2, 1991, at the peak of the Desert Shield deployment, MSC had 172 ships underway.[41]

The expansion of strategic lift capabilities, both air and sea, during the 1980s, allowed the United States to rapidly move a substantial force to the gulf in the summer of 1990. By the end of September, over 100,000 American military personnel were in Central Command's Area of Responsibility (AOR). Morocco, Egypt, and Syria had sent small detachments to Saudi Arabia to join American and gulf Arab forces confronting the Iraqis now entrenched in Kuwait. Many more troops would follow.

At sea, most of the Western European countries had sent, or were in the process of sending, warships to help enforce the embargo. On August 25, the U.N. Security Council adopted Resolution 665, calling for those nations with maritime forces "cooperating with the government of Kuwait" to use measures necessary to enforce the provisions of Resolution 661.

Despite virtually unchallenged Allied control of the seas, enforcing the sanctions against Iraq was not all that simple. Allied naval forces had to patrol 250,000 square miles of sea lanes in the Persian Gulf, Gulf of Oman, and the Red Sea. Allied air, surface, and subsurface naval assets from fourteen nations monitored traffic. Between August 1990 and March 1991, more than 165 Allied ships, of which about 80 percent were American, challenged more than 9,000 merchant vessels, boarded more than 1,100 to inspect manifests and cargos, and diverted 60 ships for violation of the United Nations sanctions.[42]

Just how effective the embargo was, or would become, soon became the subject of debate. As early as late August reports of shortages of critical items, such as spare parts for the Iraqi military, surfaced in the Western press. There followed speculation about how long Iraq could survive under the pressures of the embargo.[43] But whatever those pressures, Saddam showed no sign of yielding Kuwait. He continued to reinforce his army in Kuwait to an estimated 265,000 by late August. Nevertheless, the rapid and forceful Allied response apparently had convinced the Iraqi president not to attack Saudi Arabia. Late in August, Iraq's best units, the divisions of the Republican Guard, withdrew into reserve positions north of Kuwait.[44]

These Iraqi moves, combined with the rapid and massive buildup of coalition air, land, sea forces in the theater, marked the end of the first, most dangerous phase of Desert Shield. On August 26, General Schwarzkopf moved from Tampa to his forward Central Command headquarters in Riyadh. During his first interview, Schwarzkopf indicated that while he remained uncertain of success should the Iraqis strike south, the worst of the crisis had passed.[45] On September 4, Schwarzkopf directed elements of the 82nd Airborne Division and the marines to move northward towards the Saudi border. Saddam could no longer move south, into the Eastern Province or toward Riyadh, without encountering American ground forces backed up by a strong force of as many as 180 U.S. Air Force combat aircraft, a pair of U.S. Navy carriers, Marine Corps ground-attack aircraft, and a variety of Arab forces deployed in depth throughout the Arabian Peninsula.[46]

As Saddam's window of opportunity in the gulf closed, Allied political and military leaders began to debate what course coalition policy should take. Desert Shield was a defensive-sounding term for what was an obviously defensive operation. In August and September 1990, the Saudis stated that the Allied buildup in the kingdom did not presage a military offensive. On August 31, General Schwarzkopf told reporters, "There's not going to be any war unless the Iraqis attack."[47] The Saudi defense minister, Prince Sultan bin Abdul Aziz, stated that his country would not be "a theater for any action that is not defensive."[48] While staffs in Riyadh, Tampa, and Washington prepared contingency plans for an operation designed to drive Saddam from Kuwait, the Allies could not take offensive action until the late fall by which time the United States would have fully deployed the forces earmarked for CENTCOM.[49]

In the interim, the Allies placed their hopes on the unprecedented display of international solidarity and the U.N.-sanctioned economic embargo. Unfortunately, the expectation that international cooperation would induce Saddam to withdraw quickly dissipated. He continued to thumb his nose at his enemies and tighten his grip on Kuwait. The utility of economic sanctions was also the subject of debate. There were many who expected, or at least hoped, that economic pressure would force Saddam from Kuwait, but others either doubted the effectiveness of the embargo or believed that the coalition would disintegrate long before Saddam would yield.[50]

The embargo was clearly effective. The sanctions demonstrated Iraq's international isolation. The blockade denied Saddam access to world markets, eliminated his main source of income—oil exports—and denied his armed forces access to the spare parts needed to maintain foreign-made equipment.

But the effectiveness of these international economic measures did not necessarily mean that they would be decisive. There are few historical examples of aggressors relinquishing gains solely under the pressure of sanctions.[51] And the refusal of Saddam to cooperate fully with the Allies as late as the winter of 1991, despite his defeat in the January-February 1991 war and the fact that sanctions remained in effect, certainly supports the argument that economic measures alone would not have forced Saddam from Kuwait.

The best example of "effective" economic sanctions, and one discussed in the halls of the Pentagon in the fall of 1990, was the 1941 American effort to isolate Japan. The result, of course, was not a Japanese withdrawal from China, but an attack against the United States Pacific Fleet at Pearl Harbor. Similarly, senior Bush administration officials, among them Secretary of Defense Cheney, were concerned that if the sanctions began to squeeze Baghdad, Saddam would strike south against Saudi Arabia rather than yield.[52] Since Saddam, according to his own version of events, had invaded Kuwait in August 1990 in an effort to circumvent an economic encirclement allegedly masterminded by the United States, the proposition that he would lash out before withdrawing from Kuwait made sense. And the United States military had little desire to yield the initiative to Saddam and allow him to pick the time and place to begin active military operations.

Time was another critically important consideration: could the coalition outlast Saddam? The higher oil prices that accompanied the Iraqi invasion of Kuwait jarred the global economic system. Oil prices rose from $15.60 per barrel before the invasion to a high of $40.40 by mid-October. That increase cost the U.S. economy $2.5 billion a month, in addition to other expenditures associated with the military effort.[53] Rising energy prices and other costs also hurt the countries of the Third World. Higher oil prices and the need to repatriate workers from the gulf cost India, for example, an estimated $2.5 billion by mid-September 1990.[54] The newly democratic states of Eastern Europe lost about $4 billion in loans owed them by Iraq and suffered as well because of higher energy prices and an economic slowdown that endangered the success of reformers.[55]

Terrorism threatened to undermine a coalition that while broad, was also, to quote Secretary Cheney, a "relatively fragile, complex enterprise."[56] The allies took such threats seriously. From his Baghdad home the head of the Palestine Liberation Front called Saddam "a man of concrete actions and not slogans" and warned that if the United States attacked, Western interests in Europe and the Middle East would be targeted.[57] Concern about Iraqi or Iraqi-sponsored terrorist actions especially worried America's Arab allies.[58]

Desert Shield also placed severe pressures on the American military. General Powell assured the Congress that a large force could remain in the Arabian Peninsula for as long as a year.[59] Unfortunately, there were no indications that Iraq was likely to yield within twelve months. Saudi Arabia was not Western Europe and American troops, deployed somewhat uncomfortably in the desert, could not be maintained in the field forever.

The scope and scale of the deployment itself also ruled out an open-ended military commitment. The deployment of American ground units continued unabated well into the fall of 1990, but the initial phase air and naval buildup ended much earlier. By mid-September, U.S. Air Force assets assigned to Central Command had virtually completed their deployment to the Gulf.[60] With two Marine Expeditionary Brigades ashore and another afloat, the Marine Corps had over a third of its entire strength deployed by early October.[61] The U.S. Navy was overdeployed with three of its fourteen carriers at sea in a theater where it took seven carriers to keep one on station.

The orderly rotation of such a large force posed an extremely difficult, though not insurmountable problem for the American military. But as early as September, U.S. Navy, Marine Corps, and Air Force planners were aware that any such rotation scheme would reduce the combat effectiveness of the forces deployed in the theater beginning in the spring of 1991.

Nor were the Saudis and other gulf Arabs eager to see Western forces remain in the Arabian Peninsula indefinitely. In both Washington and Riyadh, policymakers understood that it would be best for all concerned if the crisis was resolved before the *Haj*—the traditional Islamic pilgrimage to the holy cities of Mecca and Medina in western Saudi Arabia that would begin in June 1991. Despite the Saudis' previous rejection of an offensive military option, King Fahd indicated at an early October meeting in Jidda with French President François Mitterand that he had doubts about the effectiveness of sanctions and expected a military resolution of the impasse over Kuwait.[62]

By October, the Bush administration shared the Saudi view, although few American policymakers wished to sound bellicose at a time when polls indicated that the American people opposed an offensive to drive the Iraqis from Kuwait. Media reports based on leaks from "government sources" rarely expressed the view that sanctions were likely to force Saddam to withdraw from Kuwait any time soon.[63] And while many in Congress opposed a military option, others doubted the effectiveness of the embargo. In an early September 1990 interview, Les Aspin, Wisconsin Democrat and chairman of the House Armed Service Committee, commented: "The standoff can't last forever. We build, Saddam Hussein builds, there's hyperactivity everywhere. I'd say that it comes to a head in six months, maximum, probably a whole lot sooner."[64]

But if international outrage was insufficient to convince Saddam to withdraw, and if the short- and long-term impact of the blockade was not enough to elicit a withdrawal, would the international community, U.S. allies, and most importantly, the American people support the use of military force? Despite the seemingly delicate balance between those willing and those unwilling to use force to drive the Iraqis from Kuwait, the Bush administration believed that resolute leadership on the part of the United States would produce a domestic and international consensus in support of a military option.

That assumption was well founded. As the crisis dragged on, key Arab allies seemed ever more willing to resort to force in an effort to end the standoff. Great Britain, the European state with the strongest military contingent in the Arabian peninsula, was willing to stand by its American ally. In the United States, the Bush administration based its belief that Americans would support a war to drive Saddam from Kuwait on a realistic appraisal of the patriotism of the people, albeit with the understanding that support for a bloody or endless struggle would quickly erode. Despite the scars of the Indochina war, the Americans had supported quick military actions in Libya, Grenada, and Panama. The Reagan administration had run into trouble in Lebanon where the American involvement had appeared limited, but had turned out to be bloody and open-ended. Thus, if the military chiefs could assure the president that a recourse to arms would be quick and bloodless, the administration believed that it could count on the support of the American people.

But would a military effort to drive Saddam's army from Kuwait be quick and bloodless? Projections about the costs of conflict affected not only the direction of military policy and planning, but also the international and domestic American debates about what course to pursue. The problem the Bush administration faced early in the fall of 1990 was that generals Powell and Schwarzkopf were unwilling to provide assurances that the war would not degenerate into a long, bloody campaign.

American military planning for the Persian Gulf was in a state of flux in the summer of 1990. Since the fall of 1989, under the direction of General Powell as chairman of the Joint Chiefs of Staff in Washington, and General Schwarzkopf as CENTCOM commander in Tampa, the American military had begun to change its primary planning focus for Central Command from the need to meet a Soviet drive from the Caucasus and central Asia toward the Persian Gulf, to a response to a regional threat, such as that posed by Iran or Iraq. To Powell and Schwarzkopf the Soviet threat represented less the regional military reality of the mid- and late-1980s than it did habitual Cold War worries and an early 1980s concern linked to Moscow's invasion of Afghanistan that had led to the Carter Doctrine and the establishment of Central Command's precursor—the Rapid Deployment Force.

After taking command in Tampa in November 1989, Schwarzkopf, at Powell's direction, redirected the work of the CENTCOM planners toward threats internal to the region. In the late 1980s, with Iran prostrate after eight years of war, the most likely threat was Iraq. Saddam fielded the fourth largest army in the world with nearly a million men and over 5,000 tanks.

Under Schwarzkopf, the "Iraqi Scenario" became the focus of CENTCOM planning. Wargames and studies, including the summer 1990 Global Wargame held at the Naval War College in Newport, Rhode Island, had demonstrated the difficulty the United States would have handling an Iraq drive into the Arabian peninsula. CENTCOM had itself held an Iraqi-focused exercise—Internal Look 90—during the last week of July.[65] Lieutenant General Charles A. Horner, General Schwarzkopf's air component commander, later recalled:

> We've been working this [a contingency air campaign against Iraq in the spring of 1990], from a theoretical standpoint, and I've been identifying the resources I would need to bring to the party if the party ever were to occur—in terms of command and control, in terms of types of airplanes, where you'd bed them down.
>
> Now the Air Force had about $1 billion worth of prepositioned equipment. All this stuff was over here [in Saudi Arabia] already—ammunition and fuel and things like that.[66]

On August 2, 1990, Schwarzkopf's staff was still tinkering with a draft plan—OPLAN 90-1002—that would have to guide Central Command through the coming crisis.

All of this planning and wargaming had indicated that a war against Iraq was likely to be costly, bloody, and protracted. The critical period of the campaign would be the first fortnight, during which the Iraqis were expected to drive south in an effort to overrun the ports and airfields that were needed to support an American buildup. Schwarzkopf had hoped that a prolonged regional crisis would enable the Americans to begin the buildup phase before the actual start of operations, but the Iraqis had rolled into Kuwait before a single American soldier had reached the theater. Fortunately, Saddam's army had stopped before continuing its drive into Saudi Arabia.

But if the United States had "dodged the bullet" in the gulf thanks to Saddam's limited objectives or fear of confrontation with the American military, the problem remained: how to drive the Iraqis from Kuwait. The American military services looked at this problem from very different perspectives. Senior U.S. Army leaders, facing hundreds of thousands of Iraqi troops dug into Kuwait, believed that a ground offensive could involve heavy loss of life and recognized that the bulk of these American casualties would be army personnel. Senior U.S. Marine Corps officers shared many of their army brethren's fears, although as a whole, the corps appeared less reticent about a military option. The U.S. Navy, which was already busily implementing the blockade, would play but a supporting role in any military campaign. Carrier aircraft and surface- and submarine-launched Tomahawk cruise missiles would suppport the overall air effort and provide close-air-support (CAS) for a ground attack. Navy amphibious ships could deposit marines along the Kuwaiti coast while surface combatants, most notably the old battleships such as the *Wisconsin*, provided gunfire support. Thus the navy could expect to suffer few casualties, perhaps a score of aircrew, should President Bush choose to force Saddam from Kuwait. The U.S. Air Force, while it would bear the main burden of any air war, would measure its losses in the hundreds, at worst, not the thousands expected by the army. Moreover, the air force's senior leadership believed that Saddam's military forces were grossly overrated and could be defeated, or at the minimum brought to the verge of defeat, by air power alone.

By mid-September, by which time the bulk of its planned deployable forces had arrived in the gulf, the U.S. Air Force was ready to go.[67] Staffs in Washington and Riyadh had developed detailed plans to devastate Iraq and its forces in an all-out air offensive.[68] When air force Chief of Staff General Michael A. Dugan flew to Saudi Arabia, accompanied by reporters Rick Atkinson of *The Washington Post* and John D. Morrocco of *Aviation Week & Space Technology*, Dugan elaborated on the state and nature of the planning. If the president chose the military option, under Operations Plan 90-1002 the United States would bring force fully to bear. Air power was "the only answer" to the dilemma of driving Saddam from Kuwait without heavy American casualties. "The cutting edge would be in downtown Baghdad," Dugan informed the reporters.[69] He noted that the air assets already in Saudi Arabia were about as powerful as those deployed in Europe to stop the Soviets. The air force chief of staff also dismissed the Iraqi army as "incompetent," and told the reporters that Saddam's air force had "limited military capability." "I don't mean to tell you that we won't lose any planes," Lieutenant General Jimmie V. Adams, deputy chief of staff for plans and operations cautioned, "but I think it's a manageable risk." In Dugan's view, marine and army divisions would secure bases in Saudi Arabia and launch diversions and flanking attacks. Air power would destroy the enemy's ability to resist so that the ground force can "walk in and not have to fight." Dugan also expressed concern about boredom if Desert Shield continued indefinitely.

Dugan's views were widely held within the air force and were shared by other non-U.S. Air Force aviators as well. Marine Corps Major General Royal N. Moore, Jr., commander of the Third Marine Aircraft Wing, told Melissa Healy, a *Los Angeles Times* reporter: "We have a theory, along with the Air Force and others, that we could roll back those guys, and I think we could do it very, very effectively. I'm not going to predict a cakewalk, but if we do it right, the casualties will be light, we hope."[70]

But on September 17 the secretary of defense fired Dugan. Cheney charged that the Air Force chief of staff's on-the-record remarks to the press "showed poor judgment at a sensitive time" and revealed "things we never talk about."[71] The air plan outlined by General Dugan did foreshadow the operation executed in January and February 1991. The air campaign was an all-out effort that struck downtown Baghdad on day one. And the ground war, as Dugan predicted, was a mopping-up operation.

Certainly, Dugan's frankness with the reporters, and not any interservice strategic debate, led to his dismissal. But the Air Force chief of staff's comments did reflect division within the American military hierarchy over strategy and the role accorded to air power. Dugan's publicly expressed views were at odds with those of General Schwarzkopf, the theater commander, who held the operational reins in Saudi Arabia, and the chairman of the JCS, General Powell. These U.S. Army generals were less than enthusiastic about entrusting the success of the American military effort to the U.S. Air Force and believed that army and marine corps ground troops would pay the price if the president chose to use military forces to liberate Kuwait. Schwarzkopf told one interviewer:

> Colin Powell and I understood very early on that a strategic bombing campaign in and of itself had never ever won a war and had never forced anybody to do anything if they wanted to sit it out. I don't think we ever believed exclusively that that would be it. So therefore we had already started talking about a ground campaign.[72]

Powell similarly told Congress in December:

> Many experts, amateurs and others in this town believe that this can be accomplished by such things as surgical air strikes or perhaps a sustained air strike. There are a variety of other, nice, tidy, alleged low-cost incremental, may-work options that were floated around with regularity in this town.
>
> The fundamental fatal flaw in all such strategies is that it leaves the initiative in Saddam Hussein's hands. He makes the decision as to whether or not he will or will not withdraw. He decides whether he has been punished enough so that it is now necessary for him to reverse direction and take a new political tack. Those strategies

may work. But they also may not. The initiative is left in Saddam Hussein's hands.[73]

In his public testimony before Congress, General Powell used this same line of reasoning—the problem of leaving the initiative in the hands of Saddam—in his discussion of economic sanctions.[74] But if, as Bob Woodward alleges, Powell, in fact, favored giving sanctions time to work, the chairman of the JCS was being less than frank with the American people's elected representatives.[75] Moreover, if Powell was willing to yield the initiative to Saddam in an effort to wait and see if sanctions would work, why was he unwilling to yield that same initiative to Saddam and to give the U.S. Air Force the opportunity to see if it could force the Iraqis from Kuwait with air power alone? Just what General Powell's views actually were, unfortunately, remains a mystery. Woodward's depiction of the chairman's thinking was contradicted by director of the Joint Staff, Lieutenant General Thomas Kelly, who stated that *no one* expected sanctions to work anytime soon.[76] Either Woodward or Kelly have misrepresented the views of the chairman of the JCS, or the director of the joint staff, the Congress, and the president of the United States were uninformed about what General Powell actually thought.

Whatever the chairman's views, the continued Iraqi buildup in the Kuwaiti Theater of Operations to a reputed force of over 360,000 men by mid-September, increased the concerns of Generals Schwarzkopf and Powell regarding the expected cost of a ground assault.[77] The U.S. Army did not share General Dugan's view of the "incompetence" of the Iraqi army. Fears of a bloodbath abounded. Official military estimates of casualties ran as high as 20,000, including 7,000 dead.[78] These projections were developed by the staffs of Central Command and the JCS and, not surprisingly, reflected the views, or fears, of Schwarzkopf and Powell. Ironically, the classified official estimates of casualties closely paralleled those of innumerable civilian "experts," many of whom were regular critics of United States defense policies, who also predicted heavy casualties, including as many as 10,000 American dead.[79]

But not everyone believed that the military option necessarily entailed turning Kuwait into an American abattoir. Like his predecessor General Dugan, Air Force Chief of Staff General Merrill McPeak, believed that air power could do the job. In an October meeting with General Powell, McPeak reportedly told the chairman:

Come on, Jesus . . . , this is a Third World country, a little one-city country for Christ's sake. We're making it look like World War III. We're going to get no style points at the end of this thing. We ought to be trying to make it look easy, instead of making it look hard. My worry is we wait too long.[80]

Colonel T. N. Dupuy, a noted military statistician, forecast the defeat of the Iraqi army in ten days of ground fighting, during which the United States would suffer 8,091 casualties, including 1,214 dead.[81] Joshua Epstein of the Brookings Institution, developed a model that predicted that casualties would range from 3,344 to 16,059, including 1,049 to 4,135 combat deaths.[82]

Why such disparity in casualty estimates? Perpetual defense critics who opposed the use of military force clearly had a reason to predict a bloodbath to forestall the military option. But what of the projections produced by the JCS and Central Command? Did generals Powell and Schwarzkopf, or their staffs, use casualty estimates in an attempt to influence policy?

Just how the American military came up with estimates of casualties in the 20,000 to 30,000 range remains unclear. During the Korean War, which in scale of deployment and nature of the fighting most resembled the situation faced by the United States in the fall of 1990, the American military suffered an average of about 1,000 battle deaths per month. Even using Korean War statistics, and ignoring the fact that casualty rates have declined throughout the twentieth century, it is difficult to understand how anyone, least of all the American military, could have forecast 7,000 to 10,000 killed in action.

Such dire estimates can be explained in part by the U.S. Army's gross overestimation of Iraqi military capabilities. The author of one army monograph termed Saddam's army "a devastating machine."[83] The study concluded:

At the present time were we to try to introduce American troops into a Middle East conflict, we would be placing them at great risk. To begin with, we could not field a force of the size required to adequately protect itself. We lack the necessary air and sea lift facilities to deploy troops from bases in CONUS and Europe to the area. And as discussed above, we probably could not count on the Gulf monarchs for support, which means we would have to operate from somewhere outside the region. To be sure, if we put our whole energies into the operation we could bring it off, but it would be tremendously costly.[84]

General Crosbie E. Saint, Commander in Chief, U.S. Army Europe, later admitted: "looking back, we should have known from the outset that the Iraqis were probably a pretty good tactical army, but not playing in our league."[85]

Schwarzkopf, Powell, and their staffs, at least those wearing army uniforms, reflected these views. Early in the operation, according to Schwarzkopf's own account, he gave the president "terrible advice," advising Bush that CENTCOM would need "about five times more force than I ended up getting, and that it would take seven or eight months longer than it actually took to do the job."[86] In mid-October, when Schwarzkopf's deputy arrived in Washington to brief the president, CENTCOM once again grossly overstated the difficulty of the task ahead.

By the middle of October, we had a completely robust strategic air campaign that was very executable, right down to the gnat's eyelash. We went back to Washington to brief the President, and we were told, "Oh, by the way, brief the ground plan at the same time." The ground campaign left everybody saying "umm, gee, uh," because my assessment as commander was you can't get there from here. So then the decision was made to send over the remainder of the forces.[87]

Indeed, the briefing, by Schwarzkopf's deputy, the marine commander, Major General Robert B. Johnston, on October 10, left the senior U.S. military leadership troubled.[88] The plans for the air war appeared well thought out and promising, but CENTCOM's admittedly hastily drafted outline for a ground war, which included an amphibious assault along the Kuwaiti coast combined with an Allied attack directly into the Iraqi positions in Kuwait, looked like a recipe for disaster. Schwarzkopf believed that he lacked adequate ground strength to do anything else, for example, to mount an outflanking operation around the Iraqi right. Nor did Generals Powell and Schwarzkopf believe that air power alone could win the war.

The Bush administration now faced a difficult decision. The president's patience with Saddam had been exhausted as early as late September.[89] The prospect of a quick solution to the crisis appeared to be nil. By mid-October, the first heavy units of the Army's First

Cavalry Division and the Third Armored Cavalry Regiment had reached Saudi Arabia.[90] The movement of CENTCOM's forces was nearly complete, but General Schwarzkopf considered the units thus far deployed to the gulf to be inadequate to assure success. General Powell supported Schwarzkopf and dismissed the views of those who argued that air power could force Saddam to withdraw.

The administration had little choice but to continue the buildup. As Secretary of Defense Cheney announced a few days later during a trip to Europe, reinforcement of Central Command would continue until Schwarzkopf indicated: "Okay, I've got what I need."[91] There was open discussion in the press of the decision to transfer M1A1 tanks from Germany to Saudi Arabia to replace the older M1s and M-60s of the army's 24th Mechanized Infantry Division and the Marine Corps' Seventh and First MEBs.[92] Reports now began to mention the possibility of troop movements from Europe to the gulf, although as part of a rotation plan, not as a reinforcement of Central Command.[93] But only days later, after not so subtle Saudi hints of a diplomatic settlement that might give Saddam a piece of Kuwait, the administration quickly announced that the troops headed from Europe to the Gulf would reinforce, not replace, those already there.[94]

As the administration debated policy and moved quickly to keep the coalition's hard-line toward Iraq intact, General Powell flew to Saudi Arabia to confer with Schwarzkopf.[95] Schwarzkopf wanted his forces—ground, air, and sea—virtually doubled, including the transfer of VII Corps from Germany to Saudi Arabia. Even in possession of such a force, Schwarzkopf still had doubts about the prospects of an offensive.[96] But before Powell had returned from Riyadh, the administration had announced its plans to deploy an additional 100,000 men to the gulf, although it continued to talk about troop rotation.[97]

At a White House National Security Council meeting on the afternoon of October 30, General Powell relayed Schwarzkopf's recommendations and request for substantial additional forces.[98] Secretary of Defense Cheney supported Powell. Contingency planning for such a massive redeployment had begun as early as August.[99] At the president's order, as many as 200,000 additional troops, including the U.S. Army's VII Corps in Bavaria, would move to the Persian Gulf from Europe and the United States. President Bush agreed, although the decision essentially ruled out the containment strategy and the possibility of troop rotation. Such a force would be too large to maintain in the desert forever, nor would there be sufficient forces to rotate the first wave units home. Either Saddam would draw the proper and rational conclusions and pull out of Kuwait, or there would be war.

The administration decided to delay the announcement of the decision to redeploy until November 8, after the mid-term elections. But the press sensed, and reported, the increasing likelihood of war.[100] So, too, did Saddam Hussein who placed his armed forces on "extreme alert" on October 30.[101]

Without a doubt, the decision to move additional forces to Saudi Arabia saved American lives. The extra months spent redeploying were not wasted. Planners refined their plans; the troops gained tactical and operational proficiency. Saddam's diplomatic isolation increased. International and domestic American political support for the military option grew.

Nevertheless, considering that the U.S. Army expected "to fight outnumbered and win" in Europe against Soviet forces far more capable than those of Iraq, the reticence of some American commanders to contemplate a ground war against Saddam's forces in Kuwait is surprising. By mid-November the allies had both quantitative and qualitative superiority in the air and the ratio of forces on the ground was far better than it would have been in the event of a Warsaw Pact invasion of Western Europe. Former Assistant Secretary of Defense Lawrence Korb noted that by January 1991 there would be more American military strength in the gulf facing Iraq than the United States had deployed in Europe to stop the Soviet Union.[102]

Moreover, the argument for the virtual doubling of the American forces deployed to the gulf was not based on estimates that additional assets would reduce casualties, but rather that without more units, as Schwarzkopf himself stated, "you can't get there from here." There is no indication that Schwarzkopf or Powell would have volunteered to launch an offensive had the political situation in Europe precluded moving units from Germany, or that these two army generals, denied additional ground forces, were anxious to give the green light to those air advocates who believed that air power could defeat Saddam. Moreover, the massive redeployment demanded by Schwarzkopf eliminated whatever slim chance there was of waiting out Saddam—the very policy option allegedly favored by General Powell.

After November 8, the Bush administration's gulf policy followed the traditional American two-track approach. Just as the eagle on the Great Seal holds both arrows and an olive branch in its talons, the United States prepared for war while seeking, if somewhat half-heartedly, a peaceful settlement. Reinforcements continued to pour into the Arabian Peninsula, giving the president a viable military option, while aggressive diplomacy increased the international pressure on Saddam and held the anti-Iraq coalition together.

Despite periodic reports about the unwillingness of America's allies to fight, or their eagerness to cut a behind-the-scenes deal with Saddam, once Bush decided to force the Kuwaiti issue with Saddam, coalition support increased. Late-October media reports about a Saudi-brokered settlement were soon replaced by stories about King Fahd's support for an air offensive against Iraq.[103] President Hafez al-Assad spoke openly of the need for a "military solution" and sent an additional armored division to Saudi Arabia.[104] In London, Foreign Secretary Douglas Hurd told reporters, "The crucial combination which might bring about a peaceful withdrawal is sanctions producing these shortages and the knowledge in Saddam's mind that if he doesn't go in peace he will be forced out."[105]

The Bush administration's decision to adopt a tougher line toward Iraq also found support at the United Nations. Both to increase the pressure on Saddam and to prepare the ground for a possible recourse to arms, in late November Ameican diplomats began sounding out the members of the Security Council on the possibility of passing a resolution setting a deadline for Iraqi withdrawal and allowing the use of force to liberate Kuwait.[106] High administration officials, including Secretary of Defense Cheney, speculated openly that Iraq was on the verge of developing a deliverable nuclear weapon, further restricting the window of opportunity for a diplomatic solution.[107] The United States also expressed concern about the impact of the Iraqi occupation within Kuwait. As early as August 1990, American military planners had viewed with concern the mass exodus of Kuwaitis from their country, the forced removal, disappearance, and death of thousands of others, and the movement of Iraqis and Palestinians into Kuwait. If this trend continued unabated, eventually the demographics of Kuwait would be so altered that there would be no nation to liberate. Moreover, Saddam would be able to stage and win an open plebiscite.

The U.N. Security Council responded with two additional resolutions. On November 28, 1990, the Security Council passed Resolution 677 condemning "the attempts by Iraq to alter the demographic composition of the population of Kuwait and to destroy the civil records maintained by the legitimate Government of Kuwait."[108] The following day, the Security Council passed Resolution 678 which authorized

Member States co-operating with the Government of Kuwait, unless Iraq on or before 15 January 1991 fully implements, as set forth in paragraph 1 above, the foregoing resolutions, to use all necessary means to uphold and implement resolution 660 (1990) and all subsequent resolutions and to restore international peace and security in the area.[109]

But Iraq showed no sign of backing down. On November 27, Foreign Minister Aziz told reporters: "Iraq, which believes in peace and justice, will never succumb to pressure and will struggle to achieve peace and justice in the region."[110] On the twenty-eighth, the state-controlled newspaper *Al Thawra* reported, "Any decision taken by the Security Council under the present U.S. hegemony is of no concern to us."[111] The next day, Saddam himself spoke:

If war breaks out, we will fight in a way that will make all Arabs and Muslims proud. . . . We are determined not to kneel down to injustice. . . . We don't underestimate the military might of the United States, but we belittle its evil intentions. If Allah wills that war should take place, the Americans will find that their Stealth plane is seen even by the shepherd in the desert, and is also seen by Iraqi technology.[112]

As if to underline Saddam's determination, on December 2 Iraq test-launched three Scud-type surface-to-surface missiles.[113]

Despite the tough talk, Saddam did act to relieve some of the diplomatic pressure on his country. On December 6, he announced the release of all foreign nationals, including Americans, some of whom had been held as "human shields" at various strategic targets in Iraq. If Saddam expected to receive the thanks of the Western powers, he must have been disappointed. President Bush remarked: "The release of all the hostages would be a very good thing, but the problem is the aggression against Kuwait, and the man must leave Kuwait without reservation, without condition."[114] Moreover, Saddam's minor public affairs coup was undone only days after the last hostages had left Baghdad when Amnesty International issued a report highlighting "widespread abuses of human rights" in occupied Kuwait. *The New York Times* noted:

The report lists 38 methods of torture used by Iraqi forces, including beatings while the victim was suspended from a rotating ceiling fan, rape of women and young men, stubbing out of lighted cigarettes on victims' eyeballs and tethering victims in the burning sun for hours without water.[115]

As Americans welcomed home the hostages and celebrated the December holidays, in Baghdad the Iraqi leadership gathered for a top-level meeting. Saddam continued to spout a hard line. An official newspaper warned that if attacked, Iraq would inflict a monumental defeat on the Allies leaving only "a few insane or semi-insane soldiers who had escaped the furnace of battle . . . to tell generations about the harm inflicted on them" by President Bush's decision to go to war.[116] Nevertheless, after the passage of Resolution 678, Saddam decided to accept the offer Bush had made that Foreign Minister Aziz come to Washinton and Secretary of State Baker go to Baghdad.[117]

For the next week, the diplomatic debate centered around the issue of when such meetings could take place, rather than the critically important questions at hand. Saddam wanted Secretary of State Baker to come to Baghdad on January 12. But the Bush administration believed that the Iraqis, by choosing a date so close to the January 15 deadline, were stalling.[118] Nevertheless, the president, facing a congressional debate on the war, had to demonstrate some give. As a compromise, the administration agreed to send Secretary Baker to Geneva, Switzerland, to meet with Foreign Minister Aziz on January 9.

The Geneva talks served only to demonstrate the intransigence of both Iraq and the United States. In press conferences that followed the end of the talks, both Baker and Aziz expressed disappointment at the lack of results, but gave no indication that there were any areas of potential agreement. The Iraqis refused to pull their army out of Kuwait; the Americans refused to accept anything less than a complete and unconditional withdrawal. Baker focused strictly on Kuwait. Aziz attempted to broaden the discussion to include other Middle Eastern questions, especially Palestine. Back in Washington, President Bush held a news conference and told reporters that the United States had received "a total stiff-arm, this was a total rebuff."[119] Aziz even refused to carry a letter from the president to Saddam. In the letter, President Bush had warned:

We prefer a peaceful outcome. However, anything less than full compliance with U.N. Security Council resolution 678 and its predecessors is unacceptable.

189

There can be no reward for aggression. Nor will there be any negotiation. Principle cannot be compromised. However, by its full compliance, Iraq will gain the opportunity to rejoin the international community.

More immediately, the Iraqi military establishment will escape destruction. But unless you withdraw from Kuwait completely and without condition, you will lose more than Kuwait.

What is at issue here is not the future of Kuwait—it will be free, its government will be restord—but rather the future of Iraq. This choice is yours to make [italics added].[120]

But Saddam had already made his decision. According to *Time* magazine, Saddam's half-brother, Barzan Tikriti, phoned Baghdad immediately after the meeting and told the Iraqi president that the Americans did not want a fight.[121] If accurate, the report illustrates the poor advice Saddam received from his closest advisers. The fact that *Time* magazine learned of the call may also indicate that the United States intercepted the discussion between Barzan and Saddam and knew of the latter's decision. In any event, Saddam announced: "We are not of the type that bows to threats, and you will see the trap that America will fall into. . . . If the Americans are involved in a gulf conflict, you will see how we will make them swim in their own blood."[122]

With the Geneva talks completed, the administration next focused on the pending congressional debate on the crisis. For two days senators and congressmen called for their colleagues to support or reject a resolution to authorize the president to use the armed forces of the United States to implement U.N. Security Council Resolution 678. Many of the speeches were eloquent; many were absurd. But on Saturday, January 12, the Congress passed a joint resolution giving the executive branch the authority it already believed it possessed.[123]

The die was cast. As the diplomats stumbled toward war, land and air assets continued to pour into the Arabian Peninsula. Scores of ships took up positions in the eastern Mediterranean, the Red and Arabian seas, and the Persian Gulf. By mid-January the coalition had deployed over 150 ships and 2,000 aircraft. Nearly twenty Allied divisions encircled Iraq.

In the final weeks and days before January 15, the military completed its preparations for war. Allied naval forces continued to enforce

190

the blockade against Iraq. By January 16 coalition ships had intercepted 6,960 vessels, boarded 832, and diverted 36 carrying illegal cargoes. Air, ground, and naval units conducted exercises in and around the Arabian Peninsula.

Many of these exercises were intended to do more than just improve the basic skills of allied soldiers, airmen, and sailors and to work out the problems in a complex joint and combined command structure. General Schwarzkopf later noted:

> We continued our heavy operations out in the sea because we wanted the Iraqis to continue to believe that we were going to conduct a massive amphibious operation in this area. I think many of you recall the number of amphibious rehearsals we had, to include Imminent Thunder, that was written about quite extensively for many reasons. But we continued to have those operations because we wanted to concentrate his forces—which he did.[124]

These rehearsals, observed by a press corps routinely fed information, not all of which was accurate, were part of a massive deception campaign designed to confuse Saddam and to camouflage the accurate reports that occasionally found their way into the press with cover stories.

Unfortunately for the people of Iraq, Saddam's greatest source of deception came from within. In a January 15 visit to his senior generals in occupied Kuwait, Saddam expounded on his belief in his divine destiny. The decision to invade Kuwait "was that of God Almighty," he told his commanders. Saddam then explained why he believed Iraq would triumph.

> One of the odd facts that is necessary for you to know—I personally only knew of it yesterday—is that the emblem of Bush's party is the elephant. When I heard of it I was completely surprised. I said: "Praise be to God, Praise be to God."[125]

Saddam recited a passage from the *Koran* to the generals.

> Have you not considered how Allah dealt with the Army of the Elephant? Did he not foil their strategem and send against them flocks of birds which pelted them with clay stones, so that they became like plants cropped by cattle?

Saddam's analogy was, in fact, perfect, although he had his symbolism reversed. The "flocks of birds" that would shortly appear over Kuwait and southeastern Iraq would be those of the Allies, perhaps doing Allah's will, perhaps not. The elephants were Saddam's tanks, a force that would soon be "pelted" from the air with bombs and missiles and become "like plants cropped by cattle." Saddam was as poor a prophet as he was a general.

CHAPTER TEN

A COMMANDER'S DREAM

—•—

Planning Desert Storm

Reaction in the United States to the Iraqi invasion of Kuwait reflected the long heritage of American interests and involvement in the Persian Gulf. Bush administration pronouncements about why the United States had drawn a line in the sands of the Arabian Peninsula revealed the influence of the varied impulses—commercial, missionary, strategic, and geoeconomic—that had lured Americans to the region over the course of two centuries. While interest in oil, the life-blood of the West, was without doubt the primary factor that shaped American policy, no single concern could account for the intensity of President Bush's and the American people's reaction, just as no single set of interests had drawn Americans to the gulf.

The reality of that historical heritage also revealed itself in the doubts voiced by critics of Bush's policy. Some Americans doubted the wisdom or necessity of Desert Shield, viewing the operation as nothing more than an attempt to trade American blood for petroleum, to throttle a strong Arab nationalist, and an action taken in ignorance of the realities of the Arab world. Many more Americans supported Desert Shield but opposed any offensive military action designed to oust the Iraqis from Kuwait, preferring to wait until economic sanctions forced Saddam to yield. Fears that military action would lead to a bloodbath, an environmental catastrophe, or drag the United States into a Middle Eastern Vietnam were widely held in the United States. Many experts also predicted that military action could lead to a regional and perhaps even a global wave of anti-Western violence that would more than offset whatever might be gained in a war with Iraq.

Many of these same doubts plagued the inner circles of the Bush administration and the American military. The extent to which Saddam had surprised the United States on August 2 had evoked for the administration the specter of the political and foreign policy debacles that had befallen Carter a decade earlier. Americans had been caught incognizant in the Middle East once again. What other revelations might Saddam hold in store? What unforeseen events might transpire in the gulf? How could the United States avoid being dragged into a military and political morass from which it might not be able to extricate itself without another Vietnam-like catharsis?

President Bush, like Reagan and Carter, saw no alternative to American leadership in the Middle East. For that reason the administration could not allow such worries to deflect the United States from its confrontational course with Saddam. But concerns about what directions a Middle Eastern conflict might take were not ignored and did affect administration decisions. Bush recognized that he could not turn back the clock for the United States in the gulf, but that did not mean that he wished to see an open-ended American commitment in that region. He sought to the greatest extent possible to avoid even deeper postwar political and military involvement in the region.

Bush's aversion to potentially open-ended commitments shaped American military strategy. Despite the president's predilection to compare Saddam with Adolf Hitler, American strategists and planners of 1990 and 1991 did not approach the war with Iraq as their predecessors of the 1940s had with Nazi Germany. Bush's desire to limit postwar involvement explains why the United States did not plan to march on Baghdad to eliminate Saddam. There would be no postwar occupation of Iraq, no political effort to de-Saddamize a nation, the political, ethnic, and religious divisions of which Americans could barely understand, let alone manage.

After seizing Kuwait in August 1990, Saddam yielded the diplomatic initiative to the coalition and allowed himself to slip into a rather tenuous military position. He squandered whatever chance he had to win a battlefield victory when he passed up the opportunity to attack Saudi Arabia. His accord with Iran secured his left flank and rear, but so raised the domestic political costs of his venture in Kuwait that a diplomatic settlement became extremely unlikely. Saddam's lack of diplomatic finesse and misunderstanding of the West solidified the strength and staying power of the alliance arrayed against him. By the end of the year the Allied coalition was prepared to drive Saddam from Kuwait and had built up a large force that held both a quantitative and qualitative edge over the Iraqis on the sea, in the air, and even on land.

As the January 15, 1991, U.N. deadline for an Iraqi withdrawal approached, a successful military defense of Kuwait had become problematic. Allied amphibious forces could land along the Kuwaiti Persian Gulf coast; American paratroopers and airmobile elements could conduct a vertical envelopment into the Iraqi rear; Allied mechanized forces could move through the desert bypassing Kuwait to the west. The Iraqi army's lines of communication from Kuwait back to Basra and thence along the Euphrates to Baghdad were exposed to air and ground attack. Even the security of the Iranian front remained in doubt as Teheran announced that it planned to hold military exercises in mid-January along the border with Iraq. Saddam's commanders in the KTO had to guard against all of these possibilities since once active operations began, Iraqi ground forces would be hard pressed to react in the face of Allied air superiority.

In fact, Kuwait had become a veritable death-trap for the Iraqi army. Saddam's decision to pour more and more men and equipment into his newly conquered "nineteenth province" had not been a well-thought-out military strategy designed to defeat an Allied offensive, but a political strategy meant to deter such an attack by raising the specter of a bloodbath in the minds of Allied leaders. Despite the cloak of secrecy that usually hung over Iraqi military activities, beginning in the fall of 1990 Saddam routinely disclosed the strength of the units he sent to reinforce Kuwait. For example, in November, after the Bush administration announced that additional American forces would move from Germany and the United States to the gulf, the state-run Iraqi News Agency disclosed that Saddam Hussein had decided to reinforce the 450,000 men already deployed in Kuwait and southern Iraq with an additional 250,000 men.[1]

But Saddam greatly exaggerated the strength of his forces deployed in the south and General Schwarzkopf's army never faced 700,000 Iraqis in the KTO. Nevertheless, Allied intelligence continued to produce estimates of Iraqi strength closer to Saddam's propaganda than to reality. On January 17, the Department of Defense estimated Iraqi strength at 540,000, but after the end of the war, the estimate of Iraqi forces deployed in the KTO edged closer to 350,000.[2]

Saddam's deception campaign was thus partly successful and his political strategy for the defense of Kuwait was by no means foolish. Throughout the fall and into the winter of 1990 it worked quite well.

General Schwarzkopf was reluctant to initiate offensive operations against what he viewed as a huge Iraqi army deployed in the KTO. Most of the Allied nations were gripped by what, in retrospect, was an inordinate fear of a bloodbath in the desert.

Nevertheless, once the coalition decided to strike, the Iraqi forces in Kuwait were doomed unless Saddam promptly accepted U.N. terms and pulled out. Unfortunately for thousands of Iraqi soldiers and their families, Iraq's president had no intention to withdraw.

Only Saddam Hussein knows for sure why he decided to remain in Kuwait and to await an Allied assault. While he probably understood that he could not win such a war, he most likely expected to inflict substantial casualties on coalition forces. He hoped to bring the Israelis into the war with a barrage of surface-to-surface Scud missiles. He knew that despite the weakness of the Iraqi position in Kuwait, his army, which had withstood the pressures of war for eight years with Iran, was large and armed with chemical and biological weapons.

Allied military planners were well aware of both the strengths and weaknesses of the Iraqi position. American policymakers were also aware that the United States not only had to drive Saddam's army from Kuwait, but also had to do so in a convincing fashion. A quick and easy military campaign would help the country to exorcise the demon of the Vietnam conflict and enhance the deterrent value of the hopefully limited forces the United States would maintain in the gulf after the war. Politically, the Bush administration could not afford a bloody pyrrhic victory. As Secretary of Defense Dick Cheney reportedly confided to Prince Bandar: "The military is finished in this society, if we screw this up."[3]

Fortunately, American and Allied planners had nearly a half-year to devise a plan of attack. Not since the invasion of the Normandy coast of France in June 1944 had the United States military had so much time to plan a major operation. In Washington General Powell masterfully directed a redeployment of American military forces that was unprecedented in both its scale and rapidity, while for five and one-half months, Schwarzkopf's headquarters in Riyadh had the luxury to design an offensive campaign to drive the Iraqis from Kuwait.

Saddam inexplicably did nothing to hinder the buildup of the coalition forces. There were no missile strikes against debarkation ports; no attempted air attacks against concentrations of planes and troops; no commando raids into Saudi Arabia to strike at the TransArabian Pipeline (TAPLINE) that paralleled the border. As coalition forces poured into the Arabian Peninsula, Saddam's army sat entrenched in

Kuwait as if some invisible channel separated it from the Allied units to the south.

Nor could Saddam's timing have been poorer. He invaded Kuwait just as the Cold War wound down, but before the political momentum that accompanied the end of the nearly half-century-old Soviet-American struggle had resulted in the demobilization of substantial military assets. The American military had also just completed a decade of unequaled qualitative improvements in all the services. Morale and retention rates were at record highs. In 1990 the American military was probably at the peak of its post-World War II strength and efficiency. And, thanks to Saddam, as new United States units reached Saudi Arabia, instead of being thrust into immediate battle, they had months to acclimatize themselves to the conditions in the Arabian Peninsula and to train for desert warfare.

The 1980s had also been a decade of intellectual renaissance for the American military. "Reform" had swept the services.[4] The U.S. Marine Corps had discovered "maneuver warfare."[5] The U.S. Navy had developed its Maritime Strategy. The U.S. Army had worked out the details of what it termed AirLand Battle. The U.S. Air Force had been accorded a key supporting role by both the U.S. Navy and the U.S. Army within concepts of operations that envisioned a global conventional war fought against the Soviet Union.[6]

Iraq, of course, was not Soviet Russia. Saddam Hussein was the president of a small, Third World country confronting a powerful coalition that included the United States, Great Britain, France, numerous Arab states, and an assortment of other nations. Nevertheless, as the gulf crisis dragged on after August 1990 and Saddam failed to force the United States to fight a potentially bloody ground campaign to defend Saudi Arabia, many Americans began to view air power as a "surgical" means to force the Iraqis from Kuwait. Some of these air advocates believed that air power alone could win the war. Others expected the Allied air forces to play a leading role when, and if, fighting began, but thought that a ground campaign would still be necessary to liberate Kuwait.

General Schwarzkopf's thinking was somewhat paradoxical. He maintained steadfastly that air power could not independently win the war, although he acknowledged that his advantage in the air would give him the upper hand in any campaign. But since, as late as October 1990, Schwarzkopf did not believe that he could successfully initiate a ground war, he faced a dilemma: What if President Bush, for whatever reason, ordered offensive action to drive the Iraqis from Kuwait?

Schwarzkopf also knew that Saddam's strategic assets—such as atomic, biological, and chemical (ABC) warfare facilities—were mostly located in central Iraq, not Kuwait, and could only be reached and destroyed by air. Thus to the American commander, at least until Bush's October 30 decision to redeploy the VII Corps to Saudi Arabia, offensive action implied an air effort.

For these reasons, on August 8 Schwarzkopf requested air planning assistance from General Dugan, chief of staff of the Air Force. With the threat of an Iraqi invasion of Saudi Arabia still very real, and with his own headquarters divided between Riyadh and Tampa, Schwarzkopf needed help.

In the summer of 1990, the U.S. Air Force was in the midst of its somewhat belated renaissance of thinking. Since the end of the Second World War, the air force had focused on strategic nuclear warfare to the detriment of other applications of air power. Air force–army cooperation in AirLand Battle had addressed the question of air-ground teamwork on the battlefield, that is close-air support and air interdiction. But in the late 1980s the air force began to reconsider established concepts of air power in the light of new technologies and concluded that, under certain circumstances, the United States could successfully wage an independent, strategic, conventional air campaign.

Colonel John A. Warden, III's, *The Air Campaign: Planning for Combat* epitomized the new air force thinking.[7] The book, written while the colonel was a student at the National War College and first published in 1988 by the National Defense University Press, gained wide acclaim within the air force and, in a rare development for a government publication, was republished commercially. In his preface Warden wrote:

> *The Air Campaign* is, very simply, a philosophical and theoretical framework for conceptualizing, planning, and executing an air campaign. To the extent that it assists any planners in arranging their thoughts—before they are in the thick of battle—it will have achieved its ends.[8]

Ironically, in August 1990 it was Warden who was pressed into the "thick of battle." As deputy director of War-fighting Concepts, he found himself tasked by General John Loh, U.S. Air Force Vice Chief of Staff, to develop for CENTCOM a concept of operations for an aerial campaign against Iraq.

Led by Warden, the Air Staff, not the Joint Staff, quickly put together a plan for an air campaign.[9] On August 10, Warden led an Air Staff team to Tampa to brief General Schwarzkopf. The following day Warden and company briefed General Powell back in Washington. Powell then directed Warden to bring in the other services to further flesh out the plan. As a result, the Air Staff became a defacto joint staff. Warden next briefed an expanded, joint version of the plan, now code-named "Instant Thunder," for Schwarzkopf in Tampa on the seventeenth. Warden then flew back to Washington and thence to Riyadh, where he arrived Sunday evening, August 19. The next day, Warden briefed General Horner, CENTCOM's air component commander, and other members of the CENTCOM staff.[10]

Instant Thunder's concept of operations reflected Warden's thinking about the potential of an air campaign. He believed that air power could achieve the two basic military goals established by President Bush: to get Saddam out of Kuwait and to redress the regional balance of power. In his book, Warden had outlined five possible patterns an air scenario could take and had written of the second: "*Case II*, occurs when one side is able to strike its enemy anyplace, while the enemy can do little more than reach the front."[11] When Warden examined the aerial balance of power between Iraq and the coalition, he saw a Case II scenario, what he had termed in his book "the commander's dream." "Case II," he had written, "provides the opportunity for decisive action—action so decisive that the war can theoretically be won from the air."[12]

Warden's plan identified five strategic centers of gravity or vulnerabilities and arranged these in a series of concentric circles ranging from the center to the periphery: leadership, key production facilities, infrastructure, population, and field and military forces. Warden believed that given the strength and capabilities of the Allied air forces—especially precision guided munitions and stealth—air power could bypass the front lines and strike at the enemy's brain.

The idea of overflying the outer rings to strike at the center was hardly new. After the First World War, air power advocates such as the Italian Giulio Douhet had proposed using aircraft to reach over the front lines to avoid a bloodbath and to strike at the enemy's heart.[13] But attempts during the Second World War to carry out such theories foundered because Douhet's concept of attacking the enemy's population centers proved counterproductive and morally questionable, and the bombers of the 1940s lacked the ability to target key strategic centers with true precision.

By 1990, new technologies—highly accurate navigation systems, precision-guided munitions, stealth, airborne surveillance, and control systems such as JSTARS and AWACS—and the ability of Western air forces to strike the enemy around the clock in all weather had altered the air equation.[14] Warden believed that the United States could wage the

> first of the true inside outside wars where you start at the very hub of power and work your way out as opposed to the way we have had to fight wars in the past which was to start out there with the enemy army or fleet and gradually work your way in.[15]

The choice of the codename for the air campaign—Instant Thunder—also reflected the desire of the American military to avoid a repetition of the mistakes of the Vietnam conflict. During the Indochina war, air power had been applied in a controlled, escalatory fashion, designed to gradually increase the military pressure on Hanoi in an effort to force the North Vietnamese to the bargaining table. Rolling Thunder had been the codename for one of the major air offensives of the Vietnam War. But the Bush administration and the American military planned no such "rolling" escalation in the event of hostilities with Iraq. This time, the "thunder" from the air would not roll from south to north as it had twenty-five years before, but would be applied "instantly" throughout Iraq, striking downtown Baghdad in the opening salvo. There would be no sanctuaries; there would be no bombing halts.

Despite the many attributes of "Instant Thunder," there were both conceptual and practical problems with an air plan developed in the isolation of the jury-rigged "joint" Air Staff in the Pentagon. The plan did not entirely satisfy either General Schwarzkopf in Tampa or Lieutenant General Horner in Riyadh. As a result, Horner, the CENTCOM air component commander and Schwarzkopf's on-scene deputy in Saudi Arabia, decided that Central Command had to take control of the air planning. On August 19, Horner placed a secure call to U.S. Air Force Brigadier General Buster C. Glosson.

In mid-July, Glosson had been detached from the CENTCOM staff in Tampa and sent to the Persian Gulf as Deputy Commander of the Joint Task Force Middle East. He had coordinated the combined U.S.–U.A.E. exercise—codenamed Ivory Justice—in the days before the

Iraqi invasion of Kuwait. Once the war began, Glosson had returned to Bahrain and the JTFME flagship *LaSalle* from where he had coordinated air and naval operations in the northern and central Persian Gulf.

During their telephone conversation on the nineteenth, Horner explained to Glosson that the Central Command staff had heretofore focused totally, and understandably, on the immediate defensive aspects of Desert Shield. But Schwarzkopf was both unhappy and uncomfortable relying on the Air Staff for long-range air planning. Horner wanted Glosson to fly to Riyadh, take command of the air planning staff, and develop a CENTCOM air plan. Glosson would be given a "clean sheet of paper" and would not be bound by existing plans. Horner also made it clear to Glosson that any plan would have to become Schwarzkopf's scheme for an air campaign.[16]

Glosson that same day flew to Riyadh and quickly sketched out his own concept of operations. The following morning he attended a briefing of Instant Thunder. Like Warden, Glosson believed that technology had "caught up with Billy Mitchell's vision" and that air power alone could defeat Saddam Hussein.[17] But Glosson, like Schwarzkopf, thought Instant Thunder an overly ambitious, ruthless application of air power too air force–biased to be acceptable to CENTCOM's joint staff, most especially the commander in chief, Schwarzkopf.

Glosson's concept of operations was somewhat more surgical than Warden's and less focused on Baghdad. There were few differences between Glosson's and Warden's thinking about targeting Iraq's leadership, command and control centers, facilities where Saddam's weapons of mass destruction were manufactured, and Iraq's national infrastructure—oil, electricity, and bridges. But Instant Thunder virtually ignored the Iraqi ground forces, especially the Republican Guard, and Glosson knew that Schwarzkopf would never be comfortable with such a plan. Schwarzkopf and General Horner considered the Republican Guard "a strategic target."[18] Iraq's field forces had to be weakened, by air if necessary, to meet President Bush's goal of insuring postwar regional stability. Schwarzkopf wanted Saddam's army bombed and pinned in place as soon as an air war began.[19] There were concerns that while the Allied air forces were off bombing Baghdad, Saddam might send his army south into Saudi Arabia, threatening Schwarzkopf's ground forces and the bases from which the coalition air armada operated, or, more likely in Schwarzkopf's view, that the Republican Guard would escape north once the shooting started.

201

Despite these problems with Instant Thunder, Glosson recognized that Warden had saved CENTCOM's air planners from having to start their work at "ground zero." Glosson and his staff "fleshed out" and expanded the Instant Thunder concept of operations. Of Warden's seventy-eight targets, sixty remained in Glosson's original plan. And during the course of Desert Shield and Desert Storm, Warden's "joint" air staff continued to support Glosson's.[20]

But the actual air planning for Desert Storm was the work of General Horner, Brigadier General Glosson, and CENTCOM's "strike cell." In what became known as the "Black Hole," formerly a basement storage room in the headquarters of the Royal Saudi Air Force, Glosson's staff worked out the details of the air campaign.[21] As more accurate intelligence on Iraq reached the "Black Hole," the target list grew from about 60 to nearly 400.

By mid-September, CENTCOM's rapidly expanding multi-service, multinational staff had developed an air plan in which Glosson had full confidence. On September 13, he briefed General Powell who was then on a tour of American forces in Saudi Arabia. Precision and stealth, CENTCOM's chief air planner told the chairman of the JCS, would allow the Allies to attack Iraq around the clock, especially at night when Iraqi air defenses would be weakest. Coalition air losses would thus be minimized. The impact on the Iraqi infrastructure would be devastating.

Surprisingly, Glosson had directed his staff to develop the air plan without reference to specific forces. He was convinced that his commander in chief—President Bush—would provide whatever forces were deemed necessary to execute what was already being called Operation Desert Storm. In fact, by mid-September Glosson considered the air plan "doable."[22] As additional forces arrived in theater and intelligence on Iraq and its armed forces improved, Glosson's staff fine-tuned the existing plan, although its philosophy and overall structure remained the same. Additional forces allowed significant compression and simultaneity in the execution of the phases.

Despite the fact that Glosson's original air plan remained basically unchanged even after it became part of a larger effort that included a massive ground offensive, coalition officials throughout Operation Desert Storm portrayed the air effort primarily as a preliminary bombardment designed to soften up the Iraqi Army preparatory to the beginning of the ground war. The air plan itself had no distinct codename. Officially, there was only a single joint, combined military plan, within which air power was assigned a major role.

After the end of the war, when the extent of the destruction to Iraq's infrastructure became apparent, this obvious dichotomy in the implementation of Desert Storm caused some critics to see in the course of events a secret agenda that "went beyond purely military targets."[23] For example, the Allied air campaign had targeted the Iraqi electrical power system, reducing its output during the forty-three-day air war by 96 percent, from 9,013 megawatts to 340.[24] Such attacks had a far greater impact on Iraq's civilian population than on Saddam's military machine.

But the strikes against Iraq's electrical grid were not part of any secret plan. In his undelivered letter of January 9, President Bush had warned Saddam that "the future of Iraq" was at stake. The president intended to do whatever was necessary to gain "the security and stability of the Persian Gulf," and that meant weakening Iraq's industrial infrastructure.

Most importantly, the genesis of the air plan all but predetermined the extent to which the Allies relied on air power to defeat Saddam. In the late summer and fall, General Schwarzkopf, unable to launch a ground campaign to liberate Kuwait, had to give incredible leeway to his air planners. As a result, whatever the doubts of Generals Schwarzkopf and Powell about the capabilities of air power applied independently, Glosson found himself directing the development of an air plan that hopefully would make "it unnecessary to have a land campaign." Despite the subsequent reinforcement of Schwarzkopf's command, and the beginning of serious planning for a ground attack, the basic air plan remained unaltered. "We never changed the plan after the thirteenth day of September," Glosson recalled, "the only thing we did . . . was to do more of the plan simultaneously."[25]

Thus once Desert Storm began, the Allies initiated two parallel air wars. Elements of Lieutenant General Horner's massive air armada conducted an independent strategic air effort against Iraq while other air units focused their attention on the preparation of the battlefield and direct support for the ground campaign. Regarding Allied strategic attacks, such as those against the Iraqi electrical power generating system, Colonel Warden had written:

> It is also important to note that centers of gravity may in some cases be only indirectly related to the enemy's ability to conduct actual military operations. As an example, a strategic center in most states is the power generation system. Without electric power, production of civil and military goods, distribution of food and other essentials,

203

civil and military communication, and life in general become difficult to impossible. Unless the stakes in the war are very high, most states will make the desired concessions when their power generation system is put under sufficient pressure or actually destroyed. Note that destruction of the power system may have little short term effect at the front.[26]

On the whole, the American military establishment has down-played, for parochial service reasons, the extent to which the Desert Storm air planners sought Saddam's defeat through the application of air power. Air force officers were circumspect about their expectations, especially after the dismissal of the outspoken General Dugan. For example, General McPeak, Dugan's successor, later acknowledged that he had officially predicted higher Allied aircraft losses than he had privately expected. "You know," he admitted, "air power advocates over the years have gotten themselves in trouble bragging too much about what we're going to do, so I tried to nudge that and add in a little fudge factor in there."[27] While air planners in Washington and Riyadh clearly hoped to win the war with air power, generals such as Schwarzkopf, Powell, and others, were unwilling to acknowledge the existence of an independent air campaign, or that air power could potentially win the war without the need for a ground war. Powell and Schwarzkopf repeatedly stated that air power alone could not do the job. The army's unwillingness to admit that air power was anything but an adjunct, albeit an important one, to the ground campaign was made clear in one frank memorandum from General Saint, who commanded all U.S. Army forces in Europe.

> The operational value of airpower certainly made our job easier: we should give full credit where it is due. We are even willing to allow that there was an "air campaign" in the war since the attack on Iraq's nuclear and chemical production capability achieved one of the coalition's stated strategic objectives without other service assistance. Of concern, however, is the notion that the "air campaign" was everything before the ground war began. We ought not to let that assertion go unchallenged. There was only one campaign to achieve the strategic objectives of forcing Saddam's forces out of Kuwait and destroying their offensive potential.[28]

Despite such protestations, there clearly was an independent strategic air effort to defeat Saddam with air power. In a late December interview, Air Vice-Marshal Bill Wratten, deputy commander of Great Britain's military contingent deployed to the gulf, told reporters: "the air strike, once it has started and been allowed to run to its conclusion, could be conclusive."[29] Brigadier General Glosson commented: "I knew, and still believe, that air power could have accomplished the presidential objectives if we were able to wait for it to have its impact."

As Wratten, Warden, Dugan, Moore, Glosson, and others had expected, sustained Allied bombardment did cause Saddam to agree to withdraw from Kuwait, although the details and the terms for such a withdrawal remained to be negotiated when the Allied ground offensive began. Colonel John Warden was convinced that had the ground attack been delayed a few more days, air power would have defeated Saddam.[30] Air Force Chief of Staff McPeak was frank in his assessment: "My private conviction is that this is the first time in history that a field army has been defeated by air power."[31]

In its final evolution, the Allied air plan developed in Riyadh's "Black Hole" consisted of four interrelated phases. The first would last from seven to ten days during which the Allied air forces would "disintegrate" Iraq's integrated air defense system and gain air superiority and air supremacy. Coalition aircraft and ship-launched cruise missiles would destroy Iraq's command and control system, what General McPeak termed "attacking the brains and nervous system of the Iraqi ability to control their own forces."[32] Other aircraft would strike government and military headquarters, radio, telephone, and television centers, airfields, radar sites, SAM complexes, etc. The second phase would last only a day or two and would extend the phase one treatment to the less developed Iraqi air defenses in the Kuwaiti Theater of Operations (KTO). The third, and potentially longest phase involved attacks against Iraqi army units deployed in the KTO in preparation for the Allied ground attack. During the fourth and final phase, coalition air assets would support the Allied ground assault that would liberate Kuwait. Because Horner and Glosson had so many assets at their disposal, throughout the first three phases of the campaign, all types of Iraqi targets would be subjected to attack, although the emphasis on a particular set of targets within each phase would be maintained. During phase four, the attacks against phase one, two, and three targets would continue as Allied ground forces drove into Kuwait.

While the Allied air plan remained basically unaltered, at least conceptually, between September 1990 and January 1991, planning for the ground war underwent enormous change. At first, General Schwarzkopf's understandable concern about the possibility of an Iraqi thrust south into Saudi Arabia focused the attention of his staff on the defensive. In the fall, when Washington asked for a sketch of an offensive ground campaign, CENTCOM produced a plan for a direct drive into the heart of the Iraqi defenses in Kuwait. With only a handful of dependable, well-trained, well-equipped American units in the field, Schwarzkopf had no desire to attack, but if ordered to do so, intended to undertake an offensive-defensive operation. A drive into the heart of Kuwait would force the Iraqis to move the Republican Guard divisions south from their reserve positions in Iraq to engage the Allied units. Once on the move, the Iraqis would become vulnerable to coalition air attack.[33]

But as Saddam continued to strengthen his defenses in Kuwait, and further Allied ground reinforcements reached Saudi Arabia, the possibilities of a drive around the Iraqi right flank became obvious. As early as October, Schwarzkopf and his staff began examining the problems and possibilities of the left hook through the desert. Physical reconnaissance and the presence of Iraqi units along the Saudi border west of Kuwait confirmed that the area, described on the map as "sand and gravel" cut by numerous *sabkhas* (small salt marshes), was passable by mechanized forces. Perhaps most importantly, months of experience operating in the Saudi desert had demonstrated that units equipped with satellite-linked global positioning system (GPS) receivers could find their way through such featureless, trackless terrain.

Nevertheless, General Schwarzkopf was still concerned about the risks such an operation involved and, to insure its success, directed the development of an elaborate deception effort to conceal from the Iraqis the direction of the Allies' major thrust. As Winston S. Churchill observed in 1943, "In wartime, truth is so precious that she should always be attended by a bodyguard of lies."[34]

General Schwarzkopf developed his bodyguard of lies to convince Saddam that the threat of an amphibious attack from the Persian Gulf was real and that the Allies intended to drive due north, right into the heart of Iraqi defenses in Kuwait. To achieve this end, Schwarzkopf directed his staff to keep the growing coalition ground army concentrated between the sea and the Wadi al-Batin, as if poised for a direct assault into Kuwait. Allied engineers constructed a full scale replica of the Iraqi front-line defensive system and Coalition units conducted extensive minefield-breaching and trench warfare exercises designed both to prepare the units for an actual assault into Kuwait and to convince the Iraqis that the Allies' main thrust would come directly up the coast.[35] Schwarzkopf expected that several well-publicized, large-scale amphibious exercises would force the Iraqis to defend their seaward flank. In the air, frequent operational surges conditioned the enemy to seeing large numbers of Allied aircraft airborne just south of the border.[36] If all went according to plan, the opening of the air war and the left hook through the desert would take the Iraqis completely by surprise.

The actual Allied ground plan involved several elements. The Allied command hoped that initial Allied moves would reinforce the expectations that the deception plan had planted in Iraqi minds. American amphibious forces would maneuver off the Kuwait coast; U.S. Marine Corps and Allied Arab units would drive north into Kuwait; and the American First Cavalry Division would feint an attack along the Wadi al-Batin. Simultaneously, far to the west, French and American units of the XVIII Airborne Corps, aligned along the Saudi Arabian border in a sector virtually undefended by the Iraqis, would move north into Iraq, taking up positions to shield the Allied left flank and to cut Highway 8 south of the Euphrates River. Twenty-four hours later, the main drive would begin when the Allied VII Corps pushed through the Iraqi units deployed along the Saudi border west of the Wadi al-Batin and drove north-northeast towards the Euphrates. While all of these moves were taking place, Allied air assets would continue to pound Saddam's army, weakening its defensive power and making movement difficult.

Schwarzkopf's planners incorporated the most up-to-date military doctrine into the scheme for the ground campaign. U.S. Marine Corps "maneuverists," hoping to avoid a bloody frontal assault, developed plans for the rapid penetration and infiltration of the "Saddam Line." "Jedi Knights," a cadre of U.S. Army planners trained in concepts of maneuver warfare at the School of Advanced Military Studies at Fort Leavenworth, Kansas, helped General Schwarzkopf's staff develop the plan for the march around the Iraqi right flank.[37] The powerful American VII Corps, redeployed from Bavaria to Saudi Arabia, arrived in the desert imbued with AirLand Battle doctrine, comfortable with its own "capable corps concept" that incorporated ideas about the "non-linear battlefield" and the movement of large formations over "operational distances" as a prelude to the conduct of "hasty attacks" off the march.[38]

In fact, given the state of current U.S. Army doctrine, the size of the force deployed to Saudi Arabia, and the geography of the Kuwaiti

Theater of Operations, Schwarzkopf had little choice but to go around the Iraqi right flank. While operating west of the Wadi al-Batin was an option in October and November, once the second increment of Allied troops began to reach Saudi Arabia, a left flank march became a necessity. The front along the Kuwaiti-Saudi border between the Persian Gulf and the Wadi al-Batin is about 100 miles long. According to Lieutenant General Thomas Kelly, Allied ground forces totaled about seventeen division-equivalents.[39] Such a large force could not physically be employed in an effective manner along such a narrow front. Examination of the movement of individual Allied corps during the execution of the left hook reveals that many units, especially Arab formations, were squeezed out of front line positions on days three and four of the ground war because there was insufficient room for maneuver. U.S. Army doctrine did not envision such a narrow concentration of forces in a campaign of maneuver, that is the type of campaign General Schwarzkopf and other senior American military and political leaders wanted to fight, as opposed to the set-piece, slugging match Saddam preferred.

The geography of the front also lent itself to an outflanking attack. The Iraqi lines of communication ran along the Euphrates at an angle to the front and were vulnerable to an Allied attack to the west of Kuwait. The Army's AirLand Battle operational manual—FM 100-5— offered a historical example of the effective use of maneuver against enemy lines of communication in just such a situation.[40]

Army doctrine also included two forms of potentially decisive maneuver intended to bring one's army into contact with the enemy without a head-on assault. Envelopment sought to bypass the enemy's front and to strike at his flank, assailing his force where it was weakest.[41] A turning, or encircling, movement sought to "avoid the defense entirely" and to reach deep into the enemy rear, threatening his lines of communication. Other possible elements of a turning movement included amphibious landings and airborne drops.

General Schwarzkopf, loathe to risk any undertaking that might result in high Allied casualties, chose not to employ his amphibious or airborne units. The Fourth and Fifth Marine Expeditionary Brigades, to the disappointment of many, but by no means all marines, conducted a useful feint, but performed no combat assault during the course of the campaign. The U.S. Army's 82nd Airborne Division was used as a light infantry division during the course of operations and performed no airborne assaults. Nor was Schwarzkopf willing to risk all on a sweeping, turning movement into the Iraqi rear. After reaching the Euphrates, the XVIII Corp would send only a single division—the 24th Mechanized Infantry Division—on a long flank march towards Basra, deep in the Iraqi rear. The main American thrust would involve a less risky, and potentially less decisive enfilading movement by the VII Corps, a powerful mechanized formation, capable of sustained offensive or defensive operations against the Iraqi flank.

Lieutenant General Fred Franks's VII Corps formed an armored juggernaut that General Schwarzkopf intended to sweep around the Iraqi flank. Franks's four American and one British divisions fielded over 2,000 armored fighting vehicles and comprised the most powerful formation in the theater. Nothing, not even Saddam's Republican Guard, could match the firepower and maneuverability of VII Corps. If the deception effort succeeded as planned and Iraqi reserves were drawn south into the battle along the Kuwaiti-Saudi border, Franks's corps could swing around the Iraqi right and trap Saddam's forces in Kuwait.

Surprisingly, despite the overwhelming advantages possessed by the Allies, of which complete air supremacy and Franks's VII Corps were but two, General Schwarzkopf at his now-famous briefing of February 27 termed his plan of attack a "Hail Mary play." "I think you recall," Schwarzkopf told the assembled press and millions of Americans watching television at home, "when the quarterback is desperate for a touchdown at the very end, what he does is he sets up behind the center, and all of a sudden, every single one of his receivers goes way out to one flank, and they all run down the field as fast as they possibly can and into the end zone." But on February 24, the day the ground war began, General Schwarzkopf was hardly facing a "desperate" military situation. Saddam, not Norman Schwarzkopf, stood on the brink of defeat. A far more appropriate football analogy would have been to the old "student body left" play in which an overwhelmingly powerful and dominating offensive line leads the ball carrier around the end.

Since the birth of the "Hail Mary" analogy, there has been quite a bit of hyperbole concerning the plan for, and the execution of, the ground war. Participants, most analysts, journalists, and others who have written about or discussed the war have portrayed the plan for the ground phase of Desert Storm and the deception effort as a complete success. General Schwarzkopf commented at one point: "We just went right around them." Lieutenant General William "Gus"

Pagonis, Schwarzkopf's chief logistician, termed the ground campaign "the most deceptive operation in history . . . better than D-Day every was."[42]

Given the enormity of General Schwarzkopf's accomplishments, Desert Storm must, in fact, be judged a tremendous victory. Routing such a large enemy army while taking so few friendly casualties was an incredible achievement. But that does not mean that everything went according to plan or that Desert Storm succeeded because of the success of the deception effort.

Two points must be made about General Schwarzkopf's deception plan. First, the delayed deployment of two entire corps to the west of the Wadi al-Batin, an area traversed by just a single road, was a logistical nightmare and imposed real hardship on the troops. Lieutenant General Pagonis wanted to move the units earlier. Even General Schwarzkopf has admitted that the decision to delay the move of VII and XVIII Corps bought him "a lot of guff." "They fought me all the way," Schwarzkopf commented.[43] Second, it is not clear that the deception plan worked. The official Department of Defense report on the conduct of the war concluded that Schwarzkopf's "enveloping armored thrust in the west *appears* to have been unexpected."[44] The Defense Department was wise to qualify its statement since there is evidence that the Iraqis were not entirely taken in by the Allied scheme.

For the Iraqis, the military defense of Iraq involved myriad strategic and operational problems. Saddam's troops faced threats from the sea on their left, in their center directly up the coast, and through the desert around their right, or western, flank. To guard their left and center the Iraqis garrisoned Kuwait's Persian Gulf coast with between five and seven divisions and fortified the Kuwaiti-Saudi border. To claim that these actions were the direct result of the Allied deception effort is absurd. As early as the second week of August the Iraqis had begun digging in along what became known as the "Saddam Line." And as long as the Allies had amphibious forces deployed at sea, Saddam had to guard the coast. Iraqi dispositions on the left and in the center were dictated by circumstances, not by any deception plan. The two American marine brigades kept at sea possessed far more fighting power than the five to seven Iraqi divisions strung along the Kuwaiti coast.

The Iraqi right flank posed a special problem. Saddam, whatever the size of his army, did not have sufficient forces to defend Iraq's entire border with Saudi Arabia from Kuwait to Jordan. Somewhere in the desert west of the Wadi al-Batin there had to be an exposed Iraqi flank. Historically in desert campaigns, such as those of the Second World War, attackers have struck their enemy's open desert flank.

The standard defense to meet such an assault is to refuse one's flank, that is, draw back formations on the exposed flank, and to station powerful, mobile reserves in the rear to counter any force that swings around the flank. An armored engagement then decides the course of the battle, and perhaps the campaign.

An examination of Iraqi dispositions on the eve of the ground war— evident in the charts used in General Schwarzkopf's February 27 briefing and those published in the Defense Department interim report on the war—indicate that the Iraqis were deployed to meet an Allied flanking move or, in fact, to meet any likely contingency. About eighteen of Iraq's forty-three divisions deployed in the KTO, including four of Saddam's six armored and seven of his eight Republican Guard divisions, were positioned in the path of VII Corps. The Iraqis positioned the heaviest concentration of their mobile forces not in the rear of the front in Kuwait, but to the northwest where Saddam's mechanized reserves were centrally positioned: These forces could then move south to check an advance into Kuwait or southwest to meet a drive around the army's exposed right flank. There is anecdotal evidence that at least some of these reserve Iraqi formations were facing southwest on the eve of the Allied ground offensive, as if they expected an attack from the desert.

The Department of Defense has also released images of Iraqi dispositions and movements on February 24 that belie reports that Saddam's commanders were taken in by the Allied deception plan. One picture of the front on February 24 clearly shows Allied formations closing on Iraqi defenses in southern Kuwait, while to the north Iraqi mobile columns are moving not south toward the developing battle, but west into blocking positions.[45] A similar image, taken somewhat later on the twenty-fourth, shows Iraqi columns moving into hasty blocking positions, again facing west.[46] Since the advance of the VII Corps had not yet begun, these images imply, at the least, that the Iraqi high command expected an Allied outflanking movement and that once the ground campaign commenced, began moving mobile units to meet such a thrust.

Nor does one have to accept as fact the success of the deception plan to account for Allied victory. Schwarzkopf's bodyguard of lies was meant to convince the Iraqis that the main Allied drive would

211

come directly up the coast. Yet the coalition units committed to the direct thrust north smashed through the Iraqi positions with ease. Even if Saddam had possessed a copy of the plan for Desert Storm, his army could have done little, if anything, to counter the Allied offensive.

What surprised the Iraqis the most was not the direction of the Allied advance, but its speed and violence. The Iraqis may have expected the coalition units to emerge from their trek bewildered, low on supplies, having left behind broken-down tanks and vehicles strewn for miles across the trackless desert, much as Saddam's own mechanized formations ended their assault on Kuwait. After all, since August the Iraqi president had underestimated the striking power of the American military. He had little appreciation of the power of the Allied air arsenal, or of the reality of modern, mechanized, mobile warfare. That was why in July 1990 he ignored the possibility of an American reaction and invaded Kuwait. That was why he continued to ignore the not-so-veiled threats of Allied military action. That was why in the early hours of January 17, Saddam, his senior military and political leaders, his army, and the Iraqi people were relegated to the role of targets for a coalition air effort that in its first twenty-four hours flew more sorties than the Iraqi air force had flown in the eight years of the Iran-Iraq war.

CHAPTER ELEVEN

JUST THE WAY IT WAS SCHEDULED

—•—

The Storm from the Air

As the gulf crisis developed, air power held many attractions to Americans. Reliance on an air assault offered a means to defeat Saddam without a ground war and possibly heavy casualties. But the importance of the air campaign as a component on Allied strategy also reflected the long U.S. effort to avoid engagement in the region. Air power is a standoff application of military might, an impersonal venture that can be undertaken without "getting down and dirty." Americans could not only avoid a potential bloodbath, at least for their own troops, but also protect their interests in the Persian Gulf without allowing the enemy the opportunity to grasp an American army and drag it into a quagmire of unforeseen consequences.

In the early morning hours of January 17, hundreds of Allied aircraft filled the skies over Saudi Arabia, the Persian Gulf, and the Red Sea. Similar concentrations of Allied power had taken to the air at least six times over the previous two months. But these coalition aerial displays had been part of a deception plan designed to accustom Iraqi radar operators to images of masses of approaching aircraft. The planes had always stopped short of the Iraqi border and turned away. This time they turned south again, although only momentarily, and as they did Stealth fighters—F-117A Nighthawks—peeled off and sped undetected toward their targets in Iraq.[1] H-Hour, the starting time for Desert Storm, 3:00 A.M. January 17, 1991, was at hand.

As the coalition armada took to the skies over the Arabian Peninsula, back in Washington President Bush spent the early evening hours of

213

January 16 watching the news in a small study off the Oval Office with Vice President Quayle, National Security Adviser Brent Scowcroft, Chief of Staff John Sununu, and Press Secretary Marlin Fitzwater. About 6:35 P.M., ABC and CNN reported antiaircraft fire over Baghdad. H-Hour was still twenty-five minutes off—7:00 P.M. Eastern Standard Time—and the sporadic fire indicated that the Iraqis were nervous, but also alert. Minutes later, correspondents in Baghdad reported explosions. "This is just the way it was scheduled," Bush commented. At the president's direction, Marlin Fitzwater hurried to the press room and announced that "the liberation of Kuwait" had begun. Two hours later, Bush himself addressed a nation at war.

On the morning of January 15, the president had signed, but not dated, a National Security Directive authorizing the attacks. Secretary of Defense Cheney had then sent an execute order to General Schwarzkopf.[2] Operations Order 91-001, dated January 17, listed the official objectives for the military effort: "attack Iraqi political-military leadership and command and control; gain and maintain air superiority; sever Iraqi supply lines; destroy known chemical, biological and nuclear production, storage, and delivery facilities; destroy Republican Guard forces in the KTO; and liberate Kuwait City."[3] The proverbial die was cast. The final preparations were completed. The Bush administration notified the congressional leadership as well as key allies. The months of debate and waiting had come to an end.

The aerial assault began minutes before H-Hour when F-117As and American Special Operation Forces destroyed key Iraqi radar warning sites in western and southern Iraq. These attacks blinded the defense as the coalition aerial armada penetrated Iraqi airspace.

At 3:00 A.M. local time, other F-117As began hitting their targets in and around Baghdad. The city's lights were still burning. Laser-guided bombs (LGBs) fell on communications buildings, command and control facilities, headquarters for the internal security and intelligence agencies, and the presidential palace. U.S. Navy Tomahawk cruise missiles struck soft targets such as the capital's electrical power plants and substations. Simultaneously, other Allied strike aircraft attacked sites from one end of Iraq to the other.[4]

Under the original air plan as developed back in August and early September, a massive second wave strike would have hit the capital, but following General Dugan's comments about bombing "downtown" Baghdad, Brigadier General Glosson and his staff had revised the plan. The second wave now included U.S. Navy planes carrying decoys that emitted the electronic and radar signatures of attacking aircraft, and other Allied planes armed with High-Speed Anti-Radiation (HARM) missiles designed to home in on active ground-based radars. Glosson assumed that the Iraqis, having read accounts of General Dugan's interviews with the press, would expect a massive strike and thus could be lured into turning on their equipment as the decoyled attack materialized. HARMs would then wreak havoc on the capital's air defense system.[5] The Iraqis responded as Glosson had expected and they suffered accordingly. A third wave of F-117s next struck Baghdad and met noticeably less opposition.

Not everything went as well for the Allies as first reported. A much-heralded Special Operations Forces attack against an early-warning radar site in southern Iraq, for example, was initially portrayed as a complete success. According to *Newsweek*, the operation was critical to the opening phase of the air campaign because the Special Operations Forces had to punch a hole in the Iraqi air defenses through which "hundreds" of planes would later pour. The attack, the report stated, needed "split-second timing; if it failed, the air defenses around Baghdad would light up like the Fourth of July."[6] In fact, the operation was designed to clear a route for eighteen F-15E Strike Eagles headed toward a Scud site. And while the attack was an outstanding success, the strike occurred too early and alerted the Iraqis to the developing assault. Fifteen minutes before the first F-117s reached Baghdad, the Iraqis began to fill the skies over the capital with anti-aircraft fire.[7]

Nevertheless, the initial Allied strikes were an overwhelming success. The Iraqi air defenses were blinded, confused, and then subjected to a devastating attack. The few Iraqi aircraft that took to the sky were downed or driven off by Allied fighters. Critical command and communications facilities were destroyed or badly damaged. In the judgment of U.S. Air Force Chief of Staff McPeak, "the Iraqi Air Force never recovered from this opening attack."[8] And the Allied air forces achieved these initial successes with minimal loss. The coalition flew 2,388 sorties on January 17, but lost only two planes—a U.S. Navy F/A-18 Hornet and a Kuwaiti A-4KU—over enemy territory. One French Jaguar limped home in such poor condition that it was considered lost in action.

The low number of Allied air losses came as a pleasant surprise in Washington. Many experts had predicted air losses in excess of 500 for a forty-day campaign.[9] Coalition air planners expected to lose about 150 aircraft, mostly in the early phase of the campaign before the Iraqi air defenses were degraded. The success of the initial attacks meant that the Allies could expect the loss rate to remain low. In fact, during the entire forty-three-day campaign, the coalition lost only thirty-six fixed-wing aircraft in combat.[10] The twenty-eight American aircraft lost in action represented an incredibly low attrition rate of .03 percent![11]

There were myriad reasons for the Allies' mastery in the air. In virtually every category the coalition air forces held both a qualitative and quantitative edge. The Iraqis were outnumbered by at least three-to-one and their bases were subject to attack from all directions. Of the 700 plus Iraqi aircraft, only a handful—about 75 French Mirage F-1s and 50 Soviet-made MiG-29s—were comparable to the standard Allied aircraft such as the American "Teen" fighters—the F-15 Eagle, F-16 Falcon, F-14 Tomcat, F-18 Hornet—and the European-designed Mirage 2000 and Tornado F3s. Nor were the Iraqi pilots well trained compared to their Western or Arab counterparts. Soviet flight instructors referred to their Iraqi students as "stoneheads." During the course of the campaign, the Iraqis downed more of their own planes than they did Allied aircraft. According to analyst Norman Friedman, on January 17 one Iraqi pilot flying a MiG-29 downed his flight leader, then flew into the ground himself.

> It appears the Iraqi pilots taped down the air-to-air radar button so that it locked onto the first target it acquired. They also held down the trigger so that lock-on caused immediate launch. The second pilot apparently became fixed on the fireball caused by the first MiG.[12]

Considering that the MiG-29s were the most advanced aircraft in the Iraqi arsenal, and most likely were flown by the best of the Iraqi pilots, it should be little wonder that the Iraqi air force failed to down a single Allied aircraft in air-to-air combat during the entire war while losing three-dozen of its own planes in the air.

Allied pilots were exceedingly well trained. Most American fighter and attack aircraft crews had spent time at advanced training facilities such as the U.S. Navy's Fighter Weapons School at Miramar Naval Air Station (Top Gun) and the Naval Strike Warfare Center at Fallon, Nevada, or Nellis Air Force Base, also in Nevada, where the U.S. Air Force conducted its Red Flag exercises on a range larger than Kuwait. Whereas Iraqi pilots were totally ineffective in the air, on several occasions Allied pilots scored multiple kills.[13]

A good example of the state of training and skill of Allied pilots and the flexibility of coalition aircraft came on the first day of the air war. A strike package of Carrier Air Wing 17 from the carrier *Saratoga*, operating in the Red Sea, headed for a target in western Iraq. The crew of an alert E-2C Hawkeye detected a pair of Iraqi MiGs speeding toward some of the *Saratoga*'s in-bound "shooters" and alerted the aircraft to the enemy's approach. Two F/A-18 Hornets, piloted by Lieutenant Commander Mark Fox and Lieutenant Nick Mongillo, responded, switching from air-to-ground, to air-to-air mode in their aircraft. Almost immediately, Fox's radar locked up one of the MiGs and he fired a heat-seeking, all aspect Sidewinder followed by a radar-guided Sparrow missile. Mongillo fired a Sparrow at the second MiG. Forty seconds after the Hawkeye's warning, both MiGs had been destroyed. The Hornets switched back to air-to-ground mode and resumed course to the target, which they bombed.[14]

Perhaps the Allies' most significant advantage was in the area of command and control. U.S. Air Force E-3A Sentry AWACS and U.S. Navy E-2C Hawkeyes controlled and monitored the movement of hundreds of coalition aircraft over Iraq, the Arabian Peninsula, the Red Sea, and the Persian Gulf. Not a single Allied aircraft fell to a friendly plane in a "blue-on-blue" engagement. Iraqi aircraft that took to the air were quickly detected, attacked, and usually destroyed by coalition fighters flying offensive or defensive combat air patrols.

What AWACS did for the air war, the U.S. Air Force E-8A Joint Surveillance and Target Attack Radar System (JSTARS) did for the ground war. Powerful signal processors on board the radar-equipped Boeing 707s could differentiate between the returns from wheeled and tracked vehicles, detect lines of concertina wire swaying in the breeze, and provide commanders with a comprehensive picture of the situation on the ground.[15]

JSTARS was not scheduled to become operational until 1997, although a prototype had participated in a NATO exercise—Deep Strike—during which VII Corps commander Lieutenant General Franks had used data supplied by JSTARS to identify, surprise, and counterattack an "aggressor" tank column. At Franks's suggestion, Schwarzkopf requested deployment of JSTARS and two E-8As were rushed to Saudi Arabia in time for Desert Storm.

Allied electronic countermeasures (ECM) aircraft, such as the U.S. Air Force EF-111A Raven, and U.S. Navy and Marine Corps EA-6B Prowler achieved unparalleled success fooling and blinding Iraq's defensive radar system while other aircraft destroyed surface-to-air missiles (SAM) launchers, radars, and command and control facilities, and other strategic targets. U.S. Navy aircraft, especially the Prowlers, proved particularly adept at SEAD (suppression of enemy air defense) missions.[16] American ECM did to Iraq's air defenses, albeit on a larger and more sustained scale, what they had done to Libya's on April 14, 1986, during Operation El Dorado Canyon. The Iraqis fired thousands of SAMs at Allied aircraft but scored only about ten hits during the war.[17] According to a U.S. Air Force report, after day four of the war "all allied aircraft operated with impunity in the mid and high altitude environment across the AOR."[18]

Of course, blinding the enemy's defense was a means to an end—putting bombs on target. Precision-guided munitions (PGMs) greatly enhanced the effectiveness of Allied air attacks. A PGM released during the gulf war was about 190-times more likely to hit the target than a bomb dropped by a Vietnam-era, and 9,000-times more likely than one dropped by a World War II aircraft.[19] According to official estimates, 90 percent of the 6,520 tons of PGMs dropped on or fired at enemy targets during the war were on target, whereas only 25 percent of the 81,980 tons of "dumb" bombs hit their mark. Thus, while the PGMs accounted for only 7 percent of the total delivered, they accounted for 22 percent of on-target ordnance.[20]

In the Gulf War air planners could assign a handful of PGM-capable aircraft to a target and expect a rate of success that in previous wars had necessitated the use of masses of planes. For example, strikes against enemy armored units during the Second World War generally took the form of carpet bombing, that is dropping massive patterns of bombs hoping that some would strike targets. But in the gulf, according to an air force report, "on several occasions, a two-ship of F-15Es with 16 bombs destroyed 16 tanks."[21] The air force pilots who excelled at hitting Iraqi tanks with 500-pound bombs termed the attacks "tank plinking."[22]

The low-flying, terrain-hugging U.S. Navy Tactical Land Attack Missile (TLAM) was one of several new technologies that debuted in Operation Desert Storm. Within the air tasking order, Allied air planners assigned the TLAM, known as Tomahawk, against targets in high threat areas. As a navy report noted, the missiles, "immune to human traits such as nervousness," had no problem flying in harm's way. Navy ships and submarines fired 288 Tomahawks, 98 percent of which launched successfully. About 85 percent of the missiles found their way to the target and inflicted "at least moderate damage."[23] While the TLAM's 1,000-pound warhead limited its usefulness against hardened targets, such as bunkers or concrete and steel bridge abutments, the missile's accuracy and ability to operate at night and in all-weather conditions gave mission planners added flexibility. The navy fired Tomahawks at chemical and nuclear weapons facilities, surface-to-air missile sites, command and control centers, and Saddam's presidential palace.

Without doubt, the technological star of the air campaign was the U.S. Air Force F-117A Stealth Fighter, known as the Nighthawk. The forty-two F-117As of the 37th Tactical Fighter Wing flying from "Tonopah East"—Khamis Mushait in southwestern Saudi Arabia—were the only manned Allied aircraft to strike targets in Baghdad.[24] On January 17, the F-117As comprised 2.5 percent of the "shooters in theater," but struck 31 percent of the targets.[25] During the entire war, the Nighthawks flew 1 percent of total sorties, but "covered about 40 percent of the strategic air campaign's target base."[26]

Stealth gave Allied air planners the advantages of surprise and freedom of action. Hard targets that had to be knocked out preparatory to other strikes, or targets that required extreme precision, such as the Presidential Palace, which is across the street from the Chinese Embassy, would be assigned to F-117As. The aircraft could carry a wide variety of ordnance, including bunker-busting 2,000 bombs.

Experience quickly demonstrated that the planes were so elusive that the Iraqi defenders frequently did not know Allied aircraft were overhead until bombs began exploding. Radar jamming by EF-111 Sparkvarks, for example, would often alert the Iraqis who would quickly, if blindly, fill the sky with antiaircraft fire. Even stealth technology was no defense against a random bullet. The Allies learned to delay the beginning of active electronic countermeasures until the Nighthawks had released their weapons and were making their escape. Although a few F-117As were reportedly slightly damaged by antiaircraft artillery (AAA), none were destroyed.

These Allied advantages in the air, combined with the devastating effectiveness of the initial attacks, established the tone for the remainder of the air campaign. After January 17, Iraq's defenses progressively weakened. The Allies biggest problem during the first week of the war was the weather, reportedly the worst in fourteen years. After D-Day's 2,388 sorties, the rate fell by about a quarter to a low of 1,842 on the twentieth, but then rose to 2,424 on the twenty-third.[27]

Unable to contest Allied control of the air, Saddam responded to the coalition offensive with surface-to-surface SCUD missile attacks against Saudi Arabia, Bahrain, Qatar, and most importantly, Israel. Only chemical or nuclear warheads, which Saddam apparently did not yet possess, would have made the SCUD a significant military threat. Armed with conventional, high-explosive warheads, the

SCUDs were useful only for terror attacks against large targets, such as cities.

During the war, the strikes against Saudi Arabia and the other Arab states were ineffective, except for one attack against Dhahran that killed twenty-seven Americans. Most of the SCUDs broke up during their downward trajectory, missed their target, or were downed by American-made Patriot antimissile missiles.

But eight SCUDs did strike the Israeli cities of Haifa and Tel Aviv on January 18. There were nervous moments in Washington as the initial reports from Israel indicated that the missiles had been armed with chemical warheads. The possibility of Israeli retaliation or entry into the war was the joker in the Allied deck. Israeli intervention might spread the conflict to Jordan and would have unpredictable repercussions among America's Arab allies.

Fortunately, the warheads were, and would remain, conventional. The damage inflicted upon Israel was more psychological than real. The United States responded quickly to insure Israel's restraint, sending a high-level diplomatic team to Jerusalem and rushing Patriot batteries from Europe to Israel. Central Command assigned additional assets to hunt mobile SCUD launchers, the number of which Allied intelligence had grossly underestimated. And the Israelis, well aware that Saddam's SCUD strikes were meant to provoke retaliation, wisely refused to play the Iraqi dictator's game.

There was nothing Saddam could do to reverse the inexorable course of the air war. Broadcasting "interviews" with obviously beaten Allied airmen who had been unfortunate enough to fall into Iraqi hands only further inflamed Western opinion and sparked discussion of war crimes trials. Day and night, missiles and bombs continued to fall on targets throughout Iraq and Kuwait.

After the first week of the air war, Secretary of Defense Cheney and Chairman of the Joint Chiefs of Staff Powell declared that the Allies had achieved air superiority. But Powell also stated clearly that the air war was part of a larger plan: "Our strategy to go after this army is very, very simple. First we're going to cut it off, and then we're going to kill it."[28] The campaign was proceeding, and would continue to proceed, as planned.

In Baghdad, the Iraqis recognized that after a week of war they could no longer put up an effective defense and had to change their tactics. Unable to contest control of the air, Iraqi radars started to go off the air on day eight. Because of the effectiveness of Allied Suppression of Enemy Air Defense missions, the environment for Iraqi SAM radar operators had become so lethal that it was suicidal to emit active signals.[29] The Iraqis had been reduced to area AAA fire and blind firing of SAMs.[30] They also undertook their biggest, and most successful operation of the war—the exodus to neutral Iran. By the end of the war, about 140 aircraft had taken refuge in Iran.

A frustrated Saddam's next move was to initiate a campaign of environmental terrorism, pumping an estimated 120 million gallons of oil into the Persian Gulf from Kuwait's Sea Island Terminal. But, again, air power provided the Allies with an effective response. On January 27, U.S. Air Force F-111 Aardvarks hit the manifolds that controlled the flow of oil from the storage tanks to the pumping station offshore.

By the end of January, the focus of Allied air attacks had shifted from strategic targets to battlefield preparation—phase III had begun. During a briefing on January 30, General Schwarzkopf detailed some of the results of the 30,000 plus sorties flown thus far. About 75 percent of Iraq's command and control centers and the electrical power system had been attacked, and about 60 percent of those had been either "severely damaged or destroyed." One-fourth of Iraq's electrical-generating facilities were "completely inoperative, and another 50 percent suffered degraded operations." These and other strategic targets would continue to be subjected to "systematic destruction." About 75 percent of Iraq's command and control system had likewise been struck. As the result of these attacks, Schwarzkopf told the press, "the Iraqis have abandoned centralized control of their air defense within Iraq and Kuwait."[31]

With phase III, the air war over the KTO began in earnest. By February 3, aircraft from the four American carriers operating in the central Persian Gulf had rendered Iraqi naval forces "combat ineffective."[32] Ashore, Allied attack aircraft from the A-10 Warthog tank-busters to the B-52 Big Uglies began turning the positions of the Iraqi army into a living hell.

The demands of air operations over the KTO forced some alterations in the management of the air campaign. Against static targets during phases I and II, the detailed air tasking order had been central to the implementation of a truly joint, integrated air effort. But an overly detailed plan was inadequate against more mobile targets, such as the Iraqi mechanized units in the KTO. The Allied command established "killing boxes" to which aircraft were directed. Within an individual box, fast, low-flying forward air controllers would identify targets and vector on-hand strike aircraft to the mark.[33]

The vigorous prosecution of the air war over the KTO was closely tied to Desert Storm's psychological warfare plan.[34] Allied aircraft "bombed" Iraqi frontline units with leaflets illustrating Arab brotherhood and promising good treatment to POWs. Some units were warned before they were attacked in an effort to spread panic and to promote desertion or surrender. The Allies worked diligently to maintain the physical and psychological pressure on the enemy. One air planner commented: "our bombing schedules on the Iraqi Republican Guard made sure that they never had more than a couple of hours sleep. In this war, our PsyOps [psychological operations] went well beyond that of just dropping leaflets on the enemy troops."[35]

As phase III continued, more and more Iraqis fled to the safety of Allied lines. On February 20, four days before the beginning of the ground war, four U.S. Army helicopters raided an Iraqi bunker complex, making quick work of thirteen of the fifteen positions. About 400 enemy soldiers promptly ran into the open to surrender. Heavy-lift CH-47D Chinook helicopters extracted the POWs from the midst of the Iraqi border defenses.

Despite the worsening situation at the front and throughout Iraq, Saddam refused to yield. During a January 20 Baghdad radio broadcast he warned:

In the coming period, the response of Iraq will be on a larger scale, using all means and potential God has given us and which we have so far only used in part. Our ground forces have not entered the battle so far. . . . The army's air force has not been used, nor has the navy. The weight of our missile force has not yet been applied in full.[36]

But Saddam's air force and navy were on the verge of total destruction. Allied aircraft and special forces were hunting down his Scud launchers. Saddam's threats that "the scale of death and the number of dead will, God willing, rise among the ranks of atheism, injustice, and tyranny" rang hollow, as did the prediction that "the 'God is Great' banner will flutter with great victory in the mother of all battles."

On January 26 Saddam visited the front and, as he had so many times before, demonstrated his incredibly poor sense of timing. Just as the Allies began phase III, filling the skies over Kuwait with coalition strike aircraft, Saddam directed his troops to leave their protective bunkers and to attack south into eastern Saudi Arabia.

Because of Allied control of the air, degraded command and control abilities, and possibly poor staff work, the attack did not begin until the night of January 29 when an Iraqi mechanized column drove south from the border's "elbow" while another attacked along the coast.[37] Elements of the Third Marine Regiment drove back the inland column southwest of Wafra, but the second Iraqi group reached the undefended Saudi town of Khafji. The following morning, two additional Iraqi columns struck south, but both were stopped in their tracks by Allied ground formations and air attacks. During the thirtieth and thirty-first, Saudi and Qatar troops, well supported by U.S. Marines and Allied aircraft, slowly and carefully drove the Iraqis from Khafji, taking 450 prisoners.

A definitive account of the battle of Khafji remains to be written. The purpose of the Iraqi offensive is unclear. The effort may have been planned as a raid. Saddam may have hoped that a small ground engagement initiated by his army might escalate into a larger battle and then into a full-scale ground campaign that would result in the bloodbath he needed to achieve "victory." Or Saddam may have been testing the fighting power of the Arab troops deployed in the area, hoping to break them and weaken the coalition.

Whatever Saddam's intentions, Khafji was a disaster for the Iraqis, although that fact was not always evident in press reports. Saddam's troops captured the town only because it was undefended. Khafji was within artillery range of Iraqi positions in Kuwait, had been shelled earlier in the war, and lying just north of a salt marsh, was difficult to approach from the south. Allied commanders had judged it indefensible and evacuated the Saudi inhabitants. The Iraqis also lost far more men and equipment than the dozen tanks and the 450 men of an infantry battalion ultimately trapped in Khafji. The columns of the overstrength Fifth Mechanized Division, with nine rather than the usual three brigades, were backed up for miles north of the border and subjected to constant and effective Allied air attacks. The battle also demonstrated that the coalition's Arab forces, operating with powerful air support, were more than a match for Saddam's veterans.

After their repulse at Khafji, the Iraqis remained immobile awaiting the coalition's death blow in the vain hope that a ground war would produce huge casualty lists that would undermine the political will of the United States. As they waited for the attack, the Iraqi units deployed in the KTO began to feel the noose tighten around their necks. According to CENTCOM estimates, about forty of the fifty-two major bridges critical to the supply of the KTO had been heavily damaged or destroyed.[38] Movement of supplies into the theater had been reduced in some areas by 90 percent. While Allied intelligence analysts were unsure just how badly the Iraqi army had been hurt, much to the distress of General Schwarzkopf, there was some hard evidence and much anecdotal information to indicate that the situation was becoming intolerable.[39]

Schwarzkopf was now ready to unleash his ground forces. Since January 17, the first day of the air war, the troops of the XVIII Airborne and VII Corps had been trekking west into attack positions. Along the border with Kuwait, Allied units stepped up their activity, pushing small reconnaissance teams into the Iraqi rear and conducting artillery raids to keep the enemy's attention rivetted to the south. Off the coast, the U.S. Navy continued its activity, seized offshore oil wells, a small island, and maintained an amphibious threat to the Kuwait coast. On January 24 the navy staged an exercise—Sea Soldier IV—that included the largest amphibious force assembled since the Inchon landing in 1950 during the Korean War.

By mid-February, after a month of pounding from the air, Iraqi resistance was beginning to crack. Saddam, slowly and belatedly, recognized the extent of his miscalculation. At the eleventh hour, perhaps more accurately only minutes before midnight, Saddam made a vain attempt to end the war before the Allies launched their ground assault. Much like the Japanese who in the summer of 1945 unwisely tried to find some face-saving way out of their war with the United States by using the Soviet Union as an intermediary, Saddam, too, worked through Moscow in an effort to escape death and destruction from the air, and an invasion of his homeland.

Once the air war began, the Kremlin recognized that its former client, despite billions of rubles in military aid, was headed for disaster. President Mikhail Gorbachev, to spare Iraq the embarrassment of total defeat, and no doubt also eager to see the world's attention once again focused on events in Europe, advised Saddam to cut his losses and end the war. In Baghdad on February 12, special envoy Yevgeni Primakov warned Saddam that if he did not end the war soon, an Allied ground attack would complete the destruction of Iraqi forces in Kuwait. Primakov advised Saddam to announce his readiness to withdraw.

Moscow's diplomatic initiative generated some movement toward peace. Saddam declared his willingness to work with the Soviets in an effort to end the war. But the Allies, especially the United States, doubted Saddam's sincerity and considered his diplomatic pronouncements an effort to avoid complete defeat. The Bush administration was also wary of the Soviet Union's involvement. Despite the new relationship that existed between Washington and Moscow, many Americans believed that the Russians were working to deny the United States the complete victory it had earned in the gulf, and to save a regime that for decades had been Moscow's ally in that region.

Whatever the sincerity of Soviet and Iraqi intentions, Saddam once again proved himself inept. He made abysmal use of the good offices of President Gorbachev. Given the delays caused by Saddam's unwillingness to allow his foreign minister, Tariq Aziz, freedom to negotiate while in Moscow, the need to shuttle between Moscow and Baghdad via Teheran, and the breakdown in Iraqi communications caused by Allied bombing, valuable time was wasted.

Nevertheless, as a result of the Soviet efforts, there began in mid-February a steady, daily stream of reports concerning offers and counteroffers emanating from Baghdad, Moscow, and Washington. Rumors were rife that Saddam was about to announce a withdrawal from Kuwait. Then on February 15, Iraq's Revolutionary Command Council issued a statement accepting U.N. Security Council resolution 660, the resolution that had called for a withdrawal. Unfortunately, the Iraqis simultaneously issued their own set of demands: an immediate cease-fire; the end of the embargo; the "abrogation" by the United Nations of all the relevant resolutions passed subsequent to 660; the simultaneous withdrawal of Allied forces, including the removal of the Patriot missile batteries sent to Israel after the initial Scud attacks; an Israeli withdrawal from the "Arab" territories occupied since 1967; and an agreement by the coalition to "rebuild what the aggression has destroyed."[40]

Not surprisingly, President Bush immediately denounced the statement as a "cruel hoax."[41] The eight Arab members of the alliance rejected Saddam's plan outright. French President Mitterand termed the Iraqi proposal "unacceptable." British Prime Minister John Major called it a "bogus sham."[42] Even the Soviets appeared taken aback by Saddam's response. Vitaly Churkin, Soviet Foreign Ministry spokesman, told the press: "The chief thing, in our view, consists of the fact that the Iraqi leadership is speaking of withdrawal from Kuwait." But Churkin added, "Unfortunately, this principled provision is linked to many conditions which could render it meaningless."[43]

Undeterred, Gorbachev unveiled his own secret "plan of action" in Moscow on February 17 when Iraqi Foreign Minister Tariq Aziz arrived for discussions.[44] Gorbachev personally took part in the talks and warned that Saddam had to make up his mind to withdraw without conditions as quickly as possible. But Aziz was not authorized to speak for Saddam and returned to Baghdad with the proposed plan. He promised a quick response.

But the days passed without word from Baghdad. Either Saddam could not make what was for him a difficult decision, misjudged the need for alacrity in his deliberations, or was just, as the Americans feared, trying to delay the beginning of the ground war. Saddam's silence did not trouble President Bush, who held little hope that Gorbachev's efforts would bear fruit and believed that the Soviet plan fell "well short" of what the coalition considered necessary to end the war.[45]

Finally, on February 21, the Iraqis accepted the Kremlin's proposal and announced that they agreed to a "full and unconditional withdrawal" from Kuwait that would begin the second day after a cease-fire and would be completed within a fixed, but as yet undetermined, time frame. But the Iraqi acceptance was not, in fact, unconditional. Once the withdrawal was completed, Saddam insisted that the remaining U.N. resolutions end.[46] There would be no postwar embargo and the Iraqis would not have to pay reparations.

The Soviet plan was not satisfactory to the Allies, especially the United States.[47] On the threshold of victory, President Bush saw little reason to grant a defeated Saddam conditions. On February 22, Bush, speaking for the Alliance, issued a set of demands of his own and issued a deadline for their acceptance—noon, Washington time, Saturday, February 23, 1991.[48] Saddam would have to agree to an immediate and rapid withdrawal and accept all the relevant U.N. resolutions, without conditions.

Allied reluctance to delay or to accept less than complete Iraqi acceptance of the U.N. resolutions was understandable. The VII and XVIII Corps had completed their movements to assault positions deep in Saudi desert. Holding the troops there would have jeopardized whatever hopes General Schwarzkopf had to achieve strategic and operational surprise, and the logistic burden would have been enormous and would have undermined any subsequent northward drive. The Bush administration was also well aware that while Saddam was talking peace, he was systematically destroying Kuwait. As early as January 30, General Schwarzkopf had lamented the purposeful Iraqi destruction of Kuwait's infrastructure. On February 12, the Pentagon announced that as many as fifty Kuwaiti oil wells had been set afire by the Iraqis. By February 22, when Saddam finally agreed to his "unconditional" withdrawal, Allied intelligence reported that about half of Kuwait's oil wells—more than 150 of 363—had been torched.[49] Each day, more wells were burning.[50] On February 17, black rain fell in western Iran as the newest environmental scourge unleashed by Saddam spread.[51] There were also reports that the Iraqis were rounding up tens of thousands of Kuwait's long-suffering civilians.[52] Some were apparently being used as shields, others were being transported to Iraq for reasons unknown. The Allies could hardly drop demands for reparations while Saddam was purposefully destroying Kuwait.

Time had run out for Saddam, and for the Iraqi army. Primakov believed that the differences separating the Allies and Saddam "were not so substantial that they justified a further escalation of the war." Perhaps not, but before any further efforts could be made, including a Soviet call for an emergency United Nations session, G-Day, as the day the ground war was scheduled to start was known, had arrived. Saddam and the Soviets had had two weeks to work out an arrangement. Saddam had had five months to face facts and withdraw. With Kuwait quite literally burning, to delay the ground war would itself have been a crime. In fact, the ground campaign mercifully shortened the war. In 100 hours General Schwarzkopf's army achieved what might have taken a week to ten days, or more, to do from the air.

CHAPTER TWELVE

THE MOTHER OF ALL BATTLES, THE MOTHER OF ALL RETREATS

———•———

The Storm on the Ground

By mid-February, the Coalition's reluctance to launch a ground war had disappeared. Concern that the air campaign and Soviet diplomatic initiatives might end the "party" before the ground forces had weighed in grew. Senior Allied military leaders began to recognize that they had grossly overestimated Iraqi capabilities and underestimated the deadly effectiveness of air power. Saddam's search for a cease-fire was evidence of the destructiveness of the coalition air attacks. The Iraqi air force had been smashed, or had fled to Iran. The Iraqi navy had been destroyed, primarily by strikes from U.S. Navy carrier aircraft operating in the Persian Gulf.

Most importantly, the Iraqi Army was breaking and beginning to look like a paper tiger. Reconnaissance of the front revealed that many of the Saddam Line's minefields had been unimaginatively laid, often with unmined corridors clearly marked. Nor had the minefields been adequately maintained. Allied soldiers observed that mines set off by wandering camels were not relaid. Many of the mines protruded from the ground as the winter weather eroded the covering sand. As G-Day approached, raids conducted by American marines demonstrated that despite their vaunted artillery superiority the Iraqis were slow to respond and unable to return fire effectively when they did. The increasing number of deserting Iraqi soldiers reaching Allied lines spoke of abysmal conditions, poor morale, and mass desertions that may have reached 50 percent in some units. Of the forty-one formations displayed on the charts used by General Schwarzkopf during his February 27 briefing, thirteen were estimated to be at less than 50 percent, and a dozen at less than 75 percent strength. Allied air forces had destroyed thousands of Iraqi tanks, armored personnel carriers, and guns. The battlefield had been "prepared." At 4:00 A.M. local time, February 24, 1991, Desert Storm's fourth phase, the ground offensive, began.

General Schwarzkopf's forces were deployed in six major groupings. About 18,000 American marines of the amphibious-capable Fourth and Fifth Marine Expeditionary brigades and 13th Marine Expeditionary Unit (Special Operations Capable) remained afloat in the Persian Gulf, forcing the Iraqis to garrison the Kuwaiti coast. Ashore, assigned to the easternmost corps sector, was the Arab Joint Forces Command-East (JFC-E) which consisted of three division-sized "task forces" made up of Saudi, U.A.E., Omani, Bahraini, Qatar, and Kuwaiti units. Next in line was the American First Marine Expeditionary Force—the First and Second Marine divisions and the U.S. Army's First "Tiger" brigade of the Second Armored Division. To the marines' left was the major Arab contingent, Joint Forces Command-North (JFC-N), which included the Egyptian Ranger Regiment and Third Mechanized and Fourth Armored divisions, the Syrian 45th Commando regiment and Ninth Armored Division, the Saudi Fourth Armored and 20th Mechanized regiments, and the Kuwait Shaheed and Al-Tahrir brigades. JFC-N's forces were aligned along the Kuwaiti border from the Wadi al-Batin to the "armpit" where the border curved to the southeast. To the west of the Wadi al-Batin the powerful VII Corps deployed the American Second Armored Cavalry Regiment (ACR), the First Infantry, First Cavalry, and First and Third Armored divisions, and the British First Armored Division. On the extreme western flank of the Allied line was XVIII Airborne Corps, which included the French Sixth Armored Division, the U.S. Third Armored Cavalry Regiment, and the American 82nd and 101st Airborne, and 24th Mechanized Infantry divisions.

Not surprisingly, command of such a large, disparate force that included air, land, naval, and support units from thirty-eight countries posed something of a problem. Disputes over just who was in charge reportedly surfaced in late August 1990, when the Saudi commander, Lieutenant General Prince Khalid bin Sultan bin Abdul-Aziz told reporters that the Americans would not launch offensive operations until President Bush had first conferred with, and received the approval of, King Fahd. The Saudis had accepted American support to defend the kingdom, not to strike at Iraq, and any change from defensive to offensive operations would have to have the king's sanction. General Schwarzkopf, according to these reports, believed that such a cumbersome system would tie his hands and prohibit an effective counterattack should the situation demand one.[1] Schwarzkopf took his complaints to the president who had to intercede with the Saudis and smooth ruffled feathers.

While Schwarzkopf denied the press's melodramatic version of the Saudi-American dispute,[2] there were, quite obviously, problems with the Desert Shield command structure. The Arabian peninsula was not Western Europe and Schwarzkopf's Central Command, for manifest political reasons, included no combined command structure akin to NATO's. While the Goldwater-Nichols Act may have strengthened Schwarzkopf's control over the American services, the wisdom of the United States Congress was not as readily apparent to the Arabs of the Persian Gulf. The principle of unified command, the sine qua non of the American military, could not be other than a stumbling block in Saudi Arabia. To be sure, neither President Bush nor Norman Schwarzkopf were about to turn over the operational control of several hundred thousand American servicemen and women to the Saudis. Nor were the Saudis, or the other Arabs, prepared to relinquish control of their troops to the infidel Americans.

Two factors insured that such problems did not become a major political or military problem for the coalition. While Schwarzkopf undoubtedly believed that, purely from a military standpoint, the alliance would function best if he were the sole commander, he also recognized that Saudi sensibilities ruled out such a course. Senior Saudi leaders, who no doubt believed that, for political reasons at home and within the Arab world, a Saudi general should command all forces deployed in Saudi Arabia, knew that no American president would direct Schwarzkopf to relinquish operational authority over American forces.

Over the following months, as additional units reached the theater, the Allies gradually developed a workable command structure in an atmosphere more notable for its compromises, than its confrontations. Arab states preferred to see their forces placed under Saudi command. In mid-September, the British agreed to place theirs under American tactical command.[3] Then in late October, after high-level United States–Saudi meetings, General Schwarzkopf announced that he and Lieutenant General Prince Khalid bin Sultan had agreed on a "very, very comprehensive, integrated defensive plan."[4] Under the compromise plan, dual lines of authority ran from the Saudi and United States governments through Khalid and Schwarzkopf respectively, thence to Islamic and non-Islamic forces. Placed between these two tracks was the Coalition Coordination Communication and Integration Center (CCCIC). The job of the CCCIC was to ensure that the absence of a supreme commander "did not disrupt operations."[5]

Despite the obvious deficiencies of such a system, it worked well enough during a campaign that proceeded so successfully that events never really tested the command structure. Most importantly, whatever the organization looked like on paper, General Schwarzkopf called the shots during Desert Storm and, through the CCCIC, directed the operations of the Islamic, as well as the non-Islamic forces. As one senior American officer assured Associated Press correspondent Richard Pyle, United States forces "would not be paralyzed by 'sheer unadulterated bullshit.'"[6]

At 4:00 A.M. on February 24, at Schwarzkopf's direction, coalition troops launched four supporting attacks designed to breach the front along the Kuwaiti border, break into the enemy's rear, and pin or draw south Iraqi operational reserves and Republican Guard formations.

The First Marine Division led off the offensive, striking the elbow of the Kuwait-Saudi border and with surprising ease breached both the first and second lines of the Iraqi defenses. On the left of the First Marine Division, the Second Marine Division, reinforced by the U.S. Army's Tiger Brigade, hit the line at 5:30 A.M. and made similar progress. Throughout the day the marines continued to advance. The First Marine Division reached and secured the Ahmed Al Jaber air base and the Al Burqan oilfield, destroying twenty-one Iraqi tanks and taking 4,000 prisoners en route. To the west, the Second Marine Division engaged and destroyed an advancing Iraqi tank column, taking 5,000 prisoners.[7]

On the marines' right and left flanks, Arab forces made satisfactory progress. At 8:00 JFC-E broke through Iraqi defenses along the coast and advanced north. Later in the day, after General Schwarzkopf decided to accelerate JFC-N's attack, Arab forces struck north, advancing deliberately but, given the nature of Iraqi defense on February 24, making relatively poor progress. The official Defense Department account noted: "The Egyptians, concerned about an Iraqi counterattack, established a blocking position in sector."[8] In other words, at day's end the Egyptians, far from advancing, had gone over to the defensive.

On the Allies extreme left flank, elements of Lieutenant General Gary Luck's XVIII Airborne Corps struck north at the same time that the First Marine Division hit the Saddam Line. At 4:00 A.M. the French Sixth Light Armored Division from Nimes, part of France's Force Action Rapide (FAR), moved north from its assault positions east of Ratha. The French division, known as the division d'Aguet (the division of observation), reinforced by a brigade of the American 82nd Airborne Division, numbered about 13,000 men. Division d'Aguet's initial objective was As Salman, an old fort near a road junction midway between the Saudi border and the Euphrates. The French formation's job was to cover the left flank of the Allied advance and to secure several roads needed to supply XVIII Airborne Corps.[9]

The French drove north in two columns and made excellent progress. The Iraqis had deployed elements of their IX Corps of three divisions between An Nasiriyah and As Salman, but the Iraqis engaged by the French were reservists who, in most cases, fled at the approach of Allied troops. Division d'Aguet's right-hand column reached Objective Rochambeau, a road junction near Thaqh ál Hajj midway between the border and As Salman, by nightfall. The French could have moved on As Salman but decided to delay their attack until the following morning to avoid civilian casualties in what could become a confusing night firefight. The left-hand column advanced further and was positioned to swing in behind the Iraqi defenses at As Salman if the enemy put up any kind of defense.

The following morning the French advanced into the town, meeting little resistance. They had already taken over 3,000 prisoners, who were proving to be a logistical burden. Fortunately, only 15 of As Salman's 2,000 civilians remained to be cared for; the rest had been evacuated some time before. A captured Iraqi colonel later told French Brigadier General Daniel Gazeau that the presence of the French across the border had been no secret. When asked at a press briefing if the colonel's remarks, the evacuation of the town, and the placement of Iraqi troops in As Salman area did not indicate that Saddam's commanders expected some kind of Allied thrust into the area, Brigadier General Gazeau simply answered, "Sorry!"

On the French right the American 101st Airborne Division conducted a heliborne assault against an old, small, abandoned Iraqi airbase at Al Ubayyid. Objective Cobra, as the captured airfield was codenamed, would become a forward base for further XVIII Airborne Corps operations into the Euphrates River Valley. The "Screaming

Eagles" surprised elements of the Iraqi 26th Infantry Division at Al Ubayyid and took 500 prisoners.

Since the Allied offensive was going so well, Lieutenant General Luck received permission from General Schwarzkopf to advance the attack of the XVIII Airborne Corps' heavy unit, the 24th Mechanized Infantry Division, scheduled to begin its assault at 6:00 A.M. on the twenty-fifth. Instead, Major General Barry McCaffrey's division struck north at 3:00 P.M. on the twenty-fourth. From positions around Ash Shubah, opposite the western end of the Iraqi-Saudi neutral zone, the soldiers of the "Victory" Division made immediate and rapid progress. Iraqis surrendered in large numbers, begging for food.

Schwarzkopf also decided to accelerate the attack of Lieutenant General Frederick Franks's VII Corps, originally scheduled to move out on the night of February 24–25. The reasoning behind this decision remains unclear. Accounts heretofore published or released cite the excellent and unexpected progress made elsewhere along the front. But the delayed advance of VII Corps was designed to give the Iraqis time to react to the Arab-Marine Corps drive into Kuwait, an assault intended to draw the Iraqi reserves toward the south. The JSTAR images released thus far indicate that by the afternoon of the twenty-fourth the Iraqis were not responding as expected. Saddam's commanders were not moving their armored reserves south to counterattack the advance of the marines, but west into positions directly in the path of the VII Corps. To delay the attack of the 24th Mechanized Infantry Division and Franks's VII Corps would have given the Iraqis additional time to reposition themselves and prepare to receive the Allied attack. Thus the altered timetable for the offensive may have been in part the result of the partial failure of the deception plan.

Whatever the reason, during the afternoon of the twenty-fourth, fifteen hours ahead of schedule, the VII Corps rolled into Iraq, sweeping aside elements of the Iraqi VII Corps. While the First Cavalry Division feinted an attack along the Wadi al-Batin, Franks's First and Third Armored divisions and the First Mechanized Infantry Division, "bunched in a big fist," attacked along a sixty-mile front with the elements of the corps stretching back into Saudi Arabia to a depth of 120 miles. After making a clean break through the Iraqi front, the Second Armored Cavalry Regiment passed through the lines and by the end of the day was 45 miles inside Iraq.

The first day of Desert Storm's ground campaign had been an unqualified success. Everywhere Allied forces had advanced. Except for scattered enemy units that put up a spirited, if short-lived, defense, the Iraqi Army teetered on the edge of collapse. About 5,000 Iraqis had surrendered and thousands more were wandering the battlefield hors d'combat. Allied casualties numbered in the tens.

By the morning of the twenty-fifth, it had become apparent to most senior Allied commanders that their original plan had become obsolete. The situation was extremely fluid. Opportunity beckoned on all fronts. The marines of First Expeditionary Force were now routinely changing plans, drawing diagrams in the sand or, as with the plan for the assault on Kuwait International Airport, on the back of a carton of C-rations.

Along the coast, JFC-E continued to advance, its march north aided by an amphibious feint conducted by the marines of the Fourth Marine Expeditionary Brigade. The Arabs' biggest problem was traffic management. Unlike the Europeans, Egyptians, and Syrians, the small Arab contingents that made up JFC-E were not accustomed to moving large formations across a battlefield. The swarms of Iraqi POWs that jammed the roads only made a bad situation worse.

To the left of JFC-E, the marines of First Marine Expeditionary Force found themselves operating in the permanent twilight caused by smoke from hundreds of burning Kuwaiti oil wells. Undeterred, the marines continued to advance. The First Marine Division, after securing the Al Jaber airfield, pushed north to within ten miles of Kuwait City. The Second Marine Division pushed through Al Abdallya. Throughout the twenty-fifth, both marine divisions repulsed several armored counterattacks and destroyed or captured almost 200 tanks, mostly from the Iraqi Fifth Mechanized Infantry Division. To the rear, the Fifth Marine Expeditionary Brigade conducted an administrative landing and became the reserve of the First Marine Expeditionary Force.

On the marines' left, the units of JFC-N began to break through the Iraqi front. The Third Egyptian Division alone took over 1,500 prisoners. By the end of the day, JFC-N was poised to strike toward Kuwait City.

The VII Corps' advance accelerated on the twenty-fifth. While the First Cavalry Division continued its operations in the triborder area, the British First Armored Division passed through a gap opened in the Iraqi front by the American First Mechanized Infantry Division. As they emerged into the open, the British division's two armored brigades, with about 150 Challenger Main Battle Tanks, engaged and destroyed the Iraqi 12th Armored Division. On the British left, the

American Second Armored Cavalry Regiment led the advance of the Third and First Armored Divisions. By the end of the day, tanks and mechanized infantry of the latter division had secured the road junction at Makhfar al Busayyah, about fifty miles from Highway 8 and the Euphrates.

On the left, Lieutenant General Luck's XVIII Airborne Corps continued its operations to secure the flank of the coalition advance. Division d'Aguet drove elements of the Iraqi 45th Infantry Division from As Salman and secured the vital road junction. Already, the roads to the south were lined with Allied supply convoys moving north. Bad weather hindered the 101st Airborne Division's buildup, but the heliborne troopers drove north nonetheless and about dusk cut Highway 8 southwest of An Nasiriyah. The 24th Mechanized Infantry Division also made excellent progress northward, and late in day after a sharp four-hour engagement with an Iraqi commando regiment seized Talil airfield.

By the evening of the twenty-fifty, the extent of the Allied triumph had become clear for all to see. Even Saddam at last recognized that his game was up. At 1:35 in the morning of the twenty-sixth, Baghdad radio announced that Iraq's armed forces, having "completed their duty of jihad," and having "engaged in an epic, valiant battle which will be recorded by history in letters of light," would begin to conduct "an organized withdrawal" from Kuwait.[10] Later in the day, Hussein himself spoke, bombastically proclaiming victory. "You have won," he told the Iraqi people, "you are victorious."[11]

Saddam's call for a withdrawal probably accelerated the collapse of an already tottering army. Along many sectors of the front, roads jammed with prisoners and minefields were far more of a hindrance to the continued Allied advance than the "victorious" Iraqi army.

JFC-E secured its corps sector and advanced to the outskirts of Kuwait City, while the marines of the Fourth Marine Expeditionary Brigade conducted amphibious demonstrations against Faylaka and Bubiyan Islands. The First Marine Division advanced on Kuwait International Airport and began a major tank battle that lasted into the early morning hours of February 27. The Second Marine Division pushed to the head of Kuwait Bay, reaching the town of Al Jahra and Mutla Ridge, high ground that dominated the road out of Kuwait City. On the marines' left, elements of JFC-N reached and secured Ali Al-Salem airbase, less than ten miles from Al Jahra.

But the important action on February 26 took place back in Riyadh where General Schwarzkopf decided the moment had come for

Franks's VII Corps to turn east. As the Department of Defense report on the war notes: "The [VII] Corps executed a right turn and changed its focus."[12]

Saddam's order to his troops in Kuwait to withdraw, and the rout that had begun in southern Kuwait, placed a premium on cutting off the remaining Iraqi forces before they could withdraw to the Euphrates. Allowing Franks's powerful VII Corps to roll on toward the northeast and Basra might have trapped the Iraqis. In fact, on the maps included in the Defense Department's official interim report on the war, until February 26, the VII Corps boundaries extended northwest toward Basra.[13] Schwarzkopf may have decided that it was too risky to continue to push VII Corps forward to the Euphrates while relatively intact Iraqi mechanized divisions, including at least three of the Republican Guard, remained unengaged on Franks's flank. Redirecting the VII Corps advance toward the east was the less risky course, but far from bypassing Saddam's remaining effective forces, was destined to bring on the massive, head-on engagement.

Several factors may have contributed to the decision to alter VII Corps' axis. Despite the comments of General Schwarzkopf and others, the deception plan quite obviously failed, either because the Iraqis were not fooled or because they simply were unable, in the face of Allied air power, to react to the feints in the manner Schwarzkopf and his staff desired. As the campaign unfolded, the Iraqi reserves, including the Republican Guard divisions, were well placed to threaten any Allied advance to the Euphrates, and to cover the retreat from Kuwait. Nor had JFC-N, because of its relatively slow advance, engaged and tied-down the Iraqi forces deployed in northwestern Kuwait. Logistical considerations and problems involved in the movement of large armored formations through the trackless desert terrain south of Basra may also have influenced Schwarzkopf.

The alteration of VII Corps's direction of advance involved far more than the redrawing of a few lines and the movement of a handful of symbols on a map. As the DOD account of operations indicates, the redirection of VII Corps was "a very difficult maneuver."[14] The First Mechanized Infantry Division, for example, had to pass through the Second Armored Cavalry Regiment at night. Major General Paul Funk, the commander of the Third Armored Division, and Colonel William Nash, who led the unit's First Brigade, reportedly worked out the change in the axis of division's advance in fifteen minutes on maps spread out on the hood of a Humvee.[15] The ability of Franks's divisions to execute Schwarzkopf's change of plans without losing the momentum of the advance and to promptly engage the enemy off the march was, without doubt, one of the most remarkable operational performances of the war.

On the night of February 26, as the VII Corps completed its turn, Franks's divisions began to encounter Iraqi forces, including the Republican Guard's First Hammurabi and Second Medina Armored divisions and the Third Tawakalna Mechanized Division. Elements of the American First and Third Armored divisions and the First Mechanized Infantry Division worked throughout the night and into the morning of the twenty-seventh, to engage and destroy the Iraqis and open a route to the east to complete the destruction of Iraqi forces retreating from Kuwait.

Schwarzkopf's decision to redirect the VII Corps to the east, meant that Lieutenant General Luck's forces were solely responsible not only for covering the left flank of the Allied advance, but also for cutting off the Iraqi retreat by advancing to Basra, which lay within the XVIII Airborne Corps's sector. Division d'Aguet, screening the Allies' extreme left from As Salman, reported little Iraqi activity. The American 101st Airborne Division easily scattered elements of the Iraqi 49th Infantry Division and entered An Nasiriyah along the Euphrates. The 24th Mechanized Infantry Division continued its advance north on a front from Tallil on the left to Jalibah on the right.

By the morning of February 27, the Iraqi situation had become hopeless. Twenty-two Iraqi divisions had been destroyed, about half of the units Saddam had deployed to the KTO. Most of the rest were near collapse. Conditions at the front were so bad that forty desperate, pitiful Iraqis had tried to surrender to an American Remote-Controlled Pilotless Vehicle (RPV) by running about, frantically waving their arms, as the targeting drone flew overhead.[16] The coalition already held an estimated 30,000 prisoners of war.

In Kuwait on February 27 organized resistance ended. Saudi and Kuwaiti forces entered the capital. The First Marine Division secured Kuwait International Airport after destroying more than 300 Iraqi tanks, including 70 T-72s. The marines of First Marine Expeditionary Force held controlling positions around Kuwait City. Arab units of JFC-N linked up with other Allied troops near the Kuwaiti capital. The remnants of Iraqi forces fled north along the main highway to Basra, shortly to become known as "the highway of death," or the "highway to hell." U.S. Marine Corps Harrier pilots termed the situation along the road as "a smorgasbord of military vehicles," "a parking lot," and the proverbial "target-rich environment."[17] Overhead, Allied jets bombed, rocketed, and strafed the highway which quickly became an abattoir as Iraqis fled for their lives.[18]

Throughout the day the divisions of Lieutenant General Franks's VII Corps battled their way to the east as Allied mechanized forces demonstrated their qualitative edge over the Iraqis. Thermal-sight-equipped American and British tanks usually opened fire before being spotted by the Iraqis and frequently scored first-shot hits while still on the move. When the Iraqis did return fire, they had little success. There were no confirmed penetrations of either M1 or M1A1 armor by Iraqi projectiles and of the seven M1A1s reportedly struck by rounds fired by T-72s, none suffered damage. Not surprisingly, Allied-Iraqi tank engagements generally were short and resulted in destruction for Saddam's forces. In one engagement, M1A1 Abrams tanks of the First Armored Division's Second Brigade destroyed 100 Iraqi tanks and 30 armored personnel carriers in forty-five minutes—that is an Iraqi vehicle destroyed every twenty seconds![19] Such actions allowed the VII Corps to complete the destruction of the Iraqi Republican Guard formations, including the vaunted Hammurabi, and to drive towards the gulf. By the next morning, British and American mechanized units had engaged and destroyed more than a dozen Iraqi divisions and were astride the main retreat routes out of Kuwait.

While French and American forces screened to the west and north, the XVIII Corps' 24th Mechanized Infantry Division drove into the Euphrates Valley. At dawn, the division's 197th Infantry Brigade seized Tallil airfield south of An Nasiriya. To the east, Colonel Paul Kern's Second Brigade captured Jalibah, destroying ten MiGs on the ground. Major General McCaffrey quickly wheeled his division about and, supported by corps helicopter assets and the Third Armored Cavalry Regiment, drove east along Highway 8. Surprised Iraqi units, including one with fifty tanks, were quickly scattered or captured as the division's lead elements sped toward Basra. Late in the day and into the morning, the division engaged dug-in elements of the Republican Guard's Fourth Al Faw Motorized Division. By the early morning hours of the twenty-eighth, the Iraqis had been beaten and were pulling back. McCaffrey's men were ready to push forward to Basra to seal off the main Iraqi escape route. But at 8:00 A.M., all offensive operations came to an end. Desert Storm was over.

On March 28, morning papers in the United States carried the story that General Schwarzkopf, in an interview with David Frost to be broadcast that night on PBS, had stated that President Bush's "courageous decision" to stop the war after 100 hours had prevented CENTCOM from completing the destruction of the Iraqi army. "Frankly, my recommendation had been to continue to march," Schwarzkopf told Frost, because the Allies could have "completely closed the door and made it a battle of annihilation." Bush's decision, according to Schwarzkopf, "did leave some escape routes open for them to get back out."[20] The following day, after the broadcast, Bush told reporters that as far as he was concerned, there had been "total agreement in terms of when this war should end."[21]

Schwarzkopf's remarks to Frost, remarks that the general quickly retracted, are puzzling, since it was Schwarzkopf himself, at his February 27 press conference, who first publicly raised the possibility of a cessation of offensive operations. A reporter had asked: "Do you fear that you will not be able to accomplish your end, that there will be some political pressure brought on the campaign?" Schwarzkopf replied:

I think I've made it clear to everybody that I'd just as soon the war had never started, and I'd just as soon never have lost a single life out there. That was not our choice. We've accomplished our mission, and when the decision-makers come to the decision that there should be a cease-fire, nobody will be happier than me.[22]

Not long after the briefing, General Colin Powell called Schwarzkopf and asked the general his views on halting operations. According to Schwarzkopf's subsequent testimony before Congress, he agreed with the decision because "we were really wreaking great destruction upon the enemy and taking lives unnecessarily."[23]

Schwarzkopf's contradictory statements regarding the genesis of the halt order probably indicates that, whatever his own preferred course of action at the time, there was debate among senior American and Allied military figures about whether or not to stop. General McPeak, the U.S. Air Force chief of staff, later admitted, "We weren't so sure we were making the right move when our ground forces, the 24th Mech and the armored divisions up there in contact with the Republican Guard stopped and offered, really, a merciful clemency to the Iraqi ground forces."[24]

Just how bad the Iraqi situation was became evident to the Allies on March 3 during the military-to-military talks held at Safwan, Iraq, just north of the Kuwait border. At the meeting, General Schwarzkopf, Saudi Lieutenant General Khalid, and other Senior Allied commanders

239

met with the Iraqi Vice Chief of Staff Lieutenant General Sultan Hashim Ahmad Al-Jabburi and ten senior Iraqi officers to work out the details of the cessation of hostilities. During a discussion about the release of prisoners of war, Al-Jabburi asked just how many Iraqis the Allies had captured. Informed that the number exceeded 58,000, the startled vice chief of staff asked Major General Al-Dughastani, commander of the III Corps that had been deployed in Kuwait, if that number could possibly be accurate. Al-Dughastani replied that he had no idea, but that the figure could be correct. Later, while drawing a boundary to separate Allied and Iraqi troops, Al-Jabburi asked why the line had been drawn behind Iraqi units. Schwarzkopf replied that the line marked the forward positions of coalition forces. The astonished Iraqi generals were apparently unaware, even several days after the end of operations, of the depth of the Allied advance.[25]

As the talks at Safwan were underway, reports of civil unrest among Iraq's Shia population in the southeastern part of the country reached the West.[26] Fighting soon spread from Basra north to cities such as An Nasiriya and Karbala. Days later, fighting began in the far north of the country where the Kurds drove Saddam's forces from Kurdistan.

The outbreak of unrest in Iraq, and Saddam's brutal and successful efforts to suppress it, made the debate over the timing of the end of Desert Storm of more than purely academic interest. Reports that some of the units involved in repressing the revolt had escaped the debacle in Kuwait, placed in doubt the wisdom of President Bush's decision to halt operations after 100 hours.

Indeed, some of the units used by Saddam to restore his control over Kurdistan and the southeastern part of the country had been deployed in the KTO. But that does not necessarily mean that they would have been destroyed had the ground war continued. General Schwarzkopf had made clear in his February 27 briefing and during the interview with David Frost that the Iraqi army's heavy equipment deployed in the south had been destroyed or trapped. The units that had escaped destruction were the ones that had "bugged out" before the gate had closed on February 27.

By the morning of February 28, Schwarzkopf had clearly achieved his assigned objectives. Kuwait had been liberated and Saddam's army had been weakened to the extent that it no longer posed a threat to Iraq's neighbors. Neither the United Nations, the coalition, nor the United States had undertaken the ground war to totally destroy the Iraqi Army (not all of which was deployed in the south) nor to occupy and dismember Iraq. The Allies had no desire to undertake an occupation that would have given the coalition the physical and administrative responsibility to restructure and rebuild Iraq.

To President Bush and some of the American people, Saddam may have been another Hitler, but Iraq was most definitely not another Germany. In 1945, Germans were a nationalistic people who wanted to be united, whereas the Iraqis in the spring of 1991 were not a people at all, but rather disparate ethnic and religious groups, some of which wished only to separate themselves from Iraq. A postwar Allied occupation of Iraq would have been disastrous for the United States.

While the Bush administration had publicly stated its hope that the Iraqis would remove Saddam from power, the president had in mind a military or political coup, not a bloody popular mass revolt. Nor does the absence of a successful coup (as of this writing) necessarily mean that the administration's hopes were unfounded. The revolts in the southeast and in Kurdistan helped to keep Saddam in power. Any likely successor to Saddam would be another Sunni Arab who would insist on the central authority of Baghdad and the territorial integrity of Iraq. The elimination of Saddam would only have increased the centrifugal forces at work in the country and made the job of reasserting central control even more difficult for the conspirators. Any would-be conspirator also knew (and knows) that Iraq may yet be saddled with Versailles-like financial reparations and sovereignty-limiting strictures. Until Saddam agrees to a final settlement with the coalition, he will most likely remain in power.

Despite Saddam's continued rule, Desert Shield and Desert Storm did accomplish the limited goals established by the Bush administration and supported by its Allies and the United Nations, and also reflected the United States' traditional reluctance to risk deeper political and military involvement in the gulf. Bloody religious and ethnic turmoil in Iraq did take the edge off the Allies' victory, but then the United Nations' victory in Europe in 1945 did not solve all of that continent's problems either. Destruction of the Iraqi army in Kuwait not only freed the United States from having to march all the way to Baghdad to eliminate Saddam's offensive military capabilities, but also insured that minimal U.S. military forces would have to remain in the region after the war and, because of the speed and extent of their success, would possess the maximum deterrent power.

As a result of the success of Desert Storm, by the summer of 1991 the United States was at the peak of its power and influence in the Persian Gulf, but little more deeply committed than it had been before the crisis. Critics of American policy will argue, not without reason, that the United States might not have fared as well had Saddam invaded Saudi Arabia in August 1990. But the leaders of the Middle East, who saw Iraq and the world's fourth largest army dissected in a six-week war, know that the reality of American power is no desert mirage. Who, after all, would have predicted in July 1990 that Americans would be able to forge such an alliance and deploy almost 750,000 military personnel in the Persian Gulf?

CHAPTER THIRTEEN

THE GUARANTOR OF LAST RESORT

———•———

For the United States, Desert Shield/Desert Storm marked the culminating point of a process that began two centuries earlier. In the nineteenth century, many Americans believed that the United States was a nation destined to spread throughout the world the benefits of American political and economic ideals.[1] The Persian Gulf was one of many places American merchants and diplomats sought commercial opportunity. When they reached Muscat in 1833, they began to purposefully undermine the old world order and to establish what they believed would be the new. Their frankly stated aim was to see the United States displace Great Britain as the predominant economic power in the gulf; to no longer be, as Commodore Shufeldt bluntly put it, "No. 2 Englishmen."

Americans naively expected to supplant the British commercially without having to accept old-world-style political or military responsibilities. The United States was eager to trade with Persia in the 1850s, but had no desire to play the larger role in the gulf the shah at first demanded. And as long as Great Britain remained supreme in the region, Americans were able to ignore political realities while they searched for new markets.

Americans should not have so readily dismissed Great Britain's role in the gulf. The British, too, had first arrived in the Persian Gulf seeking only trade.[2] But as commercial activity increased, so, too, did the need to play an ever-wider role. The British enforced a maritime truce that was conducive to trade and by the end of the nineteenth century, they had also identified strategic interests in the region. French, German, and Russian threats prompted extensive political involvement in the affairs of the gulf, especially along its southern shore. Then early in

243

the twentieth century the development of the oil industry in Iran and Great Britain's increasing reliance on the Persian Gulf for petroleum, spawned geoeconomic interests that also had to be defended.

The evolution of American involvement in the gulf paralleled the British pattern—a long period of solely commercial, followed by the more rapid development of strategic and geoeconomic interests. By the 1940s, Americans had replaced the British as the most important economic power in the Persian Gulf. Unfortunately, though not surprisingly, with that newfound commercial dominance came considerable diplomatic and military involvement. The United States resisted this trend, trying to convince the British to remain the power "responsible" for the security of the Middle East, but to no avail.

By the late 1960s, the British had neither the strength nor the desire to guard the region. And why should they have? The nationalization of British oil companies in the gulf and the loss of India and Egypt all but eliminated Great Britain's geoeconomic and strategic stakes in the Middle East. Those commercial concerns that remained were too limited to justify a major political-military role east of Suez.

For the United States, the British withdrawal could not have come at a worse time. The Nixon administration, caught in the morass of the Indochina war, knew that the American people would not support a policy that called for the United States to replace Great Britain in the gulf. The alternative, reliance on Iran and Saudi Arabia as the West's Twin Pillars proved to be a de facto dependence on the shah of Iran, a policy that collapsed ignominiously along with the Pahlavi dynasty in 1979.

It fell to the Carter administration to face the realities of the American position in the Persian Gulf. The United States had to either wash its hands of the region or accept responsibility for securing Western interests. President Carter chose the latter, and since the pronouncement of his doctrine in 1980, Americans have, albeit grudgingly, accepted the fact that as the premier power in the gulf the United States must bear the political and military responsibilities so long borne by Great Britain.

So, like the British in the nineteenth century, Americans have become the guardians of the gulf. As historian, analyst, and commentator Fouad Ajami noted following a visit to Kuwait in the spring of 1991, that "small principality has slipped into the American orbit."[3] Decades of support for Iraq, for the Palestinians, and for Arab nationalism availed the Kuwaitis nothing in their showdown with Saddam Hussein. Totally disillusioned by their treatment at the hands of their racial and religious "brothers," many Kuwaitis now seek "protection" from a country they view as the "guarantor of last resort."

Kuwait may be an extreme example of the mood of the gulf Arabs, but despite their reluctance to admit it, they have likewise become part of a new de facto American protectorate. In the absence of U.S. support, Kuwait, Bahrain, Qatar, the Emirates, Oman, and even Saudi Arabia would probably not long survive. In the recent and not so recent past their larger and more populous neighbors—Iraq, Iran, and Egypt—have all harbored territorial aspirations in the Arabian Peninsula. The gulf Arabs recognize this reality, even if they prefer not to discuss it. That is why they welcomed the arrival of a half-million foreign troops onto their soil after August 2, 1990.

Paradoxically, the American protectorate in the gulf evolved as the result of deliberate policy and by accident. Over two centuries Americans systematically drove the British from the region. Unfortunately, when Americans finally found themselves No. 1 Englishmen, they also discovered that it was hard to distinguish between the old and the new world orders in regions such as the Persian Gulf. To their chagrin, along with economic dominance came political and military responsibilities.

Nor was the West's or the United States' own more limited dependence on the Persian Gulf for petroleum unintentional. In the 1940s American policymakers planned that, too, hoping to preserve the oil of the Western Hemisphere as a vast strategic reserve. As the United States intended, Middle Eastern oil fueled the economic recovery of wartorn Western Europe, a development that was perhaps the most important factor in preventing the spread of communism within Europe.

Thus U.S. policy in the gulf must be considered a success. Since 1945 Americans have achieved that which they sought in and of the Persian Gulf. Americans have fared rather well in the Persian Gulf, and at minimal cost, compared to their massive, fifty-plus-year-long military investment in the defense of Western Europe, sorry experience of intervention in southeast Asia, and mixed record of success and failure in Latin America.

Of course, not everything went according to plan. The assumption that oil royalties would turn an unstable, semifeudal, economic backwater into a stable, pro-Western, politically, socially, and commercially "progressive" region proved erroneous. (But how typical of Americans to believe that money would solve the gulf's problems.[4]) The region has remained pro-Western in its global orientation, but the political

245

and social advances American policymakers once anticipated have failed to materialize.

Nevertheless, all things are relative and Americans ought not to be so glib when they portray the gulf as an unstable collection of political and socially backward semifeudal regimes. Over the past half-century, the Arab states of the Persian Gulf have been far more stable than those of other Third World regions such as Africa, south or southeast Asia, or Latin and South America. Even within the Middle East, the gulf is the most stable subregion. While the Arab governments of the gulf may not conform to western ideals of democracy, they are far from totalitarian in their politics. Economically, politically, and socially, the gulf Arabs are better off than the rest of the Third World, and even parts of the first and second.

Nor should Americans make too much of the "artificiality" of borders in the Persian Gulf. All humanly delineated boundaries are artificial. For example, the "natural" boundaries of France have long been recognized as the Rhine, the Alps, and the Pyrenees, but tell that to the Germans, the Dutch, and the Belgians.

Some Americans seem to think that these "semifeudal" and "artificial" regimes in the gulf somehow lack the right to exist. Discussions during the Gulf War often centered on how the imperialist British had drawn the boundaries of and created states such as Kuwait. In the midst of the January 1991 congressional debate over the use of force, the usually eloquent Senator Daniel Patrick Moynihan rhetorically asked what had taken place in the gulf and answered the question himself: "nothing large happened. A nasty little country invaded a littler but just as nasty country."[5]

The British did draw many of the borders in the region, and without British support and protection, the smaller gulf states would never have survived the nineteenth century. But the most artificial and short-lived state in the gulf is Iraq, not Kuwait. The Kuwaiti ruling family has been running the country for centuries, long before Iraq even existed. Saudi Arabia is by far the most racially and religiously homogeneous state in the region.

In shaping Persian Gulf policy, Americans must understand that the Arab states of the gulf are not threatened because they are artificial, which they are not, but because they are small, weak, oil-rich, and located in a dangerous, but strategically important corner of the world. The dilemma Americans face is that, like the British in the nineteenth and early twentieth centuries, they must decide whether or not it is in their interest to invest the time and the resources (and American lives are one of those resources) to insure the continued survival of the gulf states.

In answering that question, Americans must note that, whatever the relative stability of the gulf, there are troubling forces at work within the Arab, or more broadly speaking, the Islamic world, forces that threaten to submerge the region into a more general chaos. In a spring 1990 review, *The Economist* noted the "lack of euphoria" in the Arab world as much of the rest of the planet seemed to be on the verge of a millennium of democracy and economic prosperity. The rapidly expanding populations of Middle Eastern states, climatic obstacles to increased food production, and the oil-related inequality of wealth within the Arab world threaten the stability of the entire region.

If factors internal to the Arab world and the Persian Gulf are in a state of flux, so, too, are external influences that have shaped U.S. policy in the past. Of the three sets of interests that have driven our diplomacy over the last two centuries, the end of the Cold War has dramatically diminished the importance of the strategic. The Soviet (Russian) threat from the north has disappeared, at least for the time being.

The end of the Cold War has also modified some elements of the geoeconomic equation. The containment of communism no longer compels the United States to insure the continued flow of oil from the gulf to Western Europe. Nevertheless, the overall significance of geoeconomic elements in American foreign policy has increased. First, American policymakers, and the majority of the American people, understand that it is not in the interest of the United States to see the economies of its major trading partners in Europe and Asia collapse. Second, the growth of the economies of the newly democratic states of Eastern Europe depends, in part, on the availability of low-priced Middle Eastern oil. Third, American "dependence" on imported Persian Gulf petroleum is likely to increase. On the whole, the American people are reluctant to approve the construction of more nuclear power plants, for fear of accidents and the problems inherent in the production of waste; to increase off-shore oil drilling, because of concerns about water and beach pollution; or to burn more coal, which would increase air pollution and acid rain.

These alterations in the nature of American interests in the Persian Gulf, the determination displayed by the Bush administration during Desert Shield/Storm, and the willingness of the American people to support such an extensive and potentially costly operation, indicate that the question of the future course of American policy in the Persian

247

Gulf has already been decided. The struggle for Kuwait was, after all, the first post–Cold War crisis, a crisis that occurred after the strategic and geoeconomic equations had begun to change. American involvement in Operation Desert Shield/Storm was consistent with the course of U.S. policy in the gulf dating back to the 1940s. Geoeconomic concerns began to outweigh the strategic as early as the mid-1970s, more than a decade before the Berlin Wall fell.

The end of the Cold War has and will continue to further enhance the relative importance of the Persian Gulf to the United States. As the necessity to defend Western Europe and east Asia declines, the importance of the Middle East will increase. The gulf is probably the only Third World region, other than America's Caribbean and Latin American backyard, in which the United States will recognize vital interests in the coming decade.

If the United States is to play the role of guardian of the Persian Gulf in the future, several historical lessons may help guide American policymakers. First, they must keep their attention focused on the Middle East. Virtually all of the crises in the region involving the United States began when American policymakers had their focus elsewhere. This was true in 1946 before the first crisis with the Soviet Union in Iran, just as it was true in 1990 before Saddam's invasion of Kuwait. Second, the military resources necessary to secure the interests of an "engaged" United States are minimal, especially compared to the burdens Americans have borne in Western Europe and east Asia. Despite the scale of Operation Desert Shield/Storm, once the United Nations and Iraq reached a final cease-fire agreement, the United States was able to withdraw virtually all of its ground and air, and most of its naval forces. The gulf Arabs want no extensive permanent American presence ashore. They prefer to see U.S. forces at sea in the gulf, steaming over the horizon, periodically putting into port. And the United States, having demonstrated its ability to respond forcibly and effectively in the gulf, should find it easier to deter the region's next Saddam Hussein.

Given the historical experience of the United States, American policymakers should also be circumspect in their encouragement of political and social change in the gulf. Americans must understand that the stereotype of theocratic, anti-Western Islamic republics does not represent the only, nor even the typical model of Islamic social organization. Historically, Islamic society has been politically, socially, and economically progressive and scientifically advanced. Despite the current situation in the Islamic world, there is nothing inherent in

Islamic doctrine, nor in past Islamic practice, that rules out a political, social, and economic renaissance.

In the interim, Americans should avoid overreaction to the perceived dangers of fundamentalism in the gulf. The phenomenon is not new, as the rise of Wahabism in the Arabian Peninsula and the Mullah-led revolt against the British tobacco monopoly in Persia demonstrate. Nor does a fundamentalist Islamic government have to be anti-Western in its political and economic orientation. Saudi Arabia is far more fundamentalist than Iran, but is nonetheless one of the more pro-Western countries in the region.

Thus, while keeping a weather eye on the ominous storm clouds that have always threatened the serenity of the Persian Gulf, Americans should set their policy course for the next century with a degree of cautious optimism. What does the future hold? Undoubtedly more of what Americans have witnessed and dealt with successfully over the past few decades. There will be problems and crises aplenty, but they should be manageable. After all, for fifty years, despite the fears of men such as James Forrestal, the United States managed to support Israel without driving the entire Arab world into the Soviet camp, a camp, moreover, that no longer even exists.

Like Great Britain in 1919, the United States in 1991 is at the apogee of its power in the gulf. And that may be another historical lesson in itself, because Britain's post–World War I dominance proved to be short-lived. But the commercial challenge of another Western power— the United States—drove the British from the gulf, not Arab or Iranian nationalists. How long the United States maintains its position in the region will most likely be determined by factors external to the Persian Gulf. Access to petroleum deposits is, after all, but a means to an end. Whether or not Americans use the oil of the gulf to fuel dynamic economic growth into the twenty-first century remains to be seen. If not, someday, perhaps not too far distant, Americans will discover that a European or Asian power, or collection of powers, is purposefully displacing the United States economically, politically, and militarily in the region. But until that day, Americans will remain the guardians of the gulf.

MAPS

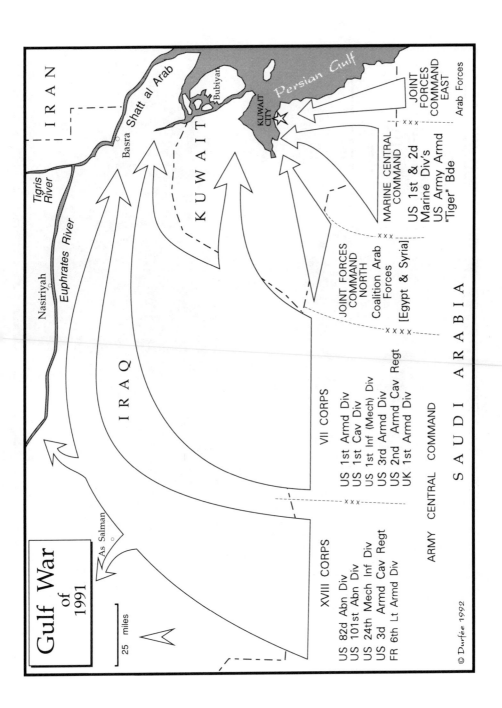

Gulf War of 1991

IRAN

I R A N

Shatt al Arab

Basra

Tigris River

Euphrates River

Nasiriyah

Persian Gulf

Bubiyar

KUWAIT CITY

K U W A I T

I R A Q

As Salman

25 miles

© Durfee 1992

JOINT FORCES COMMAND EAST

Arab Forces

MARINE CENTRAL COMMAND

US 1st & 2d Marine Div's
US Army Armd "Tiger" Bde

JOINT FORCES COMMAND NORTH

Coalition Arab Forces
[Egypt & Syria]

VII CORPS

US 1st Armd Div
US 1st Cav Div
US 1st Inf (Mech) Div
US 3rd Armd Div
US 2nd Armd Cav Regt
UK 1st Armd Div

ARMY CENTRAL COMMAND

S A U D I A R A B I A

XVIII CORPS

US 82d Abn Div
US 101st Abn Div
US 24th Mech Inf Div
US 3d Armd Cav Regt
FR 6th Lt Armd Div

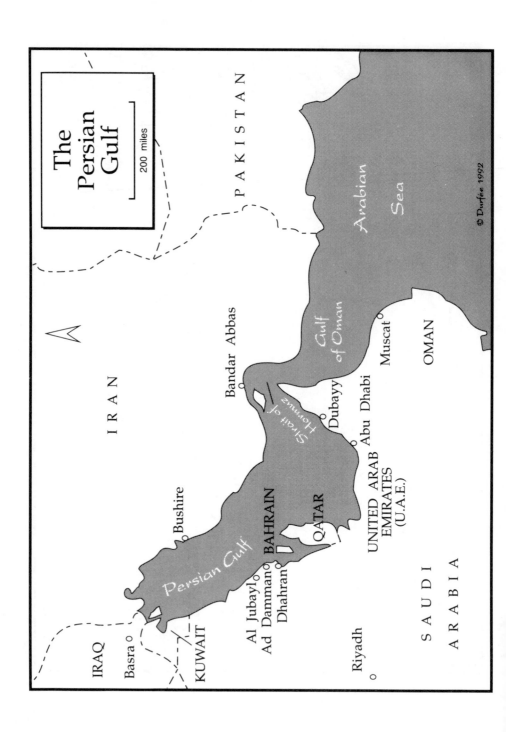

The Persian Gulf

200 miles

© Durfee 1992

PAKISTAN

IRAN

IRAQ

Basra

KUWAIT

Bushire

Al Jubayl
Ad Damman
Dhahran

BAHRAIN

QATAR

Riyadh

SAUDI
ARABIA

Persian Gulf

Bandar Abbas

Strait of
Hormuz

Dubayy

Abu Dhabi

UNITED ARAB
EMIRATES
(U.A.E.)

Gulf
of Oman

Muscat

OMAN

Arabian
Sea

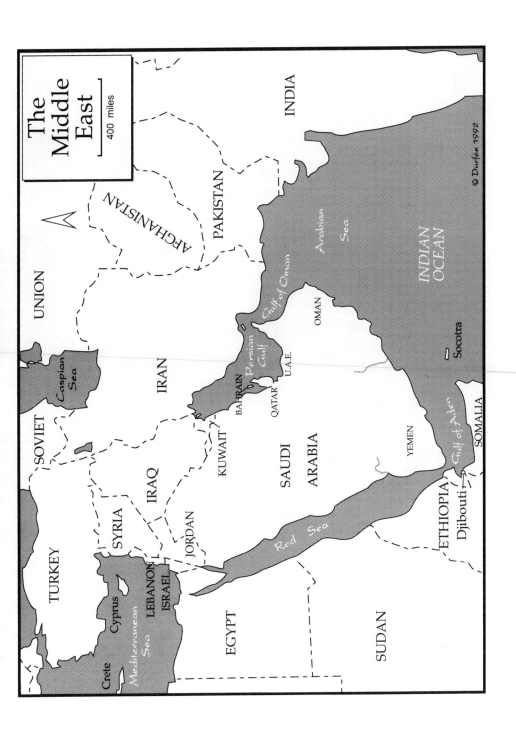

The Middle East

400 miles

© Durfee 1992

255

NOTES

ONE: AN OPEN FIELD FOR AMERICAN CAPITAL AND INDUSTRY

1. For an excellent study of the elements that drove American commercial and foreign policies in the early national period, see James A. Field, Jr., *America and the Mediterranean World* (Princeton: Princeton University Press, 1969).
2. Ibid., p. 14.
3. Before the opening of the Panama Canal in 1914, passage to the Pacific generally entailed the transit of the Indian Ocean.
4. The merchants of Salem, Massachusetts, dominated the trade in the Indian Ocean well into the nineteenth century. Captain Charles Derby brought the brig *Cadet* from Salem to Muscat, Oman, in 1795. Captain Joseph Beadle, returning to Salem in the barque *Eliza* in May 1805, reported on piracy in the gulf. See James Duncan Phillips, *Salem and the East Indies: The Story of the Great Commercial Era of the City* (Boston: Houghton Mifflin, 1947), pp. 186, 238.
5. Alfred W. Crosby, Jr., "American Trade with Mauritius in the Age of the French Revolution and Napoleon," *American Neptune* 45 (January 1965): 5–17. Mauritius and Réunion were the major trading ports for American merchants during the late eighteenth and early nineteenth centuries. In 1796, forty-nine American ships stopped at Mauritius; in 1805, ninety-eight. But wars with France (1798–1801) and Britain (1812–15), and the British conquest of Mauritius in 1810, changed the patterns of American trade in the Indian Ocean basin.
6. Michael A. Palmer, *Stoddert's War: Naval Operations During the Quasi-War with France, 1798–1801* (Columbia, South Carolina: University of South Carolina Press, 1987), p. 207.
7. Boies Penrose, *Travel and Discovery in the Renaissance, 1420–1620* (New York: Atheneum, 1971), p. 78.
8. Albert Hourani, *A History of the Arab Peoples* (Cambridge, MA: Belknap Press, 1991), pp. 243, 253, 261.
9. Even in the nuclear age, U.S. Navy vessels still take just short of a month to reach the gulf.
10. Alfred T. Mahan, *From Sail to Steam: Recollections of a Naval Life* (New York and London: Harper & Row, 1907), p. 223.
11. Ibid., p. 215.
12. Ibid.
13. Master Commandant David Geisinger to Secretary of the Navy Levi Woodbury, January 17, 1834, National Archives, Record Group 45, Masters Commandants Letters to the Secretary of the Navy, January–June 1834, #108;

Edmund Roberts, *Embassy to the Eastern Courts of Cochin-China, Siam, and Muscat; in the U.S. Sloop-of-War Peacock, David Geisinger, Commander, during the Years 1832-3-4* (New York: Harper & Brothers, 1938), pp. 351–63; J. B. Kelly, *Britain and the Persian Gulf, 1795–1880* (Oxford: Clarendon Press, 1968), p. 236; Charles I. Bevans, ed., *Treaties and Other International Agreements of the United States of America, 1776–1949*, vol. 9 (Washington, D.C.: Department of State, 1968–1976), pp. 1291–93; and David F. Long, *Gold Braid and Foreign Relations: Diplomatic Activities of U.S. Naval Officers, 1798–1883* (Annapolis: Naval Institute Press, 1988), pp. 261–62.

14. Roberts, *Embassy*, p. 363. The sultan's navy consisted of fifteen men-of-war including a 74-gun ship of the line.

15. For background on the history of the Persian Gulf, see Roger M. Savory's "The Ancient Period," "A.D. 600–1800," and Malcolm Yapp's "The Nineteenth and Twentieth Centuries," in Alvin J. Cottrell, ed., *The Persian Gulf States: A General Survey* (Baltimore and London: Johns Hopkins University Press, 1980), pp. 3–13, 14–40, and 41–69.

16. Kelly, *Britain and the Gulf*, p. 2. See Also Charles Rathbone Low, *History of the Indian Navy, 1613–1863*, 2 vols. (London: Richard Bentley & Son, 1977) for the view from the perspective of the East India Company and the Indian Navy.

17. Kelly, *Britain and the Gulf*, p. 66. Until the Indian Mutiny of 1857–58, the East India Company, not the British government, bore responsibility for the region.

18. Field, *America and the Mediterranean World*, p. 191.

19. An American consular report of December 1851 noted that ten to twelve American ships were trading in the gulf proper, using Zanzibar as their depot. See John F. Webb, William H. Jelly, and Samuel R. Masury to John Aulick, December 5, 1851, in Norman R. Bennett and George E. Brooks, Jr., eds., *New England and Merchants in Africa: A History Through Documents, 1802 to 1865* (Boston, Boston University Press, 1965), pp. 488–90.

20. Spence to Marcy, November 25, 1854, in Hunter Miller, ed., *Treaties and other International Acts of the United States of America*, vol. 7, (Washington: Government Printing Office, 1931–48), p. 459.

21. See Nicholas V. Riasanovsky, *A History of Russia* (New York, London, and Toronto: Oxford University Press, 1969); and David Gillard, *The Struggle for Asia, 1828–1914: A Study in British and Russian Imperialism* (London: Metheun, 1977).

22. Miller, *Treaties and Other International Acts*, p. 459.

23. Ibid., p. 462.

24. Ibid., p. 466.

25. Field, *America and the Mediterranean*, p. 261.

26. Miller, *Treaties and other International Acts*, p. 468.

27. Spence to Khan, June 1, 1856, ibid., pp. 469–73.

28. Spence to Marcy, December 22, 1856, ibid., pp. 474–78.

29. Ibid.

30. Ibid., p. 482.

31. Ibid., pp. 159–61; 182–86.

32. George N. Curzon, *Persia and the Persia Question*, vol. 1, (London and New York: Longmans, Green, 1892), pp. 509, 541.

33. Frederick C. Drake, *The Empire of the Seas: A Biography of Rear Admiral Robert Wilson Shufeldt, USN* (Honolulu: University of Hawaii Press, 1984).

34. Ibid., p. 220; and Kelly, *Britain and the Gulf*, pp. 775–76.

35. Drake, *Shufeldt*, pp. 220, 224.

36. In his report to the president, Secretary of the Navy R. W. Thompson noted: "[The *Ticonderoga*] was the only American man-of-war ever seen in the Persian Sea or near the mouth of the Euphrates River, and by sailing some distance up that river has brought our form of modern civilization in immediate contact with that prevailing among those who represent the oldest civilization known to history." U.S. Navy Department. *Report of the Secretary of the Navy, 1888* (Washington, 1880), p. 28.

37. Quoted in Drake, *Shufeldt*, p. 220.

38. Ibid., pp. 221, 222–23.

39. Quoted in ibid., p. 227.

40. Ibid., p. 223.

41. See Riasanovsky, *A History of Russia*; and Gillard, *The Struggle for Asia*.

42. Kasson to Evarts, July 13, 1878, United States, Department of State, *Foreign Relations of the United States* (Washington, 1878), 46–48 (hereafter *FRUS*); Foster to Blain, May 21, 1881, *FRUS, 1881*, pp. 1016–17; Benjamin to Frelinghuysen, June 13, 1883, *FRUS, 1883*, pp. 702–6.

43. Pratt to Bayard, November 29, 1886, *FRUS, 1887*, pp. 913–14.

44. Beale to Blaine, January 11, 1892, *FRUS, 1892*, pp. 356–57.

45. Mirza Ali Kuli Khan to the secretary of state, December 28, 1910, *FRUS, 1911*, p. 679.

46. See Alfred Thayer Mahan, *The Problem of Asia and Its Effect upon International Policies* (Boston: Little, Brown, 1900), p. 77; and "The Persian Gulf and International Relations," in *Retrospect & Prospect: Studies in International Relations, Naval and Political* (Boston: Little, Brown, 1902), pp. 209–51. Mahan's personal knowledge of the gulf was limited. He had visited Muscat as a young officer in the *Iroquois* in 1867, but had not actually entered the gulf proper. Mahan, *From Sail to Steam*, pp. 223–25. "Northern tier" was a term coined by Secretary of State John Foster Dulles to describe those states in the Middle East that lay close to the southern border of the Soviet Union. States frequently included in the various definitions of northern tier have included Greece, Turkey, Iran, Pakistan, and Afghanistan.

47. See Bernard Lewis, *The Middle East and the West* (New York: Harper Torchbooks, 1964), p. 9.

48. Petroleum Industry Research Foundation, Inc., *World Oil, Fact and Policy: The Case for a Sound American Petroleum Policy* (New York: PIRF, 1944), pp. 10–11, estimated the world's oil reserves in 1944 at: United States, 39 percent; Middle East, 32 percent; and the Soviet Union, 11 percent. Fifteen years later, Middle Eastern reserves were estimated at 26,000 million tons of oil, or over 62 percent of the world's total. See Stephen Hemsley Longrigg, *Oil in the Middle East: Its Discovery and Development*, 2d ed. (London, New York, and Toronto: Oxford University Press, 1961), p. 350.

49. Leonard M. Fanning, *American Oil Operations Abroad* (New York and London: McGraw-Hill, 1947), pp. 256–59. American companies alone produced between 60 and 70 percent of the world's crude between 1890 and 1918. Only

briefly, between 1898 and 1901, did Russia outproduce the United States, while the latter's proportion of world production fell to about 40 percent.

50. Longrigg, *Oil in the Middle East*, pp. 17–21.

51. Arthur J. Marder, *From Dreadnought to Scapa Flow: The Royal Navy in the Fisher Era, 1904–1919*, vol. 1 (London: Oxford University Press, 1961–70), pp. 45.

52. See Sir John Fisher, *Memoirs and Records of Admiral of the Fleet Lord Fisher*, vol. 2 (London, New York, and Toronto: Hodder & Stoughton, 1919), pp. 189–203; Sir John Fisher, *The Papers of Admiral Sir John Fisher*, ed P. K. Kemp, vol. 1 (Navy Records Society, 1960–64), pp. 80–81; and Jon Tetsuro Sumida, *In Defence of Naval Supremacy: Finance, Technology and British Naval Policy, 1889–1914* (Boston, London, Sydney, Wellington: Unwin, Hyman, 1989), pp. 259–61.

53. Longrigg, *Oil in the Middle East*, pp. 25–32.

54. Benjamin Shwadran, *The Middle East and the Great Powers* (New York, Toronto: John Wiley & Sons, 1973), pp. 197–98.

55. Longrigg, *Oil in the Middle East*, p. 25.

56. Lord Curzon's speech was reported in the November 23, 1919, *New York Times*.

57. John G. Clark, *The Political Economy of World Energy: A Twentieth Century Perspective* (Chapel Hill, North Carolina, and London: University of North Carolina Press, 1990), p. 43.

58. In the final stages of the First World War, small British forces operated in the Caucasus, first to prevent the Germans from consolidating their position in Georgia, and later to fight the spread of Bolshevism into the region. In 1920 the British withdrew and the Soviets reestablished Moscow's control over the Caucasus and Central Asia. See George Lenczowski, *Russia and the West in Iran, 1918–1948: A Study in Big-Power Rivalry* (Ithaca, N.Y.: Cornell University Press, 1949), pp. 12–41.

59. Longrigg, *Oil in the Middle East*, pp. 33–35. Historian Malcolm Yapp writes, Britain's "supremacy in the Gulf in 1919 was a flash in the pan; not the inevitable result of a steady program of historic advance, but an accident of war." Malcolm Yapp, "The Nineteenth and Twentieth Centuries," in Cottrell, ed., *The Persian Gulf*, pp. 58–59.

60. For a discussion of the Arab Revolt, rising Arab nationalism, and Arab disappointments in the post-World War I period, see George Antonius, *The Arab Awakening: The Story of the Arab National Movement* (New York: Capricorn, 1965).

61. E. H. Davenport and Sidney Russell Cooke, *The Oil Trusts and Anglo-American Relations* (New York: Macmillan, 1924), pp. 40–41; Shwadran, *Middle East, Oil, and the Great Powers*, pp. 28–29.

62. Longrigg, *Oil in the Middle East*, pp. 36–37.

63. Gerald D. Nash, *United States Oil Policy, 1890–1964: Business and Government in Twentieth Century America* (Pittsburgh, Penn.: University of Pittsburgh Press, 1968), p. 52; Herbert Feis, *Petroleum and American Foreign Policy* (Stanford, Calif.: Food Research Institute, Stanford University, 1944), pp. 8–9; Aaron David Miller, *Search for Security: Saudi Arabian Oil and American Foreign Policy, 1939–1949* (Chapel Hill, N.C.: University of North Carolina Press, 1980), p. 10; Longrigg, *Oil in the Middle East*, p. 44; and Shwadran, *Middle East, Oil, and the Great Powers*, p. 201.

64. Article 6 of the Treaty of Friendship between Iran and the Russian Socialist Federal Soviet Republic of February 26, 1921, reads: "If a third party should attempt to carry out a policy of usurpation by means of armed intervention in Persia, or if such a Power should desire to use Persian territory as a base of operations against Russia, or if a Foreign Power should threaten the frontiers of Federal Russia or those of its Allies, and if the Persian Government should not be able to put a stop to such a menace after having been once called upon to do so by Russia, Russia shall have the right to advance her troops into the Persian interior for the purpose of carrying out the military operations necessary for its defense. Russia undertakes, however, to withdraw her troops from Persian territory as soon as the danger has been removed." See Lenczowski, *Russia and the West in Iran*, pp. 317–18.

65. The Americans ran afoul both British and Russian interests in north Persia. But the main problem was geographical—moving oil from the north necessitated overland transportation either through southern Iran, where the British had an exclusive concession that included the transportation of oil, or through the Soviet Union, which claimed the rights to the concession of the northern provinces of the Persian Empire itself. Shwadran, *Middle East, Oil, and the Great Powers*, pp. 71–83.

66. Ibid., pp. 22–23.

67. Nash, *United States Oil Policy*, pp. 24–32.

68. Ibid., pp. 42, 43, 50, 53–55.

69. Ibid., p. 56.

70. Shwadran, *Middle East, Oil, and the Great Powers*, p. 219; J. B. Kelly, "Iraq's Borders: Let's Talk Turkey," *National Review* 42 (September 17, 1990): 31–34.

71. Longrigg, *Oil in the Middle East*, pp. 46, 66–70; Miller, *Search for Security*, pp. 11–12; Shwadran, *Middle East, Oil, and the Great Powers*, pp. 238 and Daniel Yergin, *The Prize: The Epic Quest for Oil, Money, and Power* (New York: Simon & Schuster, 1991), pp. 204–5.

72. Yergin, *The Prize*, pp. 390–91; Longrigg, *Oil in the Middle East*, pp. 98–105; and Miller, *Search for Security*, pp. 14–15.

73. Abbas Faroughy, *The Bahrein Islands, 750–1951: A Contribution to the Study of Power Politics in the Persian Gulf* (New York: Verry, Fisher, 1951), pp. 103–7.

74. Miller, *Search for Security*, pp. 15–16; Longrigg, *Oil in the Middle East*, pp. 110–13; and Shwadran, *Middle East, Oil, and the Great Powers*, pp. 407–9.

75. Shwadran, *Middle East, Oil, and the Great Powers*, p. 301.

76. Ibid., p. 302; Miller, *Search for Security*, p. 18.

77. Shwadran, *Middle East, Oil, and the Great Powers*, pp. 303–7; Miller, *Search for Security*, pp. 18–21; and Longrigg, *Oil in the Middle East*, pp. 106–13. Longrigg was the representative of the IPC during the negotiations.

78. The United States remained the source of about 60 percent of the world's petroleum in 1939. The percentage of total world production for the gulf region increased from .017 percent to .055 percent. Fanning, *American Oil Operations*, pp. 256–59.

TWO: THE WORLD OIL CENTER OF GRAVITY

1. For an overview of German views on the Persian Gulf see Peter Hoffmann, "The Gulf Region in German Strategic Projections, 1940–1942," *Militärge-schictliche Mitteilungen* 44 (February 1988): 61–73.
2. A 1940 long-range air attack against oil installations on Bahrain, launched from an Italian base in the Dodecanese Islands in the Aegean, caused little damage but brought the war to the gulf. Faroughy, *The Bahrein Islands*, p. 111.
3. Shwadran, *Middle East, Oil, and the Great Powers*, p. 241.
4. Fanning, *American Oil Operations Abroad*, p. 257.
5. The Trucial states, so-named because of their adherence in 1853 to a maritime truce to be enforced by the British.
6. Longrigg, *Oil in the Middle East*, pp. 117–129; 136–38.
7. From 8,298,000 barrels per year in 1938 to 6,241,000 in 1942, before recovering by war's end. Shwadran, *Middle East, Oil, and the Great Powers*, p. 392.
8. Ibid., p. 349.
9. Longrigg, *Oil in the Middle East*, p. 137.
10. Nash, *United States Oil Policy*, pp. 129–57.
11. John W. Frey and H. Chandler Ide, eds., *A History of the Petroleum Administration for War, 1941–1945* (Washington: GPO, 1946), p. 1.
12. Ibid., p. 265.
13. Nash, *United States Oil Policy*, pp. 170–72. See also The Petroleum Industry Research Foundation, *World Oil, Fact and Policy*, and Feis, *Petroleum and American Foreign Policy*. Both short studies supported a more detailed government-industry relationship in the pursuit of a coherent postwar United States oil policy. But on the issue of direct United States government participation in the construction and operation of a Trans-Arabian pipeline to carry oil from the Persian Gulf region to the eastern Mediterranean, a pet project of Secretary Ickes, Feis argued in support of the proposal, while PIRINC argued against such involvement.
14. Frey and Ides, *Petroleum Administration for War*, pp. 265–68.
15. Ibid., pp. 277–78.
16. Nash, *United States Oil Policy*, pp. 175–79; Frey and Ides, *Petroleum Administration for War*, pp. 279–87.
17. T. H. Vail Motter, *United States Army in World War II, The Middle East Theater: The Persian Corridor and Aid to Russia* (Washington: GPO, 1952), pp. 15–18, 27.
18. James A. Bill, *The Eagle and the Lion: The Tragedy of American-Iranian Relations* (New York and London: Yale University Press, 1988), pp. 29–30.
19. Ibid., pp. 162–63. The American commander was H. Norman Schwarzkopf, father of General H. Norman Schwarzkopf, Jr., commander of USCENTCOM during Operation Desert Shield/Storm in 1990–91.
20. The Persian Gulf Service Command was established in August 1942. Ibid., pp. 227, 437.
21. Motter, *the Persian Corridor*, p. 444; Lenczowski, *Russia and the West in Iran*, pp. 280–81.
22. Miller, *Search for Security*, pp. 34–36.

23. Ibid., p. 130.
24. Ibid., pp. 37–44.
25. Ibid., p. 50.
26. Foreign Petroleum Policy of the United States, April 11, 1944, *FRUS, 1944,* vol. 5, pp. 27–33.
27. Acheson to the Secretary of State, October 9, 1945, *FRUS, 1945,* vol. 8, pp. 43–48.
28. American Economic Policy in the Middle East, May 2, 1945, ibid., pp. 34–39.
29. MacVeagh to Roosevelt, October 15, 1944, quoted in Bruce Robellet Kuniholm, *The Origins of the Cold War in the Near East: Great Power Conflict in Iran, Turkey, and Greece* (Princeton: Princeton University Press, 1980), pp. 97–98.
30. Knox's speech is quoted in Vincent Davis, *Postwar Defense Policy and the U.S. Navy, 1943–1946* (Chapel Hill, N.C.: University of North Carolina Press, 1962), p. 27. American planners had no intention of maintaining postwar bases in the Mediterranean or the Middle East. See JCS 570/2, January 10, 1944, Operational Archives, Naval Historical Center (hereafter OA); Palmer, *Origins of the Maritime Strategy: American Naval Strategy in the First Postwar Decade* (Washington: Naval Historical Center, 1988), pp. 3–8, 17–18; and Elliott Vanvelt Converse, "United States Plans for a Postwar Overseas Military Base System, 1942–1948" (Ph.D. diss., Princeton University, 1984), p. 214.
31. Bernhard H. Bieri, interview with John T. Mason, Jr., pp. 211–17, United States Naval Institute Oral History, 1970. In 1944, Bieri, who would later command American naval forces in the Mediterranean, was attached to the SHAEF staff in Europe. See also Kuniholm, *The Origins of the Cold War in the Near East,* pp. 96–98.
32. Ibid., pp. 70–108.
33. Grew to Tuck, February 3, 1945, *FRUS, 1945,* vol. 8, p. 1. Roosevelt also offered to meet with King Farouk of Egypt and Emperor Haile Selassie of Ethiopia.
34. John S. Keating, "Mission to Mecca: The Cruise of the Murphy," United States Naval Institute *Proceedings* 102 (January 1976): 54–63.
35. Memorandum of Conversation between the King of Saudi Arabia and President Roosevelt, February 14, 1945, *FRUS, 1945,* vol. 8, pp. 2–3; Miller, *Search for Security,* p. 129–131; Robert E. Sherwood, *Roosevelt and Hopkins: An Intimate History* (New York: Harper & Row, 1948), pp. 871–72.
36. Eddy to the Secretary of State, March 3, 1945, *FRUS, 1945,* vol. 8, pp. 7–9; Eddy to the Secretary of State, February 22, 1945, ibid., pp. 689–90.
37. Memo, Thomas T. Handy to the Assistant Secretary of War, February 5, 1945, Annex B to Appendix A, SWNCC 19, OA.
38. Memo, State Department to SWNCC, June 14, 1945, SWNCC 19/13, OA.
39. SWNCC 19/18D, August 23, 1945, OA.
40. Report, SWNCC Coordinating Subcommittee for the Near and Middle East, September 20, 1945, SWNCC 19/20, OA. SWNCC was an attempt to coordinate the efforts of the State, War, and Navy departments and a precursor of the National Security Council.
41. Grew to Truman, June 26, 1945, *FRUS, 1945,* vol. 8, pp. 915–17.
42. Truman to Dean Acheson, September 28, 1945, SWNCC 19, OA.
43. The actual language of the article could very easily be taken to imply that the

Allies were to withdraw from Iran within six months of the surrender of Germany, and not Japan. It reads: "The forces of the Allied Powers shall be withdrawn from Iranian territory not later than six months after all hostilities between the Allied Powers and Germany and her associates have been suspended by the conclusion of an armistice or armistices, or on the conclusion of peace between them, whichever date is the earlier." In January 1942 the Soviet Union was not at war with Japan. When Germany surrendered in May 1945, the Iranians interpreted the agreement in just such a fashion and demanded Allied withdrawal. Loy Henderson was sympathetic to the Iranian interpretation and the Americans and the British ultimately offered to speed their withdrawal if the Soviets would likewise comply. See Henderson memo, 1 June 1945, *FRUS, 1945*, VIII: 374–75; and Murray to the Secretary of State, 14 September 1945, ibid., pp. 408–409.

44. Murray to Byrnes, 20 November 1945, ibid., pp. 437–38.
45. Kuniholm, *The Origins of the Cold War in the Near East*, pp. 274–75.
46. See McFarland, "A Peripheral View of the Origins of the Cold War," pp. 333–51. McFarland focuses on the substantial Iranian role in the crisis writing that they "laid the foundation for the confrontation and worked to enlarge it for Iran's advantage." Ibid., p. 351.
47. Kennan to Byrnes, 1 October 1945, *FRUS, 1945*, 8: 424. During a 19 December meeting between American ambassador to the Soviet Union Averill Harriman and Stalin the latter had defended Soviet actions in Iran by charging that the Iranians posed a threat to Baku oilfields, that the Soviet Union had the right under the 1921 treaty to intervene in Iran, that the Soviet forces were not interfering in internal Iranian affairs, and that the Iranians were stoking the crisis "to stir up trouble between Russia and the Anglo-Saxon powers." The American ambassador in Iran, Wallace Murray, later responded that the suggestion "that Iranians constitute danger to Baku oil fields is so patently absurd that it is difficult to see how the Soviets would expect it to be given any serious consideration." Wallace also pointed out that the 1921 Irano-Soviet treaty allowed Soviet intervention in the event that Iran was threatened by a third power. And the evidence clearly indicated Soviet complicity in efforts to prevent the Iranian central government from reestablishing control over its northern provinces. See Harriman to Acheson, 23 December 1945, ibid., pp. 510–11; and Murray to the Secretary of State, 28 December 1945, ibid., pp. 516–17. With regard to Soviet concerns about the status of minorities in its southern neighbor, the British ambassador in Iran, Sir Reader Bullard, aptly commented: "There is a great deal of humbug about the Soviet treatment of minorities. It may be too strong to say that it consists of folk-songs tempered by executions." See William Roger Louis, *The British Empire in the Middle East, 1945–1951: Arab Nationalism, the United States, and Postwar Imperialism* (Oxford: Clarendon Press, 1984), p. 62.
48. Almost immediately after Stalin's death in 1953, Molotov informed the Turks that the independent-minded Soviet republics of Georgia and Armenia had suddenly and inexplicably renounced their territorial claims against Turkey. In February 1953, shortly before the session of the Twentieth Party Congress during which a secret report detailing Stalin's crimes was read to party members, a *Pravda* article on the poor state of Soviet-Turkish relations quoted

remarks made by Khrushchev at a meeting of the Supreme Soviet: "We cannot say that Turkey was alone to blame. We, too, made inappropriate statements that cast a shadow on those relations." See William B. Ballis, "Soviet-Turkish Relations during the Decade 1953–1963," Institute for the Study of the USSR *Bulletin* 11 (September 1964): 3, 7.

49. Wilson to Byrnes, March 18, 1946, *FRUS, 1946*, vol. 8, pp. 818–19.

50. Harry S. Truman, *Years of Trial and Hope*, vol. 2 of *Memoirs*, (Garden City, N.Y.: 1955), p. 94.

51. JCS 1518, September 19, 1945, OA.

52. See H. W. Brands, *Inside the Cold War: Loy Henderson and the Rise of the American Empire, 1918–1961* (New York and Oxford: Oxford University Press, 1991), pp. 139–41; Henderson to Byrnes, December 11, 1945, *FRUS, 1945*, vol. 8, pp. 488–90.

53. January 31, 1946, JIC 341, *Records of the Joint Chiefs of Staff*, Part II: *1946–1953, The Soviet Union* (Washington, DC: University Publishers of America, 1979), reel 1.

54. Kuniholm, *Origins of the Cold War in the Near East*, p. 336.

55. According to Rossow, General Bagramian had replaced Lieutenant General Glinsky, the former garrison commander in Iran, in command. Rossow to Byrnes, March 6, 1946, U.S. Department of State, *Foreign Relations of the United States, 1946*, vol. 7: *The Near East and Africa* (Washington, 1969), pp. 342–43. Bagramian, a Red Army commander of Armenian descent, had commanded a front against the Germans during the latter stages of the 1941–45 war.

56. Robert Rossow, Jr., "The Battle of Azerbaijan, 1946," *The Middle East Journal* 10 (Winter 1956): 17–32.

57. Dmitri Volkogonov, retired Soviet colonel general, former head of the Institute of Military History in Moscow, and biographer of Stalin, who had access to official Soviet documentation, writes of Churchill's 1946 charge that an Iron Curtain was descending across Europe: "This was true. Soon after the war, Stalin had taken energetic measures to reduce all contact with the West and the rest of the world. A curtain, whether of iron or ideology, had decidedly come down, and henceforth for many years the Soviet people could know about the West only what officials, of Suslov's ilk, thought they should know." Dmitri Volkogonov, *Stalin: Triumph and Tragedy* (New York: Grove Weidenfeld, 1991), p. 532.

58. The text of Churchill's speech appeared in the *New York Times*, March 6, 1946, p. 4; and is excerpted in Barton J. Bernstein and Allen J. Matusow, eds., *The Truman Administration: A Documentary History* (New York and London: Harper & Row, 1966), pp. 215–83.

59. Byrnes to Kennan, March 5, 1946, *FRUS, 1946*, vol. 7, pp. 340–42.

60. Press Release, March 6, 1946, U.S. Department of State, *The Department of State Bulletin* 14 (March 17, 1946): 447. For the navy's initial plans for a show of force, see Michael A. Palmer, *Origins of the Maritime Strategy*, pp. 21–22; and Hansen W. Baldwin's "U.S Fleet Parade in Europe Dropped," *New York Times*, March 17, 1946, pp. 1, 3.

61. Rossow to Byrnes, March 5, 1946, *FRUS, 1946*, vol. 7, p. 340; Rossow to Byrnes, March 6, 1946, ibid., pp. 342–43; Rossow to Byrnes, March 7, 1946, ibid., pp. 344–45.

62. Melvyn P. Leffler, "Adherence to Agreements: Yalta and the Experiences of the Early Cold War," *International Security* 11 (Summer 1986): 88–123.

63. Walter LaFeber, *America, Russia, and the Cold War, 1945–1984*, 5th ed. (New York: Alfred Knopf, 1985), p. 35.

64. Joyce and Gabriel Kolko, *The Limits of Power: The World and United States Foreign Policy, 1945–1954* (New York: Harper & Row, 1972), p. 239.

65. John Lewis Gaddis, *The United States and the Origins of the Cold War* (New York: Columbia University Press, 1972), p. 311*n*.

66. Robert L. Meeser, *The End of an Alliance: James F. Byrnes, Roosevelt, Truman, and the Origins of the Cold War* (Chapel Hill, N.C.: University of North Carolina Press, 1982), p. 197.

67. Stephen L. McFarland's "A Peripheral View of the Origins of the Cold War," pp. 333–51.

68. See *New York Times*, March 14, 1946, p. 1.

69. See note accompanying Byrnes to Rossow, March 15, 1946, *FRUS, 1946*, vol. 8, pp. 359–60*n*.

70. See note on p. 364 of Murray to Byrnes, March 18, 1946, ibid., pp. 364–65.

71. See Archie Roosevelt, *For Lust of Knowing: Memoirs of an Intelligence Officer* (Boston and Toronto: Little, Brown, 1988), pp. 227–33.

72. See editorial note, *FRUS, 1946*, vol. 8, pp. 346–48.

73. Byrnes to Kennan, March 8, 1946, ibid., p. 348.

74. Kennan to Byrnes, March 17, 1946, ibid., pp. 362–64.

75. Kennan to Byrnes, February 22, 1946, ibid., vol. 6, pp. 696–709.

76. The Soviets informed the Iranians of their intention to withdraw on the evening of March 24. Murray to Byrnes, March 25, 1946, ibid., vol. 7, pp. 379–80. Andrei Gromyko made the official announcement before the United Nations on the twenty-sixth, ibid., pp. 381–82. See also Truman, *Memoirs*, vol. 2, pp. 95–96; and Robert James Maddox, *From War to Cold War: The Education of Harry S. Truman* (Boulder & London: Westview, 1988), p. 176.

77. CNO to CINCPAC, CINCLANT, COM7THFLT, COM12THFLT, COM-NAVMED, September 23, 1946, Box 12, Series II, Dispatch Files, Operations Division—COMINCH, OA.

78. Truman, *Year of Decisions*, vol. 1 of *Memoirs*, p. 552. A solid balanced article on the Iran crisis is Gary R. Hess, "The Iranian Crisis of 1945–46 and the Cold War," *Political Science Quarterly* 89 (March 1974), pp. 117–46. Hess concludes: "While the importance of commercial and economic objectives cannot be discounted, the dominant factor shaping American policy was that Soviet actions were seen against the background of a vivid memory of Munich. Americans thus regarded their position in Iran as a test of Western firmness and especially as a means of demonstrating the workability of the international peace-keeping system centered in the United Nations. Obviously coincidence was an important element in the shaping of American policy: the Iranian situation intensified just at the moment that disenchantment with the Soviet Union became part of the American consensus and when the convening of the United Nations presented an opportunity to prove the effectiveness of collective action to prevent war." Ibid., p. 146.

79. Truman listed Rumania, Bulgaria, Iran, the Kiel Canal, the Rhine-Danube

Waterway, the Black Sea Straits, Japan, China, Korea, and the Lend-Lease debt of the Soviet Union as areas where the United States should take a harder line.

80. Byrnes to the JCS, March 6, 1946, JCS 1641, OA. The letter was approved and signed by Truman.

81. JCS 1641/3, March 13, 1946, OA. The Joint Chiefs also used their reply as an opportunity to ask SWNCC for political guidance concerning United States Soviet policy. On August 22, the Joint Staff Planners, "on their own initiative," drew up a memorandum concerning Turkey and recommended that the Joint Chiefs forward it to SWNCC. JCS 1704, 22 August 1946, OA. The following day, the revised memorandum was sent to the secretaries of War and the Navy, who forwarded it to the acting secretary of state on the twenty-eighth. JCS, 1704/1, August 23, 1946, OA; Patterson and Kenney to the acting secretary of state, August 28, 1946, enclosing above, *FRUS, 1946*, vol. 7, pp. 856–58. The memorandum reiterated the view that Soviet demands with regard to the defense of the straits had to be rooted in interests beyond those stated since the Soviets had the capability to close the straits in any case. "The same logic which would justify Soviet participation in the defense of the Dardanelles would also tend to justify further Soviet military penetration through the Aegean." Such Soviet penetration would reduce Turkey "to a satellite Soviet State." The memorandum continued: "Strategically Turkey is the most important military factor in the Eastern Mediterranean and the Middle East. She is one of the few national entities and the only nation now possessing, according to best available information, a firm resolution to oppose the apparent Soviet policy of expansion in the area. While lacking an effective navy and air force, Turkey possesses a rugged and considerable ground army which, particularly if properly equipped and supported, is capable of offering material resistance, even to the Soviets, if the nation is attacked." The JCS concluded by recommending that military advice and assistance be provided to the Turks to maintain their will to resist.

82. Memo from the JCS to Truman, March 12, 1946, JCS 1643, OA.

83. JCS 1641/5, April 11, 1946, OA.

84. JCS 1641/6, May 18, 1946, OA.

85. JCS 1714, OA.

86. JCS 1714/1, October 4, 1946, OA. Great Britain drew 40 percent of its oil from the Abadan fields in Iran.

87. JCS 1714/3, October 14, 1946, OA. The correct date was August 23.

88. The department had prepared a policy statement in July 1946. See Policy and Information Statement on Iran, July 15, 1946, *FRUS, 1946*, vol. 7, pp. 507–9.

89. Clayton to Byrnes, September 27, 1946, *FRUS, 1946*, vol. 7, pp. 516–17; Allen to Byrnes, September 28, 1946, ibid., pp. 517–18; Allen to Byrnes, September 30, 1946, ibid., pp. 518–20; Acheson to Byrnes, October 1, 1946, ibid., p. 520; Henderson to Acheson, October 18, 1946, enclosing memorandum of the same date, ibid., pp. 533–36.

90. Memo, Loy Henderson, October 21, 1946, enclosing Memorandum on Turkey, ibid., pp. 893–97.

91. McFarland, "A Peripheral View of the Origins of the Cold War," p. 334.

THREE: MIDDLE EAST OIL AND THE DESTINY OF EUROPE

1. Loy Henderson, for example, wrote: "The most important interest of the United States in the Near East is not based, as a fairly large section of the American public appears to believe, upon American participation in petroleum extraction or in profits to be derived from trade, but upon preventing developments from taking place in that area which might make a mockery of the principles on which the United Nations Organization rests, which might lead to the impairment, if not the wrecking, of that organization, and which might eventually give birth to a third World War." Loy Henderson Memorandum, undated, *FRUS, 1946*, pp. 1–6.

2. Kolko, *The Limits of Power*, p. 236; Daniel Yergin, *Shattered Peace: The Origins of the Cold War and the National Security State* (Boston: Houghton Mifflin, 1977), pp. 179–80. Yergin quotes Henderson on the importance of the region "especially in view of the oil reserves," but Henderson's concerns were much broader. For example, his November 19, 1945, memorandum on the Iranian situation for Assistant Secretary of State Dunn, which runs for nearly two complete pages in the *Foreign Relations* series, mentions oil once, in a short concluding paragraph that reads, "Apart from our interest in the international security aspect [which was the subject of extensive discussion in the memo], this country has a direct interest in this problem because of our oil, economic, and strategic interest in this area." Henderson to Dunn, November 19, 1945, *FRUS, 1945*, vol. 8, pp. 430–31.

3. Henderson to Acheson, October 18, 1946, enclosing memorandum of the same date, *FRUS, 1946*, vol. 7, pp. 533–36.

4. The Joint War Plans Committee's "Strategic Study of the Area between the Alps and the Himalayas," conducted as part of a series of studies in the Pincher series, concluded in November 1946 that "the greatest strategic objectives in the Alps to Himalayas area, for both the Soviets and the Allies, are the control of the eastern Mediterranean area and the Middle East oil resources." See JWPC 475/1, November 2, 1946, p. 3, *Records of the Joint Chiefs of Staff*, part II, 1946–1953, The Soviet Union (Washington, 1979). Nevertheless, despite repeated studies that stressed the importance of the region in the event of war, the United States consistently resisted formal military commitment to the defense of the Persian Gulf region. JCS 1887/6 of October 1950 noted "that all of these papers [related to Middle East defense] concern geographical areas outside Western Europe. In this connection they [the Joint Chiefs of Staff] would point out that, in their opinion, the loss of Western Europe would represent a most serious blow to the Western Powers. The loss of the Middle East in the early stages of a global war would not in itself be fatal, although the recapture of the Middle East would be essential for victory. The strategic defense contemplated for the Far and Middle East indicates that those areas are, for planning purposes, now considered to be in a lower category than Western Europe." See JCS, 1887/6, October 25, 1950, OA. The JCS 1887 series consistently rejected American defence of the region through 1953.

5.

World, US, and PG Petroleum Production in Thousands of Metric Tons

Year	World	US	%	PG	%
1930	177,200	123,117	70	7,157	4
1935	200,800	134,675	67	11,445	5
1940	262,000	182,867	70	12,950	5
1945	333,000	231,575	70	25,590	7
1946	356,000	237,526	68	34,276	9
1947	390,000	254,382	65	41,012	10
1948	441,000	276,738	62	55,853	12
1949	465,000	248,919	53	68,542	15
1950	522,900	266,708	51	85,925	16
1955	772,800	335,744	43	159,779	20

Source: United Nations, *Statistical Yearbook, 1949–1950,* table 41; and 1956 and 1957 editions.

6. Office of Naval Intelligence, "The Persian Gulf," *The ONI Review* 4 (April 1949): 43.

7.

US Petroleum Exports and Imports in Thousands of bbls

Year	Imports	Exports
1930	43,489	132,794
1935	20,396	74,343
1940	41,089	78,970
1945	39,282	149,985
1946	51,610	119,687
1947	61,857	118,122
1948	59,051	94,938
1949	81,873	86,307
1950	132,547	76,483
1955	170,143	122,617

Source: Ben J. Wattenberg, ed., *The Statistical History of the United States: From Colonial Times to the Present,* pp. 596–97.

8. Some historians portray the oil problem as critical immediately after the war. See Yergin, *Shattered Peace,* pp. 179–80.
9. Walter Millis, ed., *The Forrestal Diaries* (New York: Viking, 1951), p. 272.
10. Forrestal to secretary of state, December 11, 1944, Middle East, Box 13, Political-Military Policy Division, OA.
11. Memos, Notes on Middle East Oil, April 16, 1946, and October 17, 1946, ibid. The April memorandum concluded that Soviet interests in Iran were rooted more in "political reasons than for oil and that she will use her oil

rights to seek an outlet on the Persian Gulf." Also note that while it has been United States policy since the oil embargo of 1973 to decrease American "reliance" on foreign oil supplies, American policy in the late 1940s was quite the opposite. Forrestal and other American policymakers hoped to increase American reliance on foreign suppliers, to exhaust those reserves while American petroleum reserves remained in the ground.

12. *New York Times*, January 18, 1948, pp. 1, 51.
13. Forrestal Diaries, vol. 9, pp. 2026–27, Columbia University Oral History, Privileged Manuscript Collection, OA.
14. *New York Times*, January 20, 1948, pp. 1, 14.
15. Navy press release, July 2, 1948, Press Release Files, OA. Eleven states and the District of Columbia borrowed fuel oil from the navy. According to a September 14 navy press release, "the Navy reduced its stock to a bare minimum to meet the emergency."
16. Millis, *The Forrestal Diaries*, p. 323.
17. Ibid., p. 551.
18. The publication of the *Middle East Journal* in January 1947 exemplified growing American interest in the Middle East. Modeled after the prestigious *Foreign Affairs*, the lead editorial explained that the new journal would address Americans' need to understand a region for which they had assumed "a certain amount of responsibility." The U.S. role in forcing the Soviets to withdraw from Iran, support of Turkey in the question of the Straits, and participation in the question of the fate of Palestine and the settlement of Jewish refugees, made it imperative that Americans appreciate the forces at work within the Middle East.
19. Office of Naval Intelligence, "The Persian Gulf," p. 43.
20. The navy began to buy Persian Gulf oil in late 1945, purchasing Navy Special Fuel Oil from ARAMCO refineries in Saudi Arabia for $1.05 per barrel, when the corresponding Western Hemisphere price was about $1.48. Again, the Persian Gulf rates were significantly lower than the price for Western Hemisphere oil products.

Price per Barrel, 1948

	Persian Gulf	United States
Navy Special Fuel	$1.48	$2.63
Navy Diesel	$2.11	$3.51
Motor gasoline	$3.39	$3.57

Sources: See statement by Secretary of the Navy John L. Sullivan, April 28, 1948; press release, June 24, 1948, ibid.

21. During the last half of 1946, 35 percent of the petroleum products moved by the U.S. Navy came from the Persian Gulf; during 1947, 41.5 percent; during 1948, 30 percent; during 1949, 38 percent; and during 1950, 32 percent. U.S. Navy, *Logistics Summary Reports*, Logistics Reports, Command Files, OA.

22. DCNO (Logistics) Narrative Report, July 1, 1946–June 30, 1947, p. 13, Logistics Division Reports, Command Files, OA.

23. See James A. Field, Jr., *History of United States Naval Operations in Korea* (Washington: GPO, 1962), pp. 383–84.

24. Between July 1 and November 1, 1950, "64 government owned and/or operated tankers called at Bahrein or Ras Tanura," an average of sixteen per month. During the heavier traffic of 1947–49, the number of tankers must have been about two dozen. See CINCNELM report to CNO, Operations and Conditions of Command, July 1–November 1, 1950, November 1, 1950, MEF, Command Files, OA.

25. CNO to COMNAVEU, October 17, 1946, Chronological, CNO, Command Files, OA. Conolly's headquarters, originally established early in World War II, first bore the title U.S. Naval Forces, Europe. On November 1, 1947, the command, answerable to the JCS under the Unified Command Plan, was redesignated U.S. Naval Forces, Eastern Atlantic and Mediterranean. Conolly's cumbersome title—CINCNAVEASTLANTMED—was mercifully shortened in May 1948 to CINCNELM.

26. Richard L. Conolly, interview with Donald F. Shaughnessy, 1960, p. 294, Columbia University Oral History Project, New York, NY.

27. CINCNELM Command History, October 1947–March 1948, Middle East Force, Command Files, OA.

28. CINCNELM to CNO, Annual Report of Operations, July 1, 1948–July 30, 1949 [sic], November 30, 1949, ibid.

29. CMEF to CNO (OP-09B9), July 29, 1960, enclosing Command History, from commissioning through December 31, 1958, ibid.

30. Memo, from E. T. Woolridge to Radford, April 2, 1948, A4/QG1-2 (Near East), Box 2, Operations Division–CNO, OA. Woolridge had discussed the development of the American naval force in the gulf with the State Department's Loy Henderson, who agreed.

31. Memo: OP-03 regarding NELM Conference, June 5, 1948, A4/FF7 (NELM), Box 1, ibid.

32. DCNO (Logistics), Historical Narrative, July 1, 1947–September 30, 1947, p. 11, Logistics Reports, Command Files, ibid.

33. Chief of Naval Communications, Earl E. Stone to CNO, 28 April 28, 1948, Folder 1, 1948, Chronological, CNO, ibid; I. N. Kiland to DCNO (Operations), October 1, 1948, A4 (General), Box 1, CNO, Operations Division, ibid.; CINCNELM Command History (April–September 1948), October 14, 1948, Middle East Force, Command Files, ibid.

34. CINCLANTFLT to CNO, October 24, 1947, A4/QG1-2 (Near East), Box 2, Operations Division–CNO, ibid; CNO to CINCPAC, CINCNELM, CINCLANT, January 16, 1948, ibid; memo: OP-33 to OP-03, May 24, 1948, A4 (General), Box 1, ibid.

35. Memo, OP-03 to CNO, February 15, 1948, ibid.; memo: B. H. Rodgers to OP-03, February 11, 1948, ibid.; memo: OP-33 to OP-09, May 17, 1948, A4 (General), Box 1, ibid.

36. Commander *Pawcatuck* (AO-108) to Commander Service Force, U.S. Atlantic Fleet, September 2, 1948, Report Files, ibid.

37. Report, *Greenwich Bay* (AVP-41), August 12, 1948, ibid.

38. Commander *Pawcatuck* (AO-108) to Commander Service Force, U.S. Atlantic Fleet, September 2, 1948, ibid.
39. Commander, Carrier Division Five to CINCNELM, May 3, 1948, ibid.
40. July 29, 1960, Command History of Middle East Force through 31 December 1958, Middle East Force, Command Files, ibid.
41. E. M. Eller to Sherman, Folder 2, Box 1, Sherman Papers, 1950, 00, ibid.
42. Record of discussion, September 21, 1950, *FRUS, 1950*, vol. 5, p. 207.

FOUR: THE CHIMERA OF REGIONAL DEFENSE

1. Quoted in Brands, *Inside the Cold War*, p. 277.
2. For the relevant correspondence see *FRUS, 1945*, vol. 8, pp. 1034–1218.
3. A U.S. Navy intelligence assessment of mid-1947 noted that the Arabs had to that point "sought and welcomed" American involvement in the region, but warned that "there are some indications that this attitude is not a permanent one and that eventually United States activities in the Near East will arouse Arab suspicion and countermeasures." See Office of Naval Intelligence, "The Arab League," *ONI Review* 2 (July 1947): 40.
4. Acheson, *Present at the Creation: My Years in the State Department* (New York: Norton, 1969), p. 169.
5. Compare Acheson, *Present at the Creation*, p. 169, and Millis, *The Forrestal Diaries*, p. 347.
6. Ibid., p. 169. See also Donovan, *Conflict and Crisis: The Presidency of Harry S. Truman, 1945–1948* (New York: Norton, 1977), pp. 312–31.
7. See, for example, Steven L. Rearden, *The Formative Years, 1947–1950*, vol. 1 of *History of the Office of the Secretary of Defense* (Washington: Historical Office of the Secretary of Defense, 1984), pp. 545–46.
8. SWNCC memo of June 21, 1946 in JCS 1684/1, June 18, 1946, OA. ONI considered the Palestine problem "the most powerful integrating force presently at work in the Arab League and in the Arab world." See Office of Naval Intelligence, "The Arab League," p. 39.
9. JCS 1684/3, October 10, 1947, OA.
10. For a good example see Nimitz memo to JCS of October 10, 1947, JCS 1684/6, later added to 1684/3, ibid.
11. CNO memo to JCS of February 7, 1948, in JCS 1684/8, February 9, 1948, ibid.
12. JCS 1684/11, March 31, 1948; JCS 1684/14, 13 May 1948, ibid.
13. JCS 1684/27, March 7, 1949, ibid.
14. JCS 1684/28, 6 May 1949, report of JSSC of April 1, 1949 accepted, ibid. For an Israeli view of American efforts in the region and the potential contribution of Israel, see Dore Gold, *America, The Gulf and Israel: CENTCOM (Central Command) and Emerging US Regional Security Policies in the Mideast* (Boulder, Colo.: Westview, 1988).
15. The United States also believed that Israel could pay reparations for any territory held beyond that assigned in the original United Nations partition and that an agreement ought to include the resettlement of all Arab refugees, either within Israel or neighboring Arab states. See Kenneth W. Condit, *1947–1949* vol. 2 of *The History of the Joint Chiefs of Staff: The Joint Chiefs of Staff and National Policy* (Washington: GPO, 1978), pp. 103–4.

16. Circular from the acting secretary of state, May 20, 1950, *FRUS, 1950*, vol. 5, pp. 167; Webb to Lay, August 7, 1950, ibid., pp. 176–78.
17. McGhee to Jessup, October 19, 1950, ibid., pp. 217–21.
18. Louis, *The British Empire in the Middle East*, pp. 25, 26, 583. The British proposed the establishment of an Anglo-American military command in the Mediterranean as early as 1946.
19. Report of the Near East Regional Conference in Cairo, March 16, 1950, *FRUS, 1950*, vol. 5, pp. 2–8.
20. Re-evaluation of US Plans for the Middle East, *FRUS, 1951*, vol. 5, pp. 6–11. For a good review of McGhee's role in the development of thinking, see Peter H. Hahn, "Containment and Egyptian Nationalism: The Unsuccessful Effort to Establish the Middle East Command, 1950–1953," *Diplomatic History* 11 (Winter 1987): 23–40.
21. As late as October, the State Department noted that "we understand that the JCS are opposed to any measures which would commit or tend to commit U.S. forces to the Middle East in the event of global war." McGhee to Jessup, October 19, 1950, *FRUS, 1950*, vol. 5, pp. 217–21. For evidence of the apparent lack of enthusiasm among the JCS and American military planners for Middle East defense and anything that might lead to increased American involvement see Jernegan to Henderson, November 9, 1953, *FRUS, 1952–1954*, vol. 9, pp. 424–28.
22. George McGhee, *The US-Turkish-NATO Middle East Connection: How the Truman Doctrine Contained the Soviets in the Middle East* (New York: St. Martins Press, 1990), p. 116.
23. Peter L. Hahn, *The United States, Great Britain, and Egypt, 1945–1956: Strategy and Diplomacy in the Early Cold War* (Chapel Hill, N.C., and London: University of North Carolina Press, 1991), pp. 145–47.
24. Shwadran, *Middle East, Oil, and the Great Powers*, p. 341. For an excellent discussion of Anglo-American perceptions regarding oil concessions in the Middle East and the ARAMCO agreement of December, 1950 see Louis, *The British Empire in the Middle East*, pp. 596–603.
25. Acheson to Embassy Iran, March 17, 1951, *FRUS, 1951*, vol. 10, pp. 25–26.
26. Memo from the JCS to SECDEF, October 10, 1951, ibid, pp. 220–22.
27. For expressions of Iranian concern see Allen to Marshall, March 27, June 14, and September 9, 1947, *FRUS, 1947*, vol. 5, pp. 901–2, 913–14, 948–50; Marshall to the U.S. Embassy in Iran, July 29, 1947, ibid., pp. 924–27, and 924n.
28. Jernegan to Allen, December 9, 1947, ibid, vol. 5, pp. 992–93. Secretary of State Dean Acheson reiterated the American policy five years later writing:

Irans have often expressed resentment US treatment of Iran has never been as favorable as US treatment Greece and Turkey and are inclined invidiously to compare aid rendered Iran with that under the Grk-Turk programs. Fact is that concepts Truman Doctrine apply equally to Iran as to other countries which we aid. Extent and nature of aid to each country however is based not upon what others receive but upon such factors as (a) their needs, taking into account their own resources, and (b) the extent to which such assistance can be effectively utilized. If by "no less favorably" Emb means aid programs to Iran at approximately levels in Greece and Turkey, ans question 4a Embtel 3999 wld probably

NOTES

be that while US prepared apply similar criteria in establishing Iran needs, such needs wld be less than those of Greece or Turkey. This is particularly true in view fact by settling oil controversy, Iran requirement for fon financial aid wld be limited except in initial stages resumed operations, and absorptive capacity Iran armed forces as effective instrument free world strength far less than Grk or Turk. . . . See *FRUS, 1952–1954*, vol. 10, pp. 386–89.

29. Marshall to the American Embassy in Teheran, July 29, 1947, *FRUS, 1947*, vol. 5, pp. 924–27.
30. Draft policy statement, NSC 107, March 14, 1951, *FRUS, 1952–1954*, vol. 10, pp. 21–23. Nearly a year later, as the situation in Iran continued to deteriorate, the Turkish Prime Minister informed George McGhee, then United States Ambassador to Turkey: " 'We must not remain a spectator' but must do something about the situation." McGhee had responded that "the situation was too dangerous to allow to drift, and that we must attempt to determine, rather than merely to react to the course of events." See McGhee's memo of conversation, February 10, 1952, *FRUS, 1952–1954*, vol. 8, pp. 873–880.
31. NSC 107/2, June 27, 1951, ibid., pp. 71–76.
32. For example, see Allen to Jernegan, December 26, 1947, *FRUS, 1947*, vol. 5, pp. 996–98.
33. JCS 1887/20, April 27, 1951, OA.
34. Quoted in Brands, *Inside the Cold War*, p. 235.
35. Eller to Sherman, February 5, 1951, Folder #2, Box 1, 1950, OA.
36. For example, see telegrams from Ambassador Allen to Marshall, March 27 and September 9, 1947, *FRUS, 1947*, 5: 901–902; 948–50.
37. Allen to Marshall, September 9, 1948, *FRUS, 1948*, vol. 5, pp. 948–50.
38. Allen to Marshall, June 14, 1947, *FRUS, 1947*, vol. 5, pp. 913–14.
39. Allen to Marshall, November 10, 1947, ibid., pp. 977–79.
40. JCS 1887/6, October 25, 1950, OA.
41. JCS 1887/29, December 5, 1951, ibid.
42. NSC 136/1, November 20, 1952, *FRUS, 1952–1954*, vol. 10, pp. 529–34; Robert J. Watson, *The Joint Chiefs of Staff and National Policy, 1953–1954*, vol. 5 of *History of the Joint Chiefs of Staff*, (Washington, 1986), p. 333.
43. Ibid., p. 333.
44. JCS 1714/45, November 18, 1952, OA.
45. Watson, *The JCS and National Policy, 1953–1954*, p. 333; JCS 1714/46, January 26, 1953, OA.
46. Paul H. Nitze, *From Hiroshima to Glasnost: At the Center of Decision* (New York: Grove Weidenfeld, 1989), p. 135.
47. See Gifford to SECSTATE, January 9, 1953, *FRUS, 1952–1954*, vol. 10, pp. 596–97, for positive movement in Britain. The review of the published documents in the State Department's new Iran volume make clear that an agreement seemed near in January and early February.
48. Acting secretary of state to Embassy UK, February 3, 1953, ibid, pp. 659–62.
49. J. F. Dulles to Embassy Iran, February 10, 1953, ibid, pp. 662–64.

50. Mossadegh, too, the American ambassador in Teheran noted, contemplated breaking off negotiations. Henderson to State, February 14, 1953, ibid., pp. 665–67.

51. See Henderson to State, two messages of February 28, 1953, ibid, pp. 685–88, and 688–89.

52. Nitze suggests that Mossadegh thought he could get a better deal from Eisenhower. Nitze, *From Hiroshima to Glasnost*, p. 135. More likely, Mossadegh had simply lost control of the nationalist movement and realized that any agreement that would be acceptable to the British would be considered unacceptable by many of his supporters. Even the Shah was loathe to replace Mossadegh before he had finalized an agreement with the British, fearing that the onus for the settlement would fall on the monarchy, instead of the prime minister who had engineered the crisis.

53. Brands, *Inside the Cold War*, p. 264.

54. Henderson to State, February 28, 1953, *FRUS 1952–1954*, vol. 10, pp. 688–89.

55. CIA memo, March 1, 1953, ibid., pp. 689–91.

56. Memo of discussion, 135th Meeting of NSC, March 4, 1953, ibid., pp 692–701. See also CIA Special Estimate, March 12, 1953, *FRUS, 1952–1954*, vol. 8, pp. 1125–29, which concluded: "The new Soviet regime probably fears that, while it is in the process of consolidating its power, the West may make aggressive moves against the Bloc. It would probably view with extreme suspicion any new moves made by the West, particularly involving long-range air forces or military forces close to Bloc frontiers."

57. Draft policy statement, NSC 107, March 14, 1951, *FRUS, 1952–1954*, vol. 10, pp. 21–23.

58. C. M. Woodhouse, *Something Ventured* (London: Granada, 1982), pp. 111, 117. Interestingly, the idea for a coup in Britain originated in the Foreign Office of Herbert Morrison of a Labor Government, not the Tory government of Winston Churchill that subsequently executed the plan.

59. Ibid., p. 122.

60. Ibid., p. 124.

61. Henderson to State, March 10, 1953, *FRUS, 1952–1954*, vol. 10, pp. 706–8. Kenneth Love, a *New York Times* reporter in Iran, sympathetic to the Iranian prime minister, nevertheless wrote that Mossadegh "had eliminated all means of an orderly change of government and achieved dictatorial powers before his overthrow." See *New York Times*, August 21, 1953, p. 1.

62. Henderson to State, March 6, 1953, ibid., pp. 701–2.

63. The decision to go ahead with the coup was taken in early March 1953. See Woodhouse, *Something Ventured*, p. 124.

64. Mattison to State, July 17, 1953, *FRUS, 1952–1954*, vol. 10, pp. 736–37.

65. Eisenhower to Churchill, May 8, 1953, in Peter G. Boyle, ed., *The Churchill-Eisenhower Correspondence, 1953–1955* (Chapel Hill, N.C. and London: University of North Carolina Press, 1990), pp. 52–55.

66. See Mark J. Gasiorowski, "The 1953 *Coup D'Etat* in Iran," *International Journal of Middle East Studies* 19 (August 1987): 269, 272.

67. Henderson to State, May 20, 1953, *FRUS, 1952–1954*, vol. 10, pp. 727–28. A

recent laudatory biography of Mossadegh, Homa Katouzian, *Musaddiq and the Struggle for Power in Iran* (London and New York: I. B. Tauris, 1990), pp. 266–67, portrays Mossadegh as a political philosopher and symbol of the national movement in Iran who was somewhat out of his element in government. Katouzian writes: "For all of these reasons, Musaddiq should never have become prime minister. He did not want the office and would not have captured it except for an outside chance. Like all outsiders, like Blum, like Churchill, like DeGaulle, Musaddiq was swept to power by extraordinary circumstances. Normal politics require lesser men. Yet, for the circumstances in which he and the country were caught, Musaddiq produced the best government that Iran has had this century."

68. For a contemporary view of the Soviet Union's sudden change of policy toward Turkey see Philip E. Mosely, "The Kremlin's Foreign Policy since Stalin," *Foreign Affairs* 32 (October 1953): 21–22. A CIA estimate on the probable consequences of Stalin's death somewhat ambiguously concluded:

> Specifically, in foreign policy, the new regime will probably find it more difficult to abandon positions than did Stalin and might feel itself compelled to react more strongly if moves of the West confronted it with the need for major decisions. Conversely, the new leadership will probably exercise caution in the near future in taking action which it thought would force the West to make comparable decisions.
>
> CIA Special Estimate, March 12, 1953, *FRUS, 1952–1954*, vol. 8, pp. 1125–29.

69. Woodhouse later drew a comparison between what the British and Americans feared in 1953 for Iran and what happened a quarter of a century later in Afghanistan: "The overthrow of a weak monarchy by nationalist forces, which would then be overtaken by indigenous Communists, who would then be overwhelmed by the Red Army." Woodhouse, *Something Ventured*, p. 131.

70. An August 21, 1953 *New York Times* editorial (p. 16) commented:

> There lies Iran today: weak, soft, torn by internal strife, but enormously valuable in material and strategic terms. The West would like to see her as an ally. So would Russia on the other side. Iranians dislike or even hate foreigners of any kind and want to be neutral.
>
> These power factors lend a significance to what is happening which is out of all proportion to the events within the country, but the issue will be decided in Teheran, not in Washington, London, or Moscow. Neither democratic West nor Communist East dare intervene *overtly* [my emphasis] in a situation where such vital interests are involved. If the Russians, for instance, were to enter Iran "to restore order" they would be courting World War III and they know it.

71. A record of a Dulles brothers phone conversation of July 24 makes clear that the Eisenhower administration still had doubts about the shah.

The Secy called and said in your talk about Iran yesterday at the meeting you did not mention the other matter, is it off? AWD said he doesn't talk about it, it was cleared directly with the President, and is still active.

. . . AWD said it is moving along reasonably well but the young many [man?] may pull out at the last minute, he is an unaccountable character but the sister has agreed to go.

See memorandum of telephone conversation by the secretary of state, July 24, 1953, *FRUS, 1952–1954*, vol. 10, pp. 737–38.

72. Kermit Roosevelt, *Countercoup: The Struggle for the Control of Iran* (New York: McGraw-Hill, 1979), p. 210. Roosevelt believed that the coup succeeded because "We believed—and we were proven right—that if the people and the armed forces were shown that they must choose, that Mossadegh was forcing them to choose, between their monarch and a revolutionary figure backed by the Soviet Union, they could, and would, make only one choice." Kenneth Love, *New York Times* reporter in Iran, made the same point writing: "Mossadegh's big mistake was to push the nation and the army closer and closer to a choice between him and the shah." *The New York Times*, August 23, 1953, p. 5E.

73. The British codename for the operation was "Boot." See Woodhouse, *Something Ventured*, p. 117.

74. For an excellent contemporary British account of the coup see memo on "Persia: Political Review of the Recent Crisis," 2 September 2, 1953, *FRUS, 1952–1954*, vol. 10, pp. 780–88.

75. Gasiorowski, "The 1953 *Coup D'Etat* in Iran," p. 274.

76. Ibid., pp. 128–29; Roosevelt, *Countercoup*, pp. 190–193; Helen Chapin Metz, ed., *Iran: A Country Study* (Washington: Library of Congress Federal Research Division, 1989), p. 31.

77. Woodhouse, *Something Ventured*, p. 129.

78. British memo on "Persia: Political Review of the Recent Crisis," September 2, 1953, *FRUS, 1952–1954*, vol. 10, pp. 780–88.

79. As early as August 17, Iranians were already blaming the United States for what was at that point an attempted, failed coup. See *The New York Times*, August 18, 1953, p. 1. On the twentieth, *Pravda* said that the "American agents who operated within Iran hatched new diversionary plans directed toward the overthrow of the Government." See *The New York Times*, August 20, 1953, p. 3.

80. Bill, *The Eagle and the Lion*, p. 97.

81. Katouzian, *Musaddiq*, p. 255.

82. Dulles to Wilson, November 8, 1954, *FRUS, 1952–1954*, vol. 10, pp. 1063–66.

83. Because of the ongoing crisis, MEF ships were often directed to remain in the gulf and to forego routine visits to Indian Ocean and Red Sea ports in order to maintain a presence in the Persian Gulf in the event of an emergency.

84. Watson, *The JCS and National Policy, 1953–1954*, pp. 334–35; JCS 1714/51, August 26, 1953, OA.

85. Watson, *The JCS and National Policy, 1953–1954*, pp. 335.

86. Report on the Near East by Secretary of State John Foster Dulles, *Department of State Bulletin* 28 (15 June 1953), pp. 831–35.

87. Dulles saw a MEDO as a Middle Eastern parallel to the Brussels Pact—a European alliance—that eventually matured into a broader association—NATO—and gained American adherence. See memorandum of conversation by the counselor in Pakistan, May 24, 1953, *FRUS, 1952–1954*, vol. 9, Part I: pp. 134–36. For Dulles's views on the futility of reliance on the Arab states and conviction that Turkey would have to be the "backbone"of any Pact see memorandum of conversation by the counselor of Embassy in Turkey, May 26, 1953, ibid., pp. 137–47.

88. A reappraisal of American policy in the Near East concluded: "the US must in its own interest take more initiative than it has to date in the determination of policies relative to the area." See Hoskins to Byroade, reappraisal of US policies in the NEA area, April 7, 1952, ibid., pp. 204–13.

89. The American focus on the "northern tier" represents a progression of thought that dates back to McGhee's memo of late 1950 on the need to push the West's defensive ring from outward, and to earlier concepts that originated immediately after the end of the Second World War. For example, the U.S. Navy's Sixth Task Fleet's Operation Plan 1-48 of late 1948–early 1949 stated: "Italy, Greece, Turkey and Iran form a strategic barrier against expansion by a hostile power into the Mediterranean and the Middle East." See OPLAN 1-48 (rev), Annex Dog (Intelligence), Sixth Fleet, Plans Files, OA. The commander of Sixth Task Fleet at the time was Vice Admiral Forrest P. Sherman who, as deputy chief of naval operations (Operations) had been the navy's chief strategist during 1946 and 1947, and would become CNO 1949–51. See Michael A. Palmer, *Origins of the Maritime Strategy*, pp. 21–32; and McGhee, *The US-Turkish-Middle East Connection*, pp. 54, 145–46.

90. For an Iraqi view of the shortcomings of the diplomatic effort behind MEDO, see memorandum of conversation between Dean Acheson and Mohamed Fadil Jamali, October 21, 1952, in John P. Glennon, Evans Gerakas, and William F. Sanford, Jr., eds., *Foreign Relations of the United States: Memoranda of Conversation of the Secretary of State, 1947–1952* (Washington: GPO, 1988), #1712.

91. Then Rear Admiral Arleigh Burke, Director, Strategic Plans Division in OPNAV, later CNO between 1955 and 1961, wrote that British prestige and power in the region was declining and that it appeared "that, both politically and militarily the U.S. must prepare to assume a larger burden in the Middle East if the area is not to be lost by default." See Burke to list, July 3, 1953, CINCLANTFLT, Command Files, OA.

92. See memorandum of conversation, October 1, 1952, *FRUS, 1952–1954*, vol. 9, Part 1, pp. 279–281 for Bradley's discussion of the inner and outer ring and his preference for the latter. JCS historian Robert J. Watson writes: "The futile effort to build a defense around Egypt had been abandoned. A strategy tied to the northern tier would take advantage of the excellent defensive terrain along the southwestern boundary of the Soviet Union and of the willingness of the countries of that region to cooperate with a minimum of prodding from the West." Watson, *History of the Joint Chiefs of Staff*, p. 347.

93. Statement of policy by the National Security Council, July 23, 1954, NSC 5428, *FRUS, 1952–1954*, vol. 9, Part 1, pp. 525–36.

94. Memorandum by the deputy director of the Office of British Commonwealth and Northern European Affairs, April 16, 1952, ibid., pp. 213–218. For Bradley's assessment that MEDO would be "largely political" see minutes of State-JCS meeting, November 28, 1952, ibid., pp. 319–326. See also National Intelligence Estimate, Conditions and Trends in the Middle East affecting US security, January 15, 1953, ibid., pp. 334–43, which concluded that "Middle East armed forces are incapable, individually or collectively, of effectively resisting attack by a major power."

95. Memorandum of conversation by the Politico-Military Adviser, Bureau of Near Eastern, South Asian, and African Affairs, April 24, 1952, ibid., pp. 218–221.

96. National Intelligence Estimate, Prospects for the creation of a Middle East defense grouping and probable consequences of such a development, June 22, 1954, ibid., pp. 516–20. The NIE also concluded: "Such a loose grouping would not result in any significant reduction of the area's military vulnerability. However, together with US military aid programs, it would create greater opportunities than in the past for reducing existing Middle East defense deficiencies. The requirements for outside ground forces might eventually be reduced. However, achievement of even this limited goal would be a long and costly operation, involving considerable training and equipment over a period of years, and effective Middle East defense will continue to depend for the foreseeable future on substantial Western force contributions."

97. Transcript of January 29, 1972, press conference held by the shah of Iran, in Rouhollah K. Ramazani, *The Persian Gulf: Iran's Role* (Charlottesville, Va.: University of Virginia Press, 1972), pp. 146.

98. See McGhee, *The US-Turkish-NATO-Middle East Connection*, p. xv.

99. Memorandum to the assistant secretary of state for European Affairs, January 12, 1954, *FRUS, 1952–1954*, vol. 9, pp. 450–52.

100. See Anderson to State Department, January 19, 1956, *FRUS, 1955–1957*, vol. 15, pp. 28–36; and memorandum of conversation in the White House, January 30, 1956, ibid., 101–7.

101. Gamal Abdel Nasser's nationalization speech of July 26, 1956, in Carol A. Fisher and Fred Krinsky, eds., *Middle East in Crisis: A Historical and Documentary Review* (Syracuse, N.Y.: Syracuse University Press, 1959), p. 139.

102. See Anthony Adamthwaite, "Suez Revisited," *International Affairs* 64 (Summer 1988): 449–64.

103. Memorandum of Discussion, National Security Council, August 30, 1956, *FRUS, 1955–1957*, vol. 16, pp. 324–32.

104. Memorandum of Discussion, Department of State Joint Chiefs meeting, August 31, 1956, ibid., pp. 342–44.

105. For an assessment of the situation and its impact on U.S. policy see Special National Intelligence Estimate 30-4-56, "Probable Repercussions of British-French Military Action in the Suez Crisis," September 5, 1956, ibid., pp. 382–91.

106. *Oglethorpe* cruised the eastern Mediterranean in the late summer of 1956 loaded with arms for Egypt that were to be delivered in the event of an Israeli attack. See Radford to Secretary of Defense Charles E. Wilson, September 19, 1956, ibid., pp. 523–24; and Dulles to Reuben B. Robertson, Jr., September 28, 1958, ibid., pp. 610–11.

107. David Lee, *Wings in the Sun: A History of the Royal Air Force in the Mediterranean, 1945–1986* (London: H. M. Stationery Office, 1989), p. 106.

108. Extracts from David Ben-Gurion's diary, in Selwyn Ilan Troen and Moshe Shemesh, eds., *The Suez-Sinai Crisis, 1956: Retrospective and Reappraisal* (New York: Columbia University Press, 1990), p. 322.

109. Memorandum of conversation between the president and the secretary of state, November 12, 1956, *FRUS, 1955–1957*, vol. 16, pp. 1112–14.

110. Dwight D. Eisenhower's broadcast on the Middle East crisis, October 31, 1956, in Fisher and Krinsky, eds., *Middle East in Crisis*, p. 169.

111. Kennett Love, *Suez: The Twice Fought War* (New York and Toronto: McGraw-Hill, 1969), p. 568.

112. George Lenczowski, *Oil and State in the Middle East*, (Ithaca, N.Y.: Cornell University Press, 1960), pp. 334–38.

113. Marion Farouk-Sluglett and Peter Sluglett, *Iraq Since 1958: From Revolution to Dictatorship* (London and New York: I. B. Tauris, 1990), pp. 44–45.

114. Shwadran, *The Middle East, Oil and the Great Powers*, pp. 268–71; Longrigg, *Oil in the Middle East*, pp. 262–64, 302–3, 313.

115. Resolution on the Middle East, March 5, 1957, in Fisher and Krinsky, *Middle East in Crisis*, pp. 175–176.

116. JCS 2268, Joint Middle East Emergency Defense Plan 1-57, May 8, 1957, OA.

117. Memorandum of discussion at Department of State—Joint Chiefs of Staff meeting, August 31, 1956, *FRUS, 1955–1957*, vol. 16, pp. 342–44.

118. On the eighteenth and nineteenth, the United States became aware of Soviet and Warsaw Pact troops movements along the Turkish border.

119. See Lee, *Wings in the Sun*, p. 143; George S. Dragnich, *The Lebanon Operation of 1958: A Study of the Crisis Role of the Sixth Fleet* (Alexandria, Va.: Center for Naval Analysis Research, 1970), Contribution 153, p. A-3; and Jack Shulimson, *Marines in Lebanon* (Washington: Marine Corps, 1966).

120. CMEF, Report of Operations and Conditions of Command, July 1, 1959 to February 18, 1960, January 14, 1960, MEF, Command Files, OA.

121. See Anthony H. Cordesman, *The Gulf and the Search for Strategic Stability: Saudi Arabia, the Military Balances in the Gulf, and Trends in the Arab-Israeli Military Balance* (Boulder, Colo.: Westview, 1984), pp. 111, 127–33.

122. For a recent, fresh study of crisis management during the 1967 war see Joseph F. Bouchard, *Command in Crisis: Four Case Studies* (New York: Columbia University Press, 1991), pp. 138–59.

123. MEF Command History 1967, February 25, 1968, ibid; and William B. Quandt, *Decade of Decisions: American Policy toward the Arab-Israeli Conflict, 1967–1976* (Berkeley, Los Angeles, and London: University of California Press, 1977), pp. 39–59.

124. MEF Command History 1967, February 25, 1968, MEF, Command Files, OA; and Command History, Arab-Israeli Crisis, 1967, August 26, 1967, MEF, Report Files, OA.

125. MEF Command History 1967, February 25, 1968, MEF, Command Files, OA; and Command History, Arab-Israeli Crisis, 1967, August 26, 1967, MEF, Report Files, OA.

FIVE: A TALE OF TWO DOCTRINES

1. C. J. Bartlett, *The Long Retreat: A Short History of British Defense Policy, 1945–1970* (London and Basingstoke: Macmillan, 1972). See also Kelly, *Arabia, the Gulf and the West* (New York: Basic Books, 1980), pp. 48–51, who views lack of will as the principal cause of the withdrawal; and Phillip Darby, *British Defense Policy East of Suez, 1947–1968* (London: Oxford University Press, 1973), pp. 307–26, 334, who focuses on lack of resources.
2. R. M. Burrell and Alvin J. Cottrell, *Iran, the Arabian Peninsula, and the Indian Ocean* (New York: National Strategic Information Center, 1972).
3. Darby, *British Defense Policy East of Suez*, pp. 219–21; and Charles W. Koburger, Jr., "The Kuwait Confrontation of 1961," U.S. Naval Institute *Proceedings* 100 (January 1974): 42–49.
4. Kelly, *Arabia, the Gulf and the West*, p. 49–50; Yergin, *The Prize*, p. 566.
5. Soviet concerns about a possible American naval buildup in the Indian Ocean, including the establishment of a "Fifth Fleet," dated back to the late 1950s. See Office of Naval Intelligence, "Soviet Interest in the Nonexistent Indian Ocean Fleet," *ONI Review* 14 (August 1959): 357–59.
6. By 1973 the Soviet Navy would spend four times as many shipdays than the U.S. Navy in the Indian Ocean. See "Means of Measuring Naval Power with Special Reference to U.S. and Soviet Activities in the Indian Ocean," prepared for the Subcommittee on the Near East and South Asia of the Committee on Foreign Relations by the Foreign Affairs Division, Congressional Research Service, Library of Congress, May 12, 1974, Washington, 1974, 93rd Congress, 2d Session, pp. 4–7.

U.S. and Soviet Ship Days in the Indian Ocean
(Surface Combatants and Auxiliaries)

Year	1968	1969	1970	1971	1972	1973
Soviet	1760	3668	3579	3804	8007	8543
United States	1688	1315	1246	1337	1435	2154

U.S. and Soviet Port Calls in the Indian Ocean

Year	Soviet Union	United States
1968	42	71
1969	68	71
1970	65	65
1971	47	97
1972	110	74
1973	153	115

7. *Public Papers of the Presidents of the United States: Richard M. Nixon, 1969* (Washington: GPO, 1971), p. 549. See also Richard Nixon, *RN: The Memoirs of Richard Nixon* (New York: Grosset & Dunlap, 1978), pp. 394–95.

8. *Nixon Papers*, 1970, p. 9.

9. Henry Kissinger, *White House Years* (Boston and Toronto: Little, Brown, 1979), p. 1264.

10. In testimony before the House Foreign Affairs Committee's Subcommittee on the Near East on August 8, Assistant Secretary of State for Near Eastern and South Asian Affairs Joseph Sisco testified: "In addition to the tradition of Anglo-American cooperation throughout the world and the parallel nature of American and British interests in the Persian Gulf, the United States has had a long and fruitful tradition of cooperation with the two major regional powers, Iran and Saudi Arabia." See *State Department Bulletin* 57 (September 4, 1972), pp. 241–45. See also Anthony H. Cordesman, *The Gulf and the Search for Strategic Stability*, pp. 158–62. Following the 1973 Arab-Israeli October War, when President Anwar Sadat brought his country from the Soviet to the Western camp, Egypt became the third pillar of the American position in the Middle East.

11. See Bill, *The Eagle and the Lion*, pp. 197–200.

12. William D. Brewer, "Yesterday and Tomorrow in the Persian Gulf," *The Middle East Journal* 23 (Spring 1969), p. 158.

13. Ibid.

14. Edward M. Kennedy, "The Persian Gulf: Arms Race or Arms Control?" *Foreign Affairs* 54 (October 1975): 14–35. Kennedy believed that relatively advanced Iran might be able to survive the race, but that the less advanced, smaller Arab countries, which would be forced to try to keep up, would strain both their budgets and their social fabric, perhaps to the breaking point.

15. Professor James A. Bill was an outspoken academic critic of the shah; see, for example, Bill, *The Eagle and the Lion*, pp. 245–46.

16. CNO Mideast Tripbook, 1974, memo of October 31, 1974 on US/UK talks of October 29–30, 1974, Box 263, Political-Military Affairs Division, OA. John Thomson, Britain's assistant secretary at the Foreign Office, stated that he expected that the shah would be secure for the "short term," which he defined as from three to five years.

17. Cordesman, *The Gulf and the Search for Strategic Stability*, p. 57.

18. Department of State Research Study, Bureau of Intelligence and Research, April 12, 1973, "Iran and Saudi Arabia—The Odd Couple," Box 286, Political-Military Affairs Division, OA.

19. Ibid., p. ii.

20. "Saudi Arabia-Iran: Problems of Regional Cooperation," August 3, 1973, Department of State, Bureau of Intelligence and Research Intelligence Note, Iran 1973, Box 286, ibid.

21. Defense Intelligence Agency, Defense Intelligence Estimate, April 12, 1973, "Iran's Military Buildup: Response to Apprehensions and Aspirations," p. 33, ibid.

22. Transcript of January 29, 1972 press conference held by the shah of Iran, in Ramazani, *The Persian Gulf*, pp. 143–48.

23. Defense Intelligence Agency, Defense Intelligence Estimate, April 12, 1973, "Iran's Military Buildup: Response to Apprehensions and Aspirations," pp. 31–34, Iran 1973, Box 286, Political-Military Affairs Division, OA.
24. Ibid., p. 27.
25. Intelligence note, Department of State Bureau of Intelligence and Research, January 31, 1974, Iran 1974, ibid.
26. Quoted in Monoranjan Bezboruah, *U.S. Strategy in the Indian Ocean: The International Response* (New York and London: Praeger, 1977), p. 192.
27. Kennedy, "The Persian Gulf," p. 24.
28. Iran point paper of October 23, 1974, CNO Mideast Trip Book, box 263, Political-Military Affairs Division, OA.
29. "The Imperial Iranian Armed Forces: An Assessment, September 19, 1973, draft, Office of the Director of Defense Program Analysis and Evaluation, Special Regional Studies Division, Iran 1973, Box 286, ibid.
30. See Cordesman, *The Gulf and the Search for Strategic Stability*, pp. 158–62.
31. Bezboruah, *U.S. Strategy in the Indian Ocean*, pp. 50–56.
32. *New York Times*, March 25, 1969; CNO to CINCLANTFLT, draft, c. May 11, 1968, Bahrein, Box 272, Political-Military Affairs Division, OA; VCNO memo, F. J. Blouin, August 30, 1968, ibid.; CNO to CINCLANTFLT, late 1968 draft paper, CMEF, box 261, ibid.
33. CNO to CINCLANTFLT, nd [September 1968], Bahrein, Box 272, ibid.
34. G. Warren Nutter to Joseph J. Sisco, June 18, 1968, ibid.
35. CNO Point Papers, 1970, CMEF, Box 259, ibid.
36. Secretary of the Navy memorandum for the assistant secretary of defense for International Security Affairs, October 15, 1971, Bahrein 1970, Box 272, ibid.
37. CMEF Command History, 1971, August 29, 1972, MEF, Command Files, ibid.
38. Point paper on MEF and Bahrain, May 27, 1972, Bahrein, Box 273, Political-Military Affairs Division, ibid.
39. Memo for the Director, Command Support Programs, on Political Factors Affecting Fleet Communications, Enclosure 4, Bahrain, March 1972, ibid.
40. For a study of Navy long-range planning and the Long-Range Objectives Group (OP-93) formed under Burke, see David A. Rosenberg, "Historical Perspectives in Long Range Planning in the Navy: Part I: The Planning Process Overview, 1900–1978," Draft, CNO, Command Files, ibid.
41. MEF Command History, 1968, November 21, 1969, MEF, ibid.
42. MEF Command History, 1971, August 29, 1972, ibid.
43. MEF Command History, 1972, May 1, 1973, ibid.
44. MEF Command History, 1973, April 30, 1974; CMEF Command History 1974, 15 April 1975, ibid.
45. MEF Command History, 1975, March 16, 1976, ibid.
46. Quandt, "Lebanon, 1958, and Jordan, 1970," in Barry M. Blechman and Stephen S. Kaplan, *Force Without War: U.S. Armed Forces as a Political Instrument* (Washington: The Brookings Institute, 1978), p. 285.
47. MEF Command History, 1973, April 30, 1974, Command File, OA.
48. Comment on memo on MEF "where do we go from here" session, October 30, 1973, Bahrain 1973, Box 273, Political-Military Affairs Division, ibid.

49. Draft memo for Chairman, JCS, from VCNO, November 7, 1973, ibid.
50. MEF Command History, 1975, March 16, 1976, MEF, Command Files, ibid.
51. Memo, VCNO for CNO, December 30, 1974, Bahrain 1974, Box 273, Political-Military Affairs Division, ibid.
52. Draft memo for the Secretary of Defense on U.S. Self-Imposed Indian Ocean Restrictions, File 3120, Box 58, 1974, 00, ibid.
53. MEF Command History, 1974, April 15, 1975, MEF, Command Files, ibid.
54. Memo, E. R Zumwalt, Jr., to ASD ISA, November 10–20, 1973; memo, CNO to W. D. Gaddis, DCNO (Log), November 15, 1973, uncatalogued files, Middle East, Box 130, 00, OA.
55. The embargo pushed the cost of a barrel of crude from $3 to $11 between September 1973 and January 1974.
56. *Business Week*, January 13, 1975, pp. 66–76.
57. Memo, DCNO Plans and Policy to CNO, enclosing "a survey of military options in response to an Arab oil embargo, August 24, 1974, Middle East, box 155, 1974, 00, OA; "An Examination of Direct Economic/Military Actions in Response to Arab Oil Leverage," September 12, 1974, uncatalogued Middle East, Box 156, ibid.
58. Zbigniew Brzezinski, *Power and Principle: Memoirs of the National Security Adviser, 1977–1981* (New York: Farrar, Straus, Giroux, 1983), p. 177.
59. Ibid.
60. David A. Quinlan, *The Role of the Marine Corps in Rapid Deployment Forces* (Washington: National Defense University Press, 1983), pp. 1–2.
61. OP-61 Point Paper on MEAFSA Command Evolution, November 25, 1970, MEAFSA Command Evolution File, 1960–1970, Box 254, Political-Military Affairs Division, OA.
62. James A. Bowden, "The RDJTF and Doctrine," *Military Review* 62 (November 1982): 51–64.
63. Memorandum, General David C. Jones, USAF, Chairman, Joint Chiefs of Staff to SECDEF Brown, February 28, 1979, with attached appendix, increased presence in the Red Sea and Indian Ocean, Increased Indian Ocean Presence File, Indian Ocean, Area Files, OA.
64. Zbigniew Brzezinski, *The Grand Failure: The Birth and Death of Communism in the Twentieth Century* (New York: Collier, 1990), p. 92. Brzezinski asserts that Soviet leaders decided to invade Afghanistan while intoxicated.
65. Bill, *The Eagle and the Lion*, pp. 245–46.
66. The Iranian Navy purchased oil from the Iranian National Oil Company and then sold it to the U.S. Navy, some 1.5 million barrels that the U.S. Navy sources considered "critical" to its operations. See Kissinger, *White House Years*, p. 1262; and October 23, 1974 memo on Iran, CNO Mideast Tripbook, 1974, Box 263, Political-Military Affairs Division, OA; October 16, 1974 memo on POL supplies from Iran, Iran 1974, Box 286, ibid.
67. Kissinger, *White House Years*, p. 1260.
68. Theodore H. Moran, "Iranian Defense Expenditure and the Social Crisis." *International Security* 3 (Winter 1978/1979): 181.
69. Amitav Archarya, *U.S. Military Strategy in the Gulf* (London and New York: Routledge, 1989), p. 32. The United States was well aware of many of these problems, for example, the growing problem in agriculture, and accelerating

and "worrisome" inflation that as early as 1973 had topped 10 percent. See Economic Trends Report from the American Embassy in Teheran, December 1, 1973, Iran 1973, Box 286, Political-Military Affairs Division, OA.

70. Bill, *The Eagle and the Lion*, pp. 158–61.

71. Kennedy, "The Persian Gulf," p. 19.

72. Toast by President Carter to the shah at the state dinner, Teheran, December 31, 1977, U.S. Department of State, *American Foreign Policy: Basic Documents, 1977–1980* (Washington, 1983), #328. It was during this toast that Carter issued his oft-quoted statement: "Iran, because of the great leadership of the shah, is an island of stability in one of the more troubled areas of the world."

73. The shah himself later wrote: "At the time [1977] foreign policy issues occupied most of my attention." See Mohammad Reza Pahlavi, *Answer to History* (New York: Stein & Day, 1980), p. 150.

74. See R. K. Ramazani, "Who Lost America? The Case of Iran," *The Middle East Journal* 36 (Winter 1982): 5–21. Ramazani (p. 17) writes: "The way vast oil revenues were used magnified every weakness in the Iranian economy. The grandiose economic and atomic energy development plans, the massive imports of food and consumer goods, the rapidly rising rate of inflation, the spreading corruption, the shortage of electricity, the infrastructural 'bottle-necks,' the decline of agricultural productivity, the maldistribution of wealth, etc. could not be cured by such palliative measures as increasing workers' shares in factories up to 49 per cent, or the state subsidization of social idleness in the name of social welfare. By the time the Iranian planners began to talk about a 'modest rate of growth' and the shah admitted (1976) the need for cutbacks, it was too late to do any good."

75. Khosrow Fatemi, "Leadership by Distrust: The Shah's *Modus Operandi*," *The Middle East Journal* 36 (Winter 1982): 49–61. Gary Sick, *All Fall Down: America's Tragic Encounter with Iran* (New York: Penguin, 1986), pp. 191–92, adds that the shah may have realized that his own schemes had failed to achieve what he had expected.

76. James A. Bill, "Power and Religion in Revolutionary Iran," *The Middle East Journal* 36 (Winter 1982): 28.

77. Kissinger, *White House Years*, p. 1260.

78. Cordesman, *The Gulf and the Search for Strategic Stability*, p. 213.

79. *New York Times*, November 14, 1979, p. 17; *Washington Star*, November 21, 1979, p. 1.

80. Carter State of the Union Address, January 23, 1980, State Department, *Basic Documents, 1977–1980*, #15.

81. The third carrier, the *Nimitz*, was relieving the *Kitty Hawk*, which shortly thereafter steamed for home. *Washington Star*, January 18, 1980, p. 4.

82. Address of Secretary of Defense Brown, March 6, 1980, State Department, *Basic Documents, 1977–1980*, #253.

83. For a good account of the political genesis of the operation see, Zbigniew Brzezinski, "The Failed Mission: The Inside Account of the Attempt to Free the Hostages in Iran," *The New York Times Magazine*, April 18, 1982, pp. 28–30.

84. In retrospect, the chances of Eagle Claw carrying the Americans into Teheran

were quite good, although what would have happened in the Iranian capital once the actual rescue of the Americans held at the embassy began must remain a subject of debate. Former Air Force Colonel Richard H. Kyle, in his, the most detailed account of the operation, attributed the ultimate failure to go on to Teheran to several major reasons, most notably the three abort decisions made by navy and marine corps helicopter crews. The Sea Stallion crews were the only elements of the operation that were not drawn from Special Operations units. Kyle poignantly concludes: "All that was lacking was the guts to try!" Richard H. Kyle, *The Guts to Try: The Untold Story of the Iran Hostage Rescue Mission by the On-Scene Desert Commander* (New York: Orion, 1990), p. 340.

85. *Washington Star*, September 24, 1980, p. 11; *Washington Post*, September 30, 1980, p. 14; *New York Times*, October 15, 1980, p. 14.
86. The flagship *LaSalle* and six combatants.
87. *Washington Post*, October 16, 1980, p. 1.
88. Remarks of President Carter to reporters at the White House, September 24, 1980, State Department, *Basic Documents, 1977–1980*, #256.
89. Address by Secretary of State Edmund Muskie, October 14, 1980, Muskie, ibid., #258.
90. Harold Brown, *Thinking about National Security; Defense and Foreign Policy in a Dangerous World* (Boulder, Colo.: Westview, 1983), p. 157. For a discussion of regional reactions to the development of the Rapid Deployment Force, see John W. Amos and Ralph H. Magnus, "Regional Reactions to the RDJTF," unpublished paper, October 21, 1982, Naval Postgraduate School, Monterey, Calif. and the International Studies Association, Carlisle, Penn.

SIX: NOT WHILE THIS PRESIDENT SERVES

1. Reagan's early policy toward the Soviet Union will long be associated with his remark about the "Evil Empire." Reagan also promised a new tougher line towards Iran and strong policy in the Middle East. A frequently heard joke in late 1980 was: "what's flat and glows in the dark? Iran the day after Reagan's inauguration."
2. For example, while giving testimony before the House Foreign Affairs Committee on November 12, 1981, Representative Paul Findley asked Secretary of State Alexander Haig: "President Carter made a statement that seemed to imply that the United States alone would meet any Soviet advance to the Persian Gulf. Was that a commitment?" Haig responded: "That is not our policy." But Haig remarked: "You have got to create an atmosphere of confidence in American reliability, and our willingness to share our leadership responsibility in the Middle East and everywhere, and we have been in the process of doing that. We are not seeking in the Middle East to structure archaic historic alliances, Baghdad Pacts or reestablishment of CENTO." Testimony of Haig before the House Foreign Affairs Committee, November 12, 1981, State Department, *Current Documents, 1981*, # 292.
3. Statement of Secretary of Defense Weinberger before the Senate Armed Services Committee, January 28, 1981, ibid., #23.
4. Defense Guidance for fiscal years 1983–87, May 18, 1981, 3060/1, 1981, 00,

OA. The report also called for improved capabilities of indigenous forces to respond to Soviet attack, greater access of American forces to local facilities, and out of area cooperation from America's European allies.

5. Transcript of interview with Secretary of State Haig, March 5, 1981, State Department, *Current Documents, 1981*, #280.

6. Statement by Deputy Secretary of Defense Carlucci before the Senate Armed Services Committee, March 9, 1981, ibid., #281. For examples of early 1980s studies on American interests in the Persian Gulf and the Rapid Deployment Force, see Robert J. Hanks, *The U.S. Military Presence in the Middle East: Problems and Prospects* (Cambridge, Mass. and Washington: Institute for Foreign Policy Analysis, 1982); Lewis C. Sowell, Jr., *Base Development and the Rapid Deployment Force: A Window to the Future* (Washington: National Defense University Press, 1982); Maxwell Orme Johnson, *The Military as an Instrument of U.S. Policy in Southwest Asia: The Rapid Deployment Joint Task Force, 1979–1982* (Boulder, Colo.: Westview, 1983); U.S. Congress, Congressional Budget Office, *Rapid Deployment Forces: Policy and Budgetary Implications* (Washington: Congressional Budget Office, 1983); and Alvin J. Cottrell and Michael L. Moodie, *The United States and the Persian Gulf: Past Mistakes and Present Needs* (New York: National Strategy Information Center, 1984).

7. In a February 2, 1981 interview with the *New York Times*, Reagan acknowledged that he himself had attacked the Carter Doctrine as a commitment not backed by credible force. See transcript of interview with President Reagan, February 2, 1981, State Department, *Current Documents, 1981*, #279.

8. Jeffrey Record, *The Rapid Deployment Force and U.S. Military Intervention in the Persian Gulf* (Cambridge, Mass. and Washington: Institute of Foreign Policy Analysis, 1981), pp. 1–2. Record remained consistent in his opposition to the Rapid Deployment Force concept. In testimony before the Senate Armed Services Committee in 1987 Record remarked: "The most recent example of what I would term strategic irresponsibility was the Carter administration's extension of containment to the vast and logistically remote region of Southwest Asia, a commitment that has yet to be accompanied by appropriate increases in our military power." See U.S. Congress, Senate, Committee on Armed Services, *National Security Strategy*, S. Hrg. 100–257, 100th Cong., 1st sess., 1987, p. 707.

9. In a February 2, 1981 interview with the *New York Times*, Reagan implied that the administration sought deterrence through threats of vertical, that is nuclear escalation. Horizontal escalation involves military retaliation in another theater. See transcript of an interview with President Reagan, 2 February 1981, State Department, *Current Documents, 1981*, #279.

10. Joshua M. Epstein, *Strategy and Force Planning: The Case of the Persian Gulf* (Washington: The Brookings Institute, 1987).

11. Address of Secretary of Defense Brown, March 6, 1980, State Department, *Basic Documents, 1977–1980*, #253.

12. Ibid.

13. Strategic Mobility Requirements and Programs in a Persian Gulf Contingency (SMRP-84), Joint Chiefs of Staff, p. IX–95, JCS, Command File, OA.

14. Record, *The Rapid Deployment Force*, pp. 73–74.

15. OP-60 Point Paper, Unified Command Plan and RDJTF Command Arrange-

ments, January 22, 1981, 3060/1, 1981, 00, OA. The navy did not favor the establishment of a unified command in Southwest Asia at the time, but preferred the establishment of a subunified commander under EUCOM, or the reassignment of the Persian Gulf, but not the Red Sea, to PACOM.

16. Robert C. Kingston, "From RDF to CENTCOM: New Challenges?" *RUSI Journal* 129 (March 1984): 16. USCENTCOM to differentiate between NATO CENTCOM.

17. Kingston had been the commander of RDJTF until the establishment of US-CENTCOM.

18. Kingston, "From RDF to CENTCOM," p. 16.

19. For an overview of the war and its impact on American interests see Edgar O'Ballance, *The Gulf War* (London: Brassey's, 1988); Anthony H. Cordesman, *The Iran-Iraq War and Western Security, 1984–1987: Strategic Implications and Policy Options* (London and New York: Jane's, 1987); Thomas Naff, ed., *Gulf Security and the Iran-Iraq War* (Washington: National Defense University Press, 1985); Ronald E. Bergquist, *The Role of Airpower in the Iran-Iraq War* (Maxwell Air Force Base, Ala.: Air University Press, 1988); and William J. Olson, ed., *US Strategic Interests in the Gulf Region* (Boulder, Colo. and London: Westview, 1987).

20. *Wall Street Journal*, October 2, 1981, p. 3. The attack on September 30 followed previous attacks on November 12 and 16, 1980, and June 13, 1981 and ended an oil truce between the belligerents that had been unofficially recognized after similar attacks by both sides against petroleum facilities early in the war.

21. Presidential press conference, October 1, 1981, *Current Documents, 1981*, #405.

22. *New York Times*, October 2, 1981, p. 1.

23. Statement by deputy assistant secretary of state for Near Eastern and South Asian Affairs before the House Foreign Affairs Subcommittee, September 26, 1983, State Department, *Current Documents, 1983*, #278.

24. Official State Department statement, March 5, 1984, ibid., #222.

25. Iraq's only outlet to the gulf—the Shatt al-Arab—was closed to all shipping as a result of the war.

26. Statement by the deputy representative of the United States to the U.S. Security Council, May 30, 1984, State Department, *Current Documents, 1984*, #223; United Nations Resolution 552, June 1, 1984, ibid., #224.

27. Statement by the assistant secretary of state for Near Eastern and South Asian Affairs, June 11, 1984, ibid., #225.

28. Statement by the assistant secretary of state for Near Eastern and South Asian Affairs, July 25, 1984, ibid., #197.

29. Statement by the assistant secretary of state for Near Eastern and South Asian Affairs, 18 September 1985, ibid, #256.

30. Ibid.

31. Response by President Reagan to a question asked during a June 11, 1985 interview, ibid., #245.

32. Statement by Secretary of State George Shultz, October 1, 1985, ibid., #247.

33. Shireen T. Hunter, "The Gulf Economic Crisis and Its Social and Political Consequences," *The Middle East Journal* 40 (Autumn 1986): 593.

34. Ronald O'Rourke, "The Tanker War," U.S. Naval Institute *Proceedings* 114 (May 1988): 31.

35. The shah recognized the Iranian vulnerability and accordingly built up the Iranian navy. See Pahlavi, *Answer to History*, p. 142.

36. David Segal, "The Iran-Iraq War: A Military Analysis," *Foreign Affairs* 66 (Summer 1988): 960.

37. O'Rourke, "The Tanker War," p. 34. During 1987, before reflagging, twenty-four such ships were attacked; after reflagging, sixteen. The Iranians and Iraqis together sank only a handful of ships, reaching a high of six in 1987, but more than 30 million tons of shipping had been damaged.

38. Prepared statement by the secretary of state, February 19, 1986, State Department, *Current Documents, 1986*, #172; statement by the assistant secretary of state for Near Eastern and South Asian Affairs, April 16, 1986, ibid., #203.

39. Statement by President Reagan's press secretary, May 7, 1986, ibid., #204.

40. Caspar Weinberger, *Fighting for Peace: Seven Critical Years in the Pentagon* (New York: Warner, 1990), p. 363.

41. Author's interview with Caspar W. Weinberger, Washington, DC, 24 July 1990.

42. Statement by Secretary of State Shultz, January 27, 1987, State Department, *Current Documents, 1987*, #253.

43. Statement by President Reagan, February 25, 1987, ibid., #254.

44. Weinberger, *Fighting for Peace*, p. 387. In early 1986, the Iranians had targeted Saudi Arabian shipping, but when the Saudis agreed to cooperate with Iran on OPEC oil policy, the number of attacks on Kuwaiti traffic mounted. See U.S. Congress, House of Representatives, Committee on Armed Services, "National Policy Implications of United States Operations in the Persian Gulf," July 1987, 100/1, no. 9, pp. 8–9.

45. While the Kuwaiti move was in keeping with that small Arab state's traditional unwillingness to rely exclusively on either East or West for security, they no doubt knew that the prospect of deeper Soviet involvement in the Persian Gulf would likely move the United States to react quickly and positively to the reflagging request.

46. Weinberger, *Fighting for Peace*, pp. 396–97; and Weinberger interview, July 24, 1990.

47. Ibid., p. 397. To Weinberger, the Kuwaiti request for Soviet assistance "lent a little more urgency" to the American debate, but was not the major factor in the administration's decision. Weinberger interview, July 24, 1990.

48. Statement by the assistant secretary of state for Near Eastern and South Asian Affairs, April 21, 1987, State Department, *Current Documents, 1987*, #255.

49. Statement by the assistant secretary of state for Near Eastern and South Asian Affairs, May 19, 1987, ibid., #259; statement by the assistant secretary of state for Near Eastern and South Asian Affairs, May 29, 1987, ibid., #263.

50. Murphy commented: "I think those who argue that others, not the United States, have the oil problem or should be concerned about the Gulf situation miss the point. Our economic well-being is involved, particularly since our economy is the most oil intensive of the major industrialized nations. That others may suffer more is not a persuasive argument for us to do less than our interests require."

51. Statement by President Reagan, May 29, 1987, State Department, *Current Documents, 1987,* #262.

52. See Weinberger's "The Military Underpinnings of Diplomacy: The Case of the Persian Gulf," delivered to the Portland World Affairs Council, September 21, 1987, Persian Gulf 1987, Box 10 (of 19) 1988, 00 (unprocessed), OA.

53. Statement read by President Reagan's assistant for press relations, June 30, 1987, State Department, *Current Documents, 1987,* #266.

54. U.N. Security Council Resolution 598, July 20, 1987, ibid., #268; and statement by President Reagan, July 20, 1987, ibid., #269.

55. Joint statement issued by the Venice Summit participants, June 9, 1987, ibid., #74.

56. For examples of the Soviet reaction see V. Markov, "The War in the Persian Gulf, Freedom of Navigation, and International Law," *Morskoi Sbornik* (February 1988): 83–87; M. Abramov, "U.S. Navy Aggravates Persian Gulf Situation," ibid., (March 1988): 78–81; Sergei Turchenko, "Sinister Armada," *Soviet Military Review* (July 1988): 52–54; and Norman Cigar, "The Soviet Navy in the Persian Gulf: Naval Diplomacy in a Combat Zone," *Naval War College Review* 42 (Spring 1989): 56–88.

57. Quoted in Shahram Chubin and Charles Tripp, *Iran and Iraq at War* (Boulder, Colo.: Westview, 1988), p. 217.

58. U.S. Congress, Senate, Committee on Armed Services, *U.S. Military Forces to Protect Re-Flagged Kuwaiti Oil Tankers,* S. Hrg. 100–269, 5, 11, June 16, 1987, p. 24.

59. United States Senate, Committee on Foreign Relations, *War in the Persian Gulf: The U.S. Takes Sides,* October 1987, pp. 5–8.

60. Weinberger, *Fighting for Peace,* pp. 391, 397.

61. Ibid., p. 402. Weinberger characterized the navy's concern over its prospective gulf role "understandable" given its "direct, immediate responsibility for the safety of the men and the ships," but more than "was warranted." The secretary of defense found the most support within the navy's "operational end, the people who were called on to do the job, there was no lack of eagerness there, and there wasn't much lack of eagerness at the top." Weinberger interview, July 24, 1990.

62. Statement by the assistant secretary of state for Near Eastern and South Asian Affairs, May 29, 1987, State Department, *Current Documents, 1987,* #263.

63. U.S. Congress, Senate, Committee on Armed Services, "U.S. Military Forces to Protect 'Re-Flagged' Kuwaiti Oil Tankers," S. Hrg. 100–269, June 5, 11, 16, 1987, p. 18.

64. Statement by the under secretary of state for Political Affairs, June 16, 1987, ibid., #265.

65. Caspar W. Weinberger, "A Report to the Congress on Security Arrangements in the Persian Gulf," unclassified version, June 15, 1987, p. iv.

66. To Secretary Weinberger, the reflagging of the Kuwaiti tankers itself was just a detail. "I don't think it made any difference which flag they carried. If they wanted to put them under the American flag, I was perfectly agreeable to that. If they didn't, I also thought we should protect them. It was the idea of shipping, neutral, innocent, nonbelligerent shipping in an international body of water of immense importance. And it didn't make the slightest dif-

ference to me which flag they flew, I thought they should be protected. And if they felt better about putting them under our flag, fair enough." Weinberger interview, July 24, 1990.

SEVEN: THE TANKER WAR

1. *New York Times*, June 10, 1987, p. 3.
2. U.S. Congress, Senate, *U.S. Military Forces to Protect "Reflagged" Kuwaiti Oil Tankers*, S. Hrg. 100–269, 100/1, Committee on Armed Services, June 5, 11, 16, 1987, p. 29.
3. Cordesman, *The Iran-Iraq War*, p. 558.
4. U.S. Congress, Senate, *U.S. Military Forces to Protect "Reflagged" Kuwaiti Oil Tankers*, S. Hrg. 100–269, 100/1, Committee on Armed Services, June 5, 11, 16, 1987, p. 60.
5. Ibid., p. 61.
6. Cordesman, *The Iran-Iraq War*, p. 558.
7. CMEF Command History, 1973, April 30, 1974, enclosing letter of General G. J. Eade, USA, to Chairman, JCS, December 10, 1973, MEF, Command Files, OA.
8. Scott C. Truver, "Mines of August: An International Whodunit," United States Naval Institute *Proceedings* 111 (May 1985): 95–117.
9. Robin Wright, *In the Name of God: The Khomeini Decade* (New York: Simon & Schuster, 1989), pp. 165–66.
10. Ibid., p. 167.
11. *Wall Street Journal*, February 8, 1988, p. 1.
12. "The Persian Gulf: Commitment and Objectives in Troubled Waters," OP-60 unclassified brief, March 1988, Iran-Iraq, vol. II 1988, USNATO Persian Gulf Files (unprocessed), OA.
13. Weinberger, *Fighting for Peace*, p. 390.
14. *The Independent*, September 11, 1987.
15. February 12, 1988 CNA working paper, USNATO Persian Gulf Files (unprocessed), OA.
16. Cordesman, *The Iran-Iraq War*, p. 318, states that Rear Admiral Harold Bernsen, commander Middle East Force, and Admiral Crowe, chairman of the Joint Chiefs of Staff, planned the operation in early September during the latter's tour of the gulf. According to Robin Wright, *In the Name of God*, p. 168, the *Iran Ajr* "had been tracked for several days after intelligence indicated that it had located 'suspect devices' at an Iranian port." Weinberger, *Fighting for Peace*, p. 414, noted: "That we caught the ship was no accident."
17. O'Rourke, "The Tanker War," p. 33.
18. *Wall Street Journal*, February 8, 1988, p. 1; Wright, *In the Name of God*, p. 170.
19. *Washington Times*, December 16, 1987, p. 4; *Washington Post*, December 18, 1987, p. 18; *New York Times*, December 18, 1987, p. 1.
20. Interview with Anthony A. Less, "Mideast Perspective," *Wings of Gold* 15 (Spring 1990): 50–52.
21. Ronald O'Rourke, "Gulf Ops," United States Naval Institute *Proceedings* 115 (May 1989): 44.

22. U.S. Congress, Senate, Committee on Foreign Relations, Staff Report, *War in the Persian Gulf: The U.S. Takes Sides*, p. 50.
23. For the failure of the American deployment to deter the Iranians see Janice Gross Stein, "The Wrong Strategy in the Right Place: The United States in the Gulf," *International Security* 13 (Winter 1988/89): 155 and 155n.
24. U.S. Congress, Senate, Committee on Foreign Relations, Staff Report, *War in the Persian Gulf: The U.S. Takes Sides*, p. 51.
25. O'Rourke, "Gulf Ops," p. 49.
26. "The Persian Gulf: Commitment and Objectives in Troubled Waters," OP-60 unclassified brief, March 1988, Iran-Iraq, vol. II 1988, USNATO Persian Gulf Files (unprocessed), OA.
27. Wright, *In the Name of God*, pp. 173–75.
28. The following account of Operation Praying Mantis is drawn from O'Rourke, "Gulf Ops," pp. 44–47; Bud Langston and Don Bringle, "Operation Praying Mantis: The Air View," United States Naval Institute *Proceedings* 115 (May 1989): 54–65; J. B. Perkins III, "Operation Praying Mantis: The Surface View," ibid., pp. 66–70; John H. Admire, "A Report on the Gulf," *Marine Corps Gazette* 72 (December 1988): 56–61; William M. Rakow, "Marines in the Gulf—1988," ibid., pp. 62–68; Hans S. Pawlisch, "Operation Praying Mantis," *VFW Magazine* (January 1989): 34–37; and the author's discussions with participants.
29. Statement by Secretary of Defense Carlucci, April 29, 1988, State Department, *Current Documents, 1988*, #245. Carlucci also announced continued and deeper cooperation in the gulf between the United States and its European allies.
30. Wright, *In the Name of God*, pp. 180–85.
31. Ibid., p. 176.
32. Ibid., pp. 185–86.
33. For the Airbus incident, see Norman Friedman, "The *Vincennes* Incident," United States Naval Institute *Proceedings* 115 (May 1988): 72–79; and William M. Fogarty, *Investigation Report: Formal Investigation into the Circumstances Surrounding the Downing of Iran Air Flight 655 on 3 July 1988* (Washington: Department of Defense, 1988).
34. Weinberger, *Fighting for Peace*, p. 411.
35. Author's personal recollections. See Norman Friedman, "The *Vincennes* Incident," United States Naval Institute *Proceedings* 115 (May 1989): 72–79, and especially Commander David R. Carlson's comments on Friedman's article in ibid., (September 1989): 87–92. Carlson commanded the frigate *Sides*, which was operating with the *Vincennes* on July 3.
36. Friedman, "The *Vincennes* Incident," p. 73; and author's personal recollection.
37. In addition to Friedman, "The *Vincennes* Incident," see also U.S. Congress, Senate, *Investigation into the Downing of an Iranian Airliner by the U.S.S. "Vincennes,"* HASC, 100/2, 8 September 1988. S. Hrg. 100–1035.
38. Wright, *In the Name of God*, p. 186.
39. Ibid., p. 190.

EIGHT: THE ROAD TO DESERT STORM

1. Figures derived from International Institute for Strategic Studies, *The Military Balance, 1989–1990* (London, 1989).

2. *The Economist*, September 29, 1990, pp. 19–22.

3. *New York Times*, November 12, 1990, p. A14.

4. The execution prompted sharp international protests and led Great Britain to recall its ambassador from Baghdad. In April 1991, there were claims that Bazoft was, in fact, spying for Britain, when captured. *Washington Times*, April 25, 1991, p. A8.

5. The supergun project was apparently halted by British actions and the assassination, allegedly by Israeli Mossad agents, of Gerald Bull, who had designed the gun.

6. *Wall Street Journal*, June 28, 1990, p. 1.

7. Efraim Karsh and Inari Rautsi, "Why Saddam Hussein Invaded Kuwait," *Survival* 33 (January/February 1991): 25.

8. *The Economist*, July 21, 1990, pp. 37–38.

9. See Efraim Karsh and Inari Rautsi, *Saddam Hussein: A Political Biography* (New York: The Free Press, 1991).

10. See Dilip Hiro, *The Longest War: The Iran-Iraq Military Conflict* (New York: Routledge, 1991), pp. 250–51; and Cordesman, *The Iran-Iraq War*, p. 3.

11. Sluglett and Sluglett, *Iraq*, p. 272.

12. Clark, *The Political Economy of World Energy*, pp. 348–53.

13. Ibid., p. 349.

14. Karsh and Rautsi, *Saddam Hussein*, pp. 152–53.

15. See ibid., p. 3; and David Fromkin, "How the Modern Middle East Map Came to be Drawn," *Smithsonian* 22 (May 1991): 132–49.

16. Kelly, *Arabia, the Gulf and the West*, p. 285.

17. See, for example, an excerpt from a transcript of a meeting between Saddam and Senators Robert Dole, Alan Simpson, Howard Metzenbaum, James McClure, and Frank Murkowski, on April 12, 1990, reprinted as "U.S. Senators Chat with Saddam," in Micah L. Sifry and Christopher Cerf, eds., *The Gulf War Reader: History, Documents, Opinions* (New York: Times Books, 1991), pp. 119–21.

18. *Wall Street Journal*, October 1, 1990, p. 1; ibid., December 18, 1990, p. 14.

19. *Washington Post*, July 24, 1990, p. A1; *New York Times*, July 24, 1990, p. A9.

20. A copy of the transcript appeared in *New York Times*, September 23, 1990, p. A19.

21. Glaspie appeared before the Senate Foreign Relations Committee and the House Foreign Affairs subcommittee on March 20 and 21, respectively. See *Congressional Quarterly*, March 23, 1991, pp. 759–60. Unfortunately, when Congress obtained a copy of Glaspie's official report of the meeting, several senators felt that they had been "deliberately misled" by the ambassador. *Washington Post*, July 12, 1991, p. A1; ibid., July 13, 1991, p. A1; *The New Republic*, August 5, 1991, pp. 8–10.

22. *Washington Times*, May 31, 1991, p. A2. If, on July 25, Saddam expected an American response to an invasion of Kuwait, by implication he must have already made up his mind to attack. Hence the entire meeting was a charade.

23. *New York Times*, July 26, 1990, p. A1; July 27, 1990, p. A2; July 28, 1990, p. A1.

24. Don Oberdorfer, "Missed Signals in the Middle East," *The Washington Post Magazine*, March 17, 1991, p. 40.

25. Desert Shield/Storm talk by Lieutenant General Thomas Kelly, April 24, 1991, George Washington University, Washington, DC.

26. Schwarzkopf interview with David Frost, March 28, 1991. According to Bob Woodward, *The Commanders* (New York: Simon & Schuster, 1991), p. 220, Schwarzkopf did not use the JCS briefing to predict an invasion, even a limited border crossing. Either Woodward was fed inaccurate information, Schwarz-kopf misled Frost, or the CENTCOM commander was unwilling to predict an invasion in his brief, but privately told the Chairman of the Joint Chiefs of Staff—General Colin Powell—that the Iraqis probably would cross the border.

27. *USA Today*, September 12, 1990, p. 1.

28. Oberdorfer, "Missed Signals in the Middle East," p. 40.

29. *Los Angeles Times*, September 24, 1990, p. 1.

30. *USA Today*, October 8, 1990, p. 8.

31. *Washington Post*, March 8, 1991, p. A26.

32. Deterrence: an effort by country A to convince country B not to attack country A. Extended deterrence: an effort by country A to convince country B not to attack country C.

33. While the remarks attributed to the American ambassador are suspect, those attributed to Saddam Hussein can be taken as official whether they were actually made to Glaspie at the meeting or not. The transcript was an official document released by the Iraqi government.

34. Mary C. FitzGerald, "Early Soviet Assessments of U.S. Military Success in the Gulf War," *Strategic Review* 19 (Spring 1991): 77–80.

35. *Washington Times*, October 18, 1990, p. 10.

36. *The Baltimore Sun*, March 7, 1990, p. 15.

37. Stephen C. Pelletiere, Douglas V. Johnson II, Leif R. Rosenberger, *Iraqi Power and U.S. Security in the Middle East* (Carlisle Barracks, Penn.: U.S. Army War College, 1990), p. xi.

38. John F. Antal, "The Iraqi Army Forged in the Other Gulf War," *Military Review* 71 (February 1991): 63–72. For a dissenting view, see an (in retrospect) extremely perceptive article by retired U.S. Army Colonel Wallace Franz, "Defeating the Iraqis: Saddam's Troops Are Not Ready for a War of Maneuver," *Armor* 100 (Jan-Feb 91): 8–9. Franz warned: "While it is a cardinal sin in military planning to underestimate your enemy, it is important not to overestimate your enemy and thus eliminate some viable options. There is a tendency in some circles to overestimate the capabilities of the Iraqi military, and, therefore, its ability to cause casualties to U.S. forces." Franz concluded his article by arguing that an army capable of mobile operations, like the U.S. Army, could "quickly defeat a defensive-oriented army [like the Iraqis'] without suffering excessive casualties."

NINE: SHIELD IN THE DESERT

1. For a perceptive account of the invasion see Norman Friedman, *Desert Victory: The War for Kuwait* (Annapolis: Naval Institute Press, 1991): pp. 35–42.

2. For an account of alleged Iraqi planning and preparation for the invasion, see *Los Angeles Times*, September 24, 1990, p. 1. According to reports, the Iraqis

had had a plan to invade Kuwait for five years. Such a plan was, most likely, a contingency plan. But the article also alleged that the Iraqis had been seriously preparing for the attack since 1988, and had practiced the special forces assault in mid-July in central Iraq in an area picked for its likeness to the terrain in Kuwait. If the report is accurate, this would also substantiate that Saddam had made up his mind for war before his meeting with April Glaspie.

3. For the texts of U.N. Security Council resolutions see Sifry and Cerf, eds., *The Gulf War Reader*, pp. 137–56.
4. *New York Times*, August 4, 1990, p. A5.
5. *New York Times*, August 9, 1990, p. A17.
6. *New York Times*, August 4, 1990, p. A4.
7. U.S. Congress, Senate, Committee on Armed Services, *Crisis in the Persian Gulf Region: U.S. Policy Options and Implications*, S. Hrg. 101–1071, sess. 101/2, p. 645.
8. Woodward, *The Commanders*, p. 249. Schwarzkopf, himself, gave similar figures in several postwar interviews.
9. *New York Times*, October 4, 1990, p. A15.
10. *New York Times*, August 6, 1990, p. A6.
11. *New York Times*, August 7, 1990, A10.
12. *New York Times*, August 7, 1990, p. A9.
13. *New York Times*, August 6, 1990, p. A1.
14. *New York Times*, August 6, 1990, p. A1.
15. For excerpts from King Fahd's speech see *New York Times*, August 10, 1990, p. A10.
16. Kelly talk, April 24, 1991. According to Kelly, the Saudis had made up their minds to allow the Americans in on August 3. According to Woodward, *The Commanders*, p. 254, the Saudis had in mind only air assets until the sixth.
17. *New York Times*, August 8, 1990, p. A1.
18. *New York Times*, August 9, 1990, p. A16.
19. *New York Times*, October 4, 1990, p. A15.
20. U.S. Congress, Senate, "Crisis in the Persian Gulf Region: U.S. Policy Options and Implications," SASC, S. Hrg. 101–1071, sess. 101/2, p. 645.
21. Woodward, *The Commanders*, p. 237. The author heard similar estimates being floated around the Pentagon in August 1990.
22. *Washington Post*, March 16, 1991, p. A19.
23. *Washington Post*, March 16, 1991, p. A19.
24. *New York Times*, August 10, 1990, p. A8.
25. *New York Times*, August 11, 1990, p. A6.
26. *New York Times*, August 16, 1990, p. A1.
27. *New York Times*, August 9, 1990, p. A16.
28. U.S. Air Force, *White Paper: Air Force Performance in Desert Storm* (Washington, April 1991), p. 2.
29. For an excellent discussion of the movement of Marine Corps assets to Saudi Arabia and the gulf, see Edwin H. Simmons, "Getting Marines to the Gulf," United States Naval Institute *Proceedings* 117 (May 1991): pp. 50–64.
30. See Ronald O'Rourke, *Sealift and Operation Desert Shield* (Washington: Congressional Research Service, 1990), pp. 16–17.
31. Joseph P. Hoar, "The U.S. Marines and Operation Desert Storm," presen-

tation at the Marine Corps Historical Center, Washington, DC, 1 April 1991.

32. Woodward, *The Commanders*, pp. 215–216.
33. Office of the Chief of Naval Operations, *The United States Navy in "Desert Shield" "Desert Storm"* (Washington, 1991), p. 13.
34. CNO, *The United States Navy in "Desert Shield" "Desert Storm"*, pp. 15–16, 28.
35. Douglas M. Norton, "Sealift: Keystone of Support," United States Naval Institute *Proceedings* 117 (May 1991): 44.
36. Ibid., p. 46.
37. CNO, *The United States Navy in "Desert Shield" "Desert Storm"*, p. 29.
38. U.S. Air Force, *White Paper*, p. 8.
39. CNO, *The United States Navy in "Desert Shield" "Desert Storm"*, p. 14.
40. CNO, *The United States Navy in "Desert Shield" "Desert Storm"*, p. 28.
41. Ibid., pp. 29–30.
42. Ibid., p. 25.
43. *London Financial Times*, August 21, 1990, p. 2; *Washington Times*, August 23, 1990, p. 8; *Defense News*, August 27, 1990, p. 1.
44. *Los Angeles Times*, August 29, 1990, p. 1; *Washington Times*, August 29, 1990, p. 8. The withdrawal of the Republican Guard divisions into what were obviously reserve defensive positions further north, suggests that earlier in the month, when these divisions were deployed near the Saudi border, the guard had been positioned either to invade Saudi Arabia or, at the minimum, to intimidate the Saudis. Thus Saddam had either been deterred, or had bluffed his way into a crisis of, for him, unmanageable proportions.
45. *Washington Post*, September 1, 1990, p. A26.
46. *New York Times*, September 4, 1990, p. A1.
47. *Washington Post*, September 1, 1990, p. A26.
48. *Washington Post*, September 2, 1990, p. A33.
49. Kelly talk, April 24, 1991.
50. For a sample of Congressional opinion regarding the viability of sanctions see the *New York Times*, September 4, 1990, p. 10.
51. The blockades of the Confederacy during the American Civil War, of Imperial Germany during the First World War, and of Japan during the Second World War, occurred in conjunction with active, offensive military operations. For an unconvincing effort to make a historical case for sanctions, see Kimberly Elliott, Gary Hufbauer, and Jeffrey Schott, "Sanctions Work: The Historical Record," in Sifry and Cerf, eds., *Gulf War Reader*, pp. 255–59.
52. *Washington Times*, September 5, 1990, p. A7.
53. Jonathan T. Dworken, *Economic Factors in Desert Shield Deployments: Multinational Aspects* (Alexandria, Vir.: Center for Naval Analysis, 1991), p. 11.
54. *Time*, September 24, 1990, p. 32.
55. U.S. Congress, Senate, Committee on Armed Services, *Crisis in the Persian Gulf Region: U.S. Policy Options and Implications*, S. Hrg. 101–1071, sess. 101/2, pp. 648–49.
56. Ibid., p. 649.
57. *London Sunday Times*, 23 September 1990, p. 2.
58. *Washington Times*, September 14, 1990, p. A1; ibid, September 24, 1990, p. A1; *Washington Post*, September 14, 1990, p. A1.
59. *Washington Post*, December 4, 1990, p. A1.

60. *Washington Post*, September 16, 1990, p. A1.
61. *Aviation Week & Space Technology*, September 17, 1990, p. 24; *Seattle Post-Intelligencer*, October 12, 1990, p. 1.
62. *New York Times*, October 5, 1990, p. A8.
63. *Boston Globe*, September 30, 1990, p. 26.
64. *New York Times*, September 7, 1990, p. A9.
65. John J. Yeosock, "Army Operations in the Gulf Theater," *Military Review* 71 (Sept. 91): 3.
66. Richard Mackenzie, "A Conversation with Chuck Horner," *Air Force Magazine* 74 (June 1991): 58.
67. *Washington Times*, September 11, 1990, p. A8; *Aviation Week & Space Technology*, September 17, 1990, p. 26.
68. *Newsweek*, March 18, 1991, pp. 28–29.
69. *Washington Post*, September 16, 1990, p. A1.
70. *Los Angeles Times*, September 17, 1990, p. A1.
71. *Washington Post*, September 18, 1990, pp. A1, 25.
72. *Time*, March 11, 1991, p. 27.
73. SASC, "Crisis in the Persian Gulf Region: U.S. Policy Options and Implications," p. 663.
74. Ibid., p. 664–65.
75. Woodward, *The Commanders*, pp. 299–300.
76. Kelly talk. April 24, 1991.
77. *New York Times*, September 19, 1990, p. A1; *Los Angeles Times*, September 19, 1990, p. A1.
78. Woodward, *The Commanders*, p. 349. From the author's personal experience, Woodward's figure of 20,000 is consistent with, and even lower than some, "official" estimates made in the fall of 1990.
79. See, for example, *Los Angeles Times*, September 18, 1990, p. H1. Retired U.S. Navy Rear Admiral Eugene J. Carroll, Jr., a consistent critic of Reagan and Bush administration defense policies, predicted that a full scale war would result in 10,000 American dead and 30,000 to 40,000 wounded. *Atlanta Journal & Constitution*, November 25, 1990, p. H1. Another retired U.S. Navy Rear Admiral, Gene R. La Rocque, likewise a consistent critic, estimated 10,000 dead and about 35,000 wounded, in addition to 10,000 to 15,000 allied casualties, and 100,000 civilian casualties in Iraq. See *Los Angeles Times*, November 28, 1990, p. 8.
80. Woodward, *The Commanders*, p. 314.
81. T. N. Dupuy, *Attrition: Forecasting Battle Casualties and Equipment Losses in Modern War* (Fairfax, Vir.: Hero, 1990), p. 131.
82. *Washington Post*, February 28, 1991, p. D1.
83. *Philadelphia Inquirer*, October 13, 1990, p. A6.
84. Stephen C. Pelletiere, et al., *Iraqi Power and U.S. Security in the Middle East*, p. 71.
85. CINCUSAREUR to CINCEUR, April 26, 1991.
86. *Time*, March 11, 1991, p. 27.
87. *Time*, March 11, 1991, p. 27.
88. Woodward, *The Commanders*, pp. 304–6.
89. *New York Times*, September 29, 1990, p. A1.

90. *Los Angeles Times*, October 15, 1990, p. A6.
91. *Wall Street Journal*, October 15, 1990, p. 10; *Washington Times*, October 15, 1990, p. 10.
92. *Washington Times*, September 26, 1990, p. 8.
93. *Washington Post*, October 19, 1990, p. A1.
94. *Washington Post*, October 23, 1990, p. A1; *New York Times*, October 24, 1990, p. A1; *New York Times*, October 26, 1990, p. A1.
95. *Washington Post*, October 24, 1990, p. A15.
96. Woodward, *The Commanders*, pp. 309–11.
97. *New York Times*, October 26, 1990, p. A1.
98. Woodward, *The Commanders*, pp. 318–20.
99. Kelly talk, April 24, 1991.
100. *Los Angeles Times*, October 30, 1990, p. A1; *Washington Times*, October 31, 1990, p. 1.
101. *Washington Post*, October 31, 1990, p. A1.
102. *Washington Post*, November 25, 1990, p. C-4.
103. *Miami Herald*, October 29, 1990, p. 8.
104. *New York Times*, November 2, 1990, p. A9; *New York Times*, November 5, 1990, p. A1.
105. *London Daily Telegraph*, November 1, 1990, p. 10.
106. *Washington Times*, November 26, 1990, p. 1; *New York Times*, November 26, 1990, p. A1; *Washington Post*, November 27, 1990, p. A1.
107. *Philadelphia Inquirer*, November 26, 1990, p. A1; *Boston Globe*, November 26, 1990, p. 1; *New York Times*, November 27, 1990, p. A23. Although at the time Cheney's speculations about Iraqi nuclear capabilities were greeted with a great deal of skepticism, and viewed as part of a propaganda campaign to sway public opinion, subsequent on-site inspections by United Nations teams confirmed that the Iraqis were indeed further ahead in their atomic program than had been understood before the war.
108. Sifry and Cerf, eds., *Gulf War Reader*, pp. 154–55.
109. Ibid., pp. 155–56.
110. *New York Times*, November 28, 1990, p. A14.
111. *New York Times*, November 29, 1990, p. A14.
112. *New York Times*, November 30, 1990, p. A1.
113. *The Estimate*, January 3, 1991, p. 1.
114. *Washington Post*, December 7, 1990, p. A1.
115. *New York Times*, December 20, 1990, p. A21.
116. *Washington Times*, December 26, 1990, p. A1.
117. According to Woodward, *The Commanders*, pp. 335–36, Prince Bandar, the Saudi ambassador to the United States, believed that the Bush administration's diplomatic initiative, while it may have played well with the American media, sent a signal of weakness to Baghdad, dissipating the strength of the message sent by the U.N. Security Council.
118. *Washington Post*, January 1, 1991, p. A1.
119. Sifry and Cerf, eds., *The Gulf War Reader*, pp. 172–77; *New York Times*, January 10, 1991, p. A1.
120. Sifry and Cerf, eds., *Gulf War Reader*, pp. 178–79. The emphasis is the author's.

121. *Time*, March 11, 1991, p. 32.
122. *Los Angeles Times*, January 10, 1991, p. A11.
123. Sifry and Cerf, eds., *Gulf War Reader*, pp. 287–89.
124. Schwarzkopf press briefing, February 27, 1991, p. 2.
125. This account is taken from a news report based on a transcript of a tape of the meeting discovered and smuggled out of Iraq by Kurds. *Washington Times*, June 14, 1991, p. A7.

TEN: A COMMANDER'S DREAM

1. *Washington Post*, November 20, 1990, p. A10; *New York Times*, November 20, 1990, p. A13.
2. *Washington Post*, March 17, 1990, pp. A1, A24.
3. Woodward, *The Commanders*, p. 324.
4. For an early 1980s example of reformist ideas and concepts, see the Heritage Foundation's "Green Book," Jeffrey G. Barlow, ed., *Critical Issues: Reforming the Military* (Washington: The Heritage Foundation, 1981).
5. See G. I. Wilson, "The Gulf War, Maneuver Warfare, and the Operational Art," *Marine Corps Gazette* 75 (June 1991): 23–24.
6. For an example of the air force's assigned role in supporting the ground campaign, see Richard G. Davis, *The 31 Initiatives: A Study in Air Force-Army Cooperation* (Washington: Office of Air Force History, 1987).
7. John A. Warden, III, *The Air Campaign: Planning for Combat* (Washington: Pergamon-Brassey's, 1989).
8. Warden, *The Air Campaign*, p. xvii.
9. Horner inaccurately attributes the early planning to the Joint Staff, see Mackenzie, "A Conversation with Chuck Horner," p. 58.
10. Author's interview with Colonel John A. Warden III, USAF, June 19, 1991.
11. Warden, *The Air Campaign*, pp. 16, 17.
12. Ibid., p. 33.
13. For a discussion of Douhet's ideas and those of other early advocates of air power see Edward Warner, "Douhet, Mitchell, Seversky: Theories of Air Warfare," in Edward Mead Earle, ed., *Makers of Modern Strategy: Military Thought from Machiavelli to Hitler* (Princeton, N.J.: Princeton University Press, 1943).
14. *Aviation Week & Space Technology*, April 22, 1991, p. 42.
15. Warden interview, June 19, 1991.
16. Author's interview with Brigadier General Buster C. Glosson, USAF, July 23, 1991, Washington, DC.
17. Glosson interview, July 23, 1991.
18. Mackenzie, "a Conversation with Chuck Horner," p. 60.
19. *Aviation Week & Space Technology*, April 22, 1991, p. 42.
20. Glosson interview, July 23, 1991.
21. *Newsweek*, March 18, 1991, p. 28.
22. Glosson interview, July 23, 1991.
23. See, for example, *Washington Post*, June 23, 1991, p. A1.
24. *Washington Post*, June 23, 1991, p. A1.
25. Glosson interview, July 23, 1991.

26. John A. Warden, III, "Centers of Gravity: The Key to Success in War," unpublished paper, p. 3.

27. Transcript of briefing by General Merrill A. McPeak, Air Force Chief of Staff, March 15, 1991, p. 13.

28. Saint to Galvin, March 26, 1991.

29. *Washington Times*, December 26, 1990, p. 1.

30. Warden interview, June 19, 1991.

31. McPeak briefing, p. 14.

32. McPeak briefing, p. 3.

33. *Washington Post*, March 18, 1991, p. A1.

34. Quoted in Michael Howard, *Strategic Deception*, vol. 5 of *British Intelligence in the Second World War*, (New York: Cambridge University Press, 1990), p. 107.

35. *Washington Post*, March 18, 1991, p. A1.

36. U.S. Department of Defense, *Conduct of the Persian Gulf Conflict: An Interim Report to Congress* (Washington: Department of Defense, 1991), p. 24–2.

37. Woodward, *The Commanders*, pp. 347–48; *U.S. News & World Report*, May 6, 1991, p. 31.

38. Saint to Galvin, March 26, 1991.

39. Kelly talk, April 24, 1991.

40. The manual uses the Vicksburg campaign as an example. See U.S. Army, *FM 100–5: Operations* (Washington: U.S. Army, 1986), pp. 91–94.

41. FM 100–5, pp. 101–2.

42. *U.S. News & World Report*, March 11, 1991, p. 14.

43. *Newsweek*, March 11, 1991, p. 34.

44. Department of Defense, *Conduct of the Persian Gulf Conflict*, p. 24–3. Author's emphasis.

45. *Aviation Week & Space Technology*, May 25, 1991, pp. 27.

46. *Jane's Defense Weekly*, May 4, 1991, p. 735.

ELEVEN: JUST THE WAY IT WAS SCHEDULED

1. *Aviation Week & Space Technology*, May 6, 1991, p. 66.

2. Woodward, *The Commanders*, pp. 366–67.

3. DOD, *Conduct of the Persian Gulf Conflict*, p. 2–3.

4. For illustrations of the spread of targets attacked during the first hour and the next twenty-three, see maps 5 and 6 in DOD, *Conduct of the Persian Gulf Conflict*, pp. 4–17, 4–18.

5. *Aviation Week & Space Technology*, July 22, 1991, p. 60–61.

6. *Newsweek*, June 17, 1991, pp. 20–21.

7. Brigadier General Buster Glosson, who planned the air campaign, set the record straight about the much-talked about special operation in an interview published in *Air Force Times*, July 8, 1991, p. 27.

8. McPeak briefing, March 15, 1991, p. 4.

9. Dupuy in *How to Defeat Saddam Hussein*, p. 103, forecast 505 aircraft losses during a forty-day campaign.

10. Another ten aircraft were lost to noncombat causes.

11. DOD, *Conduct of the Persian Gulf Conflict*, p. 6–1. The United States lost another seven aircraft to non-combat causes. Allied, non-American, air losses totaled

nine aircraft and no helicopters lost in combat, and two aircraft and no helicopters lost to non–combat related causes. The United States lost twenty-one helicopters, only five of which were lost in combat.

12. Norman Friedman, *Desert Victory*, p. 357.
13. *Aviation Week & Space Technology*, January 21, 1991, pp. 23–24; ibid., February 18, 1991, pp. 45–46.
14. Dirk T. Rose, "Saratoga MiG Killers: Hollywood Need not Apply," *Naval Aviation News* 73 (May–June 91): 13–14.
15. Peter Grier, "Joint STARS Does Its Stuff," *Air Force Magazine* 74 (June 91): 38–42.
16. Author's interview with Captain William H. Switzer, III, USN, June 19, 1991, Washington, DC.
17. James W. Canan, "The Electronic Storm," *Air Force Magazine* 74 (June 91): 26.
18. U.S. Air Force, *White Paper*, p. 5.
19. *U.S. News & World Report*, February 11, 1991, p. 27.
20. *Washington Post*, March 16, 1991, p. A1.
21. U.S. Air Force, *White Paper*, p. 7.
22. Mackenzie, "A Conversation with Chuck Horner," p. 60.
23. DOD, *Conduct of the Persian Gulf Conflict*, p. 6–8; U.S. Navy, *The United States Navy in "Desert Shield" "Desert Storm"*, pp. 47–48.
24. Other Allied aircraft, such as fighters and ECM aircraft, flew missions in support of F-117A strikes in and around the Iraqi capital. The home base of the F-117s in the United States is in Tonopah, Nevada.
25. U.S. Air Force, *White Paper*, p. 3.
26. U.S. Air Force, "Stealth and Desert Storm," presentation of Lieutenant General Charles A. Horner and Brigadier General Buster C. Glosson to the Committee on Appropriations, Subcommittee on Defense, United States House of Representatives, April 30, 1991, p. 2.
27. For daily sortie totals see U.S. Navy, *The United States Navy in "Desert Shield" "Desert Storm"*, p. D-2.
28. *Washington Times*, January 24, 1991, p. 1.
29. Dan Hampton, "The Weasels at War," *Air Force Magazine* 74 (July 91): p. 58.
30. *Aviation Week & Space Technology*, January 28, 1991, p. 24.
31. For a transcript of the briefing see Richard Pyle, *Schwarzkopf: The Man, the Mission, the Triumph* (New York: Signet, 1991), pp. 207–34.
32. Michael A. Palmer, "The Navy Did Its Job," U.S. Naval Institute *Proceedings* 117 (May 1991): 89.
33. *Aviation Week & Space Technology*, February 18, 1991, p. 62–63.
34. Since the Second World War, American military plans generally have included three elements—the actual strategic or operational plan, a deception plan, and a psychological warfare plan. As American military plans have been declassified over the years, only the military plans have been released. The companion deception and psywar plans have remained highly classified. Only in the last decade or so have World War II deception and psywar plans come to light. General Schwarzkopf's and other officials' public discussions regarding the deception and psywar efforts during Desert Storm is unique.
35. *Aviation Week & Space Technology*, February 25, 1991, p. 21.
36. Speech reprinted in Sifry and Cerf, *Gulf War Reader*, pp. 315–16.

37. The Saudi-Kuwaiti border includes two bends that were known during the war as the "elbow," where moving westward the border turns north, and the "armpit," where the border resumes its western orientation.
38. *Aviation Week & Space Technology*, April 22, 1991, p. 46.
39. *Washington Post*, June 13, 1991, p. A1.
40. For the text of the Iraqi statement see *Philadelphia Inquirer*, February 16, 1991, p. 7-A.
41. Ibid.
42. *Philadelphia Inquirer*, February 16, 1991, p. 7-A.
43. *Philadelphia Inquirer*, February 17, 1991, p. 18-A.
44. *Philadelphia Inquirer*, February 19, 1991, p. 1-A.
45. *Philadelphia Inquirer*, February 19, 1991, p. 1-A; ibid., February 20, 1991, 1-A.
46. *Philadelphia Inquirer*, February 22, 1991, p. 1-A.
47. *Philadelphia Inquirer*, February 23, 1991, p. 7-A.
48. *Philadelphia Inquirer*, February 23, 1991, p. 1-A.
49. *Philadelphia Inquirer*, February 23, 1991, p. 1-A.
50. *Philadelphia Inquirer*, February 13, 1991, p. 1-A.
51. *Philadelphia Inquirer*, February 18, 1991, p. 8-A.
52. *Philadelphia Inquirer*, February 21, 1991, 15-A.

TWELVE: THE MOTHER OF ALL BATTLES, THE MOTHER OF ALL RETREATS

1. *Washington Post*, September 4, 1990, p. 1.
2. Pyle, *Schwarzkopf*, p. 98.
3. *London Financial Times*, September 21, 1990, p. 2.
4. *Atlanta Journal & Constitution*, October 28, 1990, p. 1.
5. DOD, *Conduct of the Persian Gulf Conflict*, p. 15–1.
6. Ibid.
7. For a good synopsis of the marines' activities, see Edwin H. Simmons, "Getting the Job Done," U.S. Naval Institute *Proceedings* 117 (May 1991): 94–96.
8. DOD, *Conduct of the Persian Gulf Conflict*, p. 4–8.
9. The account of French operations has been drawn from press reports and the televised briefing of Brigadier General Daniel Gazeau of February 28, 1991.
10. *Philadelphia Inquirer*, February 26, 1991, p. 5-A.
11. *Philadelphia Inquirer*, February 27, 1991, p. 6-A.
12. DOD, *Conduct of the Persian Gulf Conflict*, p. 4–9.
13. See maps 14 and 15 in DOD, *Conduct of the Persian Gulf Conflict*, pp. 4–26, 4–27.
14. DOD, *Conduct of the Persian Gulf Conflict*, p. 4–8.
15. *Wall Street Journal*, March 11, 1991, p. A16.
16. *Time*, March 11, 1991, p. 27.
17. Dale R. Cooper, "Young Guns: Harrier Pilots in the Persian Gulf," *Leatherneck* 74 (July 1991): 46.
18. For a vivid first-hand description of the "highway to hell" see Michael Kelly, "Highway to Hell," *The New Republic*, April 1, 1991, pp. 11–14.
19. DOD, *Conduct of the Persian Gulf Conflict*, p. 6–5.

20. These quotes are drawn from my own notes of the broadcast and the Reuters wire service story that appeared in *Philadelphia Inquirer*, March 28, 1991, p. 8-A.
21. *Philadelphia Inquirer*, March 29, 1991, p. 1-A.
22. Schwarzkopf February 27, 1991 briefing transcript, p. 16.
23. *Washington Post*, June 13, 1991, p. A-1.
24. McPeak briefing, March 15, 1991, p. 14.
25. DOD, *Conduct of the Persian Gulf Conflict*, pp. 4–9, 4–10.
26. *Philadelphia Inquirer*, March 4, 1991, p. 1-A.

THIRTEEN: THE GUARANTOR OF LAST RESORT

1. For an excellent discussion of American political beliefs and their relationship to commercial expansion, see Field, *America and the Mediterranean World*, pp. 3–26.
2. For an excellent discussion of the development of British involvement in the Gulf, see L. B. H. Haworth to the foreign secretary of the Government of India, September 10, 1927, University Publications of America, *From the First to the Second World War Turkey, Iran, and the Middle East*, Part II, Series B, vol. 5 of *British Documents on Foreign Affairs*, part II: p. 384.
3. *U.S. News & World Report*, June 24, 1991, p. 45.
4. One of the usually missed lessons of our experience in the Persian Gulf is this failure of economic beneficence to cure political and social ills.
5. Sifry and Cerf, eds., *The Gulf War Reader*, pp. 284–86.

BIBLIOGRAPHY

MANUSCRIPT SOURCES

(Washington, DC)
National Archives, Record Group 45:
    Masters Commandants Letters to the Secretary of the Navy, January–June 1834
Naval Historical Center, Operational Archives Branch:
    Records of the Immediate Office of the Chief of Naval Operations, the 00
        (Double Zero) file
    Political-Military Affairs Division Records
    Files of the CNO Secretariat, Joint Staff (JCS files)
    Dispatch Files, Operations Division, COMINCH
    Command Files
    Plans Files
    Report Files
    Privileged Manuscript Collection
    Press Release Files

PRINTED PRIMARY SOURCES

Bennett, Norman R., and George E. Brooks, Jr., eds. *New England Merchants in Africa: A History Through Documents, 1802 to 1865*. Boston: Boston University Press, 1965.

Bernstein, Barton J., and Allen J. Matusow, eds. *The Truman Administration: A Documentary History*. New York and London: Harper & Row, 1966.

Bevans, Charles I., ed. *Treaties and Other International Agreements of the United States of America, 1776–1949*. 13 vols. Washington: Department of State, 1968–1976.

Carter, Jimmy. *Public Papers of the Presidents of the United States: Jimmy Carter*. 12 vols. Washington: Government Printing Office, 1977–1982.

Joint Chiefs of Staff. *Records of the Joint Chiefs of Staff, 1946–1953*. Washington, DC: University Publications of America, Inc., 1979.

Miller, Hunter, ed. *Treaties and Other International Acts of the United States of America*. 8 vols. Washington: Government Printing Office, 1931–1948.

Nixon, Richard M. *Public Papers of the Presidents of the United States: Richard M. Nixon*. 6 vols. Washington: Government Printing Office, 1971–1975.

United Nations. *Statistical Yearbook, 1949–1950*. New York: United Nations, 1950.

U.S. Congress. House. Committee on Armed Services. *Investigation into the Downing of an Iranian Airliner by the U.S.S. "Vincennes."* 100th Cong., 2d sess, 1988.

U.S. Congress. Senate. Committee on Armed Services. *U.S. Military Forces to Protect "Re-flagged" Kuwaiti Oil Tankers*. 100th Cong., 1st sess., 1987.

U.S. Congress. Senate. Committee on Armed Services. *Crisis in the Persian Gulf Region: U.S. Policy Options and Implications*. 101st Cong., 2d sess., 1990.

U.S. Congress. Senate. Committee on Armed Services. *National Security Strategy*. 100th Cong., 1st sess., 1987.

U.S. Department of State. *American Foreign Policy: Basic Documents, 1977–1980*. Washington: Department of State, 1983.

U.S. Department of State. *American Foreign Policy: Current Documents*. Washington: Department of State, 1982–.

U.S. Department of State. *Foreign Relations of the United States*. Washington: Government Printing Office, 1861–.

———. *U.S. Department of State Bulletin*.

Wattenberg, Ben J., ed. *The Statistical History of the United States: From Colonial Times to the Present*. New York: Basic Books, 1976.

INTERVIEWS AND ORAL HISTORIES

Interviews with the author:
　Glosson, Buster, July 23, 1991.
　Swartz, Peter M., August 24, 1990.
　Switzer, William H., June 26, 1991.
　Warden, John A., III, June 19, 1991.
　Weinberger, Caspar W., July 24, 1990.
United States Naval Institute Oral History Collection. Annapolis, Maryland:
　Bieri, Bernhard H. Interview with John T. Mason, Jr., 1970.
Columbia University Oral History Project. New York, New York:
　Conolly, Richard L. Interview with Donald F. Shaughnessy, 1960.

SECONDARY SOURCES

Books

Abrahamsson, Bernhard J., and Joseph L. Steckler. *Strategic Aspects of Seaborne Oil*. Beverly Hills and London: Sage, 1973.

Acharya, Amitav. *U.S. Military Strategy on the Gulf*. London and New York: Routledge, 1989.

Acheson, Dean. *Present at the Creation: My Years in the State Department*. New York: W. W. Norton, 1969.

Antonius, George. *The Arab Awakening: The Story of the Arab National Movement*. New York: Capricorn, 1965.

Barlow, Jeffrey G., ed. *Critical Issues: Reforming the Military*. Washington: The Heritage Foundation, 1981.

Bartlett, C. J. *The Long Retreat: A Short History of British Defense Policy, 1945–1970*. London and Basingstoke: Macmillan, 1972.

Baylis, John. *Anglo-American Defense Relations, 1939–1984: The Special Relationship*. 2d ed. New York: St. Martin's, 1984.

Bergquist, Ronald E. *The Role of Airpower in the Iran-Iraq War*. Maxwell Air Force Base, Alabama: Air University Press, 1988.

Best, Richard A., Jr. *"Cooperation with Like-Minded Peoples": British Influences on*

306

American Security Policy, 1945–1949. New York, Westport, Conn., and London: Greenwood, 1986.

Bezboruah, Monoranjan. *U.S. Strategy in the Indian Ocean: The International Response.* (New York and London: Praeger, 1977.

Bill, James A. *The Eagle and the Lion: The Tragedy of American-Iranian Relations.* New Haven and London: Yale University Press, 1988.

Blechman, Barry M., and Stephen S. Kaplan. *Force Without War: U.S. Armed Forces as a Political Instrument.* Washington: The Brookings Institute, 1978.

Bouchard, Joseph F. *Command in Crisis: Four Case Studies.* New York: Columbia University Press, 1991.

Boyle, Peter G., ed. *The Churchill-Eisenhower Correspondence, 1953–1955.* Chapel Hill, N.C., and London: University of North Carolina Press, 1990.

Brands, H. W. *Inside the Cold War: Loy Henderson and the Rise of the American Empire, 1918–1961.* New York and Oxford: Oxford University Press, 1991.

Brown, Harold. *Thinking about National Security; Defense and Foreign Policy in a Dangerous World.* Boulder, Colo.: Westview, 1983.

Brzezinski, Zbigniew. *Power and Principle: Memoirs of the National Security Adviser, 1977–1981.* New York: Farrar, Straus, Giroux, 1983.

———. *The Grand Failure: The Birth and Death of Communism in the Twentieth Century.* New York: Collier, 1990.

Burrell, R. M., and Alvin J. Cottrell. *Iran, the Arabian Peninsula, and the Indian Ocean.* New York: National Strategy Information Center, 1972.

Campbell, John C. *Defense of the Middle East: Problems of American Policy.* Rev. ed. New York: Praeger, 1960.

Carter, Jimmy. *Keeping Faith: Memoirs of a President.* New York: Bantam, 1982.

Chubin, Shahram, and Charles Tripp. *Iran and Iraq at War.* Boulder, Colo.: Westview, 1988.

Clark, John G. *The Political Economy of World Energy: A Twentieth Century Perspective.* Chapel Hill, N.C., and London: The University of North Carolina Press, 1990.

Condit, Kenneth W. *1947–1949.* Vol. II of *The History of the Joint Chiefs of Staff: The Joint Chiefs of Staff and National Policy.* Washington: Joint Chiefs of Staff, 1978.

Cordesman, Anthony H. *The Gulf and the Search for Strategic Stability: Saudi Arabia, the Military Balance in the Gulf, and Trends in the Arab-Israeli Military Balance.* Boulder, Colo., and London: Westview Press/Mansell, 1984.

———. *The Iran-Iraq War and Western Security, 1984–1987: Strategic Implications and Policy Options.* London and New York: Jane's, 1987.

Cottrell, Alvin J., ed. *The Persian Gulf States: A General Survey.* Baltimore and London: The Johns Hopkins University Press, 1980.

Cottrell, Alvin J., and Michael L. Moodie. *The United States and the Persian Gulf: Past Mistakes and Present Needs.* New York: National Strategy Information Center, 1984.

Curzon, George N. *Persia and the Persia Question.* 2 vols. London and New York: Longmans, Green, 1892.

Darby, Phillip. *British Defense Policy East of Suez, 1947–1968.* London: Oxford University Press, 1973.

Davenport, E. H., and Sidney Russell Cooke. *The Oil Trusts and Anglo-American Relations.* New York: Macmillan, 1924.

Davis, Richard G. *The 31 Initiatives: A Study in Air Force–Army Cooperation*. Washington: Office of Air Force History, 1987.

Davis, Vincent. *Postwar Defense Policy and the U.S. Navy, 1943–1946*. Chapel Hill, N.C.: University of North Carolina Press, 1962.

Donovan, Robert J. *Conflict and Crisis: The Presidency of Harry S. Truman, 1945–1948*. New York: W. W. Norton, 1977.

Dragnich, George S. *The Lebanon Operation of 1958: A Study of the Crisis Role of the Sixth Fleet*. Alexandria, Vir.: Center for Naval Analysis, 1970.

Drake, Frederick C. *The Empire of the Seas: A Biography of Rear Admiral Robert Wilson Shufeldt, USN*. Honolulu: University of Hawaii Press, 1984.

Dupuy, T. N. *Attrition: Forecasting Battle Casualties and Equipment Losses in Modern War*. Fairfax, Vir.: Hero, 1990.

Dworken, Jonathan T. *Economic Factors in Desert Shield Deployments: Multinational Aspects*. Alexandria, Vir.: Center for Naval Analysis, 1991.

Earle, Edward Mead, ed. *Makers of Modern Strategy: Military Thought from Machiavelli to Hitler*. Princeton, N.J.: Princeton University Press, 1943.

Epstein, Joshua M. *Strategy and Force Planning: The Case of the Persian Gulf*. Washington: The Brookings Institution, 1987.

Fanning, Leonard M. *American Oil Operations Abroad*. New York and London: McGraw-Hill, 1947.

Faroughy, Abbas. *The Bahrein Islands, 750–1951: A Contribution to the Study of Power Politics in the Persian Gulf*. New York: Verry, Fisher, 1951.

Farouk-Sluglett, Marion, and Peter Sluglett. *Iraq Since 1958: From Revolution to Dictatorship*. London and New York: I. B. Tauris, 1990.

Feis, Herbert. *Petroleum and American Foreign Policy*. Stanford, Calif.: Food Research Institute, Stanford University, 1944.

Field, James A., Jr. *America and the Mediterranean World, 1776–1882*. Princeton, N.J.: Princeton University Press, 1969.

———. *History of United States Naval Operations in Korea*. Washington: Government Printing Office, 1962.

Fisher, Carol A., and Fred Krinsky, eds. *Middle East in Crisis: A Historical and Documentary Review*. Syracuse, N.Y.: Syracuse University Press, 1959.

Fisher, Sir John. *Memoirs and Records of Admiral of the Fleet Lord Fisher*. 2 vols. London, New York, and Toronto: Hodder and Stoughton, 1919.

———. *The Papers of Admiral Sir John Fisher*. Edited by P. K. Kemp. 2 vols. Navy Records Society, 1960–1964.

Fogarty, William M. *Investigation Report: Formal Investigation into the Circumstances Surrounding the Downing of Iran Air Flight 655 on 3 July 1988*. Washington: Department of Defense, 1988.

Freedman, Robert O. *Soviet Policy Toward the Middle East since 1970*. New York: Praeger, 1975.

Frey, John W., and H. Chandler Ide, eds. *A History of the Petroleum Administration for War, 1941–1945*. Washington: Government Printing Office, 1946.

Friedman, Norman. *Desert Victory: The War for Kuwait*. Annapolis, Md.: Naval Institute Press, 1991.

Gaddis, John Lewis. *The United States and the Origins of the Cold War*. New York: Columbia University Press, 1972.

Gillard, David. *The Struggle for Asia, 1828–1914: A Study in British and Russian Imperialism.* London: Metheun, 1977.

Gold, Dore. *America, The Gulf and Israel: CENTCOM (Central Command) and Emerging US Regional Security Policies in the Mideast.* Jerusalem and Boulder, Colo.: The Jerusalem Post and Westview, 1988.

Hahn, Peter L. *The United States, Great Britain, and Egypt, 1945–1956: Strategy and Diplomacy in the Early Cold War.* Chapel Hill, N.C., and London: The University of North Carolina Press, 1991.

Halberstadt, Hans. *NTC: A Primer of Modern Land Combat.* Novato, Calif.: Presidio Press, 1989.

Hanks, Robert J. *The U.S. Military Presence in the Middle East: Problems and Prospects.* Cambridge, Mass., and Washington: Institute for Foreign Policy Analysis, 1982.

Hay, Rupert. *The Persian Gulf States.* Washington: The Middle East Institute, 1959.

Hiro, Dilip. *The Longest War: The Iran-Iraq Military Conflict.* New York: Routledge, 1991.

Hough, Richard. *Admiral of the Fleet: The Life of John Fisher.* New York: Macmillan, 1969.

Hourani, Albert. *A History of the Arab Peoples.* Cambridge, Mass.: Belknap, 1991.

Howard, Michael. *Strategic Deception.* Vol. 5 of *British Intelligence in the Second World War.* New York: Cambridge University Press, 1990.

International Institute for Strategic Studies. *The Military Balance, 1989–1990.* London: IISS, 1989.

Johnson, Maxwell Orme. *The Military as an Instrument of U.S. Policy in Southwest Asia: The Rapid Deployment Joint Task Force, 1979–1982.* Boulder, Colo.: Westview, 1983.

Joss, John, and George Hall. *Strike: U.S. Naval Strike Warfare Center.* Novato, Calif.: Presidio Press, 1989.

Karsh, Efraim, ed. *The Iran-Iraq War: Impact and Implications.* New York: St. Martin's, 1989.

Karsh, Efraim, and Inari Rautsi. *Saddam Hussein: A Political Biography.* New York: The Free Press, 1991.

Katouzian, Homa. *Musaddiq and the Struggle for Power in Iran.* London and New York: I. B. Tauris, 1990.

Kelly, J. B. *Arabia, the Gulf and the West.* New York: Basic Books, 1980.

———. *Britain and the Persian Gulf, 1795–1880.* Oxford: Clarendon, 1968.

Khadduri, Majid. *The Gulf War: The Origins and Implications of the Iran-Iraq Conflict.* New York and Oxford: Oxford University Press, 1988.

Kissinger, Henry. *For The Record: Selected Statements, 1977–1980.* Boston and Toronto: Little, Brown, 1977–1981.

———. *White House Years.* Boston and Toronto: Little, Brown, 1979.

Kolko, Joyce and Gabriel. *The Limits of Power: The World and United States Foreign Policy, 1945–1954.* New York: Harper & Row, 1972.

Kuniholm, Bruce Robellet. *The Origins of the Cold War in the Near East: Great Power Conflict and Diplomacy in Iran, Turkey, and Greece.* Princeton, N.J.: Princeton University Press, 1980.

Kyle, James H., with John Robert Edison. *The Guts to Try: The Untold Story of the Iran Hostage Rescue Mission by the On-Scene Desert Commander.* New York: Orion, 1990.

Kyle, Keith. *Suez*. New York: St. Martin's, 1991.

LaFeber, Walter. *America, Russia, and the Cold War, 1945–1984*. 5th ed. New York: Alfred A. Knopf, 1985.

Ledeen, Michael, and William Lewis. *Debacle: The American Failure in Iran*. New York: Alfred A. Knopf, 1981.

Lee, David. *Flight from the Middle East: A History of the Royal Air Force in the Arabian Peninsula and Adjacent Territories, 1945–1972*. London: Her Majesty's Stationery Office, 1980.

———. *Wings in the Sun: A History of the Royal Air Force in the Mediterranean, 1945–1986*. London: Her Majesty's Stationery Office, 1989.

Lenczowski, George. *Oil and State in the Middle East*. Ithaca, N.Y.: Cornell University Press, 1960.

———. *Russia and the West in Iran, 1918–1948: A Study in Big-Power Rivalry*. Ithaca, N.Y.: Cornell University Press, 1949.

Lewis, Bernard. *The Arabs in History*. New York: Harper Collophon, 1966.

———. *The Middle East and the West*. New York: Harper Torchbooks, 1964.

Long, David F. *Gold Braid and Foreign Relations: Diplomatic Activities of U.S. Naval Officers, 1798–1883*. Annapolis, Md.: Naval Institute Press, 1988.

Longrigg, Stephen Hemsley. *Oil in the Middle East: Its Discovery and Development*. 2d ed. London, New York: Oxford University Press, 1961.

Louis, William Roger. *The British Empire in the Middle East, 1945–1951: Arab Nationalism, the United States, and Postwar Imperialism*. Oxford: Clarendon, 1984.

Love, Kennett. *Suez: The Twice Fought War*. New York and Toronto: McGraw-Hill, 1969.

Low, Charles Rathbone. *History of the Indian Navy, 1613–1863*. 2 vols. London: Richard Bentley, 1877.

McGhee, George. *The US-Turkish-NATO Middle East Connection: How the Truman Doctrine Contained the Soviets in the Middle East*. New York: St. Martin's, 1990.

Mackay, Ruddock F. *Fisher of Kilverstone*. Oxford: Clarendon, 1973.

Maddox, Robert James. *From War to Cold War: The Education of Harry S. Truman*. Boulder & London: Westview, 1988.

Mahan, Alfred Thayer. *The Problem of Asia and Its Effect upon International Policies*. Boston: Little, Brown, 1900.

———. *Retrospect & Prospect: Studies in International Relations, Naval and Political*. Boston: Little, Brown, 1902.

———. *From Sail to Steam: Recollections of Naval Life*. New York: Harper & Row, 1907.

Marder, Arthur J. *From Dreadnought to Scapa Flow: The Royal Navy in the Fisher Era, 1904–1919*. 5 vols. London and New York: Oxford University Press, 1961–70.

Maull, Hanns, and Otto Pick, eds. *The Gulf War: Regional and International Dimensions*. New York: St. Martin's, 1989.

Meeser, Robert L. *The End of an Alliance: James F. Byrnes, Roosevelt, Truman, and the Origins of the Cold War*. Chapel Hill, N.C.: University of North Carolina Press, 1982.

Metz, Helen Chapin, ed. *Iran: A Country Study*. Washington: Library of Congress Federal Research Division, 1989.

Miller, Aaron David. *Search for Security: Saudi Arabian Oil and American Foreign Policy, 1939–1949*. Chapel Hill, N.C.: University of North Carolina Press, 1980.

Millis, Walter, ed. *The Forrestal Diaries*. New York: Viking, 1951.

Motter, T. H. Vail. *United States Army in World War II, The Middle East Theater: The Persian Corridor and Aid to Russia*. Washington: Government Printing Office, 1952.

Naff, Thomas, ed. *Gulf Security and the Iran-Iraq War*. Washington: National Defense University Press, 1985.

Nash, Gerald D. *United States Oil Policy, 1890–1964: Business and Government in Twentieth Century America*. Pittsburgh, Penn.: University of Pittsburgh Press, 1968.

Nitze, Paul H. *From Hiroshima to Glasnost: At the Center of Decision*. New York: Grove Weidenfeld, 1989.

Nixon, Richard. *RN: The Memoirs of Richard Nixon*. New York: Grosset & Dunlap, 1978.

O'Ballance, Edgar. *The Gulf War*. London: Brassey's, 1988.

Olson, William J., ed. *US Strategic Interests in the Gulf Region*. Boulder, Colo.: Westview, 1987.

O'Rourke, Ronald. *Sealift and Operation Desert Shield*. Washington: Congressional Research Service, 1990.

Pahlavi, Mohammad Reza. *Answer to History*. New York: Stein and Day, 1980.

Palmer, Michael A. *Origins of the Maritime Strategy: American Naval Strategy in the First Postwar Decade*. Washington: Naval Historical Center, 1988.

———. *Stoddert's War: Naval Operations during the Quasi-War with France, 1798–1801*. Columbia, South Carolina: University of South Carolina Press, 1987.

Pelletiere, Stephen C., Douglas V. Johnson, II, and Leif R. Rosenberger. *Iraqi Power and U.S. Security in the Middle East*. Carlisle Barracks, Penn.: U.S. Army War College, 1990.

Penrose, Boies. *Travel and Discovery in the Renaissance, 1420–1620*. New York: Atheneum, 1971.

Petroleum Industry Research Foundation, Inc. *World Oil, Fact and Policy: The Case for a Sound American Petroleum Policy*. New York: Petroleum Industry Research Foundation, 1944.

Phillips, James Duncan. *Salem and the East Indies: The Story of the Great Commercial Era of the City*. Boston: Houghton Mifflin, 1947.

Pyle, Richard. *Schwarzkopf: The Man, the Mission, the Triumph*. New York: Signet, 1991.

Quandt, William B. *Decade of Decisions: American Policy Toward the Arab-Israeli Conflict, 1967–1976*. Berkeley, Los Angeles, and London: University of California Press, 1977.

Quinlan, David A. *The Role of the Marine Corps in Rapid Deployment Forces*. Washington: National Defense University Press, 1983.

Ramazani, Rouhollah K. *The Northern Tier: Afghanistan, Iran, and Turkey*. New York: D. Van Nostrand, 1966.

———. *The Persian Gulf: Iran's Role*. Charlottesville, Va.: University Press of Virginia, 1972.

Rearden, Steven L. *The Formative Years, 1947–1950*. Vol. 1 of *History of the Office of the Secretary of Defense*. Washington: Historical Office of the Secretary of Defense, 1984.

Record, Jeffrey. *The Rapid Deployment Force and U.S. Military Intervention in the*

Persian Gulf. Cambridge, Mass., and Washington: Institute for Foreign Policy Analysis, 1981.

——. *Revising U.S. Military Strategy: Tailoring Means to Ends.* Washington: Pergamon-Brassey's, 1984.

Riasanovsky, Nicholas V. *A History of Russia.* New York and London: Oxford University Press, 1969.

Roberts, Edmund. *Embassy to the Eastern Courts of Cochin-China, Siam, and Muscat; in the U.S. Sloop-of-War Peacock, David Geisinger, Commander, during the Years 1832–3–4.* New York: Harper & Brothers, 1837.

Roosevelt, Archie. *For Lust of Knowing: Memoirs of an Intelligence Officer.* Boston and Toronto: Little, Brown, 1988.

Roosevelt, Kermit. *Countercoup: The Struggle for the Control of Iran.* New York: McGraw-Hill, 1979.

Rosenberg, David A. *Historical Perspectives in Long Range Planning in the Navy: Part I: The Planning Process Overview, 1900–1978.* Washington: Office of the Assistant Secretary of the Navy, 1980.

Saivetz, Carol R. *The Soviet Union and the Gulf in the 1980s.* Boulder, Colo.: Westview, 1989.

Seager, Robert II. *Alfred Thayer Mahan: The Man and His Letters.* Annapolis, Md.: Naval Institute Press, 1977.

Sherwood, Robert E. *Roosevelt and Hopkins: An Intimate History.* New York: Harper & Row, 1948.

Shulimson, Jack. *Marines in Lebanon.* Washington: Headquarters, Marine Corps, 1966.

Shwadran, Benjamin. *The Middle East, Oil and the Great Powers.* New York and Toronto: John Wiley; Jerusalem: Israel Universities Press, 1973.

Sick, Gary. *All Fall Down: America's Tragic Encounter with Iran.* New York: Penguin, 1986.

Siegel, Adam, Karen Domabyl, and Barbara Lingberg. *Deployment of U.S. Navy Aircraft Carriers and Other Surface Ships, 1976–1988.* Alexandria, Vir.: Center for Naval Analysis, 1989.

Sifry, Micah L., and Christopher Cerf, eds. *The Gulf War Reader: History, Documents, Opinions.* New York: Times Books, 1991.

Skrine, Clarmont. *World War in Iran.* London: Constable, 1962.

Sowell, Lewis C., Jr. *Base Development and the Rapid Deployment Force: A Window to the Future.* Washington: National Defense University Press, 1982.

Stoff, Michael B. *Oil, War, and American Security: The Search for a National Oil Policy, 1941–1947.* New Haven, Conn., and London: Yale University Press, 1980.

Sumida, Jon Tetsuro. *In Defence of Naval Supremacy: Finance, Technology and British Naval Policy, 1889–1914.* Boston, London: Unwin Hyman, 1989.

Szaz, Z. Michael, ed. *The Impact of the Iranian Events upon Persian Gulf & United States Security.* Washington: American Foreign Policy Institute, 1979.

Thomas, Hugh. *Suez.* New York: Harper & Row, 1967.

Troen, Selwyn Ilan, and Moshe Shemesh, eds. *The Suez-Sinai Crisis, 1956: Retrospective and Reappraisal.* New York: Columbia University Press, 1990.

Truman, Harry S. *Memoirs.* 2 vols. Garden City, N.Y.: Doubleday, 1955.

Ullman, Richard H. *Anglo-Soviet Relations, 1917–1921.* Princeton, N.J.: Princeton University Press, 1962–1972.

U.S. Air Force. *White Paper: Air Force Performance in Desert Storm.* Washington: U.S. Air Force, 1991.

U.S. Army. *FM 100–5: Operations.* Washington: U.S. Army, 1986.

U.S. Congress. *Means of Measuring Naval Power with Special Reference to U.S. and Soviet Activities in the Indian Ocean.* Washington: Congressional Research Service, 1974.

U.S. Congress. Congressional Budget Office. *Rapid Deployment Forces: Policy and Budgetary Implications.* Washington: Congressional Budget Office, 1983.

U.S. Congress. Senate. Committee on Foreign Relations. *War in the Persian Gulf: The U.S. Takes Sides.* Washington: Senate Foreign Relations Committee, October 1987.

United States. Department of Defense. *Conduct of the Persian Gulf Conflict: An Interim Report to Congress.* Washington: Department of Defense, 1991.

U.S. Navy. *The United States Navy in "Desert Shield" "Desert Storm."* Washington: Office of the Chief of Naval Operations, 1991.

United States. President's Special Review Board [Tower Commission]. *Report of the President's Special Review Board.* Washington: Government Printing Office, 1987.

Vance, Cyrus. *Hard Choices: Critical Years in America's Foreign Policy.* New York: Simon & Schuster, 1983.

Volkogonov, Dmitri. *Stalin: Triumph and Tragedy.* New York: Grove Weidenfeld, 1991.

Warden, John A., III. *The Air Campaign: Planning for Combat.* Washington: Pergamon-Brassey's, 1989.

Watson, Robert J. *The Joint Chiefs of Staff and National Policy, 1953–1954.* Vol. 5 of *History of the Joint Chiefs of Staff.* Washington: JCS Historical Division, 1986.

Weinberger, Caspar. *Fighting for Peace: Seven Critical Years in the Pentagon.* New York: Warner Books, 1990.

——. *A Report to the Congress on Security Arrangements in the Persian Gulf.* Unclassified version. June 15, 1987.

Woodhouse, C. M. *Something Ventured.* London: Granada, 1982.

Woodward, Bob. *The Commanders.* New York: Simon & Schuster, 1991.

Wright, Robin. *In the Name of God: The Khomeini Decade.* New York: Simon & Schuster, 1989.

Yergin, Daniel. *Shattered Peace: The Origins of the Cold War and the National Security State.* Boston: Houghton Mifflin, 1977.

——. *The Prize: The Epic Quest for Oil, Money, and Power.* New York: Simon & Schuster, 1991.

Articles

Abramov, M. "U.S. Navy Aggravates Persian Gulf Situation." *Morskoi Sbornik* (March 1988): 78–81.

Adamthwaite, Anthony. "Suez Revisited." *International Affairs* 64 (Summer 1988): 449–64.

Admire, John H. "A Report on the Gulf." *Marine Corps Gazette* 72 (December 1988): 56–61.

Aldrich, Richard, and Michael Coleman. "Britain and the Strategic Air Offensive against the Soviet Union: The Question of South Asian Bases, 1945–9." *The Journal of the Historical Association* 74 (October 1989): 400–26.

Antal, John F. "The Iraqi Army Forged in the Other Gulf War." *Military Review* 71 (February 1991): 63–72.

Atherton, Alfred L. "The Soviet Role in the Middle East: An American View." *The Middle East Journal* 39 (Autumn 1985): 688–715.

Ballis, William B. "Soviet-Turkish Relations during the Decade 1953–1963." Institute for the Study of the USSR *Bulletin* 11 (September 1964): 3–16.

Bill, James A. "Power and Religion in Revolutionary Iran." *The Middle East Journal* 36 (Winter 1982): 22–47.

Bowden, James A. "The RDJTF and Doctrine." *Military Review* 62 (November 1982): 51–64.

Brewer, William D. "Yesterday and Tomorrow in the Persian Gulf." *The Middle East Journal* 23 (Spring 1969): 149–58.

Canan, James W. "The Electronic Storm." *Air Force Magazine* 74 (June 1991): 26–32.

Cigar, Norman. "The Soviet Navy in the Persian Gulf: Naval Diplomacy in a Combat Zone." *Naval War College Review* 42 (Spring 1989): 56–88.

Cooper, Dale R. "Young Guns: Harrier Pilots in the Persian Gulf." *Leatherneck* 74 (July 1991): 40–46.

Crosby, Alfred W., Jr. "American Trade with Mauritius in the Age of the French Revolution and Napoleon." *American Neptune* 25 (January 1965): 5–17.

DeForth, Peter W. "U.S. Naval Presence in the Persian Gulf: The Mideast Force since World War II." *Naval War College Review* 28 (Summer 1975): 28–38.

Dekmejian, R. Hrair. "The Anatomy of Islamic Revival: Legitimacy Crisis, Ethnic Conflict and the Search for Islamic Alternatives." *The Middle East Journal* 34 (Winter 1980): 1–12.

Fatemi, Khosrow. "Leadership by Distrust: The Shah's *Modus Operandi*." *The Middle East Journal* 36 (Winter 1982): 49–61.

Fish, M. Steven. "After Stalin's Death: The Anglo-American Debate over a New Cold War." *Diplomatic History* 10 (Fall 1986): 333–55.

Fitzgerald, Mary C. "Early Soviet Assessments of U.S. Military Success in the Gulf War." *Strategic Review* 19 (Spring 1991): 77–80.

Franz, Wallace. "Defeating the Iraqis: Saddam's Troops Are Not Ready for a War of Maneuver." *Armor* 100 (January/February 1991): 8–9.

Friedman, Norman. "The *Vincennes* Incident." United States Naval Institute *Proceedings* 115 (May 1988): 72–79.

Fromkin, David. "How the Modern Middle East Map Came to be Drawn." *Smithsonian* 22 (May 1991): 132–49.

Gasiorowski, Mark J. "The 1953 *Coup D'Etat* in Iran." *International Journal of Middle East Studies* 19 (August 1987): 261–86.

Grier, Peter. "Joint STARS Does Its Stuff." *Air Force Magazine* 74 (June 1991): 38–42.

Hahn, Peter H. "Containment and Egyptian Nationalism: The Unsuccessful Effort to Establish the Middle East Command, 1950–1953." *Diplomatic History* 11 (Winter 1987): 23–40.

Hampton, Dan. "The Weasels at Work." *Air Force Magazine* 74 (July 1991): 56–59.

Hess, Gary R. "The Iranian Crisis of 1945–46 and the Cold War." *Political Science Quarterly* 89 (March 1974): 117–46.

Hoffmann, Peter. "The Gulf Region in German Strategic Projections, 1940–1942." *Militärgeschictliche Mitteilungen* 44 (2/88): 61–73.

Horner, Charles A. "The Air Campaign." *Military Review* 71 (September 1991): 17–27.

Hunter, Shireen T. "The Gulf Economic Crisis and Its Social and Political Consequences." *The Middle East Journal* 40 (Autumn 1986): 593–613.

Karsh, Efraim and Inari Rautsi. "Why Saddam Hussein Invaded Kuwait." *Survival* 33 (January/February 1991): 18–30.

Kelly, J. B. "Iraq's Borders: Let's Talk Turkey." *National Review* 42 (17 September 1990): 31–34.

Kennedy, Edward M. "The Persian Gulf: Arms Race or Arms Control?" *Foreign Affairs* 54 (October 1975): 14–35.

Khadduri, Majid. "The Problem of Regional Security in the Middle East: An Appraisal." *The Middle East Journal* 11 (Winter 1957): 12–22.

Khalidi, Rashid. "Arab Views of the Soviet Role in the Middle East." *The Middle East Journal* 39 (Autumn 1985): 716–32.

Kingston, Robert C. "From RDF to CENTCOM: New Challenges?" *RUSI Journal* 129 (March 1984): 14–17.

Koburger, Charles W. Jr., "The Kuwait Confrontation of 1961." U.S. Naval Institute *Proceedings* 100 (January 1974): 42–49.

Langenus, Peter C. "Moving An Army: Movement Control in Desert Storm." *Military Review* 71 (September 1991): 40–51.

Langston, Bud, and Don Bringle. "Operation Praying Mantis: The Air View." United States Naval Institute *Proceedings* 115 (May 1989): 54–65.

Leffler, Melvyn P. "Adherence to Agreements: Yalta and the Experiences of the Early Cold War." *International Security* 11 (Summer 1986): 88–123.

Less, Anthony A. "Mideast Perspective." *Wings of Gold* 15 (Spring 1990): 50–52.

Little, Douglas. "Cold War and Covert Action: The United States and Syria, 1945–1958." *Middle East Journal* 44 (Winter 1990): 51–75.

McFarland, Stephen L. "A Peripheral View of the Origins of the Cold War: The Crises in Iran, 1941–1947." *Diplomatic History* 4 (Fall 1980): 333–51.

Mackenzie, Richard. "A Conversation with Chuck Horner." *Air Force Magazine* 74 (June 1991): 57–64.

Markov, V. "The War in the Persian Gulf, Freedom of Navigation, and International Law." *Morskoi Sbornik* (February 1988): 83–87.

Moran, Theodore H. "Iranian Defense Expenditure and the Social Crisis." *International Security* 3 (Winter 1978/1979): 178–98.

Mosely, Philip E. "The Kremlin's Foreign Policy since Stalin." *Foreign Affairs* 32 (October 1953): 20–33.

Norton, Douglas M. "Sealift: Keystone of Support." United States Naval Institute *Proceedings* 117 (May 1991): 42–49.

Office of Naval Intelligence. "The Arab League." *ONI Review* 2 (July 1947): 37–41.

———. "The Persian Gulf." *ONI Review* 4 (April 1949): 39–44.

———. "Soviet Interest in the Nonexistent Indian Ocean Fleet." *ONI Review* 14 (August 1959): 357–59.

315

O'Rourke, Ronald. "Gulf Ops." United States Naval Institute *Proceedings* 115 (May 1989): 42–50.

———. "The Tanker War." U.S. Naval Institute *Proceedings* 114 (May 1988): 30–34.

Pagonis, William G., and Harold E. Raugh, Jr. "Good Logistics is Combat Power: The Logistics Sustainment of Operation Desert Storm." *Military Review* 71 (September 1991): 28–39.

Palmer, Michael A. "The Navy Did Its Job." United States Naval Institute *Proceedings* 117 (May 1991): 88–93.

Pawlisch, Hans S. "Operation Praying Mantis." *VFW Magazine* (January 1989): 34–37.

Perkins, J. B. III. "Operation Praying Mantis: The Surface View." United States Naval Institute *Proceedings* 115 (May 1989): 66–70.

Rakow, William M. "Marines in the Gulf—1988." *Marine Corps Gazette* 72 (December 1988): 62–68.

Ramazani, R. K. "Who Lost America? The Case of Iran." *The Middle East Journal* 36 (Winter 1982): 5–21.

Rose, Dirk T. "Saratoga MiG Killers: Hollywood Need Not Apply." *Naval Aviation News* 73 (May–June 1991): 13–14.

Rosenberg, David Alan. "The U.S. Navy and the Problem of Oil in a Future War: The Outline of a Strategic Dilemma, 1945–1950." *Naval War College Review* 29 (Summer 1976): 53–64.

Rossow, Robert Jr. "The Battle of Azerbaijan, 1946." *The Middle East Journal* 10 (Winter 1956): 17–32.

Ryan, Paul B. *Diego Garcia.*" United States Naval Institute *Proceedings* 110 (September 1984): 132–136.

Sapozhnikov, B. "The 'Rapid Deployment Force' as a Weapon of U.S. Neocolonialism." *Morskoi Sbornik* (December 1983): 70–75.

Scharfen, John C. "Interview with Gen. George B. Crist, Commander in Chief, U.S. Central Command." *Marine Corps Gazette* 70 (December 1986): 30–37.

Segal, David. "The Iran-Iraq War: A Military Analysis." *Foreign Affairs* 66 (Summer 1988): 946–963.

Simmons, Edwin H. "Getting Marines to the Gulf." U.S. Naval Institute *Proceedings* 117 (May 1991): 50–64.

———. "Getting the Job Done." U.S. Naval Institute *Proceedings* 117 (May 1991): 94–96.

Stein, Janice Gross. "The Wrong Strategy in the Right Place: The United States in the Gulf." *International Security* 13 (Winter 1988/89): 142–67.

Tibi, Bassam. "The Renewed Role of Islam in the Political and Social Development of the Middle East." *The Middle East Journal* 37 (Winter 1983): 3–13.

Truver, Scott. "Mines of August: An International Whodunit." United States Naval Institute *Proceedings* 111 (May 1985): 95–117.

Turchenko, Sergei. "Sinister Armada." *Soviet Military Review* (July 1988): 52–54.

Wilson, G. I. "The Gulf War, Maneuver Warfare, and the Operational Art." *Marine Corps Gazette* 75 (June 1991): 23–24.

Yeosock, John J. "Army Operations in the Gulf Theater." *Military Review* 71 (September 1991): 3–15.

Newspapers and Magazines

Air Force Times
Atlanta Journal & Constitution
Aviation Week & Space Technology
Baltimore Sun
Boston Globe
Business Week
Congressional Quarterly
Defense News
Economist
Independent
Jane's Defense Weekly
London Daily Telegraph
London Financial Times
London Sunday Times
Los Angeles Times

Miami Herald
Newsweek
New York Times
Philadelphia Inquirer
Seattle Post-Intelligencer
The Estimate
The New Republic
Time
USA Today
U.S. News & World Report
Wall Street Journal
Washington Post
Washington Star
Washington Times

Dissertations and Unpublished Papers

Converse, Elliott Vanvelt. "United States Plans for a Postwar Overseas Military Base System, 1942–1948." Ph.D. dissertation, Princeton University, 1984.
Warden, John A., III. "Centers of Gravity: The Key to Success in War."

INDEX

Fahd, 166; unwillingness to march on Baghdad, 194; warns Saddam, 203
Byrnes, James F., 31–32, 34, 36

California Arabian Standard Oil Company, 25
Camp David, 110
Capella, 172
Carlucci, Frank, 113, 144
Carney, Robert B., 62
Carter, Jimmy, 163, 194: and access to Persian Gulf oil, 107, 109; at Camp David, 110; enthusiasm for shah, 92; redirects American Persian Gulf policy, 101–11, 112, 244; and shah's fall, 105; and Soviet invasion of Afghanistan, 106–7; visits Iran, 105
Carter Doctrine, 106, 113, 149, 178: announced, 110, 111; criticism of, 114–15; Reagan Corollary to, 118
CENTCOM: *See* United States, Central Command
Center for Naval Analyses, 133
Central Intelligence Agency: in Iran crisis, 67–72; in Kuwait crisis, 158–59, 160
Central Treaty Organization, 81, 88, 117, 130
Chamoun, Camille, 79, 80
Chandler, 134, 138
Cheney, Richard: and air war, 220; authorizes Desert Storm, 214; concern about terrorism, 176; fears Iraqi nuclear capability, 187; fires Dugan, 181; and Iraqi ouster from Kuwait, 159, 196; and Iraqi threat to Saudi Arabia, 165, 168; and Jidda talks with Saudis, 166–67; supports CENTCOM buildup, 185
Chester, Colby, 14
Churchill, Winston S., 206: and Iran crisis, 68; Iron curtain speech, 32; meets Ibn Saud, 28; at Teheran Conference, 24–25
Churkin, Vitaly, 225
Coalition Coordination Communication and Integration Center, 231
Conolly, Richard L., 46–47
Coronado, 134, 138
Crist, George, 132, 138
Crowe, William: accelerates buildup in

gulf, 132; assurances about Iranian mine threat, 129; hope to deter Iran, 129; orders *Vincennes* to gulf, 146; proposes retaliation against Iran, 133; on reflagging decision, 126
Cuba, 164, 170
Currivan, Gene, 33

D'Arcy, William Knox, 13
Denfeld, Louis E., 55
Dhahran: as airhead for Desert Shield, 170, 172; decision to build air base at, 27–29; importance of, 168
Diego Garcia, 101, 171: base for Middle East Force, 98; expansion of, 113; supports operations during Desert Shield, 96; supports operations during tanker war, 96; U.S. Navy develops base at, 95–96
Djibouti, 96
Douhet, Giulio, 199
Dugan, Michael A., 180, 181, 182, 198, 204, 205, 214
Dulles, John Foster: in Iranian crisis, 66–67, 71; in Suez crisis, 76–77
Dwight, Timothy, 11–12
Dyess, 80

Eade, George J., 130
Eastern and General Syndicate: *See* Holmes, Frank
Ecevit, Bulent, 158, 159
Egypt, 21: aspirations in Arabian peninsula, 245; British seeks bases in, 53; at Camp David summit, 110; confrontation with Britain, 59; contribution to Desert Shield/Storm, 173; intervention in North Yemen, 81, 84; and 1958 landing in Lebanon, 80; membership in Arab Cooperation Council, 151, 152; military forces in Desert Storm, 229, 231, 234; response to Red Sea mining, 131; in Six Day War, 82–83; strategic importance to Britain, 59, 73; in Suez crisis, 75–77; and Yom Kippur War, 97, 98
Eisenhower, 165, 167, 170
Eisenhower, Dwight D.: in Iran crisis, 66–72; Middle East policy, 78, 85; in Suez crisis, 76
Eisenhower Doctrine, 78

Iraq (*cont.*)
wait, 163, 164; and Iran arms buildup, 89; and Iranian threat, 151; Iran-Iraq War, 120, 144–45, 153–54, 169; at Khafji, 223; military forces destroyed, 228, 234; military of on wartime footing, 151; and Nasser, 77; nuclear capability, 187; oil production, 21–22; plans attack on Kuwait, 159–60; political grip of Saddam on, 154; possible intelligence coup, 161; post–Iran-Iraq War relationship with U.S., 151; pro-Axis sentiment, 20; Republican Guard, 201, 206, 211, 214, 231, 236–37, 238; returns territory to Iran, 169–70; Scuds test-fired, 188; seeks conditional terms for withdrawal, 225; seeks Soviet intercession, 224–26; *Stark* attack by, 123; Syrian threat to, 151; threatens Kuwait, 86; threatens Persian Gulf, 134; threatens Saudi Arabia, 165, 168; transships oil, 121; UN embargo against, 174–76; U.S. tilt toward, 119, 156
Iraqi Petroleum Company, 17
Israel, 107, 121: American policy and, 42, 55–57; at Camp David summit, 110; *Intifada* and, 151; invades Lebanon, 117; 1948 war, 55–56; Scud attacks on, 219–20; in Six Day War, 82–83, 85; in Suez crisis, 75–77; in Yom Kippur War, 97, 98
Italy, 21, 124, 131, 132
Ivory Justice, 200

al-Jabburi, Sultan Hashim Ahmad, 240
Jack Williams, 140, 142
Japan, 21, 133, 164
Jarrett, 133
Jedi Knights, 207
Jernegan, John D., 61
Johnson, Lyndon B., 85, 86
Johnston, Robert B., 184
Joint Forces Command-East, 229, 231, 234, 235
Joint Forces Command-North, 229, 231, 234–37
Jordan, 220: in Arab Cooperation Council, 151; British intervention in, 79; crisis of 1970, 97; fears of Nasser, 77; Six

Day War and, 82; supports Saddam, 170
Joseph Strauss, 140, 143
Joshan, 142, 143
JSTARS, 200, 217, 233
Jubayl, 168, 171, 172
Jufair, 48

Kelly, John, 159
Kelly, Thomas, 159, 182, 208
Kennan, George F., 30–31, 34–35
Kennedy, Edward, 88–89, 91, 114, 125
Kennedy, John F., 81
Kern, Paul, 238
Khafji, 222–23
Kharg Island, 108
Khomeini, Ruhollah, 105, 128, 150, 153
Kingston, Robert C., 115–17
Kissinger, Henry: fall of shah and, 104, 105; gulf policy, 87–88, 92; on "oil grab," 100; Yom Kippur War and, 97
Kitty Hawk, 106
Knox, Frank, 27
Korea, 45, 52, 58, 64, 69, 72, 73, 101
Krug, Julius, 43
Kurdistan, 30, 32, 151, 240–41
Kuwait, 136: American guardianship of, 149, 245; assists U.S. in gulf, 132; fears for Westerners in, 166; Iranians attack ships bound to, 119; Iranians bomb, 118; Iraq destroys, 187, 226–27; Iraqi human rights abuses in, 188–89; Iraq invades, 163; Iraqis plan attack on, 159–60; Iraq threatens, 86, 153; and 1958 landing in Lebanon, 80; military forces in Desert Storm, 229, 237; oil development, 14, 18, 21–22; oil revenues decline, 120; requests reflagging, 122–24; response to Suez invasion, 77; transships Iraqi oil, 121; U.S. response to Iraqi invasion of, 193

LaSalle, 201
Leahy, William D., 37
Lebanon: civil war, 79–81, 117, 118, 151; Nasser and, 77; Iranian involvement in, 150; Israel invades, 117; U.S. intervention, 79–81, 102; U.S. support, 54
Lend-Lease, 21, 22, 24
Less, Anthony A.: commands JTFME